W9-DCN-572

Perceptions of Palestine

Perceptions of Palestine

Their Influence on U.S. Middle East Policy

KATHLEEN CHRISTISON

University of California Press

BERKELEY   LOS ANGELES   LONDON

University of California Press
Berkeley and Los Angeles, California

University of California Press, Ltd.
London, England

© 1999 by the Regents of the University of California

Parts of this book first appeared in the *Journal of Palestine Studies*
as follows: "Splitting the Difference: The Palestinian-Israeli Policy
of James Baker" (autumn 1994); "U.S. Policy and the Palestinians:
Bound by a Frame of Reference: (summer 1997); "Bound by a Frame
of Reference, Part II: U.S. Policy and the Palestinians, 1948–88" (spring
1998); and "Bound by a Frame of Reference, Part III: U.S. Policy and the
Palestinians, 1988–1998" (summer 1998). Reprinted with permission.

Library of Congress Cataloging-in-Publication Data

Christison, Kathleen, 1941–.
    Perceptions of Palestine: Their Influence on U.S. Middle East Policy /
Kathleen Christison.
        p.   cm.
    Includes bibliographical references (p.) and index.
    ISBN 0-520-21717-9 (alk. paper)
        1. United States—Foreign relations—Palestine.   2. Palestine—
Foreign relations—United States.   3. United States—Foreign
relations—Israel.   4. Israel—Foreign relations—United States.
5. United States—Foreign relations—20th century.   I. Title.
E183.8.P19C48   1999
327.7305694—dc21   98-41413
                                                                                              CIP

Manufactured in the United States of America
08 07 06 05 04 03 02 01 00 99   10 9 8 7 6 5 4 3 2 1

The paper used in this publication is both acid-free and totally chlorine-
free (TCF). It meets the minimum requirements of ANSI/NISO Z39.48-
1992 (R 1997) (Permanence of Paper).

To Bill

Contents

Acknowledgments		ix
Introduction		1
1.	Palestinians in the Nineteenth-Century Mind	16
2.	Woodrow Wilson: "Rising Above" Self-Determination	26
3.	Franklin Roosevelt: Locked In	45
4.	Harry Truman: History Belongs to the Victors	61
5.	Eisenhower, Kennedy, Johnson: Possession Is Nine-Tenths of the Law	95
6.	Richard Nixon and Gerald Ford: An Unrecognizable Episode	124
7.	Jimmy Carter: Making a Difference	157
8.	Ronald Reagan: Missed Opportunities	195
9.	George Bush: No Illusions	242
10.	The Pictures in Our Heads	274
	Notes	295
	Selected Bibliography	339
	Index	351

Israel and Territories Occupied by Israel since June 1967

Acknowledgments

I owe many thanks to many people for their help. This book grew out of a suggestion by Philip Mattar for an article on the mind-set, or "frame of reference," from which policymakers usually approach the Palestinian-Israeli conflict. The idea intrigued me, but as I began to look into the mind-set of current policymakers, then in the Bush era, I found I was led farther and farther back into history before I could adequately explain what had gone into shaping the impressions, the assumptions, and the preconceptions that each administration's policymakers brought to their jobs. I first went back as far as the Truman administration, which encompassed the period of Israel's birth and the Palestinians' dispersal, but then discovered that I needed to investigate even earlier periods before I could satisfy myself that I had truly found the origins of today's "frame of reference." I am deeply indebted to Philip Mattar for his initial imaginative idea, for his patience in waiting for the finished product, for his encouragement, and for his sharp comments on the manuscript.

Ann M. Lesch also read the manuscript and made many perceptive comments. John Ware read through the first few chapters. My thanks to both. I also deeply appreciate the assistance of those former policymakers who allowed me to pick their brains and helped me gain some sense of what it's like inside the policymaking environment. Particular thanks go to John Sherman for his help, given just out of friendship, and special thanks also to Don Lamm. It goes without saying that any mistakes and misinterpretations are my responsibility entirely.

I also thank Lynne Withey and Rose Anne White of the University of California Press for their encouragement and help, and Pamela Fischer for her excellent editing.

Above all, I thank my husband, Bill—for everything.

Introduction

Malcolm Kerr, the late scholar of the modern Arab world, wrote in 1980 that the conventional wisdom about the Arab-Israeli conflict had become so entrenched in the United States that diplomats were severely inhibited in their ability to formulate policy. Kerr maintained that a body of assumptions and misconceptions, rarely challenged or debated, had grown up around the origins of the conflict, and serious discourse had ceased among the public and except in rare instances among policymakers as well. Policymakers tend in general, he observed, to try to avoid controversy, and, with regard to the Arab-Israeli conflict, it had thus become the natural inclination of the very people inside government whose job it was to study the issues to fall back instead on the analysis prevailing in Congress, in the press, and among the general public.[1]

Kerr's observations remain widely applicable today, despite progress toward resolving the Arab-Israeli conflict. Two of the elements that he identified as constituting the conventional wisdom relate specifically to the Palestinian-Israeli issue: the notion that Palestinian national claims are "artificially and mischievously inspired" and thus may be ignored and the notion that the only real issue in the Arab-Israeli conflict is an unreasonable Arab refusal to accept Israel's existence—not, as Arabs contend, a real grievance against Israel arising from the Palestinians' displacement.[2] The perception that the Palestinians have no rational basis for their hostility to Israel and no legitimate national claim to the land of Palestine is fundamental to the misconceptions surrounding this conflict. It has essentially been a given for most of the twentieth century that Palestinians are contesting the Jews' inherent right to exist in Palestine—not that Palestinians, as a native population with centuries of residence and title deeds to the land, have their own claim to patrimony in Palestine.

1

For the half century before the 1993 Palestinian-Israeli peace agreement, and in large measure still, the assumption that the Arab and Palestinian position was "mischievously inspired" has constituted a nearly unchallengeable vantage point for observing the Arab-Israeli conflict. This vantage point has constituted what might be called a frame of reference within which the conflict has been contained in public and diplomatic discourse. The frame of reference defines and sets boundaries around thinking on Palestinian-Israeli issues. It is for the most part Israel-centered, approaching the conflict generally from an Israeli perspective and seldom recognizing the existence or the legitimacy of a Palestinian perspective.

The dispossession and dispersal of the Palestinians in 1948 has always been and to a great extent remains "an unrecognizable episode," as Kerr put it, even for most informed Americans[3]—unrecognizable in the sense not only that the dispossession has been forgotten but also that it is seldom recognized to be the ultimate cause of the conflict. A well-known Israeli historian has remarked that history is in a real sense "the propaganda of the victors," and because Israel won the contest for Palestine, Israel's version of that contest, of the rights and claims that underlay it, and of the justice of the outcome has prevailed in most international discourse.[4]

For the vast majority of Americans, including the reasonably well informed, Palestinians have never had a history; they were never there until, apparently out of the blue, they began preying on Israel. A U.S. journalist working in Saudi Arabia in the early 1980s recalls a U.S. senator asking a Saudi official where on earth the Palestinians had come from "to begin with."[5] The senator's ignorance is not unusual by any means. The conventional wisdom generally holds that the conflict originated not because Palestinians lost land and homes and a national locus in their native territory and have been attempting to recover a lost heritage but because Arabs have an innate hatred for Jews. The notion that the conflict involves not unreasoned hatreds but competing nationalisms finds little accommodation within the frame of reference, even today.

In its Israel-centeredness, the frame of reference assumes a unique bond between Israel and the United States arising from a common biblical heritage, from a shared belief that because of the Holocaust and earlier centuries of suffering Jews must have a homeland, and from U.S. identification with what some have called Israel's "national style," particularly its pioneering beginnings and its commitment to Western democracy.[6] For some, particularly those U.S. Jews in whom Israel arouses an intense emotional identification, the relationship is symbiotic. "Americans and Israelis are bonded together like no two other sovereign peoples," notes Peter Grose in his 1983 book, *Israel in the Mind of America*. "As the Judaic heritage flowed through the minds of America's early settlers and helped to shape the new American republic, so Israel restored adopted the vision and the values of the American dream. Each, the United States and Israel, grafted the heritage of the other onto itself."[7] Grose accurately reflects the depth and quality that supporters of Israel have tried to achieve in the relationship. Another historian has observed that the emotional and cultural identification of the United States with Israel is so close that Israel takes part "in the 'being' of American society."[8]

In a frame of reference that so enthusiastically envelops Israel and so automatically approaches the conflict from the Israeli point of view, there has been little room for the Palestinian perspective. This is clearly the case in the public consciousness, and, for the same reasons, policymakers have paid little heed to the Palestinian viewpoint. The emotional bond with Israel, the perception that has prevailed to one degree or another throughout every administration since Harry Truman's that Israel is strategically important to the United States, a strong and ingrained reluctance among policymakers to spark controversy or generate change by giving any advantage to Arabs perceived to be "difficult" or ready to upset the status quo, and the militant and uncompromising nature of the Arab and Palestinian reaction to Israel's creation and the Palestinians' dispossession—all these factors have combined to give Israel overwhelming predominance in U.S. policy considerations and to push concern for the legitimacy of Palestinian claims to the background.

The idea that an event as significant as the displacement of over seven hundred thousand people from homes and native land could have become an "unrecognizable episode," forgotten by policymakers as the source and motivation for that people's anger and hostility, would seem preposterous. But a mind-set is by its nature an outlook that is fixed, accepting of the status quo, and often closed to new or unconventional perspectives. As will be seen, so many factors combined so quickly in the wake of the Palestinians' displacement in 1948 to put the Israeli case prominently before the U.S. public, to make the assurance of Israeli security the central concern of U.S. interest, and, perhaps most significant, to push the Palestinian case to the background that the development of a mind-set and an all but immutable frame of reference was virtually immediate.

In his classic study of Western perceptions of the Orient, *Orientalism*, Palestinian American intellectual Edward Said describes the life cycle of a mind-set in a graphic way. "Fictions," he observes, "have their own logic and their own dialectic of growth or decline." Learned texts, media representations, any supposedly authoritative body of knowledge have a self-reinforcing tendency. Having gained a certain perspective from something they have heard or read, audiences come to have particular expectations that in turn influence what is said or written henceforth. Said notes:

> [If] one reads a book claiming that lions are fierce and then encounters a fierce lion, . . . the chances are that one will be encouraged to read more books by that same author, and believe them. . . . A book on how to handle a fierce lion might then cause a series of books to be produced on such subjects as the fierceness of lions, the origins of fierceness, and so forth. . . . A text purporting to contain knowledge about something actual . . . is not easily dismissed. Expertise is attributed to it. The authority of academics, institutions, and governments can accrue to it, surrounding it with still greater prestige than its practical successes warrant. Most important, such texts can *create* not only knowledge but also the very reality they appear to describe.[9]

Like the notional literature on lions and their fierceness, the conventional wisdom on the Palestinian-Israeli conflict has grown exponentially as it has been iterated, reiterated, embellished, and expanded on. Each scholarly text, each novel and movie and media representation, each piece of data added to the framework has helped create reality. Former Secretary of State Henry Kissinger, in a 1996 op-ed article criticizing Hollywood director Oliver Stone for distorting history in the movie *Nixon*, notes that, once put forth in a big-budget movie, "a caricature of history" is virtually impossible to counter in the public mind. Actual history is usually too complex for a simplified dramatic presentation.[10] And so a new body of knowledge is created.

A prime example of a significant misrepresentation in the Palestinian-Israeli situation that has had the effect of creating false knowledge, through a spiraling process of constant repetition and supposedly authoritative reinforcement, is the widely believed but untrue story that Palestinian civilians left their homes in 1948 because the Palestinian leadership broadcast instructions over the radio that they leave in order to give Arab military forces a clear field to drive the Jews out of Palestine. This misconception began to be circulated in the midst of the 1948 war and quickly became an enduring staple of Israeli lore and U.S. perceptions.

In fact, no broadcast orders from any Arab authority were ever issued to the Palestinian populace, and, except in a few local instances, no Arab military commanders gave orders to clear areas of Palestine of civilians. A U.S. author, Dan Kurzman, whose 1970 book, *Genesis 1948: The First Arab-Israeli War*, recounted the events of 1948 as seen by both Arabs and

Israelis, searched Israeli military archives and the British Broadcasting Corporation's radio monitoring files and found no record of either Arab military communications ordering a civilian evacuation or any broadcast radio instructions.[11] Virtually no heed was paid to Kurzman's findings, which constituted the first refutation of the "broadcasts myth" to appear in a popular medium in the United States.[12] Almost two decades later—forty years after the Palestinian flight—Israeli historian Benny Morris concluded in *The Birth of the Palestinian Refugee Problem,* an exhaustive study using declassified Israeli archival material, that no Arab authority issued "blanket instructions, by radio or otherwise, to Palestine's Arabs to flee," that Palestinian flight was induced to a great extent by a "general sense of collapse" that permeated Arab Palestine, and that a "small but significant proportion" of the flight resulted from explicit expulsion orders issued by Jewish forces.[13]

The broadcasts myth became a central element in Israeli and U.S. images of the 1948 conflict. It was used to demonstrate that the Palestinians' attachment to their land and homes was weak, that by clearing the way for Arab military forces to "drive the Jews into the sea" the Palestinians showed that they were bent on Israel's destruction, and that in the end Israel bore no responsibility for the Palestinians' displacement and homelessness. Although it has been discredited in most scholarly circles, the myth remains widely believed outside academia.

Historians have often noted the difference between events and the memory of them, the dichotomy between how a historical event actually unfolded and how it is remembered. Nowhere has this been more true than in the Arab-Israeli conflict, where both sides have built an elaborate structure of myths and warped memories. And with no other country has the United States more completely absorbed the entire catalog of myths than it has with Israel. Israeli commentator Meron Benvenisti has noted that national myths, made up of a mixture of real and legendary events, are "the building-blocks from which a society constructs its collective self-image" and, once absorbed, "become truer than reality itself."[14] In a real sense, Israel's self-image has become a part of the U.S. self-image, as Israel is a part of the "being" of the United States.

The Israel-centeredness of the framework of thinking on Palestinian-Israeli issues, even today, is clearly illustrated in the way the media treated the Palestinians' May 1998 commemoration of the fiftieth anniversary of their dispersal. Palestinians call this dispossession the *nakba,* the catastrophe, in recognition of the national and societal disaster caused by their expulsion and flight from Palestine in 1948. The Israeli press, however, indicating a wholly self-absorbed point of view, reported that the word *nakba* referred to Israel's creation—"the Arab designation for the founding of the State of Israel"—rather than to the Palestinians' dispossession. Reflecting a similarly Israel-focused perspective, even the *New York Times* reported that Israel's creation was "an event [the Palestinians] call the 'catastrophe.'"[15] A neutral press would have described the *nakba* from the perspective of those who coined the term, not from Israel's viewpoint.

The prevalence of the Israeli perspective is further illustrated by an encyclopedia of the Arab-Israeli conflict published in 1996. Edited by the well-known scholar Bernard Reich, *An Historical Encyclopedia of the Arab-Israeli Conflict* approaches most issues from an Israeli perspective despite what Reich describes as a deliberate attempt to be nonpartisan and to select scholars with a wide range of perspectives. Bias is notable not only in terminology but also in the selection of data and in interpretation. The 1948 war, for instance, is called the War of Independence, the 1967 war is the Six-Day War, and the 1973 war is the Yom Kippur War—all Israeli terms for these conflicts that Arabs consider offensive. In articles on Palestinians involved in terrorism, each incident is detailed and words such as *slaughter* and *murder* are used repeatedly. Yet none of these terms is used in the articles on Menachem Begin and the Irgun, the pre-state terrorist organization that Begin headed, and Begin's involvement in political violence, including the 1946 bombing of the King David Hotel and the massacre of Palestinian civilians at the village of Deir Yassin during the 1948 war, is not mentioned at all. Irgun involvement at Deir Yassin is briefly mentioned, but the incident is described as an attack "which resulted in 240 Arab civilian casualties."[16]

Two articles cover Jerusalem: one, three pages in length, devotes one paragraph each to the city's Muslim and Christian connections, leaving the entire remainder of the article to Jewish matters; the second, also three pages long, is devoted solely to the Jewish Quarter of Jerusalem's Old City. The treatment given Hebron, a West Bank town of great religious significance to both Jews and Muslims, where fewer than 500 Israelis live among 120,000 Palestinians, is similarly skewed toward the town's Jewish aspects. Reich and his authors also use virtually none of the revisionist history of 1948 published since the mid-1980s by such Israeli historians as Benny Morris, Avi Shlaim, and Ilan Pappé. As a result, the encyclopedia contains nothing about the pre-1948 cooperation between the Zionist leadership and Transjordan's King Abdullah to prevent the formation of a Palestinian Arab state and nothing about the expulsion of Palestinians in 1948.[17]

Terminology such as that used in Reich's encyclopedia has always played a major role in shaping perceptions of Palestinian-Israeli issues. Terminology is the basic material for constructing the framework through which we view any situation—the shaper, in the words of Israeli sociologist Baruch Kimmerling, of our cognition and patterns of thinking.[18] In the Middle East, terminology shapes reality; it becomes a way of seeing reality, and, finally, it is reality. Terminology often determines, for instance, who is thought of as a terrorist and who is not. British journalist Robert Fisk relates that the Marine colonel who commanded the U.S. contingent of the multinational force in Lebanon in 1982 referred in a press briefing to a group of Palestinians who attacked Israeli armor near Beirut as terrorists. When Fisk asked why he had used that particular word, the colonel responded sarcastically that he could also have called them outlaws. But Fisk thought the colonel had missed the point of the question. Either word implied that the Israelis, although a foreign army, had a right to expect immunity from attack in Lebanon and that anyone who shot at them was automatically a terrorist.[19] The Americans, by using either "terrorist" or "outlaw," had bought into the concept that Israel's presence in Lebanon was more legitimate than that of its enemies, some of whom were also foreign, some indigenous. The use of these terms automatically defined the U.S. frame of reference for dealing with anyone who shot at Israelis.

Terminology can also determine who owns a piece of land—or who the speaker believes owns it. In the case of the West Bank, the land can be called by the name Arabs and most of the international community use or by the names Judea and Samaria, used by Israelis who believe it is irrevocably Israeli land. Imposing place names is part of imposing control and passes judgment on ownership, according to Palestinian American scholar Rashid Khalidi. "This process of naming," Khalidi says, "is an attempt to privilege one dimension of a complex reality at the expense of others, with the ultimate aim of blotting the others out, or decisively subordinating them to Israeli domination."[20]

Kimmerling observes that through their use of certain words and concepts Israeli historiographers often predetermine their conclusions—and, it might be added, help to predetermine the perceptions that Americans also hold about Israel and the Palestinians. Many Israeli historians, for instance, indiscriminately use the term Eretz Israel—the Land of Israel—to apply to all historical periods, no matter what power ruled it at the time. The practice effectively grants Jews an "eternal title" over the land, obscuring and in some fashion delegitimizing other populations and other governments, Kimmerling notes. During the British Mandate, Israeli historiographers handled the Palestine issue "as an almost exclusive 'Jewish bubble.'" Britain and the Arab population of Palestine either were not included or, if dealt with, were "treated as external forces and residual categories."[21] In many respects, this exclusion, particularly of the Palestinian Arabs, spilled over into U.S. perceptions of the Palestine situation, and many Americans, in and out of government, came to see the Palestine issue primarily in "Judeo-centric" terms, despite Palestine's Arab majority and British government.

The frame of reference that defines the limits of discourse on the Palestinian-Israeli issue is not a matter solely of terminology and of false knowledge but also of knowledge withheld. The Palestinians have always to a great degree been politically invisible. This has been true since the days of Woodrow Wilson, when the United States endorsed Britain's Balfour Declaration; this first policy statement by a Western government on the Palestine situation supported the establishment of a Jewish homeland in Palestine and largely ignored Palestine's Arab inhabitants, referring to them merely as "non-Jews." From more recent times, a few examples suffice to demonstrate how the frame of reference functions to withhold knowledge.

- In the mid-1980s, the executive producer of the ABC television program *Nightline* acknowledged to an interviewer that the Arab point of view was underrepresented in comparison with the Israeli viewpoint because, he said, there was a dearth of "credible Arab guests" who were as interesting from a programming standpoint as Israel's spokespeople. Other television programs and networks similarly ignored Arab spokespeople thought to be radical, uninteresting, or not credible for one reason or another, particularly before 1990.[22] As a result, in its search for program material that is entertaining rather than necessarily balanced, television only rarely gave audiences an opportunity to hear the Arab and Palestinian points of view at all until the 1990s.

- In June 1988, at the height of the Palestinian uprising, the *intifada*, in the West Bank and Gaza, a close adviser to Palestine Liberation Organization (PLO) Chairman Yasir Arafat passed out to the press corps covering an Arab summit meeting in Algiers a statement affirming Palestinian agreement with Israel's desire for direct peace talks. Expressing Palestinian understanding for "the Jewish people's centuries of suffering," the statement affirmed a belief that "all peoples—the Jews and the Palestinians included—have the right to run their own affairs, expecting from their neighbors not only non-belligerence but the kind of political and economic cooperation without which no state can be truly secure." The statement, one of the most conciliatory by a Palestinian official to that point, was reportedly rejected when submitted to the *Washington Post* as an op-ed article and when distributed to journalists at Algiers was reported on only by the *Wall Street Journal,* which placed the story on page nineteen. It was another two weeks before other major newspapers mentioned the statement and then only in articles whose principal focus was anti-Arafat fringe groups that rejected its moderation. *New York Times* columnist Anthony Lewis praised the statement's moderation two weeks after its issuance.[23] The U.S. State Department did not respond to it.

• Many Americans have been equally reluctant to hear news and opinions about Israel that do not fit what has come to be the conventional wisdom. On a visit to the United States in 1983 Israeli journalist Danny Rubinstein met with representatives of the major U.S. Jewish organizations and was rebuffed when he argued that the principal danger Israel faced was not Arab military threats but the potential for internal "moral destruction" because of its occupation of the West Bank and Gaza. A leader of one organization told Rubinstein he was not interested in hearing the journalist's argument because he could not use it with his audiences. Rubinstein concluded that only the notion of Israel facing external threats would sell in the United States. Moderate positions, he wrote in an article for the Israeli press, went unheard and did not bring in contributions.[24]

• The reluctance to publish or to hear the viewpoint of Israel's opponents has extended beyond the Palestinians and to areas beyond politics. A Columbia University professor of comparative literature recalls being asked in 1980 by a New York publisher to suggest a list of Third World novels to be translated and included in a planned new series. The professor gave the publisher a long list that included two or three books by Egyptian novelist Naguib Mahfouz, who was awarded the Nobel Prize for literature eight years later but was then hardly known in the United States. Asked after a few weeks which novels he intended to have translated, the publisher said that none by Mahfouz had been selected because "Arabic is a controversial language." [25]

Studies of the foreign-affairs decision-making process have shown that, not unlike the general public, policymakers usually operate on the basis of a set of assumptions, often inherited from predecessors, and do not scrutinize or challenge those assumptions. Analysis of failed policies shows that policymakers make errors because they have not asked the right questions or examined preconceived notions. Underlying assumptions are often so widely shared that anyone who questions them is regarded as troublesome, so there are few incentives for debating an issue on which everyone seems generally agreed. This has been the case with the Palestinian issue for virtually all of its history. When an issue has a long history, in fact, as with the Palestinian-Israeli conflict, policymakers are particularly reluctant to seek out opposing views, feeling that everyone's position is known and everyone is in tune with the prevailing policy line.[26]

The mind-set with which most policymakers approach the Middle East tends in fact to be self-reinforcing in the sense that officials usually seek only those opinions that fit with the views they already hold. According to one former government official who is still a close observer of the Washington scene, most administrations go through the motions of consulting outside academic experts during their election campaign or early in their tenure but soon limit this contact because most academics do not tell them what they want to know or do not give them information in a context they can use. Those more policy-oriented academics whom policymakers do listen to tend to be co-opted by the administration and become insiders.[27]

Harold Saunders, a senior State Department official who was involved in Arab-Israeli peace negotiations under Presidents Richard Nixon, Gerald Ford, and Jimmy Carter, states that it is normal to reexamine assumptions and policy directions at the beginning of an administration but equally normal to ride along with the initial judgments unless a major development causes rethinking or a particularly difficult situation requires repeated midcourse corrections. Saunders notes that sometimes in his experience, once an initial review had been completed, basic choices with regard to the direction of policy were made instinctively rather than through a further formal decision-making process and that often no one took the time to examine the consequences of a position taken. Saunders also indicates that a president's or senior policymaker's approach to Middle East questions has almost always been influenced by the particular lens through which he or she views the world. Kissinger, for instance, saw the world in a traditional, power-centered way; as a result, he was receptive to Israeli Prime Minister Yitzhak Rabin because they could talk in terms of the international balance of power. Carter and his secretary of state, Cyrus Vance, by contrast, viewed the world more in the context of human rights, making them better able to see the Palestinian perspective. When Ronald Reagan took office, he and his policymakers put the strategic lens back on, diminishing the importance of regional issues like the Palestinian question.[28]

Studies of the decision-making process show that statesmen who have formed a certain image of another country are able to maintain that image even in the face of large amounts of information that should alter it. The very human inclination among policymakers and their subordinates is to ignore information that does not fit basic assumptions.[29] For example, before the October 1973 war, both Israeli and U.S. intelligence analysts saw evidence of military preparations by Egyptian and Syrian forces but assumed the military moves were exercises because it was so universally believed that the Arabs would not launch a full-scale war. In the aftermath of Israel's stunning victory in the 1967 war, Israeli analysts had constructed a doctrine, which came to be called *ha-Konseptzia*, "the Concept," that maintained that the Arabs were inherently inferior and would never launch a war because they knew they could not win.[30]

Policymakers do consult with outside experts when doing so reinforces their viewpoint. A few prominent academics have become part of the policymaking milieu; they often obtain a hearing with policymakers because they have gained a reputation as scholars with the right political bent and an ability to talk in terms that are relevant to policy. One of these is the well-known historian of the Arab world Bernard Lewis. "This was a guy," according to a former government official, "who had all the appropriate credentials: knowing the Arab world, speaking Arabic better than most Arabs—and being pro-Israeli. It's an amazing combination." Another is Arab scholar Fouad Ajami, whom the former official describes as also combining a knowledge of the Arab world with a pro-Israeli tilt. "That combination has somehow worked," the official notes, "whereas somebody who is 'an Arabist' and sympathizes with the Arabs tends to be dismissed as pleading for a client."[31] Scholars like Lewis and Ajami reinforce a policymaker's mind-set. It is an exaggeration to say they are bluntly pro-Israeli or anti-Arab, but policymakers are often comfortable with them because they reinforce the tendency to view the Middle East through an Israeli-oriented prism, and they are generally either outspokenly critical of or patronizing toward the Arabs.

As the people in government who are supposed either to be or to rely on the Middle East experts, policymakers above all would perhaps not be expected to base serious Arab-Israeli policy on an incorrect or insufficient reading of history or on ephemera such as an impression or a public perception. Ultimately, however, policymakers are members of the general public who grow up with and base their fundamental attitudes on the same impressions and perceptions that inform the public. As one student of the policymaking process has noted, because people tend to absorb the values and beliefs that dominate society at the time they first begin to think about politics and because the concerns and events that are most important in any period pervade society, all those who come of age at that time are similarly affected. The orientation or framework originally formed is not easily replaced but instead "structures the interpretation of later events." [32]

Thus it has been a rare policymaker in the late twentieth century who has not taken office thinking as the general public does on Palestinian-Israeli issues: basically ignorant of the Palestinian situation and feeling, at least subconsciously, that Palestinians are backward, warlike, perhaps pitiable, and, especially, different from Americans, while Israelis are enterprising, progressive, under siege by Arabs, and "like us." In a substantive sense, until the 1990s it was also a rare policymaker who did not automatically exclude Palestinians from policy considerations simply because the Israelis constituted a sovereign nation and the Palestinians did not.

Any body of perceptions that has evolved into conventional wisdom is tenacious and extremely difficult to alter, and so these impressions have tended to remain popular throughout most administrations. Policymakers are not as a rule historians or students of any geographical area of the world. They come to their jobs with a general impression and at best a casual knowledge of a given issue and usually do not have the time while on the job to delve into the historical background or into those aspects that do not appear immediately relevant to policy. In fact, many of the bureaucrats and policymakers concerned with, and usually totally absorbed in, fast-breaking current developments tend to exhibit a clear disdain for history. History is often regarded as a leisure pursuit, a luxury that a busy policymaker or bureaucrat has little or no time for. [33]

There is often academic expertise, including scholarship in languages and the humanities, at the working level of the bureaucracy, but the impact of these low-level experts is minimal. Evidence that presidents and key policymakers often, perhaps usually, ignore this expertise is voluminous, and it has historically been the case that those working-level bureaucrats whose analysis occasionally does reach the president or his aides are as likely as not to have no academic expertise in or historical knowledge of the conflict. Richard Parker, a long-time Foreign Service officer and former ambassador to several Middle East countries, studied policymaker behavior through Middle East crises spanning sixteen years and involving three U.S.

administrations; he concluded that in each instance in which the United States miscalculated there was a tendency to ignore expertise. Decisions were made by a few people at the top, Parker found. Policymakers listened selectively, ignoring what they did not want to hear, and they consulted little and debated little. Decisions tended to be personal rather than collegial and to be based more often on intuition than on hard evidence.[34] Other studies have found that the greater the urgency of the situation, the fewer the participants in the decision-making process. "Although it may be liberating to get away from predictable and self-interested departmental views," one expert notes, "small high-level groups also get away from expertise."[35]

Policymakers also generally lack any continuity on the Arab-Israeli conflict that might compensate for a lack of historical background. Presidents and bureaucrats come and go, and neither is likely to pass on knowledge to a successor. Occasionally, a key policymaker from one administration remains in the next administration; for example, in the 1970s, Saunders made the transition from the Nixon-Ford administrations to the Carter administration, and, again in the 1990s, Dennis Ross served in a central policymaking role first in the George Bush and then in the Bill Clinton administrations. But this kind of continuity is rare. As a result, the policymaker who may once have known the background of a conflict has long since been replaced by a policymaker who cares little how the conflict originated and whose focus on the present situation makes him or her reluctant to look beneath the surface. The result of all these influences and pressures on policymakers, as has been noted, is to make them fall back on the easy analysis, the facile explanation, the common, superficial impression prevalent among the general public, in Congress, and in the media.

This book will describe in some detail the impact that the so-called frame of reference has had on policymaking on the Palestinian issue in each U.S. administration since Woodrow Wilson's—which coincided with the issuance in 1917 of Britain's Balfour Declaration promising support for the establishment of a Jewish national home in Palestine. The book will analyze (1) the state of knowledge of the president and key policymakers in each administration and the preconceptions with which these policymakers entered office, as gleaned through their writings, if any exist, or through the writings of those individuals who most influenced their thinking, or as deduced from a knowledge of what might be called their style—their religious inclinations, for instance, or their susceptibility to pressure from special-interest groups or their general policy outlook; (2) the state of public knowledge of the Palestinian-Israeli conflict in the United States and the prevailing set of public perceptions in each period, as determined by images and impressions conveyed in the media, in popular literature and movies, and by public, particularly congressional, figures; and, finally, (3) the ways in which policies in each administration have been influenced by the conventional wisdom on this question. There has been an extremely slow but evident evolution in U.S. policy toward the Palestinians since 1917, as there has been a definite evolution in the prevailing frame of reference; both phenomena will be discussed as they relate to each other.

The Palestinians' own actions have inevitably had some impact on how popular and policymaker perceptions have been formed and on how the policymaker frame of reference has changed over the years, and these actions will be examined for their impact on each administration. But the book will concentrate not only on how perceptions of the Palestinians have evolved over the years but also on popular perceptions of Israel and the roots of the U.S.-Israeli alliance, for the Palestinian image has to a great extent been a function of the Israeli image. Because the framework within which policy is made is determined as much or more by how Israel is perceived as by how Palestinians are perceived, it is important to look beyond the Palestinian image.

The intent of this book is to demonstrate how a body of perceptions can evolve into a seldom-challenged set piece and a tightly bound framework for thinking, to the point that public discourse and U.S. policymaking are profoundly affected. In his criticism of the movie *Nixon*, Kissinger asks, "But what if public discourse becomes warped by powerful engines of myth, big budgets and outright falsehoods?"[36] This book will not delve deeply into the "what ifs" of U.S. policy on the Palestinian-Israeli conflict, for they are endless: What if the United States had not acquiesced in Jordan's seizure of the parts of Palestine that were to have constituted a Palestinian state under the 1947 United Nations partition resolution? What if the United States had in some way forced Israel to permit the repatriation of Palestinians who fled their homes in 1948? What if the United States had treated the Palestinian problem as a political issue rather than as an issue simply of refugee relief from the beginning, after the 1948 displacement? What if the United States had encouraged rather than ignored the signs of Palestinian flexibility that began to emerge in the mid-1970s and grew apace throughout the 1980s? What if the United States had not waited almost three decades to recognize that the Palestinian issue was the heart of the Arab-Israeli conflict, as it finally reluctantly did in 1975? And so on.

Finding definitive answers to these questions is impossible, but, in suggesting the questions, the book will raise the possibility—indeed, the likelihood—that in a different, more open, and more all-encompassing frame of reference, many wars might have been avoided and peace in some form might have been possible much earlier. If public discourse had not been warped, policy might have been quite different.

1   Palestinians in the Nineteenth-Century Mind

Humorist Mark Twain's bitter cynicism and cleverness as a wordsmith combined to make him a popular commentator in mid-nineteenth century United States. His jaundiced observations of Palestine and Palestinians, publicized in his 1869 account of travels through Europe and the Holy Land, *The Innocents Abroad,* have made him a favorite with proponents of Israel ever since. Of the land of Palestine, he wrote, "Of all the lands there are for dismal scenery, I think Palestine must be the prince. . . . It is a hopeless, dreary, heartbroken land. . . . Palestine sits in sackcloth and ashes." Of its Arab inhabitants, he wrote that they were "all abject beggars by nature, instinct, and education." Describing an Arab village, he wrote that it was "thoroughly ugly and cramped, squalid, uncomfortable and filthy—just the style of cities that have adorned the country since Adam's time." When he rode into the village, he said, "the ring of the horses' hoofs roused the stupid population, and they all came trooping out—old men and old women, boys and girls, the blind, the crazy, and the crippled, all in ragged, soiled, and scanty raiment."[1]

In modern times, Twain's exaggerations have become grist for the mills of those who propagate the line that Palestine was a desolate land until settled and cultivated by Jewish pioneers. Twain's descriptions are highlighted in Israeli government press handouts that present a case for Israel's redemption of a land that had previously been empty and barren.[2] His gross characterizations of the land and the people in the time before mass Jewish immigration are also often used by U.S. propagandists for Israel.

Mark Twain's was only one of literally hundreds of travel books about the Middle East published in Europe and the United States throughout the nineteenth century that conveyed an image of Palestine and its Arabs; the image was almost without exception derogatory, although often less dramatically drawn than Twain's. In fact, the frame of reference within which Palestinian-Israeli issues have been perceived in the late twentieth century began forming when this image took hold—not when Israel was created in 1948 or even when Zionism became a force in Palestine fifty years earlier but in the mid-nineteenth century, when Western orientalist historians, geographers, and ethnographers, as well as Western Christian missionaries, religious pilgrims, and ordinary travelers like Twain, began visiting Palestine and conveying their impressions of the land and its people to readers and congregations throughout the Western world.

During the nineteenth century, particularly the latter half, interest in the Orient and especially in the Middle East flourished. The area became a favorite destination for travelers, scholars, and imperial agents—"layer upon layer of interests, official learning, institutional pressure, that covered the Orient as a subject matter and as a territory."[3] As many as twenty thousand visited Jerusalem alone every year.[4] Learned societies sent archaeological expeditions and geographical survey teams throughout the area, missionaries proselytized, and travelers wrote guides and memoirs that became bestsellers. At a time when the population of the United States was only about twenty million, the travelogue *Incidents of Travel in Egypt, Arabia Petraea, and the Holy Land,* by adventurer John Lloyd Stephens, sold over twenty thousand copies in the first two years after its publication in 1837.[5] Two decades later, missionary William Thomson published a long work on the Holy Land, *The Land and the Book,* that went through multiple editions and eventually sold almost two hundred thousand copies, said to be more than any U.S. title other than *Uncle Tom's Cabin* had sold to that point.[6] Twain's travelogue sold sixty-seven thousand copies in the first year after its publication.[7]

Travel books were the most popular genre at that time in the United States, according to one contemporary publisher; they did not sell fast, like novels by well-known authors, but they sold longer and more steadily and in the end sold best.[8] Americans also avidly read myriad periodicals that published travel articles, and travelers were well received on the lecture circuit. Works of fiction from the Middle East were also widely popular. In 1873, author Harriet Beecher Stowe edited a collection of nine works of fiction judged to be most popular at the time. Two of these, almost one-quarter, were Middle Eastern. Parts or all of *The Arabian Nights* were frequently reprinted in the United States throughout the nineteenth century. Stowe wrote that stories like "Aladdin's Lamp" and "Sindbad the Sailor" were so exotic that they gave "a start to the imagination, . . . a powerful impulse to the soul," particularly transporting impressionable children to a magic place "among genii and fairies, enchanted palaces, jewelled trees, and valleys of diamonds."[9]

Edward Said calls orientalism "the corporate institution for dealing with the Orient—dealing with it by making statements about it, authorizing views of it, describing it, by teaching it, settling it, ruling over it." Nineteenth-century orientalism imposed "a kind of intellectual *authority* over the Orient," became an instrument for imposing actual imperialist authority, and always operated from the assumption of Western superiority over the East and its dark-skinned peoples.[10] Orientalism perceived itself as a civilizing mission, a set of texts and observations that would assist the West in bringing modernity and civilization to primitive "natives." Westerners sometimes viewed the natives with affection, romanticizing them as "noble savages" or exotic remnants of the past, the fantastic genii of Stowe's imagination. Most often, however, native populations were scorned, and always they were regarded as uncivilized. The Orient in the nineteenth century, Canadian scholar Thierry Hentsch has observed, became all that the West was not, "the antithesis *par excellence* of modernity."[11]

The mere fact of categorizing and differentiating between the Western and the Oriental created a polarization between the two. Each became more so—more Western, more Oriental—and a barrier was thrown up to any kind of human encounter between different cultures, traditions, and societies. Without a human and personal element, orientalism became stylized; the people studied became objects, and their characteristics were typed. Characteristics became generalizations, and generalizations became part of an immutable framework about the Oriental nature, temperament, and mentality. Orientalism distilled certain "ideas about the Orient—its sensuality, its tendency to despotism, its aberrant mentality, its habits of inaccuracy, its backwardness—into a separate and unchallenged coherence," so that the mere mention of the word Oriental came instantly to convey an impression.[12] The impression was negative.

U.S. orientalism had elements of both religion and politics about it. Like the doctrine of Manifest Destiny, which encouraged westward expansion in North America, the nineteenth-century impulse to extend U.S. influence to the Orient was based on a desire to bring Christianity and "civilization" to the benighted infidel native populations of the Orient. For Americans who thought in these terms, the United States seemed centrally placed, between backward nations to the east and the west, to extend its reach in all directions, bringing enlightenment and the word of God to lands perceived to lie in darkness. As far as many Americans were concerned, it was the will of God that the United States should "stand as sure in Asia as in America." U.S. sights fastened on Palestine—the Holy Land, the land of the Bible—as the place where Christianity and the ancient kingdom of Israel must be restored and repossessed from Muslim intruders.[13]

Islam, and the West's perception of it, strengthened the barrier to understanding between the West and the East. Islam had been regarded as the enemy of Europe, the quintessential "Other," from its earliest days, when its emergence split the unity of the Mediterranean world; through the Dark Ages, when its learning and scientific accomplishments challenged Europe's ignorance and backwardness; through the Crusades, when Europe fought the infidel; and into the eighteenth and nineteenth centuries, when Europe began attempting to "recapture" the Orient from Islam and dominate it.[14] Only in this last period, however—coinciding with the rise of colonialism and of orientalism—did Europe begin to exhibit a sense of superiority over the Orient and to deny the intellectual, linguistic, and cultural debt it owed to Islam and the Arab world.[15] In this later period, it became politically expedient in Europe to portray Arabs and Muslims—the two became interchangeable in the Western mind—in derogatory terms. European travelers and merchants, abetted by the translation into European languages of *The Arabian Nights,* began to identify Arabs and Muslims with the images from those tales, and in European eyes all Arabs became indolent, obstinate, sensual—"wild, cruel, savages or robbers, in greater or lesser degree." These were the images and impressions passed on to Americans, even before they began to read *The Arabian Nights* for themselves.[16] As the nineteenth century went on, U.S. writers began to take on Islam directly, writing about the religion and the Prophet Muhammad for the express purpose, as one writer puts it, of exposing Islam as "a heap of rubbish," an imposture, and Muhammad as an evil schemer.[17]

In this orientalist framework, Palestine's Arabs were equated with "uncivilized" American Indians.[18] Moreover, because the Holy Land had special significance for Western Christians, Palestine's Arabs and Muslims were represented, uniquely among Oriental peoples, as aliens in their own land. To the missionaries, pilgrims, and other travelers who went to the Holy Land attempting to "reclaim" it and "restore" it to their preconceptions of its biblical state, Palestine's Arabs appeared to be foreign—not biblical, not Christian or Jewish, and therefore alien to Palestine's "true" Christian and Judaic heritage.

Nineteenth-century missionaries and other travelers and writers considered it a "shame that the Turk is permitted to keep and desecrate the

Holy Land,"[19] and historians ignored Muslim history, focusing on Palestine's biblical period or skipping ahead to the Crusades, leaving a thousand years of Arab and Muslim history untouched.[20] One scholar has noted that "the idea that the true Palestine lay buried beneath the rubble of the contemporary scene" became so common in the nineteenth century that the assumption that the Holy Land contains secrets waiting to be uncovered by Western science or by Israeli archaeologists remains today largely unquestioned.[21] Because Palestine was so widely regarded as belonging to Western Christians, there was, as one historian has observed, "a sense of injured pride, of molested personal property, when the Western Christian traveler arrived in Hebron, Jerusalem, or Constantinople after a long journey, with great expectations, only to find that the guardians of 'his' holy places" were Muslims or strange Eastern Christians. Americans railed against the alien "occupiers," often seriously advocating that Muslims be expelled from the Holy Land.[22]

If not reviled, Palestine's Arabs were often ignored altogether. Stephens had little to say one way or the other about the Arabs in his 1837 book, concentrating instead on Palestine's Christian holy sites and its Jewish inhabitants. In this period, Muslim Arabs made up well over 90 percent of Palestine's population, and the vast majority were not nomadic Bedouin, as one would gather from Stephens, but inhabitants of towns and villages. Thomson was similarly oblivious to Palestine's Arab and Muslim character. His chief concern in the 1859 book *The Land and the Book*, as the title suggests, was to relate Palestine's physical features to the Old and the New Testaments, and while he gave lengthy descriptions of the country's flora and fauna, people rarely figured in the book's seven hundred pages. Twain's description of the all-Arab town of Nablus is typical of how travel writers dealt with Arab localities. Calling the town Shechem, its biblical name, he described in detail the ancient roots of Jews there but never mentioned an Arab presence and only once used the name Nablus.[23]

Palestinians were sometimes romanticized as quaint evidence of Palestine's unchanging biblical aspect. The illustrated religious books, postcards, and stereoscopic slides popular in the late nineteenth and early twentieth centuries regularly captioned landscape pictures and photographs of the most ordinary village and town scenes with biblical citations.[24] Although not unsympathetic, these depictions portrayed the Palestinians simply as props—a bit unreal, backward, and above all different from the modern European and U.S. audiences at whom these portrayals were directed. It was only a short step from these stylized depictions to the kinds of unfavorable stereotypes that originated in nineteenth-century travel books and the press and that have clung to Arabs until today: the lascivious pasha, the harem girl, the devious rug merchant, the murderous tribal chieftain.

Western Christian travelers did not find Palestine's local inhabitants any less distasteful because some were Christian. The fact that these Arabs were the descendants of Jesus Christ's followers seemed in fact to escape the notice of most modern Western visitors, who, ignoring the local Christian communities themselves, were often repelled by the Eastern, Byzantine opulence of orthodox churches. Stephens lamented that the "parti-colored marble" and "gaudy and inappropriate ornaments" that marked the points of Christ's life in Palestine were wholly unlike descriptions from the New Testament and seemed to have been "intentionally and impiously" super-imposed by local Christian sects "to destroy all resemblance to the descriptions given in the sacred book."[25] Other writers criticized the Byzantine propensity for "gewgaw" and found the Eastern liturgies nothing more than "curious humbug" and "disgusting mummeries."[26] The animosity extended beyond the aesthetic. An active hostility developed between pros-elytizing Western Protestant missionaries and the clergy of local Christian orthodox sects, which strenuously resisted the Protestants' conversion efforts.[27]

The disappointment Stephens felt upon discovering that Jerusalem's churches did not live up to his mental image of New Testament Palestine is characteristic of much orientalist literature. For many nineteenth-century travelers, the actual Middle East was not as glamorous or romantic as in their imaginings. French artist Gérard de Nerval, who produced the classic *Voyage en Orient* after an 1843 trip to Egypt, Lebanon, Syria, and Turkey, complained to a friend that he would never find the "real Egypt" under the dust of Cairo; in the end, he said with no apparent sense of irony, "it is only in Paris that one finds cafés so Oriental."[28] The frame of reference from which these travelers approached Palestine was essentially the Parisian café scene or the English countryside or the small-town verdure of Mark Twain's Missouri, and what did not match these scenes was condemned.

The assumption that the real Orient lay somewhere beneath the surface, that the real Palestine was Christian or Jewish (or both) rather than Arab or Muslim, constituted a symbolic dispossession of the Palestinians. The notion that there were no Arab inhabitants in the Holy Land or that they were alien interlopers became a part of the popular imagination in the West, at least among the informed public and the religiously aware, well before the first Zionist settlers ever conceived of migrating to Palestine in the 1880s. The assumption fit perfectly with the prevailing orientalist and col-onialist notion that backward non-Western lands everywhere lay ready for the taking by more capable Western powers and peoples. Zionist writers and intellectuals seized on this idea with the well-known slogan that Palestine was a "land without people for a people without land," [29] and early Zionist writings planted and widely promoted the idea among Western Christians that a Jewish return to Palestine would be a fulfillment of biblical prophecies.

By contrast, the Arabs of Palestine did nothing to put forth their case in the nineteenth century. The wave of nationalism that swept Europe in this period did not reach the Arab world until later. In addition, because there was no separate Palestinian administrative entity during Ottoman rule, Palestinian Arabs did not yet have a well developed sense of living in a territorial unit called Palestine or of being "Palestinians," and they therefore also perceived no need to enunciate a specifically Palestinian nationalism.[30] Although this perception would change soon thereafter, as a greater sense of territorial nationalism began to develop early in the new century, nineteenth-century Palestinians, having no sense of what was about to happen to them, lacked awareness that they needed to defend their place in Palestine.[31]

Palestinians in these early years, in fact, were at a great disadvantage vis-à-vis the Zionists precisely because they lived in Palestine and therefore perceived no need to organize, propagandize, or publicize in order to advance their goal of continuing to live and form a nation in Palestine. By the time of the First Zionist Congress in 1897, 117 local Zionist groups existed throughout the world; a year later, at the time of the Second Congress, there were 900.[32] The Zionists' organizational efforts benefited in some measure from the very fact of the Jews' dispersal. The Palestinians—not dispersed, not reaching out for anything, minding their own business in their homeland—had already lost a major battle in the war to keep that homeland. The Palestinians also did not feel a need to intellectualize their right to remain in Palestine. Whereas Zionist writings defined a conscious and highly articulated sense of place, specifically because Zionists longed for a land they did not possess, the Arabs of Palestine as insiders, as possessors, felt no need in this early period to give expression to their attachment to the land.[33] The great outflow of poetry and prose in honor of home and land that today makes up the large body of Palestinian literature would come much later, when the land had been lost.

Certainly not all Westerners in the nineteenth-century Middle East were scornful of Palestine's Arab population or oblivious to its existence. Some U.S. missionaries in this era became deeply attached to the Arab world, began a tradition of educating local Arabs, and, at the post–World

War I Versailles peace conference, became active advocates for Arab independence. Among the most notable U.S. Protestant educators were those who founded the Syrian Protestant College, later renamed the American University of Beirut, and the Quakers who operated separate girls' and boys' elementary and secondary schools in Ramallah in Palestine. U.S. Protestants established educational missions throughout Ottoman Anatolia and Syria from the mid-nineteenth century onward and by the beginning of World War I had developed a larger network of these schools than any other Western nation. This missionary-led educational effort, with its mission presses, contributed at least a small part to a late-century resurgence of interest throughout the Arab world in Arabic-language publishing, from scientific textbooks to ancient Arabic literature.[34] The large U.S. mission and educational effort also produced the well-known families whose names (Dodge, Bliss, and others) are still associated with education in Lebanon—and because many missionary children entered the Foreign Service, with what supporters of Israel charge was a pro-Arab bias in U.S. State Department diplomacy for decades before and after Israel's creation.

Nonetheless, throughout the nineteenth century, whatever favorable images of Arabs these few missionaries may have transmitted to U.S. congregations and readers were largely buried under the weight of the more voluminous writings of those who were decidedly unsympathetic. In any case, Arabs were but a small part of the missionary effort. Missionary educators concentrated their efforts much more heavily in non-Arab Christian areas of the Ottoman empire, particularly in Armenian areas in the north, where the number of American-run schools was more than four times the number in Syria and Palestine. When they did work in the Arab world, missionaries tended to focus their proselytizing on the small Arab Christian communities, whom they tried to turn away from orthodoxy, rather than on Muslims, who were considered too difficult to convert.[35]

That the missionary effort in the Middle East was not entirely sympathetic to the Arabs is attested to by the fact that one of the earliest U.S. attempts to generate support for Jewish settlement in Palestine came from a Protestant missionary in the late nineteenth century. In 1889, a Presbyterian minister from Chicago, William Blackstone, visited Palestine and Syria, saw Palestine's potential for agricultural and commercial development, and concluded that it should be given to the Jews as a national home to alleviate their suffering. Two years later, he presented a petition to President Benjamin Harrison for which he had collected the signatures of 413 prominent non-Jewish Americans, including governors, congressmen, judges, clergymen, editors, and business leaders, among them John D. Rockefeller.[36]

The prevalence of anti-Semitism in the United States at the turn of the century did not by any means lead to an enhancement of the Arab image, although many have tried to demonstrate otherwise. Peter Grose, writing in his popular 1983 book, *Israel in the Mind of America*, notes that many of the State Department officials who staffed the Division of Near Eastern Affairs[37] in the 1920s, 1930s, and 1940s and opposed Israel's creation in 1948 were raised in the late nineteenth and early twentieth centuries on a diet of anti-Semitic children's literature that portrayed Jews as "routinely ridiculous figures." This literature made an early and largely indelible impression on young Americans and specifically on these policymakers in their youth, Grose believes. "Nothing they, or others like them, would learn or hear in their maturity," he says, "could wholly erase its effects."[38]

Grose does not exaggerate the extent of anti-Semitism in the United States or the lasting impact of impressions and mind-sets gained in childhood. As a people, Jews in the early twentieth century suffered grievous prejudice, and in a political sense they were only slightly less invisible than the Arabs of Palestine. Jews faced an anti-Jewish prejudice that came as second nature to most Americans, and, in an age totally unconcerned with political correctness, this prejudice was rarely hidden or camouflaged.

Nonetheless, among Americans the picture of Arabs conveyed by travelogues from Palestine was no better than the image of Jews, and may have been worse. Because Jews lived throughout the United States and because individual Jews had risen to positions of public prominence, they may have had a somewhat more human face among the U.S. public than those strange storybook Arabs from far away. The notion of sending the Jews to Palestine found favor with many Americans—both for cynical reasons, because the idea of decreasing the number of Jews in the United States was welcomed in the minds of many, and for the more compassionate reason of providing Jews with a home and a sanctuary from persecution. Furthermore, the thought of Jews returning to the Promised Land inspired among many Americans imbued with biblical teachings a kind of religious and emotional passion with which Palestinians in their invisibility could not hope to compete. Jews, in short, had a place in the mind of Americans, for better or worse, whereas Palestinians had virtually no place at all, and certainly no favorable place, in the public consciousness.

Although Grose is undoubtedly correct in believing that anti-Semitic children's literature made a lasting impact on many of those who later became involved in making policy on the Palestine issue, it is equally true that those U.S. policymakers who supported the Zionist program in Palestine and ultimately supported the creation of Israel must have read the same children's literature and been able to throw off its invidious influences. Furthermore, it must be assumed that the substantial body of derogatory writings on the Arabs of Palestine made at least as enduring an impression on young minds in the late nineteenth and early twentieth centuries as anti-Semitic literature had. Indeed, Massachusetts Senator Henry Cabot Lodge spoke stirringly during a speech on the Senate floor in 1922 of having read Sir Walter Scott's stories *Ivanhoe* and *The Talisman* as a young boy and come away with an intense admiration for the Crusaders who freed Jerusalem from Muslim rule. "The dominant impression of the boyish mind," he said, "was hostility to the Mohammadan."[39]

To the extent, then, that early twentieth-century policymakers in the United States thought about the Palestine situation at all, it was within an orientalist framework in which Palestine stood forth as a holy and biblical land destined by divine writ for reclamation by Christians and Jews and in which the native Arab inhabitants were unimportant. As the Zionist movement grew in strength, this framework was increasingly reinforced by Zionist intellectuals and lobbyists. There was no counterpoint; no one brought the Arab and Muslim presence and lineage in Palestine to Western attention or refuted the paternalistic assumption that Western, including Jewish, stewardship must necessarily be better for Palestine than Arab/Muslim stewardship. Within this framework, Arabs, simply put, did not fit.

2 Woodrow Wilson
"Rising Above" Self-Determination

A frame of mind in which Arabs essentially played no part, in which they were politically invisible, patronized, disdained, or ignored altogether—this is the mind-set with which the policymakers who made the first official decisions on Palestine for the United States after World War I grew up. President Woodrow Wilson was a devout Christian, son of a Presbyterian minister, a man for whom prayer and Bible reading were daily routines.[1] Like most U.S. Christians of his day, he had grown up well tutored in the biblical history of Jews and Christians in Palestine. For Wilson, the notion of a Jewish return to Palestine seemed a natural fulfillment of biblical prophecies, and so influential U.S. Jewish colleagues found an interested listener when they spoke to Wilson about Zionism and the hope of founding a Jewish homeland in Palestine. Few people knew anything about Arab concerns or Arab aspirations; fewer still pressed the Arab case with Wilson or anyone else in government. Wilson himself, for all his knowledge of biblical Palestine, had no inkling of its Arab history or its thirteen centuries of Muslim influence. In the years when the first momentous decisions were being made in London and Washington about the fate of their homeland, the Palestinian Arabs had no place in the developing frame of reference.

Wilson was more than usually free of bigotry for the period in which he lived and was considerably more compassionate and progressive in his attitude toward other peoples than most of his well educated, well-to-do U.S. and European contemporaries. During his tenure as president of Princeton University from 1902 to 1910, he appointed the first Jew and the first Roman Catholic to the faculty; he appointed the first Jew to the New Jersey Supreme Court when he was New Jersey's governor from 1910 to 1912; and his appointment of Louis Brandeis to the U.S. Supreme Court in 1916 marked the first time a Jew had been named to the Court.[2]

Wilson is best remembered today for his doctrine of self-determination, enunciated in January 1918 as part of his Fourteen Points for bringing World War I to a peaceful conclusion. As envisioned by Wilson, the principle of self-determination would guarantee a virtual end to colonialism, to the domination of "subject peoples" by outside powers, and it would grant these peoples a role in determining their own future when power alignments were reordered in the aftermath of the war. His greatest obsession in the years between the beginning of U.S. involvement in the war in 1917 and the stroke that caused his withdrawal from an active role in the presidency in 1919 was trying to ensure that the Allied victors imposed a compassionate peace on the vanquished. Although he failed in large part, his concern was to guarantee that harsh, vengeful terms were not imposed on Germany, that the peoples formerly dominated by the defeated Central European and Turkish powers were freed from subjugation, and that world order and peace would be ensured by the formation of a general association of nations, the League of Nations, that would mutually assure political independence and territorial integrity.

Despite his compassion and marked lack of religious bigotry, however, Wilson was not entirely free of at least an unconscious bigotry and was not as concerned as he might have been to ensure the universal application of his vaunted universal principles. If he had no problem giving Jews and Catholics equal rights and high-level appointments, he was unready to do the same for blacks—or, in the end, for most colonial subjects around the world. He seems to have had a paternalistic view of dark-skinned peoples, seeing them as deserving of kindness and compassion but not of equality.[3] This attitude no doubt accounts for why, as will be seen, he was inconsistent in his view of how the principle of self-determination should be applied.

Biblical nostalgia played some part in Wilson's decision to back the Zionist program in Palestine, but practical political reasons were the primary impetus. In point of fact, Wilson did not care deeply one way or the other about Palestine's political fate. He certainly gave no thought to the fate of the Palestinian Arabs or to the impact on them of Zionist plans. His support for the Zionists was not a high priority either, although he ultimately played a pivotal part in the advancement of Zionism by virtue of being the first U.S. president to support the notion of a Jewish homeland in Palestine. When he gave his endorsement in October 1917 of Britain's plan to issue a statement in support of the Zionist movement—a statement issued a month later as the Balfour Declaration, which promised British support for the establishment in Palestine of a Jewish "national home"—his primary purpose was to support an ally in wartime. At the height of World War I, Britain hoped to win the political and financial backing of the Zionist movement and world Jewry in general, which were being wooed by Germany, and the British were under some pressure from leading Zionists such as Chaim Weizmann to promise Palestine to the Zionists in return for that support. Although Palestine was still at that point under Ottoman control, the Balfour Declaration was conceived in anticipation of an Allied victory over Turkey, which would give Britain control of the territory. The British expeditionary force commanded by General Edmund Allenby captured Palestine a month after the declaration's issuance.

From Wilson's standpoint, his endorsement was a gesture of wartime support; it cost him nothing and must have seemed to him to be of little consequence, while at the same time showing him to be responsive to the desires of his U.S. Zionist friends. When he did finally endorse the British declaration, he did so casually, a month after Britain had requested his support and only upon being reminded of the request. He apparently did not know or particularly care about the precise content of the declaration in advance, and, probably in order not to antagonize Turkey, with whom the United States was not at war, he did not speak out publicly in favor of the Zionist enterprise in Palestine for another several months.[4]

If Wilson did not care deeply about Palestine, some of his closest political colleagues did. Their pressure on behalf of the Zionist cause following issuance of the Balfour Declaration and during the peace conference that rearranged colonial alignments in the aftermath of World War I made him, for all intents and purposes, a strong Zionist and committed the United States to supporting the notion of a Jewish homeland in Palestine. His friend and political ally Brandeis had been among the founders of the Zionist Organization of America in 1915 and was serving as its president when Wilson appointed him to the Supreme Court in 1916.[5] Wilson's friendship with Brandeis was probably what most heavily influenced him to give active support to Zionist goals. Zionist leaders abroad, such as Weizmann, as well as prominent U.S. Jews like Rabbi Stephen Wise used Brandeis as an entree to Wilson on matters regarding Palestine. In the last year of the war and the first year of the Versailles peace conference, before Wilson's illness forced him from active participation in the presidency, Brandeis and other U.S. Zionists approached the president frequently with requests for public and private reassurances of continuing U.S. support for the Zionist cause.[6]

Zionist pressures on Wilson were not completely unopposed, but forces supporting the Arab cause were far less effectual, and most pro-Arab activity did not focus in any case specifically on the Arabs of Palestine. Like the Zionists, Protestant missionary supporters of the Arab cause had easy access to Wilson, in this case through industrialist Cleveland Dodge, a long-time friend and former schoolmate. Dodge's family had been heavily involved since the nineteenth century in educational efforts in the Ottoman Empire, including the founding of the Syrian Protestant College in Beirut. Dodge had been a close personal friend of Wilson since their student days at Princeton University. He refused a formal appointment in Wilson's administration but maintained frequent informal contact and is said to have had a great deal of influence on the president to the point, early in Wilson's term, of helping prevent Brandeis's appointment as attorney general.[7]

Dodge was deeply involved in the wartime relief effort for the Middle East led by the American Board of Commissioners for Foreign Missions. Because the mission board feared for the safety of Americans and U.S. property in the Ottoman Empire, as well as for the continued operation of the relief effort, Dodge and his colleagues actively pressed Wilson to remain officially neutral toward Turkey, persuading him, for instance, not to declare war on the Ottoman Empire when he submitted his message to Congress declaring war on Germany in April 1917. During and after the war, Dodge and his associates on the mission board became involved with the Arab independence movement in Syria, where the U.S. relief effort had won many friends among Syrian nationalists. When President Wilson established a commission of scholars and area experts in early 1918 to provide political and economic analyses of colonial areas of the world to help determine the postwar governance of these areas, missionary spokesmen had a significant input. Mission officials wrote studies for the commission, which came to be called "the Inquiry." They also heavily lobbied Inquiry members and after the war lobbied the U.S. peace-conference delegation, urging that Arab wishes be taken into account in postwar governing arrangements. They actively promoted the idea of a U.S. mandate over Syria and Armenia.[8]

In the end, however, Dodge and his missionary associates had virtually no impact on U.S. postwar policy toward the Middle East and particularly on Wilson's support for the Zionist project. First and foremost, their interest was centered on Armenia rather than on the Arab portions of the Ottoman Empire. When they did deal with Arabs, they did so almost exclusively with Christian Arabs, and in Syria rather than in Palestine. Palestine played but a small part in the considerations of any of the missionary spokesmen, as indeed it did in the policy considerations of the United States, which was dealing in the larger scheme of things with postwar arrangements in areas of the Middle East well beyond Palestine and in areas of the world well beyond the Middle East. Second, U.S. Protestants were not unanimous or single-minded in their support for the Arab cause, as witnessed by the fact that the Presbyterian General Assembly passed a resolution in 1916—sponsored by the same Reverend William Blackstone who had organized the pro-Zionist petition sent to President Benjamin Harrison in 1891—favoring establishment of a Jewish homeland in Palestine.[9]

Indeed, the missionaries' support for the idea of Arab independence, centered as it was on Syria rather than Palestine, was not necessarily inconsistent with support for Zionism. In an era in which it was judged appropriate for the Western world to determine the political reordering of the East, the possible inconvenience of fitting a Jewish national home into the small piece of Arab land that was Palestine would most likely have gone wholly unnoticed even by the most Arabophile of missionaries. As ever, the Arabs of Palestine fit into virtually no one's calculations.

Zionism and Woodrow Wilson's principle of self-determination were never really reconcilable. Self-determination was rooted in an ingrained U.S. aversion to colonialism that viewed the domination of other peoples as unethical, as well as in the pragmatic belief that political stability throughout the world would be better assured if subjugated peoples were freed from colonial domination. This was not a workable proposition with regard to Palestine, however. The impossibility of ever reconciling Zionism, which proposed to form a more or less exclusively Jewish homeland or state, with self-determination for Palestine's established Arab population has always since Wilson's day forced the United States into an ambivalent position about the universal application of this anticolonial principle.[10]

Wilson himself may never have confronted the inconsistency, but his secretary of state, Robert Lansing, clearly recognized the problem, and Wilson's legal counselor advised him that true self-determination would prevent establishment of a Jewish state in Palestine.[11] When Brandeis, in a notable conversation with British Foreign Secretary Arthur Balfour in Paris during the peace conference in 1919, was asked how Wilson could reconcile support for Zionism with the principle of self-determination, Brandeis observed that Zionism proposed to deal with a "world problem"—the fate of worldwide Jewry—that transcended the interests of any existing local community.[12] Balfour had already concluded that commitment to Zionism obviated any possibility of achieving numerical self-determination in

Palestine—that is, allowing Palestine's Arab majority to exercise self-government[13]—and he was undoubtedly relieved that Wilson was also willing to disregard his commitment where Palestine and its Arab inhabitants were concerned.

Three months after this conversation, Balfour wrote a memorandum frankly acknowledging that "in Palestine we do not propose even to go through the form of consulting the wishes of the present inhabitants of the country." The Allies were already committed to Zionism, he wrote. "And Zionism, be it right or wrong, good or bad, is rooted in age-long traditions, in present needs, in future hopes, of far profounder import than the desires and prejudices of the 700,000 Arabs who now inhabit that ancient land." Balfour forthrightly acknowledged that "so far as Palestine is concerned, the Powers have made no statement of fact which is not admittedly wrong, and no declaration of policy which, at least in the letter, they have not always intended to violate."[14]

Britain had backed away from a promise to the Arabs once before. In 1914, in an effort to enlist the aid of Sherif Hussein of Mecca in leading an Arab revolt against Turkish rule, Britain formally instructed its high commissioner in Egypt, Henry McMahon, to promise Hussein that Britain would support Arab independence after the war in a large area encompassing parts of Greater Syria and what are today Jordan, Iraq, and Saudi Arabia, excluding only the coastal area of Lebanon, which was to be under French influence. The exchange of letters in which this promise was contained became known as the McMahon correspondence. The Arabs, including leaders of the Palestinian Arabs, believed they had reason to expect that Palestine was included in the area to be granted independence since the only areas specifically excluded were all located north of Beirut and well outside Palestine, but the British immediately hedged and ever afterward maintained that they had never intended to include Palestine within the future Arab state.[15]

In a colonialist era in which native peoples were believed to have no capability for governing themselves and not even much interest in self-rule, failure to live up to political promises made to them was not seen to be out of order. Even as Wilson championed self-determination, he qualified the principle by noting that "undeveloped peoples" were not yet ready to take on "the full responsibilities of statehood" and should be given friendly "guidance" in the form, for instance, of the British and French mandates imposed on Palestine, Iraq, Lebanon, and Syria.[16] In regard to Palestine, the colonial powers considered neither Jews nor Arabs to be ready for the "full responsibilities of statehood," but Jews, being European, were regarded as educable, whereas Arabs—dull and inarticulate as they were thought to be—were not so perceived; they were not, in fact, considered even to want self-rule. The overriding of Arab interests was thus done carelessly, without thought.

Indeed, it has become so much a part of the conventional wisdom that the Arabs of Palestine were neither ready for nor even aware of the possibility of independence in the early 1920s that popular historians molding and reinforcing the Palestinian-Israeli frame of reference more than half a century later accepted as a matter of course colonialism's disregard for Arab interests. Historian Peter Grose, for instance, after citing Balfour's memorandum, frankly praises the British foreign secretary for being "willing to rise above" the principle of self-determination.[17]

Wilson found it easy to ignore Palestinian interests, even when presented with clear evidence of Palestinian opposition to the Zionist program. In 1919, at the behest of his missionary friends, Wilson dispatched a commission to investigate the views of the inhabitants of the former Ottoman Empire, including Palestine. Led by a college president, Henry King, and a businessman and former Wilson campaign contributor, Charles Crane, who both began with what they called a "predisposition" in favor of Zionism, and staffed by several others with connections to the missionary effort in Turkey, the King-Crane Commission spent two weeks in Palestine interviewing over two hundred Muslim, Christian, and Jewish individuals and groups. The commission concluded that the full Zionist program would be a "gross violation" of the principle of self-determination, as well as of the Palestinian people's rights, and should be modified.[18]

The report noted that in its conversations with Jewish representatives and from its reading of the literature on Zionist goals provided by Zionists in Palestine, the King-Crane entourage had gained the clear impression "that the Zionists looked forward to a practically complete dispossession of the present non-Jewish inhabitants of Palestine, by various forms of purchase." The Christian and Muslim Arab population of Palestine, constituting 90 percent of the total in 1919, was, the commissioners learned, virtually unanimously opposed to the Zionist program in its entirety. British officers consulted by the commission believed that the Zionist program could be carried out only by force, and it was the commission's view that decisions "requiring armies to carry out . . . are surely not gratuitously to be taken in the interests of a serious injustice."[19]

The King-Crane Commission's conclusions on Palestine had no impact on Wilson administration policy. The report went unpublished for three years until Wilson, already out of office, authorized its publication in July

1922. Even then, the State Department published it only unofficially.[20] There is no evidence that Wilson, who had a stroke two months after the report was issued, ever read it, certainly none that he took its conclusions seriously. In fact, the commission's recommendations were probably doomed from the start. Britain and France disagreed with the decision to send the commission in the first place and refused to appoint their own delegates. Allied disapproval was compounded by the fact that the commission's major recommendation was that all of the former Ottoman Empire except Mesopotamia (Iraq) be placed under a U.S. mandate,[21] which flew directly in the face of British and French designs in Palestine and Syria.

As for the recommendations on Palestine, by the time the commission was appointed, the United States already felt itself to be committed to supporting Zionist goals, so the recommendations on this territory were predestined to fall on deaf ears. Wilson regarded his support for the Balfour Declaration as an unbreakable solemn promise and told the commissioners even before their departure that the Palestine question had already been virtually closed by the Allies.[22] Even so, U.S. Zionists, fearing that Wilson's resolve would slip, exerted strong pressure. A leading Zionist, Judge Felix Frankfurter, wrote Wilson that the commission's investigation was causing world Jewry the "deepest disquietude," prompting a reassuring response from Wilson.[23]

By 1920, the frame of reference in which the Arabs of Palestine were viewed was already firmly set. Palestine had begun to be considered a Jewish land, the Arabs of Palestine had all along been ignored or disdained, and the United States was committed, in the absence of any pressing interest to the contrary, to supporting Zionism. Wilson's public statements on behalf of the Zionist program took on a new and more enthusiastic tone, as he began to pledge U.S. support not simply for a Jewish homeland in Palestine but for a Jewish commonwealth.[24] U.S. Zionists began insisting that the Balfour Declaration was committed to making all of Palestine a Jewish national home rather than simply, as the declaration actually stated, to forming a Jewish national home *in* Palestine. During his 1919 Paris meeting with British Foreign Secretary Balfour, Justice Brandeis spelled out the distinction, pointing out that if the Zionist program were to be successful, all Palestine would have to be the Jewish homeland.[25] It was another three years before Britain issued a white paper clarifying its position that the declaration had not been intended to grant the entirety of Palestine to the Jews.[26] Wilson himself did not use the broader formulation, but other officials and the media tended to use it interchangeably with the more restrictive language of the declaration. This interpretation and Wilson's own carelessness with the terms *homeland* and *commonwealth* indicated at least a casual disregard for how much of Palestine the Jews might receive and in what form, and how much the Arabs might lose.

Wilson's successors were equally committed to the Zionist program. By 1922, the year the League of Nations confirmed the British Mandate for Palestine, United States policy was firmly pro-Zionist. President Warren Harding's secretary of state, Charles Hughes, told Balfour early in the year that the United States interpreted the idea of a homeland for the Jews in Palestine to mean establishment of a Jewish state.[27] In 1924, Britain and the United States concluded the Anglo-American Convention, which regulated U.S. trade with Palestine and guaranteed the protection of U.S. citizens there. The convention formalized U.S. endorsement of Britain's control over Palestine and, by reiterating provisions of the Balfour Declaration and of the British Mandate instrument, formally accepted Zionism in Palestine.[28] •

Although the State Department has long had a reputation for opposing the Zionist enterprise, there is little evidence in this early period of any strong resistance to Zionist plans from any level of the U.S. bureaucracy. In fact, the dismissal of the King-Crane Commission report was an early indicator of the fate of most of the opposition to Zionist settlement in Palestine posed over the years by lower-level functionaries within the U.S. foreign-policy bureaucracy. The overriding concern of the United States in these early postwar years was to avoid any foreign entanglements, and although the United States supported Britain and regarded its endorsement of the Balfour Declaration as a more or less binding commitment, the obligation did not extend to active intervention in the affairs of Palestine. One scholar who has studied State Department memoranda throughout the 1920s notes that although internal State communications contain many examples of grumbling against Zionism and Zionist pressures, these complaints were never translated into active opposition to or lobbying against the Zionist project. Because official U.S. policy was noninterventionist, the State Department rebuffed both the frequent representations of U.S. Zionists for active support of the Zionist project and the far less frequent requests from Arab American groups urging diminished support for the Balfour Declaration and the British Mandate.[29]

It was in these early days that the State Department's refusal to give Zionism active backing became identified in the minds of many Zionist supporters with active anti-Zionism. Anti- or non-Zionism then came to be equated with anti-Semitism. The term *Arabist*, meaning by strict definition anyone who speaks Arabic and knows Arab culture, has come to be used more loosely in common parlance to label any State Department official who has spoken for the Arab perspective or against the Zionist/Israeli perspective on the Arab-Israeli conflict, whether or not that person is an expert in the Arabic language or Arab affairs. The image of power that has grown up around these so-called Arabists has been exaggerated from the beginning. The first "Arabists" undoubtedly included some anti-Semites, but most opposed giving active U.S. support to Zionist settlement in Palestine for practical reasons: because they foresaw that this support would lead to bloodshed or simply because they felt it was not in the U.S. interest to become involved in matters that were at that time more properly Britain's concern. Whatever their motivation, their views carried little if any weight.

There are numerous instances from the earliest days in which the views of State Department officials opposed to U.S. promotion of Zionism were ignored, as there are numerous instances, on the other side of the issue, in which State functionaries at all levels fully supported Zionist goals in Palestine. Among the first group, Robert Lansing, Woodrow Wilson's secretary of state at the time the Balfour Declaration was issued, is a prime example. Lansing opposed Zionism because he believed the United States should not alienate Turkey, which controlled Palestine until December 1917, but Wilson did not allow him a role in making policy on this issue. Lansing was so thoroughly bypassed in fact that when the Balfour Declaration was issued, fully a month after Wilson's secret endorsement of it, he had to inquire of the U.S. ambassador in London what the background of the declaration was.[30]

Lansing was not the only official whose opposition to aspects of the Zionist program went unheeded. More than one U.S. official on the scene in the Middle East warned over the years that Arab opposition to the Zionist program was widespread and would ultimately lead to bloodshed between Arabs and Jews, but the warnings were ignored.[31] In 1922, during the administration of President Warren Harding, Allen Dulles, then head of the State Department's Division of Near Eastern Affairs, later to become the director of the Central Intelligence Agency in the Eisenhower administration, and not a Middle East expert except by avocation, wrote a memorandum to an assistant secretary of state expressing his "strong" feeling that the State Department should not officially support the positions of either Zionists, anti-Zionists, or Arabs. Zionism, he observed, had "a certain sentimental appeal," but this appeal had to be measured against "the cold fact" that Jews made up only 10 percent of Palestine's population. Dulles's call for political neutrality fell on deaf ears.[32]

Not by any means was the State Department in this early period unanimously opposed to Zionism. William Yale, an oil explorer temporarily employed as an intelligence agent at the end of the war, had initially predicted a bitter Arab reaction to Zionism but soon changed his attitude and began sending pro-Zionist views to U.S. policymakers. As a member of the King-Crane Commission, he wrote a dissent to the majority conclusion, saying that, despite Arab opposition to Zionism, the Arabs of Palestine and Syria did not have a strong national history, and "due consideration" should be given to the Jews because they did have "a national history, national traditions, and a strong national feeling." Retracting the promises made to the Jews in the Balfour Declaration would be, he thought, "unjust and unwise." Reflecting the widespread view that Zionism equaled Western values equaled civilization, whereas Arabs and the East equaled the absence of civilization, Yale said that a Palestine controlled by Jewish genius would be a bastion of Western ideals in the East.[33]

Diplomatic historian Frank Manuel believes that Wilson's preference for a Jewish Palestine "soon seeped through" all levels of the Foreign Service. He gives as what he calls a typical example the change of heart experienced by a young vice consul whose memoranda were anti-Zionist in the first few months after issuance of the Balfour Declaration but who soon "began to take an autonomous Jewish Palestine for granted." Assuming that a Jewish state was all but a *fait accompli,* he set about devising strategy on this premise, even drawing a map of possible boundaries for the use of the Versailles conference delegation and suggesting ways of mollifying Palestine's Arab population.[34]

Another State Department official, serving as director of Near Eastern affairs in Allen Dulles's temporary absence in 1922, wrote in the aftermath of a flare-up of intercommunal violence between Jews and Arabs in Palestine that the British had not been firm enough with the Arabs, who, he said, possessed "a tendency to loot and kill" and who had not been "as severely treated as their known tendencies might require."[35] This view, a variation on the theme that the Arabs understand nothing but force, was already at this early stage a part of the conventional wisdom. The memorandum is an indication that the pro-Arab, anti-Zionist attitude so often attributed to the State Department had not in fact taken hold. The experience of the young vice consul who went along with President Wilson's pro-Zionism because it was the established policy was very much the norm.

The U.S. Congress, even at this early date, was fairly enthusiastic in its support for Zionism. Zionist activists worked closely with members of Congress in 1922 to pass a joint resolution favoring establishment of a Jewish national home in Palestine. A Jewish delegation from Massachusetts, prompted by the Zionist Organization of America, started the process when it approached Massachusetts Senator Henry Cabot Lodge and requested that he sponsor a Senate resolution supporting the Zionist program. In one of the early examples of organized pro-Zionist lobbying, other Zionist groups urged their members throughout the country, according to the *New York Times*, to make the issue of support for the resolution "a local issue with Representatives and Senators who sought election." New York Congressman Hamilton Fish sponsored a resolution simultaneously in the House, which passed in June 1922, and three months later, Lodge's Senate resolution was combined with Fish's and passed as a joint resolution of Congress.[36]

Lodge's efforts on behalf of the resolution were apparently made in direct response to Zionist requests. Because he was an isolationist and had taken no previous interest in Zionist goals in Palestine, the *New York Times* criticized him in repeated editorials for suddenly discovering an enthusiasm for Zionism in search of Jewish votes.[37] Lodge was not influenced by the criticism and continued his vigorous support for the Palestine enterprise. Expounding a common theme, he gave a speech at one point during Senate debate on the resolution in which he hailed Jewish influence in Palestine as a vast improvement on its native Arab influence. "I never could accept in patience," he said, "the thought that Jerusalem and Palestine should be under the control of the Mohammedans." The very idea that these territories might remain in the hands of "Turks" was, he believed, "one of the great blots on the face of civilization, which ought to be erased."[38] *Ivanhoe* had clearly had a lasting impact on him.

Similarly, Fish, speaking at a dinner given by U.S. Zionist leaders to express thanks for his work on the joint resolution, observed that he foresaw a Jewish "state" in Palestine that would stand as a peaceful, democratic bastion between the "warlike races" of Muslim Africa and Asia.[39] Zionists may or may not have suggested these lines of argument to Lodge and Fish, but they probably had no need to prompt the congressmen. Casting slurs on Palestine's Arabs was politically risk-free, and Lodge and Fish were enunciating what had already become a basic tenet of the conventional wisdom: the notion that Arabs and Muslims were incompetent, lacking in civilization, and warlike.

Among the informed public, as in Congress, the emerging view of the Palestine issue was, for lack of virtually any input from the other side, largely Zionist-centered. While the public at large undoubtedly had no knowledge of any of the political issues involved in Palestine and at most possessed only an ill-defined sense of Palestine as a place in the Bible related to Jesus Christ and somehow related to the Jews, that small segment of the population who read the country's major newspapers did know something of the issues involved, and they learned it from an almost entirely Zionist perspective.

One study of articles on Palestine appearing in 1917 in four leading U.S. newspapers—the *New York Times,* the *Los Angeles Times,* the *Chicago Tribune,* and the *Washington Post*—shows that editorial opinion almost universally favored the Zionist project and condemned Muslim/Turkish rule. Considering the low level of interest in the issue among the general public, coverage was heavy throughout the year, averaging as many as two articles a week in the *New York Times.* Editorials and news stories alike applauded Jewish enterprise, heralding a Jewish return to Palestine as "glorious news" and "one of the wonderful romances of all history," a pioneering event similar to the opening of the American West. Britain's capture of Palestine in December 1917 and the prospect of a Jewish return were hailed as events that would "deliver" the Holy Land from the Muslims' "bloodstained" hands and from "the thousand-year dominion of the infidel." With a fervor befitting a pulpit rather than a newsroom, the papers portrayed the capture of Jerusalem, a city deemed holy to Christians and Jews but not to Muslims, as a modern-day crusade that had "redeemed" and "reclaimed" the city from pagan defilement.[40]

Ironically, an anti-Turkish editorial campaign launched by the very Protestant missionaries who most effectively advocated the Arab cause in the war and immediate postwar years had the effect of adding to the general impression of Arabs as rapacious and marauding. In the aftermath of the Armenian massacres of 1915–1916, the mission-led relief effort headed by Dodge sent a barrage of press dispatches to wire services and editors across the country. The specific intent of the effort to expose Turkish atrocities was, as one of the missionary leaders said, to "create a sentiment" throughout the country. Headlines detailing the atrocities and specifically attributing the horrors to Turkish brutality began appearing all over the United States. The mission board also saw to it that copies of a book detailing the Armenian massacres published in mid-1917 made their way to the desks of all members of Congress and many of the country's opinion molders.[41] Arabs did not figure at all in this propaganda campaign, and the issue had nothing to do with Palestine, but as is evident from Lodge's reference to the "Turks" who inhabited Palestine, in those days only the most sophisticated Americans, and not many of them, knew the difference between a Turk and an Arab. They were all subjects of the Turkish Ottoman Empire,

and, in the minds of most Americans, they were all infidels and all unde-
sirable. The U.S. missionaries' efforts to "create a sentiment" against the
Turks had a profound and lasting impact as well on the image of Arabs.

Other studies of articles on Palestine in leading U.S. papers during the
1920s indicate that coverage, often front-page coverage, remained frequent
even after Zionism had become a less pressing issue for the United States.
Articles on Palestine in the *New York Times* averaged just under one a week
throughout much of the decade, and, in periods of crisis, coverage was much
heavier. In 1922, for instance—a year that saw Britain's submission to the
League of Nations of a draft Mandate for Palestine and, later in the year,
Arab strikes and demonstrations in Palestine protesting the Mandate—the
Times averaged an article almost every other day. In 1929, when differ-
ences over Jewish access to the Western Wall in Jerusalem led to violent
Arab demonstrations and the massacre of more than sixty Jews in Hebron,
coverage in the *Times* and other leading papers soared.[42]

Throughout the decade, the coverage continued to be, as it had been in
the early postwar years, favorable to the Zionist program, supportive of
British control over Palestine, and either highly disdainful of Arabs and
Arab capabilities or prone to ignore them altogether. For the most part, editorials took the line that Zionists were pioneers building a land and a society very much as pioneers had done in the United States. Zionists were
widely seen to be carrying on the work of Western civilization. They were
assumed to share Western values, Western intellectual capabilities, and
Western energy, whereas Arabs were considered hopelessly uncivilized.[43]

The Arab point of view was basically ignored in the press. During the
first seven months of 1929, for instance, the *New York Times* ran fifty-one
articles on Palestine but carried only a single paragraph enumerating the
demands of Palestinian Arabs. In the last five months of that year, after the
start of Arab rioting, which grew out of Arab objections to increasing Zionist and British control of Palestine, only 5 percent of the numerous articles
in the *Times* and three other leading papers addressed the perspective of the
Arabs of Palestine on events there.[44] Editorialists generally believed that
the Arabs opposed Zionism and the Jewish influx to Palestine because they
were naturally warlike, had been duped by hate-mongering Muslim propagandists, or were simply obtuse. It would be ideal, the *Los Angeles Times*
wrote in 1929 in an editorial that succinctly captured the essence of the
anti-Arab stereotype, if "the wild Arabs of the desert [were] to open their
hearts to moral suasion," but "unhappily sweet reasonableness does not
seem to be the strongest point of the Bedouin sheik. What he does thoroughly understand and appreciate . . . is the song of the bullet." No account

was taken of Arab political grievances, and the notion of an independent Palestinian Arab state was, in the *New York Times*'s estimation, "fit for Bedlam only."[45]

In its editorials the *Times* did oppose the formation of a specifically Jewish state in Palestine. Owner Adolph Ochs, although Jewish, was an avowed non-Zionist and believed the establishment of a state on the basis of religion or race was wrong. But the paper favored allowing Jews seeking refuge from oppression and persecution elsewhere in the world to settle in Palestine in large numbers, never questioned Britain's right to continue its domination of Palestine, and rarely expressed interest in the fate of Palestine's Arabs.[46]

Given the relative unimportance of the Palestine issue to the United States in the 1920s, the fact that the country's major newspaper devoted one or two articles a week to the subject for years on end, even in the absence of a crisis, and much more during crisis periods, is of considerable significance. The issue was so minor a part of the larger postwar issues in which Wilson became deeply involved that his biographers mention Palestine only in passing or, more often, not at all. For his successors in the 1920s, it was an even less important issue. The relatively heavy press coverage is an indicator of the extent of Zionist influence even in this early period. One scholar has estimated that, as of the mid-1920s, approximately half of all *New York Times* articles were placed by press agents,[47] suggesting that U.S. Zionist organizations may have placed many of the articles on Zionism's Palestine endeavors. The *Times* and many other papers also received a large portion of their information on Palestine from the Jewish Telegraphic Agency wire service, and the *Times* in addition had a resident correspondent who for many years in the 1920s exhibited strong Zionist sympathies in his articles.[48]

While newspapers played a large role in this era in shaping the image among informed Americans of Jews and Arabs and their relative worth, movies probably had a greater impact on a broader spectrum of Americans in creating an unflattering, if largely nonpolitical, image of Arabs. Motion pictures began to come into their own in the 1920s as a major form of entertainment and a major shaper of public perceptions, reaching audiences vastly broader than the readership of newspapers and periodicals. Movies caricaturing Arabs became an instantly successful genre, giving further substance to the derogatory picture of Arabs first drawn almost a century earlier.

In the 1920s, a total of almost ninety U.S. films dealt in some way with Arabs. No list of early movie classics is complete that does not include such films as Rudolph Valentino's *The Sheik* and *Son of the Sheik*, *The Thief of Bagdad*, *Beau Geste*, *The Desert Song*, or *Kismet* or, in the 1930s, Eddie Cantor's *Ali Baba Goes to Town* or Boris Karloff's *The Mummy* and its sequels. The most engaging Arab portrayed in these movies was a buffoon or a charming rogue. Most were lawless and violent, oversexed, and without honor.[49]

In the 1920s, the motion picture took up where the travel books of the nineteenth century left off, capitalizing on what has apparently always been a popular U.S. fascination with foreign villains and carrying the dark image of the Arab to a much wider audience than books would ever do. The movie screen, as one expert has noted, "is where America has met most of its Arabs."[50]

In this early period of U.S. policymaking on Palestine, Zionist activists were the prime movers in the formulation of both the public view of the Palestine issue and the official policy that emerged. But they were building on a base of anti-Arab sentiment that had begun to be created a century earlier, well before the Zionist program in Palestine came into existence. The two factors were equally important, for while it is clear that the strength of the official U.S. commitment to Zionism in this period arose directly from the strength of the Zionist lobbying effort, it is equally clear that Zionist activists would not have been as successful in pressing their case with Wilson and other U.S. policymakers and members of Congress had public perceptions of the Arabs not been quite so unfavorable and had the Arabs mounted a significant lobbying campaign of their own.

U.S. Zionists were skilled, well organized, and numerous even at this early date. Brandeis's easy access to both Wilson and Balfour was a factor of inestimable importance in shaping U.S. and British policy. The Zionists mounted a multipronged effort, simultaneously attempting to shape the views of the public through frequent and well placed media stories, of Congress through direct lobbying, and of key policymakers themselves through personal contact. The Zionist effort marked the already fairly sophisticated beginning of what was to become an extensive, well-organized pro-Zionist and pro-Israeli lobby.

Membership in U.S. Zionist organizations ebbed and flowed in the 1910s and 1920s, but enthusiasm was at a peak precisely when it needed to be— in the war years and immediate postwar years, when government and congressional support was most necessary and the United States was making crucial decisions. Membership in the Zionist Organization of America grew tenfold, from twenty thousand before World War I to almost two hundred thousand during the war, but dropped again to about eighteen thousand by 1929.[51] I. L. Kenen, who founded the modern pro-Israeli lobbying organization AIPAC (American Israel Public Affairs Committee) decades later, credits passage of the joint congressional resolution supporting Zionism in 1922 to "a pioneering Zionist lobby"[52]—a lobby strong and numerous enough to make support for the resolution an election issue for congressmen. Even late in the decade, when formal membership was at a low point, Zionists could mobilize large numbers of supporters for demonstrations and letter-writing campaigns. When anti-Zionist demonstrations broke out in Palestine in August 1929 and Jews were murdered in Hebron, U.S. Zionists organized multiple demonstrations of fifteen thousand and twenty thousand in New York City. During the first few weeks of the Palestine disturbances, the State Department received a thousand letters from Zionist supporters.[53]

Arab American lobbying efforts were insignificant by contrast. A handful of Palestinian, Lebanese, and Syrian individuals, leaders of two small Arab American organizations, actively protested British and U.S. policies favoring Zionism after World War I and throughout the 1920s. These activists organized demonstrations, wrote letters to their representatives in Congress and U.S. officials, and in one instance testified before the House of Representatives during its 1922 debate on a resolution endorsing the Balfour Declaration. The Arab American lobbying effort was minuscule, however, particularly compared with the strong effort being made by Zionist supporters, and U.S. officials paid little or no attention to the Arab representations.[54]

Even without their organizational strength, Zionists would have had a relatively easy sell. Palestine was an issue of minor significance at this point to the U.S. government and to the public; the public, in fact, knew virtually nothing about its politics. But Americans nonetheless had a general impression of Arabs as a primitive race of people with few redeeming qualities and as profoundly different from Americans. To Christians whose only knowledge of Palestine came from the Bible, a Palestine inhabited by Jews seemed much more natural than one inhabited by Muslims. Incidents of intercommunal violence in Palestine such as occurred in 1922 and 1929, whose origins in serious political grievances were never understood by Americans or even fully appreciated by most U.S. officials, tended simply to reinforce the prevalent image of Arabs as uncivilized and prone to violence.

Politically, the Arabs were virtual nonentities. The extent of their political invisibility was strikingly demonstrated when the Balfour Declaration referred to them—at a time when they made up over 90 percent of Palestine's population—as one of the "existing non-Jewish communities." Identifying Palestine's Arabs according to what they were not—not Jews— became common in official and unofficial parlance, thus establishing their political nonexistence as a principal element of the conventional wisdom on the Palestine question. The Mandate instrument submitted by Britain for ratification by the League of Nations in 1922 incorporated the Balfour Declaration into the preamble, confirming in international terms the Palestinian Arabs' negative designation as a people who existed not in themselves but only in relation to the people they were not. The Mandate was, by most reckonings, a document and a governing instrument "framed unmistakably in the Zionist interest." Like the Balfour Declaration, the document assured the civil and religious rights (but not the political rights) of "existing non-Jewish communities" but did not once use the term *Arabs*.[55]

The frame of reference on the Palestine question as a political issue was thus Zionist-centered from the beginning. Given the extent of anti-Semitism in the United States at this time, it was not a particularly pro-Jewish phenomenon. Indeed, some have suggested that much of the support for Zionism arose out of a desire to rid the United States of Jews, either for blatantly anti-Semitic reasons or to prevent immigrants from swamping the U.S. labor market.[56] The frame of reference was, however, strikingly non-Arab and therefore, almost by default, emerged as pro-Zionist. The Arabs were historical and biblical oddities, not real people. Jews, however, had a central place in the common Christian conception of how the Holy Land should be peopled. The Arabs also did little to put their own case forward or to counter the Zionists' effective lobbying. As a result, Jews and not Arabs were at the forefront of the public mind when political issues regarding Palestine arose. Simply by having proposed a change in the status quo in Palestine, and having succeeded in achieving it, Jews attracted a kind of attention to themselves never accorded the Arabs of Palestine.

Scholar Mark Tessler, a student of the Palestinian-Israeli conflict, has noted that at the early stages in Arab political development, political activity was expressive, emerging through such vehicles as periodicals, speeches, discussion groups, and congresses. Political expression did not reach the stage of mobilizing popular support, building institutionalized mass movements, and engaging in the kind of activism that could directly confront political adversaries until the years between the world wars. Only then did Arab nationalists begin to command popular loyalty and to mobilize mass support around strategies for throwing off autocratic and foreign rule and moving toward self-rule.[57] Thus, although the Zionists failed to understand the true nature of Arab nationalism—dismissing Palestinian aspirations and mistakenly assuming that Palestinians were no different from other Arabs and could find political expression and a political identity as part of the Arab world—it is quite true that Palestinian political development was slow compared with that of the Zionists and was unready in these years to confront Zionism on an equal footing.[58]

As far as Americans were concerned, the Arabs of Palestine were political ciphers. Arab lobbyists were not strong or numerous enough to counter the sophisticated intercessions of Zionist lobbyists. No Arab bloc of voters influenced American politicians, no newspapers or books or travelers to Palestine juxtaposed favorable images of Palestine's Arabs with the increasingly common images of pioneering Zionists in Palestine, and no one ever thought it necessary to take the Palestinian Arabs seriously.

3 Franklin Roosevelt
Locked In

Franklin Roosevelt made no major policy decisions with regard to Palestine, but because he perpetuated what had already become a firmly set frame of reference at a critical time in the history of Palestine, his tenure was pivotal. Elected in 1932, he was in office from the era of increased Jewish immigration to Palestine prompted by Hitler's rise to power in Germany, through the Holocaust, to the beginning of serious discussion of statehood for the Jews in Palestine. The United States accepted Zionism virtually by rote, having inherited from Wilson a commitment to promote a Jewish homeland in Palestine. Policymakers did not question the real meaning or consequences of this pledge or notice that what began as a commitment to a Jewish homeland in some part of Palestine soon became a pledge to turn all of Palestine over to the Jews.

Roosevelt's outlook was shaped not by public opinion but alongside it. His views on the Palestine issue, which were, like the general public's, based primarily on a religious upbringing heavily imbued with Bible readings featuring a Jewish Palestine, were undoubtedly also deeply influenced by the widespread perception of Arabs and Muslims as primitive and pagan. In office, his views were reinforced and his policy given definition under the close scrutiny and influence of Zionist leaders who had ready access to the White House and of political colleagues, in Congress and elsewhere, who were themselves influenced by Zionist activists.

Roosevelt was not a deeply religious man and did not attend church regularly, but his Episcopal faith was a strong force in his life, and he is said to have inherited a "pious streak."[1] Like most of his contemporaries, he had an extensive knowledge of the Bible and was fascinated with biblical lands.

45

He shared the widespread view that the Holy Land was properly a Jewish place. The story is told that while en route to Tehran in 1943 to meet with Winston Churchill and Joseph Stalin, he ordered his pilot to fly low over Palestine and showed great excitement at seeing everything from "Beersheba to Dan."[2]

Knowledge of the Jews' biblical heritage did not automatically make Roosevelt a committed Zionist, and he has been severely criticized for doing virtually nothing to help the Jews during the Holocaust. Although Roosevelt did make some half-hearted attempts to deal with the relocation of Jewish refugees, he never showed much interest in the problem of rescuing the Jews, never made a serious effort to curb State Department obstruction of Jewish immigration to the United States, and never showed real concern to halt the murder of millions of Europe's Jews.[3] Nor was Roosevelt free of some anti-Semitic instincts. During a discussion of resettlement schemes for Jews in North Africa during his summit meeting with Winston Churchill in Casablanca in early 1943, for instance, he evidenced a surprising degree of bigotry, expressing sympathy with German complaints about the overrepresentation of Jews in the professions.[4] He and his wife and friends often exhibited a casual, almost thoughtless anti-Semitism, what one biographer calls a "jocular anti-Semitism" that was "nearly universal" in the circles in which the Roosevelts traveled. Franklin Roosevelt made jokes about "Hebraic noses," for instance, and Eleanor Roosevelt commented pointedly on the number of Jews in her husband's law class. According to his biographers, however, Roosevelt was not as bigoted as most of his upper-class contemporaries and not so bigoted that he did not have several close Jewish friends and political colleagues. Unlike many around him, Roosevelt was rarely vicious in his remarks or feelings about Jews, and he is said to have surprised even his wife in the extent to which he sought out Jewish colleagues. During Roosevelt's presidency, a time when Jews made up about 3 percent of the U.S. population, they constituted 15 percent of his top appointments.[5]

As a result, U.S. Zionist leaders had fairly easy access to Roosevelt in the 1930s and 1940s and exerted considerable influence. Because of disagreements among U.S. Jews over support for Zionism and disagreements over style and tactics between U.S. Zionists and European Zionists led by Weizmann, Zionism had lost considerable support in the United States during the 1920s and early 1930s. By 1935, however, Rabbi Stephen Wise— a protégé of Supreme Court Justice Brandeis and a longstanding colleague of Roosevelt in Democratic party politics—had taken control of and revitalized Brandeis's old organization, the Zionist Organization of America.

He and another Brandeis protégé, Judge Felix Frankfurter, whom Roosevelt appointed to the Supreme Court in 1939, used their access to the president to bring Zionist issues to his attention and urge his intercession on behalf of the Zionist cause.[6]

During the war, Roosevelt feared that too much public talk of Palestine would play into Germany's hands by stirring up anti-British protest among the Arabs, and as a result he avoided public statements himself and attempted to quash any public U.S. involvement with Palestine, even to the point of rejecting Frankfurter's request in July 1942 that he meet with David Ben-Gurion, then head of the Jewish Agency in Palestine, the local Zionist representative body.[7] In private, however, Roosevelt's Zionist and pro-Zionist colleagues kept the issue always before him, and he repeatedly gave them private reassurances of his continuing pro-Zionist sympathies.

There was a considerable degree of schizophrenia during these years in the attitude of the Roosevelt administration, the Congress, and the general public toward American Jews, the fate of Europe's Jews, and the political question of Palestine. Statements of support for the Zionist enterprise in Palestine, whether these were Roosevelt's private assurances or the public resolutions and platform statements of Congress and the political parties, were something altogether different from actual steps to help the Jews, and when it came, for instance, to opening doors to Jewish refugees from Europe, political support for Zionism meant nothing. Polls from the late 1930s and 1940s clearly showed that the majority of Americans were unwilling to permit more Jewish immigration to the United States, even if the result was not rescuing Jews from Hitler, and in 1942 an anti-Semitic element in Congress defeated a measure that would have given Roosevelt the power to loosen immigration restrictions for the sake of Jewish refugees. Roosevelt himself, although increasingly aware of German atrocities and frequently under pressure from his wife to do something for Jewish refugees, in fact was never deeply enough impressed by the Jews' plight to press hard. He allowed the director of the State Department office dealing with refugee issues, Breckinridge Long, to talk him into a go-slow approach on the issue of admitting Jews. A Democratic party contributor whose diaries have shown him to be a virulent anti-Semite and an elitist basically opposed to admitting refugees of any sort to the United States, Long practiced a policy of deliberate obstruction toward Jewish immigration.[8]

Political support for Zionism was clearly a great deal easier for politicians than any tangible step to help Jews, particularly admitting substantial numbers to the United States, and the cynicism and hypocrisy of many of those U.S. politicians who paid lip service to Zionism is strikingly revealed by this fact. Anti-Semitism was still alive and healthy throughout the United States even late in the war. But political support for Zionism is the point here. The political mind-set that assumed Palestine to be a Jewish place and ignored Arab rights and the Arab presence there did not require an absence of ethnic prejudice against Jews and, whatever the degree of anti-Semitism abroad in the country, Roosevelt's political support for the Zionist enterprise in Palestine throughout his administration provided vital sustenance to the project and helped hasten the political demise of the Arabs of Palestine.

Despite consistent support for Zionism, Roosevelt was never well informed about the Palestine situation. Most fundamentally, he operated under a misconception about what the Balfour Declaration had promised to the Jews. In a memorandum to Secretary of State Cordell Hull discussing a 1939 British white paper on Palestine that favored the Arab position, Roosevelt stated his own—incorrect—understanding that Britain's intention from the beginning had been that, despite Arab objections, Palestine would be "converted" into "a Jewish Home which might very possibly become preponderantly Jewish within a comparatively short time. Certainly that was the impression given to the whole world at the time of the Mandate." Given that intent, he said, he did not believe that the British could legally limit Jewish immigration, as they proposed in the white paper to do.[9]

Roosevelt was no doubt correct in assuming that the Balfour Declaration was widely perceived throughout the world to be unambiguous in its grant of all of Palestine to the Jews, but the British themselves did not have such a sweeping intent. A white paper issued in 1922 for the specific purpose of clarifying British policy stated that Britain had not "at any time contemplated . . . that Palestine as a whole should be converted into a Jewish National Home."[10] Not unusually, the clarification had escaped the notice of the United States, and by the time Roosevelt came to office, the Zionist interpretation had taken firm hold. The British had in fact made commitments to the Arabs that the Arabs regarded as of a solemnity equal to that of the Balfour Declaration, but Roosevelt and most of the U.S. government were unaware of these assurances.

Roosevelt was ignorant both of the actual facts on the ground in Palestine and of the Arabs' attitudes. In the memorandum to Hull on the 1939 British white paper, one of whose provisions was to limit Jewish immigration to Palestine to seventy-five thousand over a five-year period, Roosevelt discounted Arab objections to the influx of Jewish immigrants. The Jews could be easily absorbed, he thought, because the number of Arab immigrants to Palestine since 1920 had "vastly exceeded" the number of Jewish immigrants for that period.[11] He was seriously mistaken. According to British demographic statistics, Jewish immigration from 1920 through 1938, totaling 306,049, was more than ten times the level of Arab immigration, which totaled 23,407.[12] Jewish immigrants had averaged ten thousand a year throughout the 1920s, but the number soared in the early 1930s in response to Hitler's rise in Germany, trebling in 1933 and doubling again in 1935.[13] Moreover, heavy Jewish immigration in these years had drastically altered the Arab-Jewish population balance—from 90 percent Arab and 10 percent Jewish in 1920, to 69 percent Arab versus 31 percent Jewish in 1939.[14]

Although he had a deep appreciation of the Zionists' attachment to Palestine, Roosevelt apparently had no understanding of the Palestinian Arabs' feeling for their native land and seemed oblivious to the impact the Zionist program was having on them. Without any thought for the justice of forcibly expelling an entire population, he devoted considerable thought to devising ways of accommodating Jewish control of Palestine by moving the Arabs aside. In a 1939 conversation with Brandeis, for instance, Roosevelt discussed sending 200,000–300,000 Palestinian Arabs to Iraq. He repeated the idea to the British and a year later to Weizmann.[15] Well into the war, he was still thinking about the possibility and told a cabinet member that he wanted to begin moving the Arabs to some other part of the Middle East so that eventually 90 percent of Palestine would be Jewish.[16]

Perhaps because he was so poorly informed, Roosevelt seems to have had little understanding of the dilemma the British faced in Palestine. In fact, it is ironic that throughout the 1930s, as the United States became more solidly pro-Zionist despite having no direct responsibility for Palestine, the commitment to the full-scale Zionist program began to erode in Britain, where the responsibility lay. As the British became more acutely aware of the problems involved in ignoring the Arab position in Palestine, they began to back away from the kind of political surety that the United States, in its relative ignorance, had come to feel. It was the British who had to deal with the recurrent Arab riots and, between 1936 and 1939, the Arab Revolt waged to oppose British control and protest dramatically increased Jewish immigration. After each crisis, the British government, recognizing Arab alarm at the prospect of becoming a minority in their native land and at the increasing Zionist economic and political influence in Palestine, sent an investigative commission to report on local conditions, and each time it issued a report or white paper recommending limitations on Jewish immigration, restrictions on Jewish land purchases, or increased Arab participation in local government. There is virtually no evidence that Roosevelt or any other

U.S. policymakers understood the basis for Britain's increasing sense that unqualified support for the full Zionist program could not be reconciled with the reality of a majority Arab population in Palestine.

The by now fairly long legacy in the United States of disdain for Arab competence and civilization made it all but impossible for most Americans, even at the policymaking level, to fathom the political content of Arab protests against the Jewish influx to Palestine. Arab rioting and terrorist attacks on Jews and Britons in Palestine appeared to Americans only to confirm the longstanding view of Arabs as naturally bloodthirsty and too primitive to be concerned about issues like independence or political control. To Roosevelt, the Arabs of Palestine were simply part of a sea of "seventy million Mohammedans" surrounding the small Jewish enclave who desired nothing more than to "cut [the Jews'] throats the day they land," as he once wrote to a colleague by way of explaining his decision to continue minimizing public attention to the Palestine issue. Jews, he said, are "of all shades—good, bad and indifferent"; Arabs were undifferentiated cutthroats.[17] He put the Arabs' discontent down to ethnic hostility and economic deprivation and believed they could be mollified with economic incentives. Shortly before his death in 1945, he told a friend that the reason the Middle East was "so explosive" was that the people were so poor. When the war was over and he was out of office, he said, he intended to look into the possibility of establishing something like the Tennessee Valley Authority in Palestine, which "will really make something of that country."[18]

This view is an extension of the argument that gained currency in the media and in Congress shortly after World War I: a Jewish presence in Palestine would bring such economic prosperity to the Arabs that they would accept the Jews gratefully. Indeed, such thinking had a long colonialist history. Roosevelt's talk of using economic incentives to smother political impulses is also an indication of how firmly rooted and enduring a conventional wisdom can become, for despite the fact that a quarter century of Western economic and social practices introduced to Palestine by Jews and the British had demonstrably done nothing to quiet Arab political concerns, U.S. officials persisted in believing that the Arabs' problems were economic.

Little of the State Department's input in this period did much to enlighten Roosevelt or to change public or policymaker perceptions in general. One review of State Department communications between 1939 and 1948 indicates that, contrary to the common belief that the so-called Arabist diplomats in this period were knee-jerk Arab sympathizers, in reality the State Department never showed particular concern about which side would ultimately control Palestine.[19] At least one high-ranking State Department official in fact was a Zionist sympathizer. Sumner Welles, who served as undersecretary of state under Hull until 1943, has been described as having "pronounced Zionist sympathies" and served as one of the principal high-level government contacts for Zionist leaders on the Palestine issue.[20]

The State Department did have its share of anti-Semites. As noted, the office that dealt with refugee issues in the early 1940s was in the hands of a strong anti-Semite, Breckinridge Long, who tried to obstruct the immigration of Jewish refugees. But Long did not work on Middle Eastern affairs and did not make policy on Palestine. More to the point, however anti-Semitic any of these officials were, anti-Semitism did not translate into support for the aims of the Palestinian Arabs. The chief concern of diplomats in State's Division of Near Eastern Affairs in the early 1940s was the effect the Arab-Zionist conflict would have on U.S. and British pursuit of the war. Palestine itself was recognized to be primarily a British problem, and the State Department was interested only in the impact the conflict would have on U.S. interests.[21] Contrary to the prevailing view, State was not, either in this period or later, particularly interested in the justice or morality of either side's position in Palestine or the relative merits of either side's historical or legal claim to the land. Diplomats rarely spoke up for Arab concerns about what Zionism meant for Palestine's Arab population.

As the war went on, Zionist leaders became increasingly active in lobbying outside the White House, particularly in Congress. In 1941, the Zionist leadership tapped New York Senator Robert Wagner, a close Democratic political ally of Roosevelt, to chair a newly revived organization of prominent pro-Zionist Gentiles whose mission was to keep the issue of Palestine as a Jewish homeland before the public. Wagner was an active campaigner on behalf of Zionism whom historians class as both genuinely interested in the fate of the Jews during World War II and politically aware of the large numbers of Jewish voters in his state.[22] Despite Roosevelt's efforts to limit public discussion of the Palestine issue, by the time the new organization, called the American Palestine Committee, was formally reconstituted in April 1941 (it had originally been formed in 1932 by several congressmen and gone inactive),[23] it had among its members sixty-eight senators, including the majority and minority leaders, as well as two hundred congressmen, several governors, and two cabinet members. Within a year, its membership included eight hundred "distinguished citizens" in several local chapters throughout the country. Although the organization was

non-Jewish, it was run out of Zionist offices in New York, and Zionist functionaries wrote Wagner's correspondence and in one instance an article for
publication.[24]

The U.S. Jewish community itself was not wholly supportive of Zionism
and the concept of a Jewish state in Palestine at this stage. The largest Jewish organization, the American Jewish Committee, representing 1.5 million
U.S. Jews, was opposed to Zionism, and even some Zionists hesitated to
press the issue of statehood in Palestine at a time when many believed the
rescue of European Jews, rather than politics, should be U.S. Jewry's first
priority. In opposition to these anti-Zionist and moderate Zionist schools,
a group of Zionist maximalists led by Rabbi Abba Hillel Silver, who pushed
openly for Jewish statehood in Palestine, rose to prominence and soon
wrested the leadership of U.S. Zionism from the moderates. The maximalist view carried the day when Silver's group won the support of a Zionist
convention held in May 1942 at the Biltmore Hotel in New York for a plan,
henceforth called the Biltmore Program, presented by Ben-Gurion to establish a Jewish state.[25] This marked the first time U.S. Zionism had formally taken a unified position in favor of full statehood.

In 1943, the brash Silver set about organizing an aggressive grass-roots
campaign to win congressional and popular support for the Zionist cause.
He formed the American Zionist Emergency Council (AZEC), organizing
local chapters in every community in the country with a Jewish population, as well as in the hometown of every influential member of Congress.
Within little more than a year, AZEC had four hundred local committees.
Members were instructed to keep in constant touch with their representatives in Congress by writing them and holding dinners and luncheons in
their honor. Approaching the non-Jewish community at the local level,
AZEC activists successfully organized local rallies supporting Jewish statehood in Palestine and in 1944 generated pro-Zionist resolutions and telegrams to Congress from as many as three thousand organizations, from labor unions and Rotary clubs to church groups and granges.[26]

The Zionist lobby had the wholehearted support of Congress and most
politicians. In 1939, twenty-eight senators signed a pro-Zionist statement
inserted in the Congressional Record. Three years later, the support in Congress was far more resounding. On the twenty-fifth anniversary of the Balfour Declaration in November 1942, at Zionist urging and despite Roosevelt's efforts to downplay public references to Palestine, sixty-three senators
and almost two hundred members of Congress issued a statement noting
the urgent need to establish a Jewish national home in Palestine in view of
Nazi persecution of Jews in Europe. By 1944, the assumption that Palestine

should be Jewish was so prevalent in the United States that both the Democratic and the Republican party platforms, using nearly identical language, called for establishment of "a free and democratic Jewish commonwealth" and urged that Palestine be opened to unrestricted Jewish immigration. Both Roosevelt, breaking his usual silence on this issue, and his Republican opponent issued similar endorsements.[27]

Sympathy for Zionism among the country's politicians did not imply particular knowledge of what Zionism stood for or of the situation in Palestine, any more than it did for Roosevelt himself. Even the Zionists lamented congressional ignorance about the complexities of the situation. Among themselves, Zionist leaders remarked on the high level of sympathy for Zionism they had found throughout Washington, but they were disconcerted by how little anyone actually seemed to know about Zionism, about Palestine, and about British promises to the Zionists. One Zionist leader complained that although most members of Congress were "astoundingly sympathetic" and the Zionist cause enjoyed support "in every sector of Washington," every politician had to be instructed in Zionism, "for it is a closed book to them."[28]

Knowledge of the Arabs was even more limited. None of the several congressional declarations on Palestine issued through the war years showed any indication that Congress knew that more than two-thirds of Palestine's population was Arab or understood the nuances of the British and U.S. commitment—that is, to support establishment of a Jewish homeland in some part of Palestine rather than to give all of Palestine to the Jews. Political discourse in the United States entirely discounted Arab opposition to the prospect of Palestine's becoming a Jewish land, either ignoring the opposition altogether or, in the words of one historian, explaining it away as "baseless, minimal and perverse."[29]

Throughout the extended period of Roosevelt's presidency, the public's generally unfavorable impression of Arabs—whether a clearly defined perception or merely a vague sense of Arabs as distasteful—and the favorable public perception of the Zionist program were both further reinforced by movies and the media. Roguish Arabs continued to be a popular theme in motion pictures, which grew in popularity as a form of entertainment in the 1930s. Media coverage of the Palestine question also continued throughout the 1930s and into the 1940s to reflect the generally pro-Zionist, Jews-as-pioneers, Arabs-as-primitives viewpoint that had marked coverage throughout the 1920s. In addition, the terrible plight of Europe's Jews increasingly became a theme that aroused sympathy for Zionist plans. During the Arab Revolt against British rule in Palestine, from 1936 to

1939, newspaper articles often emphasized the Jews' legal and historic rights to settle in that territory, and as the extent of the Nazi atrocities became increasingly known, emphasis was placed on Palestine as a refuge for the Jews.[30]

This is not to say that public interest in the Palestine question, outside political circles, had grown significantly by the late 1930s. Although the issue was covered in the major newspapers, it was not of major interest to the vast majority of Americans, particularly during the Depression, when concerns closer to home were paramount. But Zionism was already a part of the national mind-set on Palestine. Officially, the United States had for some time felt itself, in the absence of any opposing pressure, to be automatically committed to the Zionist program. The assumptions that Palestine was soon to be Jewish, that Jews had an unlimited right to immigrate there, and that they would ultimately gain numerical predominance and political control had been an integral and generally unquestioned part both of official policy and of the general mind-set for many years before Americans became aware of the Jews' desperate plight in Europe and before the question of Jewish statehood in Palestine began to be debated in international forums.

Public knowledge of the Palestine situation increased markedly in the war years, thanks to the grass-roots efforts of Zionist activists and the heavy coverage given the situation of Europe's Jews, and by the end of World War II the notion that the Jews could find a refuge in Palestine had become commonplace. Polls taken in the two years after the war generally indicated that fully 80 percent of Americans had at least heard or read about Palestine and that as many as half followed developments there.[31] As the Jewish claim to Palestine rose to prominence in the minds of Americans, the knowledge that Arabs inhabited the land and also had a claim was generally pushed aside. The Arab perspective did not fit into the postwar frame of reference.

Roosevelt did gain a glimpse of real Arab concerns just two months before his death, but it was too late. He met with Saudi Arabian King Abdul Aziz, known in the West as Ibn Saud, aboard the cruiser USS *Quincy* in the Suez Canal on February 14, 1945, the first time a U.S. president had ever met an Arab leader. Roosevelt's planned postwar aid package for Saudi Arabia was the principal impetus for meeting Abdul Aziz, but much of the discussion apparently centered on the Palestine problem, Roosevelt appealing to the Saudi king for understanding of the European Jews' suffering and their need for a haven in Palestine. Unable to understand the justice of giving the Jews Arab land rather than lands belonging to the defeated Germans who were the Jews' oppressors, Abdul Aziz argued with Roosevelt that Palestine was not the place for the Jews. He was effective enough to wrest from Roosevelt an undertaking to consult fully with both Arabs and Jews on all Palestine decisions and to "do nothing to assist the Jews against the Arabs." In early April, Roosevelt followed up with a letter to Abdul Aziz formally putting the seal of the presidency on the pledge.[32]

Roosevelt was sending mixed signals by now, however, and may well have been deeply confused about the Palestine issue. On the one hand, he was clearly impressed by Abdul Aziz's representations and on the plane home told Secretary of State Edward Stettinius that he wanted to meet with congressional leaders to "re-examine our entire policy in Palestine." In an address to Congress he said he had learned more about "that whole problem, the Muslim problem, the Jewish problem, by talking with Ibn Saud for five minutes than I could have learned in the exchange of two or three dozen letters."[33] On the other hand, Zionists in the United States were outraged by the meeting, and probably with some justification, for Abdul Aziz was accustomed to regaling anyone who would listen with lengthy anti-Jewish diatribes, and one may properly be suspicious of the notion that Roosevelt learned anything about "the Jewish problem" or very much of a positive nature about Arab aspirations from the Saudi king.

What may have most impressed Roosevelt was the forcefulness of Abdul Aziz's hostility to a Zionist presence in Palestine. If he did not necessarily learn what the Arabs of Palestine wanted in a positive sense, he did come away with an understanding that trying to implement the Zionist program could well lead to war, and he tried to warn some U.S. Jewish leaders against a head-on collision, emphasizing in private his belief that establishing a Jewish homeland just then was impossible. At the same time, in response to Zionist complaints about the meeting with Abdul Aziz, he authorized Rabbi Wise to issue a public statement in March—midway between the meeting and the follow-up letter to Abdul Aziz—to the effect that he continued to support unlimited Jewish immigration and the establishment of a Jewish state.[34]

The State Department had to scramble to explain away Roosevelt's inconsistencies, lamely telling its Middle East posts that by authorizing Rabbi Wise's statement Roosevelt really meant to indicate his hopes for the long-term future and that he still intended to consult both Arabs and Jews before making any decisions.[35] In the event, Roosevelt died only days later, and his successor, Harry Truman, was easily able to ignore any commitments to consult seriously with Arabs. The incident demonstrates, however, the basic ignorance in which the United States operated in this period: ignorance of the precise British promises to Jews and Arabs, ignorance of who among the Arabs should properly speak for the Arabs of Palestine, ignorance not only of how an off-hand pledge to consult with the Arabs would affect domestic U.S. politics but of how seriously it would be taken by the Arabs.

The Arabs did little to raise the level of knowledge and sophistication among U.S. policymakers and to bring their perspective to the attention of the public. As in an earlier period, neither the people nor the politicians were exposed to the Arab viewpoint via direct lobbying or through books and newspapers. One former State Department official describes the Arab propaganda effort during the 1940s as "pitiful"; it was 1945 before an Arab Information Office was opened in Washington, D.C.[36] It was also 1945 before an Arab leader argued the Palestinian Arab case at high levels of the U.S. government—and then only at Roosevelt's invitation. The fact that Roosevelt thought to discuss Palestine with the king of Saudi Arabia rather than with any Arab from Palestine says as much about the Arabs' ineffectiveness in putting forth their position and in organizing themselves inside Palestine as it does about U.S. understanding of the issues involved. Not only did the Arabs of Palestine do little to present their case to the U.S. public or political leadership, but virtually every aspect of their behavior in the late 1930s and early 1940s reinforced the already prevalent image of Arabs as militant, politically unsophisticated, and unfit for self-government.

Numerous factors contributed to this impression. Most significant was the image of the Palestinian Arabs' principal leader, the Mufti of Jerusalem, Haj Amin al-Husseini. Although, contrary to the common perception, Husseini had played a moderate role and cooperated with the British throughout the first half of the Mandate, frustration over the growing strength of the Zionists and the Arabs' inability to influence Britain radicalized him by the mid-1930s. He became embittered and inflexible when the British forced him into exile in 1937 for his role in the Arab Revolt of 1936–1939, a countrywide rebellion against British rule and against vastly increased Jewish immigration. So hostile to the British that he threw in his lot with the Axis powers, the Mufti spent the last several years of the war in Germany assisting Nazi propaganda efforts through radio broadcasts to the Arab world and attempts to stir up further Arab rebellion against Britain. His actions were never very effective, and he never participated in atrocities against the Jews, but in acting out his frustration and anger with the British he all but irretrievably damaged the Arab image, seeming to lend substance to Zionist and later Israeli claims that Palestinians wanted the destruction of all Jews.[37]

Britain and the Zionists vilified the Mufti as a Nazi collaborator with the "blood of millions of Jews" on his hands.[38] Philip Mattar, the Mufti's foremost biographer, has concluded that although the Zionists, eager to prove him guilty of war crimes, have exaggerated his connections with the Nazis, the Mufti himself and many of his defenders were "so busy justifying his statements and actions in the Axis countries that they ignored the obvious and overwhelming fact that the Mufti had cooperated with the most barbaric regime in modern times."[39]

To the extent that Americans knew anything about the Mufti and his policies, they knew him as a radical, not as the reasonable leader he had been when he was trying to win his country's independence from a colonial power and preserve his society from what Arabs perceived to be a massive influx of European settlers. Even the Arab Revolt, so similar to the *intifada*, the West Bank–Gaza uprising of the late 1980s, and like the *intifada* constituting a plea for freedom from foreign domination, had no impact on Americans. In the absence of the kind of television coverage that brought the *intifada* to everyone's living room and gained the Palestinians considerable sympathy in the United States and the West, the Arab Revolt went almost unnoticed in the United States

Moreover, the revolt and Britain's harsh response took a heavy toll on the Arabs' economy, society, and political structure, from which they never fully recovered. Over three thousand Arabs were killed and thousands were arrested—huge numbers out of a population of under a million.[40] More seriously, Britain's exile or arrest of the entire local Arab political leadership during the revolt left the Arabs in political disarray. Even a decade later, they were unable to recover any semblance of unity and no new political leadership emerged, lending credence to the widespread belief that Arabs were incapable of governing themselves. The lack of credible political institutions at a time when issues of statehood and local self-governance were at the top of the political agenda was all the more striking when juxtaposed with the Zionists' highly organized local administration in Palestine.[41]

In the absence of an effective leadership of their own, the Palestinian Arabs came during the 1940s to depend heavily on the Arab states for political guidance, and this dependence in turn reinforced the widespread belief, a notion being heavily promoted by the Zionists, that for all intents and purposes all Arabs were interchangeable—that Palestine was not a distinct political entity, that Palestinians had no separate nationalism, and that they could therefore easily be absorbed elsewhere in the Arab world, leaving the small piece of land that was Palestine to the Jews. Few Americans in the mid-1940s understood that local Palestinian nationalism was a phenomenon that had existed in some form for decades.[42] Even the Zionist leadership in Palestine, although living alongside the Palestinian Arabs and in frequent contact with them, refused to acknowledge their sense of nationalism. As one scholar notes, the Zionists "had little comprehension that the Arabs' ties to Palestine were as profound as their own and would be guarded as zealously."[43] That Americans did not appreciate Palestinian nationalism either is hardly surprising.

As World War II was ending, the inability of the Arabs of Palestine to speak for themselves and enunciate clearly a goal that was specific to Palestine and not rooted in pan-Arabism became critical. During this period the Jews' situation was most pressingly in need of solution, and the Zionists had given up vague formulas for "homelands" and "commonwealths" and begun openly to press for establishment of a definitive "state." The Arabs' indecisiveness about who spoke for Palestine and whether Palestine was an entity distinct from the Arab states or part of the "greater Arab nation," made it difficult for the United States to distinguish a Palestinian from a Syrian from a Saudi Arabian. The Arab states did not help the situation. Pan-Arabists, particularly in Syria, had always seen Palestine as part of "Greater Syria" and did not have a clear sense of Palestine as a distinct entity. Transjordan's King Abdullah had visions of a broader hegemony as well and was being quietly but actively encouraged by Britain and the Zionists to prepare to absorb any part of Palestine left outside a future Jewish state.[44]

Thus, as the struggle for Palestine approached a critical stage at the end of World War II and the drive for Jewish statehood gathered steam, U.S. policymakers had virtually no concept of the strength of Palestinian attachment to the land, little notion that even without a leadership the Arabs of Palestine felt and professed a distinctly Palestinian nationalism, and little understanding that their struggle was as much a nationalist struggle as it was an anti-Zionist one.

This conclusion begs the question of whether a concerted effort by the Arabs of Palestine to bring their position to the attention of the United States could have made a significant difference. The answer has to be no. Certainly a more skillful Arab propaganda effort and a better organized leadership would have forced on U.S. policymakers some awareness of Palestinian concerns—of the danger of completely excluding Palestinians from the frame of reference in which policy was made. But it is extremely doubtful that, given the circumstances, this awareness would have been enough to alter the course of events. Everything militated against the Palestinians obtaining a hearing: the frame of reference that automatically assumed a Jewish place in Palestine and assumed the Arab claim to be inferior was so deeply rooted in a century of orientalist literature and anti-Arab stereotyping that little could have fundamentally altered it; the Jews of Europe had suffered horrific persecution and urgently needed a refuge somewhere; U.S. Zionist activists were highly skilled, extremely well organized, and well connected at high levels of the policymaking establishment and the Congress, and they represented a segment of the U.S. population several times the size of the small Arab American population; and even the Arab states were conspiring to undercut Palestinian nationalist claims. Against this combination, a more charismatic Palestinian leader or a more clever public-relations effort would have had little impact.

One of the major factors in perpetuating the mind-set on Palestine in the Roosevelt era was simple policy inertia—the kind of inertia that follows past practice almost by rote and resists challenging or questioning accepted notions. Basic policy decisions, particularly ones that have little or no direct impact on U.S. interests, often tend to become cast in concrete, forming a fundamental body of policy that is never questioned and, essentially through inertia, never changes. Thus did U.S. support for the formation of a Jewish homeland in Palestine, enunciated almost carelessly as a favor to an ally in wartime and to political colleagues at home in 1917, become an unalterable and unassailable pillar of policy ever after. Even by the time of Roosevelt's election, but particularly by the end of World War II, the Jewish right to possess some or all of Palestine was assumed, with virtually no consideration given to the impact on the Arabs of Palestine.

Years after her husband's death, Eleanor Roosevelt defined what had long before become the official American mind-set on the Palestine issue. Speaking during a trip to Damascus in 1952 to a group of Syrian reporters who questioned her about her support for Israel, she replied that U.S. support for the Balfour Declaration's promise of a Jewish homeland had, from the beginning, "practically committed our government to assist in the creation of a government there eventually, because there cannot be a homeland without a government." [45] In retrospect, it became easy enough to acknowledge that in the minds of most U.S. and British policymakers the promise of a Jewish national home had all along been intended to lead to statehood.

In actuality, nothing the U.S. government did through the end of the Roosevelt era had much of a direct impact on the situation on the ground in Palestine. But the further reinforcement of the pro-Zionist frame of reference that occurred in this era had a profound effect in establishing a mind-set in the United States that made it relatively easy, when the time came in which U.S. policy decisions did have a direct effect, to ignore the Arabs and the impact Jewish statehood would have on them. If the United States had known more about the Arab viewpoint and had more direct responsibility for Palestine, U.S. policymakers might have reacted more nearly as the British did in recognizing that Arab aspirations had to be somehow accommodated. Because the United States knew little and had no responsibility, however, policymakers followed the lines of least resistance, responding to those who brought direct pressure on them and molding views and policies according to that perspective.

What if any difference a greater knowledge of the Palestinian Arab viewpoint might have made in the policy decisions taken with regard to Palestine in the United States, in Britain, and at the United Nations in the three years leading up to Israel's creation is a moot point. But it is not unreasonable to assume that if the Palestinians had had a presence in the U.S. policy-making mind-set, their input in the decision-making process about Palestine might have been sought out and taken into account. Some partition arrangement for Palestine was undoubtedly inevitable, but the particular division ultimately decided on—which allotted to the Jewish state 55 percent of the land area of Palestine at a time when Jews made up one-third of the population—might have been different. A serious effort to consult the Arabs about their fate might also have produced in them a more compromising attitude. As it was, the Arabs of Palestine approached the international debate over dividing Palestinian land without either a voice in international councils or an opportunity for equal consideration.

4 Harry Truman
History Belongs to the Victors

History, writes Israeli historian and Oxford University professor Avi Shlaim, is in a sense "the propaganda of the victors," and because Israel so resoundingly won the 1948 war, which gave it independence and determined for decades thereafter the fate of the Arabs of Palestine, Israel was able to put forth its own version of the war. It was a version that came to constitute a conventional wisdom, its own frame of reference, until the 1980s, when a group of young Israeli historians, including Shlaim, used Israel's own newly declassified archives to tell a somewhat less idealized story. The original history was written for the most part not by independent professional historians but by official state or military historians, participants in the war, politicians, soldiers, journalists and, Shlaim adds, hagiographers—few of whom, Israel's new historians contend, even pretended to objectivity.[1] Another of the young historians, Benny Morris, describes the essence of the "old" history: "that the Zionist movement, and the state it engendered, were incomparably just and moral; that the Zionist leaders were wise and humane (though also firm, when necessary); that Zionism throughout had sought an accommodation, based on 'live and let live,' give and take, with the native Arab population of Palestine and with the surrounding Arab states; but that the Arab leaders, feudal and obscurantist all, had foiled every effort at compromise, single-mindedly seeking the destruction of the burgeoning Zionist entity."[2]

Americans and, with them, most U.S. policymakers accepted this version of history because it was easy to do so. Israel as a new, small, and heavily besieged state fighting off the Arab Goliath and building a nation out of barren desert was an image that brought out Americans' memories of their own heroic revolution and pioneer history. That this nation building was being accomplished by Jews in the aftermath of the Holocaust's horrors aroused Americans' compassion as little else ever had. If this were not enough, the fact that the enemies of this courageous new Jewish nation were Arabs almost automatically put a distinguishing mark on the villains of the piece and, in the end, made it easy to forget what the 1948 war had meant to Palestinians.

By the time Harry Truman came to office after the death of Franklin Roosevelt in 1945 and certainly by the time he extended U.S. recognition to Israel three years later, Israel's creation and survival were inevitable, and no amount of State Department opposition, British obstruction, or Arab military force could have prevented it. The Zionists were so determined and skilled, the Arabs so weak and disorganized, and the world community so sympathetic that the Zionists were unstoppable. Also probably inevitable—given an international and a domestic U.S. climate that was weary of war, convinced of the need to preserve the credibility of the United Nations as a guarantor of world peace, and inclined because of Cold War tensions to view individual nationalisms as threatening to the status quo—was the Palestinian Arabs' disappearance from political calculations. Thus did the Palestinians' displacement become, as Middle East scholar Malcolm Kerr termed it, a forgotten or an "unrecognizable episode." To the victor in the first Arab-Israeli war belonged not only the actual spoils of war but, almost as important, the memory and the history of what went before it.

For half a century, Truman has been lionized by supporters of Israel as the man who made the birth of Israel possible, and Truman himself never shunned the accolades or denied their veracity. Tears ran down his cheeks when Israel's chief rabbi told him during a visit to the White House that God had put Truman in "your mother's womb so you would be the instrument to bring the rebirth of Israel after two thousand years."[3] Long after he had left the White House, he again responded with tears when Israeli Prime Minister David Ben-Gurion told him in a private meeting that his support for Israel had given him an immortal place in Jewish history.[4]

Historians and biographers differ over how deserving Truman is of these accolades and over what primarily influenced him in his decisions on Palestine. One former Palestine desk officer at the State Department has said that he believed at the time that Truman was motivated primarily by humanitarian concerns for Jewish refugees in Europe after World War II but finally concluded, after a review of documentary evidence three decades later, that domestic political considerations had a much greater impact on Truman.[5]

At the other end of the spectrum, Truman's chief White House adviser, Clark Clifford, a strong Zionist supporter, has firmly dismissed any notion that politics ever played a part in either his own views or Truman's decisions, insisting that Truman acted only out of moral and ethical considerations and in U.S. strategic interests.[6] Others have indicated disappointment that Truman was insufficiently piqued by the "romance" of Israel's creation[7] or have taken as a sign of an "unsavory prejudice" Truman's occasional anger and frustration with the more outspoken and insistent of the Zionist activists who made their case to him during the Palestine debate.[8]

Truman's support for Israel was actually more ambivalent than the accolades he has received would indicate, and his role in its creation was much more complex than simplistic explanations of either a domestic political or a moral motivation would warrant. Truman the statesman remained uncertain throughout the Palestine debate about the impact on U.S. national interests of creating a Jewish state in Palestine and therefore did take heed of the overwhelmingly anti-Zionist advice of every agency and official in the government. But Truman the man was emotionally bound up from the day he took office in the struggle to secure a Jewish haven in Palestine, and Truman the politician, grappling in an election year with a popularity rating in the range of 35 percent, was acutely attuned to the importance of accommodating the powerful Jewish vote. None of these Trumans had much concern for the Arab side of the Palestine debate.

Truman was a true lover of the Bible and knew it intimately. He told one biographer that he had read it at least twice before he started school and, because biblical heroes were real people, much preferred its stories to fairy tales or Mother Goose stories. He felt, he said, that he knew some of the people in the Bible better than he knew many of his contemporaries. Palestine had thus always been particularly intriguing to him, and he had searched out other postbiblical histories of the area. He clearly considered himself something of an expert—not only on Jews and their history but on Arabs, who he said had shown a deplorable lack of enterprise about developing the area.[9] As with his predecessors and so many of his contemporaries who were steeped in the Bible, a Jewish return to Palestine seemed to him to be historically appropriate.

Early in his administration, Truman was moved in his decisions on the Palestine issue primarily by the plight of Europe's Jews. In June 1945, only two months after he took office, he sent Earl Harrison, dean of the University of Pennsylvania Law School, as a personal emissary to investigate the situation in Europe's displaced-persons camps and was deeply affected by Harrison's descriptions of the Jews' misery. Harrison told Truman that most

Jewish displaced persons wanted to go to Palestine, that in fact from a purely humanitarian standpoint Palestine was the only "decent solution" for them, and he recommended that one hundred thousand be admitted to Palestine.[10] Believing that Jews had suffered "more and longer" than other European refugees, that they alone had no home to return to, and that the United States could not stand by while they were denied the opportunity to rebuild their lives, Truman inserted the United States into the Palestine imbroglio by passing Harrison's recommendation to the British, who had by this time stopped all Jewish immigration to Palestine.[11]

Truman apparently believed that in so doing he was not delving into political issues, but, despite his self-described expertise, he did not at this stage know the political intricacies of the Palestine situation. In particular, he does not seem to have understood that Jewish immigration was the crux of and inseparable from the political problem. However just the salvation of Jewish refugees was in absolute moral terms, admitting one hundred thousand or, as was often suggested, unlimited numbers to a country whose political fate depended directly on the demographic balance between Jews and Arabs would have prejudged the political outcome by tipping the balance overnight. It says nothing about the rights and wrongs of the Palestine situation to recognize this reality, but Truman was apparently so concentrated on the Jewish refugee situation that he did not see the broader implications.

Truman did not favor establishment of a Jewish state in Palestine in the first year or two of his administration. In these early years he made it clear that he did not like the idea of any state established on racial or religious lines, something he felt was at odds with U.S. pluralism and secularism.[12] He also repeatedly said, in both public and private statements to Jews and non-Jews alike, that he was not willing to send "half a million American soldiers" to defend the Jews in Palestine, which he thought would be necessary if a state were established.[13] But he apparently did not understand that his genuine desire to help the Jews could not possibly be reconciled with his determination to stay out of the politics of it all. Dean Acheson, who would later serve as Truman's secretary of state but who at this point was undersecretary of state, says he found himself fielding requests from other nations for an explanation of the U.S. position and becoming entangled in "baffling and circular" discussions when he tried to explain. Truman focused exclusively on the immigration issue, others regarded immigration as something that necessarily had to follow rather than precede a decision on Palestine's fate, and Truman in turn dismissed this ultimate decision as a separate issue.[14]

Truman was not unaware of the Arab position on Jewish immigration, but it apparently did not arouse his particular concern. Several Arab leaders interceded directly with Truman as soon as he took office and frankly explained the impossibility, from an Arab standpoint, of agreeing to a policy that would guarantee the Arabs of Palestine minority status in their own country. Egyptian Prime Minister Nuqrashi Pasha wrote Truman in mid-1945 asking why the one million Arabs of Palestine should have been forced over the previous quarter century to accept "immigrants of an alien race up to nearly 50 percent of their own number." (According to British census estimates, the population of Palestine at the end of 1944 stood at 1,179,000 Arabs and 554,000 Jews.)[15] Now, he went on, "the guests at the Arab's table are declaring that in any case they are going to bring in large numbers of their kinsmen, take over all of his lands, and rule to suit themselves. It is this program of setting up a Jewish State in which the Arabs will be either reduced to the inferior status of a minority or else have to leave their homes that arouses their firm determination to resist at all costs."[16]

Truman quoted this letter in his own memoirs, written a decade later, but even then did not seem to understand the real Arab concern. Pasha's letter was one of the first times that an Arab leader had brought before a top-level U.S. official the Arabs' conviction that, from their standpoint, what was occurring in Palestine was an injustice—that to them nothing, not even the Jews' suffering in the Holocaust, warranted making the Palestinian Arabs a minority in their own land or endangering their continued presence on the land. In part because the Arabs had not made their case well or cogently or often, but especially because by 1945 the horrific nature of what had happened to the Jews in Europe had captured the world's compassion, Americans in general did not understand the depth or the true nature of the Arabs' fear and sense of injustice. The widespread belief was, as it had long been, that the Arabs simply did not like Jews and were being unreasonable in trying to keep them out. Truman was acutely aware of the danger of a violent Arab reaction, but he seemed to share with most Americans an inability to grasp why the Arabs were reacting as they were. The reaction was for him a problem to be gotten around, not something to be addressed or accommodated in any way. In his memoirs, he brushed off Arab concerns with derision; commenting that the Arabs had announced following the United Nations November 1947 decision to partition Palestine that they would defend their rights, he put the word "rights" in quotation marks.[17]

The partition decision, taken when Britain concluded that it could not resolve conflicting Arab and Jewish claims and appealed for UN help, proposed to divide Palestine into a Jewish state and an Arab state. The Arabs of Palestine and most Arab countries regarded partition as unjust for several major reasons: it was imposed by fiat by an outside body without giving the Palestinian Arabs a significant voice in determining sovereignty in their own land; it designated 55 percent of the land area of Palestine for the Jewish state at a time when Jews owned 7 percent and made up one-third of the population; and the substantial Arab population left in the Jewish state would have become a minority population. Truman's derision of the idea that Arabs had rights in Palestine is an indication that he fundamentally misunderstood the Arab concern. The Arabs were unable to break through his Zionist-centered mind-set. Acheson describes a 1946 meeting between Truman and the Saudi Arabian Foreign Minister, Prince Faysal bin Abdul Aziz, later to become King Faysal, in which it appeared that the two men's minds "crossed but did not meet." Neither, Acheson observed, "really grasped the depth of the other's concern; indeed, each rather believed the other's was exaggerated." The meeting ended in platitudes, "which were seized upon as agreement."[18]

Truman's frame of reference was so centered on the Zionists that he viewed the issue of self-determination only as a principle that would benefit the Jews—which, of course, put him at cross purposes with the Arabs, who based the logic and the justice of their case on this principle. Truman turned the principle around completely. Taking note in his memoirs of the Arabs' opposition to Zionism, he said that he regarded the Balfour Declaration's promise to Jews to "re-establish" a Jewish homeland as a fulfillment of "the noble policies of Woodrow Wilson, especially the principles of self-determination."[19] By referring to the "re-establishment" of a Jewish homeland from two millennia earlier, Truman was able to ignore or mentally submerge the Arabs' place in Palestine and, because it was impossible to allow both Jews and Arabs real self-determination, to apply the principle only to Jews. Middle East scholar George Lenczowski has observed that self-determination had generally from Woodrow Wilson's time been taken to signify the right of subjugated people to gain freedom and determine their own destiny, not the right of another people to rule over an unwilling conquered people. But Truman's belief that Jews were simply restoring their past enabled him to justify their claim over that of the Arabs.[20]

This is not to say that Truman believed the Palestine problem was a simple one. The domestic and foreign political intricacies and the problems on both sides of the issue bedeviled Truman throughout the entire three years before the Israeli state was created, and the choices were so difficult that, despite what some of his biographers have written and despite the fact that his sympathies lay with the Zionists from the beginning, he never took a definite stand on any aspect of the issue except when the outcome was already inevitable. His support for the 1947 UN partition resolution came only when partition clearly appeared to be the only viable solution. In May 1948, his decision to extend immediate diplomatic recognition when Israel announced its independence came only when Jewish statehood clearly was inevitable and would be declared no matter what the United States did.

The Palestine problem posed moral, political, and strategic dilemmas for Truman. The moral dilemma involved a clash between two just causes: the Jewish claim to a homeland and a refuge from persecution versus the Palestinian Arabs' claim to continued majority status and real self-determination in their own land. Truman did not struggle with this dilemma because he had believed from the beginning that justice was on the side of the Jews. He was, however, torn by the political and strategic dilemmas. Politically, his choice was either to opt for Jewish statehood, and possibly provoke Arab military action, or to endanger his political future by not helping the Zionists; he was facing a critical election battle with low poll ratings and was opposing a Republican candidate who openly courted the Jewish vote by vowing to open Palestine to unlimited Jewish immigration. The Palestine problem posed a nearly insoluble strategic dilemma as well, involving multiple dangers: that U.S. support for partition could give the Soviet Union, newly emerging as the Cold War rival of the United States, an entree in the Middle East; that failure to oppose partition as the Arabs desired would put at risk U.S. commercial interests in the Middle East, U.S. and European access to Arab oil, and, without oil, the Marshall Plan for the postwar rehabilitation of Europe; or, conversely, that failure to support and follow through on the UN partition decision would undermine UN influence and credibility at a critical early stage in its existence.

The conflicting pressures on Truman and the stark reality that no option was without serious risks, either to the United States or to Truman himself, deeply frustrated him. His indecisiveness throughout much of the Palestine debate stemmed from the fact that he took most of the pressures on him to heart—the Zionists' pleas and the pro-Zionist advice of his closest advisers, as well as the opposing concerns of the State Department and other government agencies and the Arabs' threats of violence.

Because he had not been elected in his own right but had succeeded after Roosevelt's death and also because he was conscious of coming from "the people" rather than from the moneyed patrician class like most of his predecessors, Truman had some political insecurities that also affected his decision making. He hated being told what to do, hated even more being lectured to, bristled at the thought that anyone was infringing on his pre-rogatives as president, and deeply feared not being taken seriously.[21] This insecurity affected his relations with State Department bureaucrats as well as with Zionists.

Truman's legendary battle with the State Department did not, as is com-monly believed, arise primarily because State opposed establishment of a Jewish state but because diplomats, generally members of the patrician eastern establishment, tended to patronize the Missouri haberdasher Tru-man and, at least initially, to treat him like a country bumpkin. Truman himself derisively labeled them "striped pants boys"[22] and years later still harbored deep resentment. In the 1960s he recounted for an oral historian what he told a U.S. Zionist leader with whom he met only days after he succeeded to office in 1945. When the Zionist expressed concern that the State Department would thwart Zionist plans, "I told him I knew all about *experts*," Truman recalled. "I said that an *expert* was a fella who was afraid to learn anything new because then he wouldn't be an *expert* anymore. And I said that some of the *experts*, the career fellas in the State Department, thought that they ought to make policy but that as long as I was president, I'd see to it that *I* made policy."[23] Truman did take the State Department's concerns about creating a Jewish state seriously, particularly during the period when the highly respected World War II hero George Marshall, a strong opponent of Zionist plans, served as secretary of state from 1947 to 1949, but the condescending manner of Marshall's sometimes imperious subordinates clearly rankled.

Truman had his limits on being pressed by Zionists too. Along with con-stant expressions of concern for the Jewish refugees in Europe, his corre-spondence is replete with irritated remarks, some bordering on the anti-Semitic, about Zionist pressures and the supposed arrogance of underdogs who achieve power.[24] Rabbi Abba Hillel Silver, the outspoken leader of the American Zionist Emergency Council, so enraged Truman because he had the temerity at a meeting in mid-1946 to shout at the president and pound on his desk that Truman banned him from the White House and for some time refused to see any other Zionist leader.[25] But in the end Truman's own pro-Jewish sympathies and, eventually, the inevitability of the Jewish state's establishment combined to overcome his anger with the Zionist activists and to make him into at least a de facto Zionist.

Truman's association with long-time business partner and friend Eddie Jacobson, a devout Jew with whom the president had run a haberdashery in Kansas City before entering politics, had a strong impact on him, as did, to a much more profound extent, his own closest White House aides, who were all strongly pro-Zionist. Throughout much of the Palestine debate, Jacobson, who was not a Zionist but did view Zionism as a vehicle to save Europe's Jews, was reluctant to presume on his friendship and his ready access to the White House and played a low-key role. But at a critical time in early 1948, when Truman was telling everyone that the problem was "not solvable as presently set up," Jacobson used his friendship to persuade Truman to end the embargo on visits by Zionists and receive Zionist leader Chaim Weizmann; during the meeting with Weizmann Truman committed himself to supporting partition and Jewish statehood. Truman himself credited Jacobson with making a contribution of "decisive importance." [26]

Truman's advisers had an even stronger impact on his thinking and his decisions. Together, the three main advisers on this issue did more than any other group to shape Truman's viewpoint on the Palestine issue and mold the frame of reference from which he approached the problem. These men were Clark Clifford, a Missouri lawyer who served as a key domestic adviser; David Niles, a holdover from the Roosevelt administration who was Truman's adviser for minority affairs; and Max Lowenthal, who had played a major role in Truman's selection as Roosevelt's vice-presidential running mate in 1944 and who served during the Palestine debate as Clifford's legal adviser on Palestine. These men were so supportive of Zionism that their advice enabled Truman to believe, as he did with utter sincerity, that in making the decisions he did on Palestine he was not bowing to electoral pressure but was doing the right thing.[27] Although non-Jewish, Clifford was a strong proponent of Zionism, perhaps at the instigation and under the influence of Niles and Lowenthal, who were firm Zionists, so emotional about the cause that Truman once said he found it disconcerting that they burst into tears whenever he tried to talk to either of them about Palestine.[28] All three of these men had easy access to Truman even during those periods when he had banned other Zionist spokesmen from the White House.

It is clear from many of the memoranda the trio of advisers sent Truman that they fed him a steady diet of material designed to influence his emotions and his personal perceptions of Arabs and Jews, thereby building a mind-set. In early March 1948, the United States was in the midst of an internal debate over whether to continue support for the partition of Palestine despite the risk of provoking violent conflict or, as the State Department was suggesting, to opt for a UN trusteeship, which would have postponed a hard decision on the fate of Palestine. Truman himself was genuinely undecided and torn by the strategic implications of the two options. Clifford sent him a lengthy memorandum recommending support for partition. The memo was written in detached tones until Clifford's heated conclusion. In language that demeaned the Arabs and indirectly challenged Truman's strength of purpose, he wrote that, by its uncertainty over partition, the United States "appears in the ridiculous role of trembling before threats of a few nomadic desert tribes. This has done us irreparable damage. Why should Russia or Yugoslavia, or any other nation treat us with anything but contempt in light of our shilly-shallying appeasement of the Arabs." [29]

Niles wrote Truman a memorandum shortly after he assumed office that attempted to plant the idea that there was strife between Christian Arabs and Muslim Arabs in Palestine—not generally true in fact—and that Christians would have nothing to fear from Jews. It was "obvious," he said, that Christians, particularly Catholics, "have more to fear from the Moslems than from any other competitive religious groups," whereas Jews had always gotten along well with all Middle Eastern Christians.[30] The memos and correspondence of these aides are full of similar examples of attempts to shape Truman's thinking by building on stereotypes of Arabs and Muslims as fanatical and backward or as not so dedicated to their beliefs that they could not be bought.[31]

Niles and Lowenthal had extensive contacts in Zionist organizations and were conduits for information going both into and out of the White House. Their presence virtually guaranteed that the Arab viewpoint rarely found its way into the White House or that, if it did, it would be undermined or countered by Zionist arguments. Niles is believed to have passed on to the Zionists most of the memoranda the State Department sent to Truman opposing partition and was rated by his principal State Department opponent, Loy Henderson, director of the Office of Near Eastern and African Affairs, as "the most powerful and diligent advocate of the Zionist cause," chiefly responsible for getting the partition vote through the UN.[32] Niles was close enough to Truman that, during an early 1948 meeting in the Oval Office, he could without endangering his job threaten emotionally to resign unless Truman acted more emphatically in support of the Jewish cause, and he was bold enough to advise Truman against the pending appointment to the U.S. UN delegation of people he deemed "unsympathetic to the Jewish viewpoint" who might engender "much resentment." [33]

Niles also served as a principal entree to the White House for the Zionists. There is good evidence that the Jewish Agency considered him a friend in the White House whom they could use to urge Truman to make pro-Zionist public statements,[34] and he was a key member of or contact for several self-appointed "brain trusts"—some specifically pro-Zionist, others that included Zionist members but were designed primarily to give advice on economic or social issues—that met regularly to advise the president and used a network of contacts to exert pressure on the White House. Composed of highly influential business leaders, government officials, and Democratic Party officials, these informal but powerful groups gave political advice and substantive recommendations on key issues. Niles was a member of some of the groups, coordinating strategy with them, and a frequent contact for others, with whom he exchanged documents.[35]

One of these Zionist "brain trusts" grew out of a group that had been meeting informally, often with Niles, since 1942. During a February 1948 dinner at the home of a prominent Washington attorney, two leading officials of the Jewish Agency in Palestine met with the group to discuss how to penetrate the policymaking establishment and how best to neutralize opposition to the Zionist program coming from the State Department and elsewhere in the government. A two-track approach was decided on, to be pursued through a network of contacts and influential friends, who would in turn approach others, and so on until the word had spread through both Washington society and official Washington. On one track, a concerted effort would be made to counter the opposition to Zionism by enlisting prominent individuals to press the line at high levels of the government that the Zionist cause was compatible with U.S. national interests. Another, blunter effort would be made to impress on both Democratic and Republican party leaders the electoral danger of not supporting the partition of Palestine.[36] The likelihood that the Arab point of view could ever penetrate this thick screen of Zionist sympathizers was virtually nil.

Lowenthal served as Clifford's legal adviser on Palestine in 1947 and 1948 but was not a formal White House adviser and did not have an office there. His role in both educating Clifford and shaping Truman's views was no less critical for being anonymous. He regularly visited Zionist offices in Washington to obtain analysis and advice and, in addition to sending memoranda to the president, was able to press his views on Truman via numerous informal, off-the-record oral briefings. His carefully argued memos went directly to Truman in some cases, and he is also believed to have written all or many of the memos Clifford sent to the president. Truman was indebted to Lowenthal for several political favors and clearly respected him highly; their discussions would most likely have been friendly and informal and very political. Truman later credited Lowenthal with instructing him during the debate over recognizing Israel.[37]

Whether Clifford learned his Zionism from Lowenthal and Niles or came to the White House already a convinced Zionist, he was a strong and unwavering advocate and exerted an influence on Truman of inestimable importance. He had a private, informal, and always off-the-record meeting with Truman at the end of every day and also communicated more formally by means of written memoranda. Like Niles and Lowenthal, he became so much involved in the Zionist struggle, particularly during the critical points before the UN voted for partition and before the United States recognized the new state of Israel, that often he acted as much like a Zionist political activist as like a presidential adviser. In November 1947, for instance, during the closing debate at the UN on partition, when the delegate of the Philippines indicated that his government would oppose partition, Clifford visited the Philippine ambassador in Washington, apparently without Truman's knowledge, and told him that such a vote would endanger U.S. relations with the Philippines. Under this and other pressures from U.S. congressmen and various key U.S. Zionist leaders, the Philippines voted for partition.[38]

Clifford himself recounts in his memoirs a revealing example of his deep involvement with the Zionists during the debate over whether to extend diplomatic recognition when Israel declared its establishment. This step was intensely debated within the government. The argument came to a head during a heated but indecisive meeting in Truman's office in which Clifford strongly argued the case for recognition against Secretary of State Marshall, who was so deeply opposed that he threatened to Truman's face not to vote for the president in the next election if he opted for recognition. Following the meeting, Clifford decided on his own to force the issue by asking the Jewish Agency representative in Washington, Eliahu Epstein, to send Truman a formal request for U.S. recognition of the new Jewish state a few hours before the anticipated announcement of its creation. Clifford unabashedly states in his memoirs that Epstein "did not realize that the President had still not decided how to respond to the request I had just solicited," and when it turned out that no one at the Jewish Agency knew how to word the request, Clifford helped write it. When the request arrived at the White House, Clifford and Niles wrote the official U.S. reply, also before Truman had made a final decision.[39] The uniqueness of the U.S.-Israeli relationship from this point forward is aptly captured in this unprecedented involvement of a high-ranking U.S. official on both sides of an exchange of diplomatic correspondence.

However angry President Truman may periodically have been over the pressures exerted by some Zionist activists during the Palestine debate,

U.S. Zionist organizations undeniably played a critical and decisive part between 1945 and 1948 in creating a body of opinion in the United States, a frame of reference—among the public, in the press, in Congress, and at the White House—that assumed the rightness of the Zionist program in Palestine and ignored the reasons for Arab opposition. Effective though it had been at other points in the past, the pro-Zionist lobby truly "came into its own" during the Truman presidency.[40] It "set a tone for public discussion," as one historian has noted.[41]

By 1948, membership in the various U.S. Zionist organizations had grown to just under one million—from about 150,000 in the middle of World War II.[42] These members, making up about one-fifth of the entire Jewish population of the United States at the time, were not passive but were letter-writing, lobbying, money-contributing activists who blanketed the country. From revenues in 1941 of $14 million, the United Jewish Appeal increased its monies raised in 1947 and 1948 to an annual total of $150 million, virtually all contributed by U.S. Jews; this total was four times more than the entire nation contributed to the American Red Cross. In 1945, at Zionist urging, thirty-three state legislatures, representing 85 percent of the U.S. population, passed resolutions favoring establishment of a Jewish state in Palestine. Before Truman left for a meeting with Winston Churchill and Joseph Stalin in Potsdam in July 1945, thirty-seven governors sent him a cable, generated by the Zionists, urging that he demand that Britain lift the limits on Jewish immigration to Palestine. Over half the Congress also signed a message to this effect, which was given to Truman before he departed.[43]

Activists from AZEC left few stones unturned in their effort to obtain support, approaching national and local politicians—down to mayors and town council members—as well as newspaper editors and radio broadcasters, business leaders, labor leaders, movie stars, and writers. In addition to the obvious targets, AZEC tried the innovative. In May 1947, it sponsored an "Action for Palestine" week in which its local chapters urged radio stations to run public-service announcements suggesting that the UN debate then beginning on Palestine would decide the fate of the Jewish people and that every American "with a sense of fair play" should "side with justice" and support partition by writing to President Truman. Radio stations in over forty cities ran the spots, as did newspapers in thirty-one other cities. Mass meetings were held in almost sixty cities. The mobilizing effort clearly paid off. During the second half of 1947, the White House received 135,000 telegrams, postcards, letters, and petitions on the Palestine issue.[44]

The Arabs could not hope to match the reach or the organizational skill of the Zionists' grass-roots effort. The Arab American population was quite small—under half a million, against the Jews' five million in the United States—and it tended to be not well educated and not economically well off. Coming from diverse areas of the Arab world, Arab Americans generally lacked a sense of community unity; they were notably apolitical and, in an effort to blend into U.S. society, had always been at pains to remain so.[45] The impending partition of Palestine clearly did not galvanize the small Arab American community as the catastrophe of the Holocaust galvanized U.S. Jews.

The Zionists were most effective when they appealed to Americans' humanitarian impulses. Americans had been horrified by revelations about the Holocaust. News of the atrocities suffered by the Jews had blanketed the United States in the aftermath of the war, and Americans, including the press, were "hooked on the story," in the words of two Israeli journalists. General Dwight Eisenhower had urged that a film entitled *Nazi Atrocities* be shown in theaters throughout the nation. According to a scholar who researched the impact of World War II films on U.S. culture, audiences responded to the footage with "appalled solemnity." Some "gasped, a few hissed obscenities at the Germans, but most sat in shocked silence."[46]

Perhaps the Zionists' single most effective spokesman, Abba Eban, who came to the United States in 1947 as a member of the Zionist delegation to the UN and later served as Israel's ambassador to the United States and Israeli foreign minister, recalls that one of his first official functions—as a member of the Jewish Agency Information Department in London in 1946—was to employ his charm with a number of influential Britons. "Zionism had its own rationality," he observes, "but it was unlikely to be embraced by anyone who lacked a historic imagination and at least a modest ounce of romantic eccentricity." It was precisely the Zionists' recognition that passion and romance and an appeal to one's better instincts played far better than angry threats that made their effort so successful. In 1947, Eban was reassigned to the United States to inject some of his rhetoric and passion into the debate here. The Jewish Agency had asked a group of lawyers to prepare a brief for the Zionist case. The result was "scholarly, precise, and authoritative," Eban remembers, but it lacked any "tang," dealing with Palestine as a "problem" rather than a physical reality and with Zionism as a learned argument rather than a human drama. So Eban was brought in to add zest to the staid legal brief.[47]

Zionist propagandists also made skillful use of the fact of the Jews' national homelessness. I. L. Kenen, later to become the first formal pro-Israeli lobbyist in the United States, has recounted how the Zionists played up the fact that they had no official status at the UN at the very time that body was debating the future of Palestine. At his suggestion, all Zionist representatives decided not to attend a special UN session on Palestine in 1947, so when the press gathered to photograph the expected arrival of several Jewish leaders, Kenen himself, an American, drove up alone in a limousine and drew wide international attention to the fact that the Zionists had been denied official status. "Every such episode," Kenen believed, "bolstered our appeal for status."[48]

Zionists also scored a major propaganda success in 1947 when the Palestinian Jewish underground sailed to Palestine an old renamed cargo ship, the *Exodus 1947,* filled with forty-five hundred European Jewish refugees in order to dramatize Britain's immigration restrictions in Palestine. The British captured the ship and returned it and its desperate cargo to Europe, thus focusing attention on Britain's heartlessness and the Jews' homelessness and creating powerful pressures for finding a resolution to the problem of Palestine. The UN Special Committee on Palestine (UNSCOP), which had been established to examine the Palestine situation and recommend a solution after Britain turned the problem over to the UN, was in Palestine at the time the ship arrived in July 1947 and was able to meet with a correspondent aboard the ship. The incident apparently persuaded most committee members that resolving the fate of Europe's Jews had to be given priority over resolving Palestine's demographic realities.[49] A majority of the committee, made up of representatives of eleven nations, eventually did recommend partition into sovereign Jewish and Arab states.

A prominent newspaper editor captured the essential romance of the Zionists' story in a letter to a friend following the partition decision. *Boston Herald* editor Frank Buxton had served on the Anglo-American Committee, established by Britain and the United States in early 1946 to probe Jewish and Arab positions and investigate the situation in Palestine. (The committee ended by satisfying no one. After several months of hearings and visits to Palestine, it waffled on the area's political disposition, concluding that neither an Arab nor a Jewish state should be established, and recommended that Britain immediately lift restrictions on Jewish immigration.) Writing in late 1947, Buxton waxed eloquent on the Zionist program. "How thrilling the Palestine or Israel news is!" he wrote. "Regardless of the relative merits of the Jewish and Arab claims, here's something portentious [sic] and exhilarating—'manifest destiny,' 'the inevitability of history,' a conflict between the traditional East and the progressive West, a token of the possibilities of the United Nations."[50]

Another, British member of the Anglo-American Committee had described the Zionist appeal to Americans in somewhat more cynical terms. Noting Zionism's similarity to the pioneering spirit that developed the U.S. West, Richard Crossman, a Labor Member of Parliament who was pro-Zionist, predicted that Americans would "give the Jewish settler in Palestine the benefit of the doubt, and regard the Arab as the aboriginal who must go down before the march of progress."[51]

The sense of inevitability expressed in these two observations is key to an understanding of how easily a mind-set that excluded Arab concerns was shaped. The Zionist story was so romantic and so exciting that to most people it simply seemed right. The establishment of Zionism in Palestine fit with Western concepts of progress and modernity and the march of history and therefore should happen. "Regardless of the relative merits of the Jewish and Arab claims," as Buxton said—regardless of any question of justice—the Arabs, symbol in the West of antimodernity and the retreat of history, would inevitably be eclipsed.

In the then-universal frame of reference, the Arabs had essentially lost control of their situation. By late 1947, probably no course but compromise—that is, agreement to the partition of Palestine—could have guaranteed the Arabs a means of safeguarding even a minimal presence in and control over Palestine. They did not help themselves by refusing to compromise their political position and failing to launch any public campaign to put their case forward to the U.S. public.[52] Nonetheless, even with a conciliatory position and a skillful public-relations campaign, the most the Palestinians could have hoped to achieve was the half of Palestine allotted them by the partition decision. What was politically possible in the atmosphere prevailing at this point no longer had any relation to what the Arabs believed was just or logical.

The Arabs' failure to recognize this reality helped seal their fate, assuring that they were completely closed out of the policymaking frame of reference. Even the State Department grew impatient with what was regarded as Arab intransigence. Arabs who gave testimony before the Anglo-American Committee, reiterating their absolute refusal to permit the immigration of any additional Jews to Palestine, including the elderly and infirm, were regarded by State Department diplomats as rigid and unimaginative in the face of what virtually all Americans saw as the Jews' great humanitarian need.[53]

Perhaps the Arabs' most serious misstep came in 1947 when the special eleven-nation UN committee UNSCOP was constituted to look into the Palestine problem. The Arab Higher Committee, the organization led by the exiled Mufti of Jerusalem that functioned as the Palestinians' government, boycotted UNSCOP in the conviction that neither the UN nor any outside body had the authority to decide the fate of their land. The Palestinian boycott worked to Zionist advantage by making the Zionists appear reasonable and willing to compromise, while the Arab demand for complete control over all of Palestine appeared, in the circumstances, unreasonable and inflexible. It was a no-win situation for the Arabs, whose only choices, since they did not in fact control the fate of their land, were either to cooperate in the division of their homeland or to refuse cooperation and appear intransigent.

The Jews, in the observation of one U.S. Zionist, were "not presenting a claim as much as they were exhibiting a conclusion," for even in 1947 there was already, for all practical purposes, a Jewish state in Palestine—not legal or yet formally recognized but in existence.[54] This further indication that the eventual creation of a Jewish state was assumed by all concerned and that its creation had become so much a part of the conventional wisdom that only the formalities of state creation remained made the Palestinian Arabs' opposition appear simply as obstructionism and not as an effort to preserve their homeland intact. The UNSCOP members had not approached the problem with a strongly pro-Zionist mind-set, but their chief interest was in finding a workable, not an absolutely just, solution, and the contrasting Jewish and Arab presentations strikingly demonstrated which approach was more workable. When UNSCOP recommended partition, the Arabs rejected it and, again in the belief that the UN had no authority over Palestine, rejected as well the minority UNSCOP recommendation for establishment of a federated state with two autonomous regions. Four months later, in November 1947, the Arabs rejected the UN General Assembly's vote to partition.[55]

The decision to partition Palestine was a foregone conclusion long before it was formally voted for. It had already for so long been a part of the conventional wisdom that Jews should and would find a home in Palestine—a home it was believed they desperately needed in the wake of the Holocaust— that the question on all minds except the Palestinians' was how—no longer whether—they could do so. The Arabs, for so long politically invisible, now became a nuisance, an obstacle standing in the way of everyone —of a British government frustrated by the Palestine problem and concerned primarily to guarantee an easy exit, of a world eager to resolve the humanitarian problem of the European Jewish refugees, of a newly formed UN concerned to demonstrate that it could save the world from future wars by resolving international disputes, and of a United States eager to keep looming Cold War tensions to a minimum, to demonstrate the credibility of the UN, and to accommodate the heartfelt wishes of a politically powerful segment of the population. In these circumstances, Arab objections were not only troublesome but self-defeating, for the all-or-nothing nature of their demands, far from demonstrating that they were the victims of an injustice, as they believed, gave the impression around the world that they were the victimizers.

The romance of the Zionists' story would undoubtedly have captured the attention of the U.S. press without the impetus of a skilled Zionist information program. One analysis of the *New York Times* in the fifty days following the UN vote on November 29, 1947, to partition Palestine gives a striking indication of how central this story had become in U.S. thinking and would remain for the next year. The day after the UN vote, the *Times* ran eighteen separate stories on the issue. In the following seven weeks, a total of 360 articles appeared—a remarkably high average, over this fairly extended period, of more than seven articles every day.[56]

Both the Zionists and the Truman administration, including the State Department to some extent, actively courted the press, particularly the *New York Times*, seeing it as a principal instrument for shaping public opinion on the Palestine question. But the street was two-way, for the *Times* management saw its role in guiding public opinion as giving it a part, to some degree, in policymaking, and it valued the access and the intimate contact Truman and high government officials permitted with top levels of the policymaking establishment. Truman was an inveterate newspaper reader and had particular regard for the *New York Times*, which he viewed as the best source for learning the public mood and the principal channel for getting his message out to "elite opinion." Contact between the *Times* and the White House was quite close, and various *Times* executives have maintained that Truman and other high-level officials sought advice from them on some policy questions.[57]

On the Palestine issue, the press was to a great extent the battleground on which competing factions in the administration fought their struggle. This was particularly true in March 1948, when the State Department was advocating that the United States abandon its backing for partition and support instead the imposition of a UN trusteeship over Palestine. State believed that the impending end of the British Mandate and the imposition of partition two months hence in May 1948 would lead to violent conflict between Arabs and Jews in Palestine, endangering U.S. commercial and oil interests in the Middle East and enhancing the Soviet Union's role in the area. The trusteeship proposal was intended to postpone making a hard decision. Truman initially entertained the State Department proposal, but, under pressure from his aides and persuaded by Weizmann during a secret White House meeting, he rejected it and without informing the State Department promised the Zionist leader continued support for partition. This decision was made just as the State Department, without itself informing Truman, proceeded to announce U.S. support for trusteeship in a public speech to the UN. The ensuing confusion opened Truman to severe criticism. Press attacks on him for supporting trusteeship were fed by officials within his administration, and Truman aides Clifford, Niles, and others are reported to have encouraged press reports and a letter-writing campaign attacking the State Department.[58]

Journalist Bruce Evensen, who has studied media treatment of the Palestine question in the 1947–48 period, believes that initially media editors and commentators did not strongly favor any particular course of action in the partition debate. Editors tended to regard Palestine as an arena of competition between the United States and the Soviet Union and, in the belief that partition would lead to instability and give the Soviets an advantage, were at least somewhat receptive to the State Department's antipartition arguments. When the UN voted for partition, however, this step was regarded as an expression of world public opinion that should be supported because the survival of the UN was so vital.[59]

The *New York Times* led the way in changing its viewpoint. Although it had always opposed the idea of establishing a state based on a religious faith, when in mid-1947 the credibility of a UN committee, UNSCOP, was coupled with a recommendation for partition, the *Times* announced that it was now ready to accept "any favorable UN decision" and even to "*work for* the success of it." The *Times* viewed its task as an activist one, to build public opinion in favor of the UN's decision, and its veteran Washington correspondent, Arthur Krock, concluded that "the world having conceded the soundness" of establishing a Jewish homeland, "the good faith of Washington would be enlisted in making that homeland a reality."[60] This theme was taken up by other media. The liberal opinion weekly the *New Republic* considered that the UN's decision placed an obligation on the United States and the media. A May 1948 editorial stated unequivocally that because the UN was "our one source of world law and our one hope for world peace," its decision on partition had to be followed. "Whether it was wise or unwise, just or unjust, was from that moment on irrelevant," the editorial said. "That decision is today a part of the world law that governs all of us."[61]

Having become an advocate for partition, the press was harshly critical of Truman after the trusteeship debacle for seeming to lose control over U.S. policy. In fact, Truman appears to have misjudged the strength of public and media opinion in favor of partition, and from this point on until partition took effect with Israel's creation in May 1948 he was more often the controlled than the controlling party in the interaction between press and policymakers. The press, not only reflecting public and Zionist opinion but also actively guiding public opinion, helped to focus public indignation on the president and created a political climate in which opposition to partition became all but impossible.

The interaction between the press and the Zionists, the press and policymakers, the press and the public in this period is in fact an interesting study in the interplay at work in the creation of a conventional wisdom. For instance, Evensen notes that the surge of public and press support for partition in March 1948 in the wake of the trusteeship debacle strengthened Zionist resolve to continue insisting on nothing less than partition, while the Zionists' determination worked in turn to strengthen the media's belief that a Jewish state would come into existence when the British Mandate ended, no matter what Truman or the State Department did. In fact, the State Department solicited the views of several Middle East correspondents after the trusteeship proposal backfired and discovered that all believed the Zionists could not be prevented from establishing a state. The power to define policy alternatives on any issue is obviously not confined to policymakers but is a process in which the media and the public also participate, and in the Palestine situation the media played a key role in shaping the new conventional wisdom by serving as the place in which "definitions of what was happening in Palestine"—definitions conjured up by Zionist groups, by pro- and anti-Zionists within the administration, by the public—were formulated and debated. Because it had the power to portray and interpret, to define what it saw, the media helped reshape the events it was covering.[62]

From the moment partition was voted for at the UN, the press played a critical role in building a framework for thinking that would endure for decades. Beginning a trend of heavy coverage of Israel that was to continue into the 1990s, a total of twenty-four U.S., British, and Australian reporters converged on Palestine shortly before the scheduled end of the British Mandate on May 15, 1948, to cover the intercommunal strife that had been going on for months between Jews and Palestinian Arabs, as well as the anticipated attack on Palestine by neighboring Arab states when the British withdrew.[63]

Virtually all reporting was from the Jewish perspective. The journals the *Nation* and the *New Republic* both showed what one scholar calls "an overt emotional partiality" toward the Jews. No item published in either journal was sympathetic to the Arabs, and no correspondent was stationed in Arab areas of Palestine, although some reporters lived with, and sometimes fought alongside, Jewish settlers. Most articles used value-laden words and phrases to describe Arabs and Jews—words like "feudal," "violent," "fanatics," and "murderous" for the Arabs; words like "American-like," "heroes," "clean," "courageous," and "peaceloving" for the Israelis.[64]

The press knew early in the fighting, well before the Mandate ended and the Arab states attacked, which side would be the winner, and this belief determined to a great extent the perspective from which the media reported. Kept abreast of the military situation by Zionist leaders, the press assumed before the fact that Jewish statehood was a *fait accompli.*[65] The Zionists were confident of victory from the beginning and put the word about widely that they expected to win. As early as February, three months before the British Mandate was to end, the U.S. consul general in Jerusalem reported to Washington that Jewish officials were telling him they had no doubts about their ability to establish a state and adequately defend the coastal strip between Tel Aviv and Haifa. They expected more trouble securing other areas and were extremely worried about the fate of the Jewish population of Jerusalem, but, the consul noted, they believed that the fate of the future Jewish state was tied to the fate of the UN and that the world community would not let either one "go under."[66]

Despite later attempts to portray the Jewish forces as outnumbered and outgunned throughout the 1948 fighting and as having won by a near-miraculous show of grit, in fact the Jewish/Israeli forces generally had the upper hand in the fighting from the time they secured key lines of communication in Palestine in early April.[67] The Arab armies that invaded Palestine in May had an initial advantage in equipment, but that advantage did not last beyond the first week in June, and Jewish/Israeli forces outnumbered the combined Arab forces at every stage of the fighting. In May 1948, the Haganah had 35,780 troops mobilized—63,000 by July—while the combined strength of the regular Arab armies in Palestine was about 30,000 and never equaled the Israeli totals. Israel also demonstrated superior organization and command and control throughout.[68]

The fact that the press generally knew from the start that Israeli forces would win, that the Palestinian Arabs had nothing but some small guerrilla units, and that the Arab armies were small and disorganized hastened the disappearance of the Arabs of Palestine from consideration as serious actors in the Palestine drama. Israel's victory was the culminating point of a psychological process in which virtually all media reporting ignored the Palestinians while defining Israel as a gallant young state under constant siege from violent neighbors—a nation much like the United States in its pioneering history and its Western democratic spirit. It was in this period, during and just after Israel's creation, that an Israel-centered mind-set became so embedded in U.S. thinking that Israel became for all intents and purposes a part of the "being" of the United States.

Public opinion polls had for some time reflected the Palestinians' disappearance from consideration, even in the way poll questions were posed. In December 1944, for instance, one polling organization asked, "Do you think the Jews should be given a special chance to settle in Palestine after the war, or do you think all people should have the same chance to settle there?" No mention was made of the Arabs who already lived and constituted a majority in Palestine. Neutral questions generally elicited answers focused on the Zionists. In 1947, for instance, to the question "Can you tell me which groups of people have been having trouble in Palestine recently?" almost twice as many people (82 versus 45 percent) answered "Jews" or "Zionists" as answered "Arabs" or "Mohammedans." In reports on public opinion polls covering the years of the Palestine debate, readers could find no references to "Palestine" or "Arabs in Palestine" in the index but were referred to "Jews: Colonization." By the time of their exodus from Palestine, one scholar has noted, the Palestinians did "not register at all on the consciousness of Americans."[69]

After the 1948 war, newspapers led the way in articulating a picture of the new Palestine minus its Arabs. Leading papers featured long articles on Israel's accomplishments in state building, touting its triumph over adversity and headlining its dreams. Under a headline noting "There Is No Present Tense in Israel," for instance, one typical *New York Times Magazine* article in February 1949 described Israelis who were "in a hurry, . . . impatient of desert and its languor and determined to abolish them"; settlers who were "bold, self-conscious, high-spirited"; a "new and intense" kind of nationalism, "inspired not by love of, but lack of, nationhood"; Israelis fighting for survival "with our backs to the wall because for us there is no place of retreat." Correspondent Anne O'Hare McCormick invited readers to be intrigued by pointing out that Israel "contains the seeds of a great experiment" and thus "stirs the imagination and emotion of the world far more than bigger issues." Israel's struggle, the article concluded, was the "desperate effort of a long-suffering people to create security in a hostile environment and to build a home in an inhospitable world."[70]

The McCormick article was part of an intensive effort by the *New York*

Times to cover the young Israeli state. The *Times* ran at least two multipart series on Israel in 1949. The first included ten articles by McCormick, the second was a four-part series in the *Times Magazine* by correspondent Gertrude Samuels. This series was notable for creating a positive stereotype of the Israelis that U.S. novelists would pick up and perpetuate for years. In one article, Samuels described native-born Israelis, called *sabras*, as "bronzed, blue-eyed, tough and blond, who look for the most part like Scandinavian or 'Aryan' types."[71] In a second article, she referred to *sabras* as being, "for the most part, tall, handsome, husky and fearless young people, their blue eyes and blond or light brown hair conditioned perhaps by the climate of the sub-tropics."[72]

In one example of reporting from an Israeli perspective, the *Times* ran a two-page picture spread in its *Magazine* that showed a large panorama of Jerusalem. The caption noted that "the Old City, site of the Holy Places of three faiths and whose Jewish Quarter was destroyed in the 1948 fighting, is in Arab hands." The "New City," the caption pointed out, "is 95 per cent Jewish controlled."[73] The factual and apparently neutral wording omitted information that would have taken in the Palestinian perspective as well— primarily the fact that several Palestinian Arab neighborhoods in what became the Jewish-controlled New City were also destroyed in the 1948 fighting, as were Arab towns outside Jerusalem whose land Israel later incorporated into the city.[74]

Added to press stories about the "unbelievable courage and persistence" of the Israelis, the "superhuman effort" going into building Israel, the Israeli "miracle" of turning a "once-derelict land into an oasis," and the "romantic little state of Israel, created on the basis of determination and a dream,"[75] several books were published in the first few years after Israel's establishment that touted its accomplishments in glowing terms. One of these, written by the first U.S. ambassador to Israel, James McDonald, and published in 1951, is typical. Noting in the preface that so much about Israel's first few years was already well known, McDonald promises to refrain from "retelling the stories of Israel's heroic defense, its improvisation of Army, Navy, and Air Force, the miracles of transforming deserts into orchards, the spectacular change of the physical face of the land. . . . Only the highest literary artistry could advantageously weave new variations on these well-known themes."[76] McDonald's certainty a bare three years after Israel's establishment that these perceptions of the Jewish state's accomplishments had already taken root in the imagination of Americans is an indication of how powerful a hold the image of Israel had on the United States even at the beginning.

The Palestinians became all but lost in the headlong rush to focus attention on Israel. Another popular book at the time, Frank Manuel's *The Realities of American-Palestine Relations*, a history of Zionist settlement in Palestine published only a year after the Jewish state was established, provides an illustration of how thorough the Palestinians' exclusion had already become. The book is remarkable for the fact that the word *Arab* does not appear until page 185, and for a 361-page volume the index carries only twenty-six references to Arabs and only seven to Muslims.[77] (The term *Palestinian* for the Arabs of Palestine was not then used by anyone except the Palestinians themselves.)

The McCormick article cited above did note that Israel's accomplishments had been made possible at the "cruel price" of the exile of hundreds of thousands of Palestine's Arab inhabitants, and McCormick had written in an earlier article that if Israel had become a fact that had to be recognized, "so is the burning sense of invasion and usurpation the Palestinian Arabs feel."[78] But for most correspondents the Palestinians and their fate were of little or no interest. The general attitude, among the public and in the press, was reflected in a commentary McCormick herself wrote on May 15, 1948, the day Israel announced its independence; Israel had become a fact, its existence "irrevocable," she wrote, and it was now pointless to go back to the "old controversies" over the respective rights of Arabs and Jews.[79] Although the press had provided vivid descriptions of the displaced persons in Europe in the aftermath of World War II, the fact that over seven hundred thousand Palestinians had been displaced by the 1948 war and were living in refugee camps in Lebanon, Syria, Transjordan, and Egypt received only minimal coverage. The press carried little mention of Palestinian flight as it was occurring and little mention of the refugee camps. In March 1949, a State Department study concluded that because of limited press coverage the U.S. public was generally unaware of the refugee problem.[80]

Much of the small amount of press commentary was wholly unsympathetic to the Palestinians. Presumably following the lead of the Israeli government, which maintained that the refugees had left Palestine of their own accord and denied Israeli responsibility for them, the *New York Post* vehemently opposed helping the refugees.[81] The liberal opinion weeklies the *Nation* and the *New Republic* played the problem as one for which the Arab states, not Israel, had responsibility. In the *Nation's* only mention of the refugees in all of 1948, one article argued that Israel should not have to take responsibility for them and noted, moreover, that the exodus had serendipitously solved the problem for Israel of having too many Arabs in a

Jewish state. Why should Israelis revive the problem by taking the refugees back, the article wondered, "when, above all, they need land and houses for their own immigration and freedom from the endless vexation" of a large and unassimilable minority. "They fled," the magazine asserted. "Let them settle somewhere else." [82]

It was not long before a new and enduring mythology grew up. A major theme and probably the most important single element in the newly emerging frame of reference about which party had morality and justice on its side was the story of how the Palestinians had left Palestine. Soon after the exodus, word began to circulate that the Palestinians had been ordered by their leaders in radio broadcasts to leave their homes and land so that the way would be clear for Arab military forces to push the Jews out, after which the Palestinian inhabitants could return. The belief that the Palestinians had been ordered to leave became so widely believed that it was, and still is, part of the folklore. The point of this line of argument is to give the impression that total responsibility for the Palestinians' displacement and dispossession lay with them and that Israel had no moral obligation to take the refugees back, compensate them for property left behind, or refrain from using Palestinian homes and land to build the Israeli state.

In actuality, Israeli historians, using declassified Israeli archival materials, have concluded that there were no broadcast orders by Arab leaders and no blanket orders disseminated by any means instructing the Palestinian population to leave their homes. Morris concluded in a landmark study of the origins of the refugee problem that a multitude of factors caused the exodus, including anticipation of attack by Jewish/Israeli forces, which accounted for much of the flight occurring in the first half of 1948; outright expulsion by the Israeli military, which occurred more often in the second half of the war, during Israeli offensives in July and October; and fear induced by the lack of Arab leadership and a resulting feeling of impotence and abandonment. In most cases, Morris believes, "the final and decisive precipitant to flight" was attack by Jewish/Israeli forces or the fear of such attack.[83]

Because it so quickly and so thoroughly became a part of the conventional wisdom that the Palestinians had brought their plight on themselves, it became easy to ignore them or treat them with disdain. There is a certain disdain, for instance, in the remarks Israel's new president, Chaim Weizmann, made about the refugees to U.S. Ambassador McDonald, who publicized the remarks in his 1951 book. Declaring that the Palestinian exodus amounted to a "miraculous simplification of Israel's tasks," Weizmann said that in any case he thought the murder of six million Jews in Europe was a far vaster tragedy, and he could not understand why, if the world had done nothing to prevent the genocide of the Jews, there was "such excitement" in the UN and in Western capitals about the Palestinian refugees.[84]

Other references pointed to a widespread feeling of distaste for the Palestinians among Americans. Capturing the mind-set of significant numbers of Americans, Eleanor Roosevelt described in an autobiography a 1952 trip to refugee camps in Jordan, followed by a visit to Israel. She found that she was greatly disheartened by the sense of hopelessness she observed among the Palestinians but loved the enterprising spirit shown in Israel. The contrast struck her particularly and goes to the essence of the U.S. affinity for Israel. Crossing into the Jewish state from Arab East Jerusalem was, she declared, "like breathing the air of the United States again."[85] Americans felt at ease with Israel but were uncomfortable with the Arab world.

The simple fact of Israel's existence, as well as the affinity Americans almost instantly felt for Israel and the vastly increased distance this affinity imposed between Americans and Palestinians, all combined as a powerful force in shaping both public and policymaker opinion. It was not long before even the State Department, which had so strenuously opposed the partition of Palestine, recognized and accepted the facts on the ground— explicitly accepting the new Israeli state as a reality, criticizing the Arabs for not doing the same, and abandoning any notion of supporting the formation of an independent Arab state in those portions of Palestine not allotted to or captured by Israel.

The State Department has long been vilified as anti-Zionist and even anti-Semitic because of its opposition to partition, but in a large sense it was simply caught in what has always been a strong tension between the politicians who lead government and the nonpolitical careerists who work in government. Harold Saunders, a State Department official who worked with two secretaries of state in negotiating several Arab-Israeli peace agreements in the 1970s, has observed that whereas presidents and their political advisers engage in political maneuver and influence wielding, diplomats and career officers are encouraged to think in analytical terms and are actively discouraged from involving themselves in politics.[86]

At few times in the history of U.S. policymaking has the dichotomy between the politicians and the government careerists been clearer or the tension stronger or more bitter than in the years leading up to the establishment of Israel. It would be as simplistic to say that there was no anti-Semitism at the State Department in the period surrounding Israel's creation as it has been to charge that State's principal motivation was anti-Semitism. But concerns far broader than the ethnic prejudices of the bureaucrats and statesmen involved with the issue primarily influenced State Department thinking. Indeed, State was not alone in opposing partition; the Department of Defense, the Joint Chiefs of Staff, the National Security Council staff, and the newly established Central Intelligence Agency were united with State in fearing that partition might lead to warfare in the Middle East, force the United States to intervene militarily, enhance the Soviet position in the area, and endanger U.S. interests in the Arab world. The principal concern of the military and the government careerists was not the politics of the situation but the effect on U.S. strategic interests. Even Eban has noted in retrospect that the State Department's position was not based on "heat and passion" but was "dangerous precisely because [it] rested on a certain logic." [87]

The absence of heat and passion is abundantly evident in the alacrity with which the State Department and every other agency changed direction and supported Israel's existence when it became clear that the new state was and would remain a reality and that it had the solid backing of the White House. By June 1948, the State Department was putting it about that because the United States had officially recognized Israel, State's policy was "postulated upon the continuing existence of the State of Israel" and on the assumption that Israel's sovereignty was a fact. State also assumed that the independent Palestinian Arab state called for by the partition resolution would never come into being; that the parts of Palestine not under Israel's control, which were to have formed the Palestinian state, would be given to the neighboring Arab states (that is, to Transjordan, which was occupying the West Bank, and to Egypt, which controlled Gaza); and that populations would be exchanged where necessary to make the Jewish state and the Arab areas of Palestine each more homogeneous. [88]

Clearly, the State Department early on not only accepted Israel as a *fait accompli* but showed itself to be more than ready to give away Palestinian Arab areas to the Arab states and forcibly move a few hundred thousand Arabs out of Jewish areas. By November 1948, it became the official U.S. position that "Arab Palestine standing alone could not constitute a viable independent state" [89]—even though only half a year earlier the United States had been prepared to support an independent Palestinian state as part of the partition plan. The formulation that a Palestinian state would not be viable was to remain an official staple of U.S. policy—constantly repeated as if by rote, rarely questioned or investigated—at least through the Bush administration. The Palestinians had at this point ceased to be a part of the official policymaking frame of reference in the United States.

The Zionists and King Abdullah of Transjordan (which formally changed its name to Jordan in 1950) had for long been secretly discussing some kind of arrangement to split Palestine between them, and when Transjordan's Arab Legion invaded Palestine on May 15, 1948, its principal intent was not to fight the establishment of Israel but to secure its hold on the areas designated for an Arab state.[90] The British had also long entertained the idea of giving parts of Palestine to Transjordan, as when the Peel Commission in 1937 had proposed partitioning Palestine into a small Jewish state and an Arab state to be merged with Transjordan. So, for the United States, eager above all at this point to bring an end to the war and ensure a measure of stability in a volatile area, it seemed a heaven-sent solution to give the West Bank, most of what remained of Arab Palestine, to a friendly potentate who had ruled peacefully for almost three decades, who had served under the tutelage of the British until gaining independence in 1946, and whose military was still trained and officered by the British. The thought that anything like a true sense of nationalism existed among the Palestinian Arabs never occurred to U.S. policymakers, and in the aftermath of World War II, when huge numbers of people throughout the world were being displaced and when colonialism was only just coming to an end, the idea of shifting whole populations to suit Western needs was not at all outrageous.

Having settled on what it considered a satisfactory policy for the disposition of the Arab areas of Palestine, the State Department was unwilling to entertain any thought that these areas might come under Palestinian control. In October 1948, after the former Mufti of Jerusalem formed a provisional government in exile called the All Palestine Government, the State Department took the position that such a government was prejudicial to the best interests of the Arabs of Palestine because it had been established without prior consultation with the Palestinians. Coming at a time when the United States was actively pursuing the idea of giving the Arab portions of Palestine to Transjordan, with no thought of consulting the wishes of the Palestinians, this position showed considerable cynicism.[91]

Contrary to the commonly held view, the State Department did not advocate the position of the Arabs of Palestine when it was opposing partition. Henderson did at least once remind his superiors that partitioning Palestine against the wishes of its Arab inhabitants ignored the principles of self-determination and majority rule,[92] but there is little else in State Department correspondence that indicates sympathy for the Arabs.

When the State Department came around to accepting Israel, it quickly lost patience with the Arabs for not following suit. In a memorandum in early July 1948, one high-level State official, clearly no Arab sympathizer, observed that the Arabs had shown emotion and bad political judgment in going to war. He said he did not "care a dried camel's hump" about the Arabs' feelings but was concerned to ensure that "these fanatical and over-wrought people" not damage U.S. strategic interests. At this same time, the U.S. UN representative sent Washington a long cable in which he criticized the Arabs for "immaturity" and for the "blindspot" they exhibited that prevented even the more moderate among them from recognizing Israel as a political fact. They had been accustomed for so long, he said, to regard Jews "as the root of all evil that it is difficult for them to see contributions for good that Jews might make politically, economically, and culturally to [the] welfare of Arabs."[93] The United States had by now become so eager to be done with the whole problem of Palestine that few realized the futility of asking Arabs who were at that moment being uprooted from their homes to recognize that they could benefit from Jewish contributions to their political life.

The United States did show concern for the approximately 725,000 Palestinians displaced by the 1948 war and worked for years to achieve some resolution of the refugee problem. Initially, the U.S. concern was to relieve the immediate problem, described by some experts in refugee relief as the worst they had ever seen. Before an international relief effort was established, hundreds of thousands of refugees were living in makeshift encampments in the surrounding Arab states and the areas of Palestine controlled by Transjordan and Egypt, without adequate food, sanitation, shelter, or medical care. They overwhelmed the resources and disrupted the demographic balance of most of their Arab hosts, particularly Transjordan, an economically strapped nation where the refugees added 20 percent to the existing population,[94] and Lebanon, where the largely Muslim refugees threatened the delicate confessional balance in a nation controlled uneasily by Christian Arabs.[95]

The United States and the UN unsuccessfully pressed Israel to take back a portion of the refugees. In December 1948, the United States supported UN General Assembly Resolution 194 calling for the return to their homes of all refugees willing to live in peace with Israel, but few serious steps were taken to pursue this resolution. Specific proposals for repatriating one to two hundred thousand people were explored but never agreed on,[96] and

Israel eventually permitted only about twenty-five thousand to return.[97] The United States also conceived several resettlement schemes over the years involving incentive payments to Arab leaders and irrigation and land-reclamation projects designed to facilitate the economic integration of the refugees in their host countries by providing employment opportunities. None of these plans ever bore fruit.[98] Although large numbers of the refugees eventually made their way out of the camps, hundreds of thousands remained in Jordan, Lebanon, Syria, and Egyptian-controlled Gaza. Both in order to keep world attention on the Palestinian issue and because the refugees so taxed their own resources, most Arab states—except Jordan, the only Arab country to grant the Palestinians citizenship—made no efforts to resettle the refugees, and all Palestinians, refugees and nonrefugees alike, have lived in the Arab world under a variety of restrictions, usually without citizenship except in Jordan and with uncertain residency status and limited civil rights.[99]

Most noteworthy for the formation of a frame of reference in which future U.S. policy was to be made is that the United States, having assumed early on that the Jewish state would survive as a sovereign nation and that the Palestinian Arab state would never exist, never treated the Palestinians as anything but refugees—as a problem, without any political content, that needed somehow to be gotten around. It did not view the Palestinians as having national or political rights or any political grievances that should be addressed, and, of course, it did not support a national solution involving the formation of a Palestinian state, the return of Arab areas captured by Israel during 1948, or the return of areas of Palestine controlled by Jordan to the Palestinians.

For U.S. policymakers, as for the public at large and the press, the conventional wisdom about why the Palestinians had become refugees seemed enticingly simple: the Palestinians, viscerally opposed to having Jews in their midst and therefore deeply opposed to sharing Palestine with a Jewish state, had simply left Palestine rather than live under Jewish rule or had been ordered by their leaders to leave. This story was so simple and seemingly logical that no one challenged it or thought to look further for the evidence that Palestinians left unwillingly, in fear and panic or under expulsion orders from Jewish and Israeli forces. Whether knowing the story of the exodus from a Palestinian perspective would have changed U.S. policy is a moot point; it probably would not have, but some deeper understanding of Palestinian thinking and grievances might have prevented the Palestinians' total exclusion from the frame of reference that was to guide policymaking for the next several decades. The failure to know anything about the Palestinians except their plight as a mass of refugees made them an abstract concept, difficult to put a human face on.

Although not one of the primary actors in the drama of 1948, John Foster Dulles, who was then a member of the U.S. delegation to the UN and would become Eisenhower's secretary of state, summed up official American sentiment on the Palestine issue aptly. Speaking to two Lebanese officials at the UN in December 1948, Dulles observed:

> The American people and the Government were . . . convinced that the establishment of the State of Israel under livable conditions was a historical necessity and the United States was determined to go through with it. We realized that doing so involved certain injustices to the Arab *States*. The situation was not one where there was any solution that was totally just to all concerned. . . . Nevertheless, there had to be a solution and, we believed, a peaceful solution. . . . Therefore, our present action could be looked upon not as inaugurating a continuing policy of supporting a Jewish State as against the Arabs, but rather as completing one phase of a historical development which, when completed, would permit of better relations than ever before with the Arab *States*.[100]

The statement is notable for its assumption that Israel's creation was a historical inevitability, for its acceptance that the Arabs would have to live with some injustices, and particularly for the fact that, even before the fighting had totally ceased in Palestine, the Palestinians had been forgotten as a factor in the equation, even as the object of the acknowledged injustices, which Dulles believed had been done to the Arab states, not to the Palestinians.

Despite the adulation Truman has received over the years for helping to midwife the creation of Israel, a close look at the record indicates that Truman was an uncertain midwife, so unsure about the wisdom of partitioning Palestine and later of recognizing Israel and so concerned about the possible consequences of these actions that he was undecided in each instance until the last minute. In the end, in fact, policymakers did not make policy on the Palestine issue; they laid out options, they argued, they listened, and in the end they merely reacted. They reacted to their compassionate impulse to rescue the Jews, to heavy pressures by Zionist activists inside and outside the government, to a strong public information campaign on behalf of Zionist goals in Palestine, to the public support for Zionism that this campaign generated, to the Palestinians' refusal to cooperate with the forced partitioning of their land, to a mind-set that painted Arabs in dark colors.

There was a considerable element of bowing to the inevitable in everything the United States did throughout the Palestine debate. Although Truman did not want to become involved politically in the issue at all, he essentially had no choice, for both domestic political and international strategic reasons. He also basically had no choice about partition; some sort of arrangement to split Palestine or to permit enough Jewish immigration to create the Jewish majority that would have given the Zionists control of Palestine was in the cards no matter whether the United States gave its imprimatur or not. Finally, Israel's establishment as an independent state and its survival even in the face of Arab military attack were also already inevitable by the time Israel announced its independence on May 15; the Jewish state would have come into existence even if Truman had not rushed to extend diplomatic recognition.

Particularly striking is the ease and speed with which the United States, at all levels of the policymaking community, accepted the inevitable. By early 1949, a bare eight months after Israel's establishment, even the Joint Chiefs of Staff, which had earlier opposed partition for strategic reasons, began to look at Israel as a strategic asset. Viewing the new nation as a military power second in the Middle East only to Turkey, the Joint Chiefs suggested that support for Israel was a means of gaining strategic advantage in the area.[101] The State Department's full acceptance of Israel was even faster and, in light of the vehemence of its opposition to partition, more striking.

In a real sense, Palestinians disappeared from the scene simply because Israel came out of the Palestine debate as a sovereign state, while the Palestinians came up scattered and lacking any of the attributes of a nation. With no status in the family of nations, they were no longer a political factor, not part of anyone's strategic considerations or of the policymaking milieu. If policymakers in this era quickly forgot them as a political factor, most policymakers for decades into the future, from the White House down to middle echelons of the bureaucracy, did not know them to have been a political factor and thus did not think to learn their story, the reason for their grievances, or their perspective on the issue.

The entire Palestinian-Israeli issue, in fact, became something of a zero-sum equation in which support for Israel precluded support for any aspect of the Palestinian position. In part, this reality arose because of the uncompromising position the Palestinians took on partition. With their demand that all of Palestine become an Arab state, they offered the United States no choice that it felt it could accept, and this fact hastened their exclusion from U.S. thinking. It was human nature that, once the United States had decided to participate in the imposition of partition on Palestine, the party that opposed partition came to be seen as uncooperative and unreasonable, whereas the party that cooperated was automatically seen as reasonable. The fact that the Arabs refused to go along with a national dismemberment that no people has ever willingly agreed to or that the Zionists cooperated because they were realizing immense gains did not matter. As far as U.S. policymakers were concerned, Palestinians were trying to thwart the United States in the pursuit of an objective and Jews were not.

A strong moral corollary to this line of thinking also put the Palestinians at a severe disadvantage. All discussion of the 1948 war started, and often still starts, from the premise that the Palestinians were immoral to have opposed the creation of a Jewish state in Palestine at all—immoral to have opposed Jewish immigration, even though unlimited immigration would have meant becoming a minority in their own land; immoral to have been unwilling to share their land with a needy people, to have begun the civil war after the UN voted for partition in November 1947, to have been associated with the invasion by Arab armies, and ultimately even to have fled Palestine.

Eban, whose eloquence did so much to mold Israel's image in the world as a beacon of moral rectitude, now observes that morally the situation was not unambiguous—that Palestine posed a deep moral dilemma and that justice and morality were not all on one side.

> To assert that thousands of years of Jewish connection totally eliminated thirteen centuries of later Arab-Muslim history would be to apply a discriminatory standard to historic experience. . . . The Palestine Arabs, were it not for the Balfour Declaration and the League of Nations Mandate, could have counted on eventual independence either as a separate state or in an Arab context acceptable for them. . . . It was impossible for us to avoid struggling for Jewish statehood and equally impossible for them to grant us what we asked. If they had submitted to Zionism with docility they would have been the first people in history to have voluntarily renounced their majority status.[102]

But such acknowledgments were not common in 1948 or for many decades afterward—not from Eban or other Israelis and not from those in the United States who made policy on Israel and the Palestinians. Coming as it did on top of the widespread sense that Palestinians were somehow interlopers in the Jewish-Christian Holy Land and were primitive and violent in the bargain, the moral opprobrium that attached to them in the decades after 1948 was more than enough to eliminate them from political consideration. An Israeli official who participated in an international conference that attempted in 1948 and 1949 to find some resolution to the Palestinian refugee problem noted when the conference ended inconclusively that the refugees had become "the scapegoats, so no one takes any notice of them. No one listens to their demands, explanations, and suggestions." [103] The Palestinians had become an indistinct mass of refugees—not a nation, not a political entity, only a problem, and not a major one at that.

5 Eisenhower, Kennedy, Johnson

Possession Is Nine-Tenths of the Law

In line with the principle that what is out of sight is out of mind, the Palestinians rarely entered U.S. policy considerations throughout the 1950s and 1960s. After their dispersal in 1948, the name *Palestine* disappeared from the world's political register, primarily because for Israel and even some Arab states the name was inconvenient. The remaining parts of Palestine, taken over by Egypt and Jordan and designated the Gaza Strip and the West Bank, lost their specifically Palestinian identity.[1] The Palestinian people themselves were nameless, known only as "Arab refugees," without identity or status except as a mass of camp dwellers.

As far as the United States was concerned, the Palestinians did not exist politically—a phenomenon that continued for the duration of the administrations of Presidents Dwight Eisenhower, John Kennedy, and Lyndon Johnson—and, as a result, an entire generation of policymakers came of age not knowing, and not thinking it necessary to learn, the Palestinians' story. Israel possessed the territory, and, as the victor in 1948, Israel possessed the history. Israel was a state, as the Palestinians were not, and Israel therefore set the limits of discourse on the Palestinian-Israeli question.

The same period saw the U.S. relationship with Israel flourish in both tangible and intangible ways. Israel's hold on the hearts and minds of the U.S. public intensified, as it was portrayed repeatedly in popular books, movies, and the press as a small, heroic, pioneering nation embodying Western values, surrounded and besieged by huge armies of implacably hostile Arabs. Its victory in the 1967 war, against what were perceived to be impossible odds, captivated the U.S. public. The special emotional affinity for Israel grew among policymakers as well, Eisenhower's unsentimental detachment ultimately giving way to Johnson's deep feeling for Israel, and the strategic relationship grew in strength as the years went on. As the United

States became more deeply enmeshed in the Cold War, its concern increasingly became to ensure stability and preserve the status quo in potentially volatile areas, and so in the Middle East U.S. policymakers looked to Israel for stability and opposed any hint of revolution or the growth of local nationalisms. When the Palestinians entered into policy considerations at all, it was as a dissatisfied group with a potential for upsetting the status quo. Moreover, in the zero-sum equation by which the Arabs and Israel were measured, the image of Arabs in general worsened in direct proportion to the enhancement of Israel's public portrayal, and in their penchant for warmongering and fiery rhetoric the Arabs seemed to lend substance to the worst aspects of their poor image.

Israel did not have a champion in the White House in President Eisenhower. He had no emotional commitment to Israel; in fact, he stands out as the only president who ever exerted heavy pressure on the Jewish state for a territorial withdrawal, which occurred after Israel captured Egypt's Sinai Peninsula in the 1956 Suez War. But distance from Israel did not make Eisenhower a friend of the Palestinians.

Eisenhower had a peculiarly detached, emotionless style and virtually no passion for anything, and so the romance of Israel's story never struck him. He did not even share the sense of Israel as a fulfillment of biblical prophecies that had so taken many of his contemporaries. Abba Eban tells of meeting Eisenhower shortly before Eisenhower's election in 1952 and finding him to be amiable and highly articulate but disconcertingly aloof. Eisenhower frankly acknowledged that he knew little about Jews, having always thought of them as unreal characters who existed only in the Bible. Eban remembers Eisenhower's telling him that the Bible "spoke of cherubim and seraphim and other creatures who, to the best of his knowledge, no longer existed. He [had] thought the Jews were in this category of extinct species."[2] As late as 1956, Eisenhower's diary indicates that he referred to Israelis as Israelites,[3] as though they were still slightly imaginary characters from the past.

The stark contrast between Eisenhower's reaction to the Bible and Truman's much more personal response is a striking indication of how different the two men were, in their personalities and in their attitudes toward Israel. Eisenhower was uncomfortable with rhetoric and distrustful of abstractions, preferring plain language and concrete concepts. He had little appreciation for history, his aides have said,[4] and thus no appreciation for what Truman and so many others felt was the special appropriateness of biblical Israel's reincarnation. It was clearly beyond his general's imagination to feel a personal attachment for any nation or people. Secretary of State John Foster Dulles, a pragmatist and doctrinaire balance-of-power politician, was no more sentimental or romantic about Israel, although he did admire Israel's mettle and believed its military victory in 1948 had demonstrated its moral strength.[5]

As a result of this aloofness, Eisenhower, probably alone among modern presidents, did not feel the need to play electoral politics with Israel, and his administration was highly resistant to pressures from any special-interest group. During the Suez crisis in 1956, when he openly opposed the Israeli-British-French military action against Egypt and with an election imminent, Eisenhower wrote to a friend that he had given "strict orders to the State Department that they should inform Israel that we would handle our affairs exactly as though we didn't have a Jew in America. The welfare and best interests of our own country were to be the sole criteria on which we operated."[6] Neither U.S. Jewish leaders and lobbyists nor Arabists in the government bureaucracy had much access to the White House. There was no "Jewish portfolio," another stark contrast with the Truman era, and Eisenhower made it known that he believed no group should have a "caretaker" at the White House.[7]

Eisenhower, and to a lesser extent Dulles, genuinely believed that in order to resolve the Arab-Israeli conflict the United States had to be friendly with both sides. "To take sides," Eisenhower wrote in his diary in 1956, "could do nothing but to destroy our influence" with all the parties. He felt it was vital that the Arabs' interests and self-respect be preserved. The arguments of Israeli supporters, particularly in Congress, that distance between Israel and the United States only encouraged the Arabs to challenge Israel's existence aroused little interest at the White House.[8]

Yet it is a particular irony for the Palestinians that by this time they had been so thoroughly removed from the picture that the Eisenhower administration's impartiality meant little from their standpoint. The Palestinians never figured in Eisenhower's strategic calculations—or, most likely, in his consciousness at all. It was clear as early as 1948, when Dulles dismissed the injustices done to the Arab *states*, that the Palestinians were not in his frame of reference either. Dulles seems to have had no interest in the Palestinians except as a discontented and possibly disruptive mass of refugees, and no sense that whatever injustice was done in 1948 was to the Palestinians, not to the Arab states.

Eisenhower's impartiality actually worked against Palestinian interests, for it assumed continuance of the status quo that had existed since the end of the 1948 war—that is, no Palestinian entity; Jordanian and Egyptian control respectively of the West Bank and the Gaza Strip, the only areas of former Palestine still in Arab hands; and the continued existence of Israel within the borders established by the 1949 armistice agreements. U.S. acceptance of this status quo had already been a fact for over four years before Eisenhower took office, and this reality effectively meant that any effort to resolve the Arab-Israeli conflict, no matter how impartial the approach, would not resolve the Palestinian problem. This is a critical point with regard to the perpetuation of the frame of reference surrounding the Palestinian-Israeli conflict, for from 1948 onward the U.S. definition of peace always included a guarantee of Israel's existence within the armistice borders, as well as an interest in Jordan's existence—which together automatically excluded a political solution to the Palestinian issue. By the time Eisenhower took office, it literally no longer occurred to policymakers to think of Palestinians in a political context. Throughout his two terms, decision makers made virtually no effort to deal with or even identify groups or individuals with authority to speak for the Palestinians.[9]

The overriding U.S. concern in the Middle East throughout Eisenhower's presidency was to prevent Soviet penetration of the area and maintain guaranteed access to oil supplies, and the administration took an activist position in pursuing these often overlapping objectives. Any disruption of the status quo was seen to contribute to Soviet designs and was vigorously opposed, whether it originated from allies like Britain and France, from Israel, or from Arab nationalists. Eisenhower generally opposed signs of lingering Western colonialism because it generated anti-Western hostility, which gave the Soviets an advantage. As a result, he supported Egyptian President Gamal Abdel Nasser's right to nationalize the Suez Canal, although not his right to block Israeli passage through the canal, and he opposed the British-French-Israeli invasion of the canal zone in 1956. He also opposed what he deemed Israel's excessive use of force in retaliation for cross-border guerrilla raids by small groups of Palestinians from Gaza and Jordan because heavy retaliation intensified Arab hostility to Israel and the West. For this reason he forced Israel to withdraw from the Egyptian Sinai Peninsula following the 1956 invasion.

At the same time, Eisenhower feared the rise of stridently nationalist governments in many Middle East countries because this phenomenon gave the Soviets direct inroads to the area. Thus, when a militantly nationalist premier, Muhammad Mussadegh, rose to power in Iran and seemed to be encouraging the rise of a strong local Communist party, Eisenhower enlisted the Central Intelligence Agency (CIA) in 1953 to overthrow Mussadegh and restore authority to the Shah. When Egypt's Nasser began espousing a revolutionary ideology and fomenting trouble in other Arab countries, Eisenhower and Dulles first pulled back from their early courtship of him and then began actively opposing his actions. In 1958, when leftist pan-Arabists inspired by Nasser threatened a pro-Western government in Lebanon, Eisenhower sent a contingent of Marines to signify U.S. support for the established government.[10]

The Arab countries and the question of how to win their friendship and keep them and their vast potential out of Soviet hands intrigued and disturbed Eisenhower and Dulles throughout much of their time in office. Early in Eisenhower's first administration, Dulles lamented after a tour of the Middle East that the Arab peoples were more afraid of Zionism than of communism. It disturbed him that he had found "deep resentment" against the United States among the Arabs as a result of Israel's creation and the Arabs' fear that the United States was backing Israel in expansionist schemes. The United States had always previously had such good relations with the Arab world, he said, and could not now afford to be distrusted by "millions who could be sturdy friends of freedom." [11] Five years later, in 1958, when instability and revolutionary fervor seemed to have intensified in the Arab world despite the best U.S. efforts to keep the lid on, Eisenhower was still trying to figure the Arabs out. Still concerned to ease Arab hostility to the United States, he mused with several foreign visitors at the height of the 1958 Lebanon crisis about how to "get at the underlying Arab thinking" and whether to work with it or try to change it.[12]

In the end, he more or less ceased trying to get into the Arabs' heads. Nothing he tried had worked to win the friendship of the majority of Arabs: not the Baghdad Pact, a defensive alliance that Eisenhower sponsored in 1955 to thwart the Soviet threat; not the Eisenhower Doctrine in 1957, which proposed economic and military aid, as well as the possibility of U.S. military intervention, to advance U.S. interests in the region; not his pressure on Israel; and neither efforts to woo revolutionary Arab leaders nor armed intervention against them. After the Suez crisis, Eisenhower deemphasized efforts to find a solution to the Arab-Israeli conflict, and for his last two years in office he took a less activist role in the Middle East in all respects.

The Palestinians did not figure at all in these policy initiatives. Six months after Eisenhower took office, in July 1953, the National Security Council officially laid out U.S. policy objectives in the Middle East. The need to resolve the "Arab refugee problem" was acknowledged perfunctorily, in what was to become a rote formula calling for resettlement in the

Arab countries, repatriation to Israel "to the extent feasible," and economic-development programs. Politically, the document was remarkable for how studiously it ignored the Palestinians, focusing all recommendations on Israel and the established Arab states. It called for settlement of major issues "between the Arab *states* and Israel." In a tone intended to be reassuring to the Arabs, it promised that Israel would not receive preferential treatment "over any Arab *state*," that U.S. policy toward Israel was limited to assisting Israel in becoming a viable state "living in amity with the Arab *states*," and that U.S. interest in the well-being of "each of the Arab *states*" was basically identical to its interest in Israel.[13] Neither Eisenhower nor Dulles, nor indeed most others in the administration, had any sense that an attempt to solve the Arab states' conflict with Israel should address Palestinian political aspirations. Policymakers faced no pressure from any quarter in the 1950s to politicize the issue. Even the Arab states were more interested in their own unresolved territorial issues with Israel and never seriously pressed in these early years for a national solution for the Palestinians. The Palestinians themselves—dispersed all over the Middle East, economically destitute, socially and culturally shattered, and lacking any political leadership—languished in a state of political lassitude and were unable throughout the 1950s to articulate their political aspirations. Small-scale Palestinian commando attacks were launched against Israel from Gaza and Jordan in the 1950s, but the first organized guerrilla group, Fatah, was not formed until 1959, and organized political activity did not begin on a significant scale until well into the 1960s.

The United States focused on schemes that would effectively sweep the Palestinian problem away, either by inducing Israel to accept the repatriation of some of the refugees and to compensate the remainder or by resettling the majority in neighboring Arab countries. Although Washington often made representations to Israel on the repatriation issue and annually cosponsored UN Resolution 194, advocating the repatriation of any refugee willing to live in peace under Israel's sovereignty, the administration never strenuously opposed Israel's adamant stand against repatriation and compensation. Eventually, having run out of proposals, it stopped pushing these ideas.[14] Resettling the refugees in the Arab countries was a more comfortable notion for the United States, for it did not involve arguing with Israel and it fit with the old colonialist notion, still widely subscribed to, that if the Arab states and the refugees were made economically content, the politics of the problem would vanish. But Eisenhower administration resettlement schemes, like those that went before and would come after, became deeply embroiled in the politics of the Arab-Israeli conflict after all and ultimately went nowhere.

Abba Eban, who was Israel's first ambassador to the United States, serving throughout the 1950s, believed that the key to Israel's strength and prosperity lay with U.S. public opinion. He viewed his principal task as making Israel, as he put it, "so acceptable to the American public" that, if ever a disagreement arose between Israel and the United States, any administration would be reluctant to carry the disagreement to the point of confrontation. U.S. Jewish organizations, including the several popular organizations and the formal lobby group AIPAC, formed the core of Eban's efforts with the U.S. public. He met regularly with the leaders of these groups to exchange views and impressions about the U.S.-Israeli relationship and has said in retrospect that he finds it "hard to imagine" that Israel would ever have been as effective as it was in Washington without their active support. These Jewish leaders in turn served as Eban's ambassadors to the general public, and Eban himself spent what he calls a "frenzied existence" going from Washington to "college campuses to Jewish meetings to state houses to lecture platforms, to foreign policy councils and associations, and above all, to the electronic media." [15]

This network of support gave Eban, and all future Israeli ambassadors, a distinct advantage in their dealings with whatever administration was in office. The fact that an Israeli ambassador was known to have substantial backing behind him when he appeared at the White House or the State Department gave added weight to Israel's representations, Eban points out, and "elevated the level at which American-Israeli affairs were transacted." This popular backing for Israel, and policymakers' knowledge that it was always there, helped shape a particular frame of reference for dealing with Israel, which developed at the very period when Palestinians were stuck in a political limbo. By the time Eban resigned as ambassador in 1959, he and Israel had become so well known throughout the United States that a special committee of tribute was formed that included the top leaders from both political parties, and dozens of editorials praising his accomplishments appeared in newspapers across the country, including some of the most obscure. The significance, as Eban points out, is that while few Americans could name the ambassador of any country, they knew his name and they knew about Israel. Israel, he says, operated in the United States on an "entirely original basis." [16]

From the earliest days of Israel's existence, U.S. Jewish activists were also Eban's lobbyists in Congress, and their influence served, to an even greater extent than Israel's popular support, to foreclose policymakers' options. AIPAC was formed in 1951 under the leadership of I. L. Kenen, an American who had done extensive lobbying for the Zionists during the Palestine debate in the 1940s. The occasion for organizing a lobby was Israel's need for economic assistance to absorb the vast numbers of Jewish immigrants moving into the new state, and because the State Department was reluctant to give the aid, the Israelis went directly to Congress through AIPAC. The lobbyists were so successful that Israel had already secured the support of congressional leaders in both houses before Eban formally approached Secretary of State Dean Acheson. Since that time, Eban notes, all U.S. administrations have been "willing to understand" that the Israeli embassy does not confine its contacts to the executive branch.[17] The lobbying produced strong congressional friends. During the Suez crisis in 1956, Congress, showing what two Israeli authors call an "almost stunning tilt" toward Israel, strongly opposed Eisenhower's pressure to withdraw from the Sinai. Israel's clout with Congress had become so much a given by 1958 that when Eisenhower sent Marines to Lebanon, Dulles asked Eban to press Congress for support.[18]

The intensity of U.S. public support for Israel waxed and waned in the first two decades after its creation, but throughout this period there was a steady base of support among the informed public, fed by newspapers, books, movies, and Israel's legions of organized supporters. Palestinians had no base of support, and as Israel's popularity grew, not only did the Palestinians fall farther into political obscurity, but Arabs in general were increasingly demonized as Israel's enemies, even as latter-day Nazis bent on another Holocaust. Typical of the prevalent attitude was historian Henry Steele Commager's comment at a rally held in 1958 to celebrate Israel's tenth birthday. In the inevitable comparison of Israel with its Arab neighbors, Commager called Israel's nationalism benign and devoted to peace, while Arab nationalism, he said, was committed to "chauvinism, militarism, and territorial and cultural imperialism."[19]

Commentators across the political spectrum in the United States began to vilify the Arabs. In the aftermath of the 1956 Suez war, the liberal journal the *Nation* depicted Arabs as greedy, sly "old-fashioned sheikhs" driven to oppose the West and Zionism by the "fanatical ideology of their religion," while the conservative magazine *National Review* took a similar approach toward President Nasser's nationalization of the Suez Canal. Calling him a "strutting fanatic" who wielded dictatorial power over twenty million "diseased and starving illiterates" through a handful of "landlords and grafters," the journal raged that Nasser not only had "dared to hijack one of the world's great strategic prizes" when he nationalized the canal but then had flung insults at the canal's "rightful owners," the French and British.[20]

By the late 1950s there had come to be what some observers have called a "cultural convergence" between Israel and the United States, promoted particularly by the movie industry. Relations were "wonderful," recalls Teddy Kollek, who did much to promote the Hollywood-Israel connection and later became the popular and long-serving mayor of Jerusalem. Movie stars, television producers, and writers, attracted by the story of Israel's accomplishments and by its open and easy-going atmosphere, began flocking to Israel, much as another generation of travelers had streamed into the Holy Land a century earlier. The entertainers were well taken care of in Israel—wined and dined, taken on special tours by the Israeli army, lent military equipment for movies, and introduced to Israeli officials for photo opportunities and autographs. When they returned home, they could be relied on to appear at fund-raisers for Israel.[21]

Movies became a popular vehicle for portraying Israel's story, and Arabs continued to be depicted as the villains and rascals they had been since the dawn of movie making in the 1920s, but now they were the enemies of Israel and took on a more sinister cast. The 1960s saw at least ten movies in which Israelis or Arabs or both figured, the Israelis almost always favorably, the Arabs unfavorably.[22] But few pieces of fiction have had as deep an impact on the U.S. public as did the 1960 movie *Exodus* and the 1958 Leon Uris novel on which it was based. The idea for the book began with a prominent public-relations consultant who in the early 1950s decided that the United States was too apathetic about Israel's struggle for survival and recognition, selected Uris, and sent him to Israel with instructions to soak up the atmosphere and create a novel.[23]

It was an astute public-relations scheme. Already a well-known novelist, with a talent for evoking powerful emotions, Uris approached his task like a crusade. It was the most fulfilling experience of his life as a writer, he told interviewers. "I was just plain pissed off about the Holocaust, and I wanted to hurl that in the face of the Christian world." When he went to Israel, he realized he had "a lightning story" in his hands, something Americans would take to immediately. The book has sold more than twenty million copies over the years, and the movie has reached hundreds of millions, educating a generation of Americans, along with a great many in succeeding generations, about the Israeli version of the Palestine story.[24]

Exodus is the story of Holocaust survivors and Jewish pioneers who fight and toil to build the Israeli state against incredible odds. Both book and movie capture a people and their spirit, inspiring awe at their suffering and their accomplishments, stirring emotions and bringing tears. The Israelis in this story are strong, determined not to give up, and, as Uris describes himself, "pissed off" enough at the world to hurl their achievements in its face. Palestinians and Arabs in general are portrayed in *Exodus* as the fanatical successors to the Nazis, preying on Jewish settlers and Israelis. The two Palestinian characters who come closest to evoking sympathy are weak. The land, Uris writes, "had lain neglected and unwanted for a thousand years in fruitless despair until the Jews rebuilt it," and Palestinians did not have the wit to be grateful. Arab Palestine was "known for vile underhanded schemers." Palestinian men let their women till the fields while they lay about in coffeehouses smoking hashish. People lived in squalor, sharing quarters with farm animals. Villages were malodorous; coffeehouses reeked with vile aromas; one group of women, heavily robed and "encased . . . in layers of dirt," smelled worse than the goats in their vicinity. No Palestinian in this montage cared about Palestine, had a legitimate reason for objecting to being dispossessed—a dispossession that was not mentioned at all—or acted out of any sentiment except raw hatred of Jews.

Little wonder that the many millions of Americans who read the book or sat enthralled through three and a half hours of the movie ended up not only loving Israel but revolted by the Palestinians. And little wonder that policymakers, who also read books and went to movies and listened to the pulse of the country, imbibed the same excitement about Israel and the same revulsion for Palestinians and the other militant Arabs with whom they were lumped together.

Much about the brief administration of President Kennedy was like the policy equivalent of rediscovering the wheel. He tried all over again to win the friendship of Egypt's President Nasser and other nationalist Arab leaders and started again from the beginning on repatriation and resettlement schemes for the Palestinian refugees. But Kennedy's style and approach were markedly different from Eisenhower's, and in the area of relations with Israel his instincts, his emotional commitment, and his policy were worlds apart from his predecessor's.

Like Eisenhower, Kennedy believed friendship with the Arab states was essential to prevent Communist inroads, although the East-West rivalry was not his primary emphasis. He believed Eisenhower had placed his own efforts to befriend Nasser too exclusively in an East-West context and that the United States should instead rid itself of all vestiges of colonialism and befriend rather than try to repress Arab nationalism. The rise of nationalism throughout the world was inevitable, Kennedy felt, and because it would affect the global political balance, the United States should try to capitalize on it. Shortly after taking office in 1961, Kennedy wrote to the leaders of Egypt, Jordan, Lebanon, Iraq, and Saudi Arabia pledging help in resolving the Arab-Israeli conflict and the refugee problem and promising moral and economic support for all states "determined to control their own destiny and to enhance the prosperity of their people." He made particular overtures to Nasser and carried on a personal correspondence with him.[25] In the end, however, Kennedy's different approach was no more successful than Eisenhower's. The Arabs suspected that his overtures concealed a trap and were so divided themselves that they could not coordinate a response or a general stance toward the United States. In the end it proved impossible both to accept Nasser's pan-Arabism and to maintain friendly ties with the conservative regimes he was trying to subvert.[26]

Kennedy's efforts to solve the Palestinian refugee problem were equally unsuccessful. As a senator, he had called for the repatriation of all refugees willing to live in peace in Israel, along with resettlement of the rest in the Arab states, and he emphasized the need for repatriation and compensation for lost property in his May 1961 letters to Arab leaders. His efforts, never close to his heart in any case, became mired in Arab-Israeli politics. As before, Israel resisted repatriation and favored resettlement in the Arab states, which would have relieved it of the problem, while the Arab states feared that Kennedy's resettlement schemes and economic-development proposals would end up permanently consigning the refugees to their care. Not only would absorption of the refugees have been economically difficult for the Arab states, but final resolution of the refugee issue in the absence of a comprehensive peace settlement would have signified Arab acceptance of the post-1948 status quo—that is, acceptance of the Palestinians' dispossession without recompense and of the permanence of Israel's presence in Palestine.[27]

Kennedy did not have a good understanding of the refugee issue or a real appreciation of the depth of feeling on both sides. His desire to resolve the problem was sincere but pro forma, something he thought should be attempted but that took second or third place to other interests in the Middle East, and he failed to understand either the vehemence of Israel's objection to taking back substantial numbers of Palestinians or the intensity of Arab fears of what they called "liquidating the Palestine problem" without actually solving it.[28] The Palestinians themselves appear to have escaped

Kennedy's notice altogether. It almost goes without saying at this stage in U.S. policymaking on the Middle East that he had no appreciation for the Palestinians as "a people" or a political entity. Kennedy and policymakers in his administration dealt with Israel and with various Arab states, but they did not deal with and, it seems, rarely thought about Palestinians. They talked around the Palestinians, who were a problem, not a people.

Although he made some attempt to accommodate both sides in the Arab-Israeli conflict, relations with Israel generally took precedence in Kennedy's mind over relations with the Arab states and over the effort to resolve the refugee problem. The warm and enduring nature of the U.S.-Israeli tie essentially began with Kennedy. He saw the tie as a true attachment, a bond in which emotions and not just strategic interests were engaged, and he began a pattern, which has continued virtually uninterrupted until the present, of ever-increasing warmth and closeness in the relationship. Given the zero-sum nature of most Arab-Israeli issues, this bond with Israel left little room for a serious focus on Arab or Palestinian concerns.

Kennedy's attachment to Israel was genuine, but he was also acutely aware of the domestic political advantages of establishing close ties. He made a conscious effort to play to Jewish audiences during his 1960 presidential campaign, received considerable financial backing from the U.S. Jewish community, and held a strategy meeting with a large group of Jewish leaders as one of his first acts after receiving the nomination in 1960. In the election, it is estimated that he received 80 percent of the Jewish vote, which he was frank to acknowledge, apparently somewhat to the chagrin of Israeli leaders. During his first meeting with Israeli Prime Minister David Ben-Gurion, he took Ben-Gurion aside and said he knew he had been elected by the votes of U.S. Jews and wanted to do something for the Jewish people. Ben-Gurion privately reported being somewhat put off by Kennedy's openly political approach.[29]

Because Kennedy was so frank about the politics, it is difficult to know where true emotional commitment left off and domestic political considerations began, but the effect, a strengthened relationship with Israel, was the same either way. The commitment to a "tradition of friendship with Israel," he once said, went back to the time of Wilson and was based on a U.S. affection for "all free societies that seek a path to peace and honor and individual right." Friendship for Israel was not partisan but was a "national commitment," he said in a campaign speech, foretelling the tone of future election campaigns on this question.[30]

Whether arising out of politics or emotion, Kennedy's bond with Israel was not simply a matter of nice speeches and eloquent phrases, for he was the first president to give substance to the relationship—the first to call it a "special relationship," which has been the term of art ever since, and the first to give meaning to the term. He was the first president to appoint a full-time aide to maintain contact with the U.S. Jewish community, thus giving Jewish leaders, Israeli embassy officials, and pro-Israeli congressmen immediate access to the White House, which they had been denied during the Eisenhower years.[31]

Most important, Kennedy was the first president to sell arms to Israel, agreeing in 1963 to Israel's request to purchase Hawk antiaircraft missiles. Following the 1948 war, the United States had embargoed military aid to both sides in the hope of maintaining some kind of military balance in the area, but when the Soviet Union began arms shipments to Egypt in the mid-1950s, Israel and its U.S. supporters began to argue for military assistance for Israel.[32]

The Hawk sale put the U.S.-Israeli relationship on a wholly new footing and established a pattern of military cooperation that has continued and intensified over the years, but the true significance of the 1963 arms deal extends far beyond the usual military cooperation. Although the surface perception at the time, and the conventional wisdom among many historians since then, has been that the Hawk sale righted a tilt in the military balance toward the Arab side after the Soviet weapons sale to Egypt had put that balance in jeopardy, in fact Israel already enjoyed military superiority, and top-level U.S. officials knew it. In reality, the Hawk sale constituted a failed attempt to induce Israel to stop development of its nuclear-arms capability.

The intricate story of the Hawk sale and its relationship to the U.S. discovery that Israel was secretly building a nuclear-weapons production facility provides a striking illustration of how thoroughly Israel-centered the policymaking frame of reference had become by the time Kennedy came to office, how unwilling the United States was to challenge Israel seriously even on issues of vital strategic importance, and how relatively insignificant the Palestinians and issues such as their resettlement or repatriation and their frustrated nationalism appeared by comparison.

In December 1960, after Kennedy had been elected but before he had taken office, photographs from a U.S. U-2 reconnaissance aircraft showed that Israel was constructing a nuclear complex at Dimona in the Negev desert. U.S. analysts at the CIA and the Atomic Energy Commission concluded that the complex probably included a reactor capable of producing weapons-grade plutonium. Particularly concerned in this period to prevent nuclear proliferation, the United States repeatedly asked Israel for assurances that it would not produce a nuclear weapon. The U.S. representations were low-key, however, and ultimately ineffectual.

Kennedy expressed his concern to Ben-Gurion during a meeting in May 1961, but the representation could not have had much impact, as this was the meeting at which Kennedy expressed his desire to do something for the Jewish people in gratitude for Jewish votes. The next time the subject was broached with Ben-Gurion was a year later, at the same time a presidential envoy informed the Israelis that the United States would grant Israel's request for Hawk missiles. The issue was raised for a third time in April 1963, the same month the Hawk sale was concluded.[33] The United States was not fooled about Israel's nuclear-weapons production despite Israeli efforts to hide its production facilities and deceive U.S. inspectors, but the United States was easily maneuvered into going along.[34]

The CIA produced an internal memorandum in March 1963 that described, with considerable foresight, the likely Israeli strategy for dealing with the Arabs and enmeshing the United States in a military relationship. Noting that "Israel already enjoys a clear military superiority over its Arab adversaries, singly or combined," the memo predicted that acquisition of nuclear weapons would greatly enhance the Israelis' feeling of security and would render their policy toward the Arabs "more rather than less tough." Israel would probably, the CIA believed, use knowledge of its nuclear capability to intimidate the Arabs psychologically; the Arabs would react by turning to the Soviet Union for additional help against the heightened Israeli threat; and Israel would then put pressure on the United States for more assistance and acquiescence in its possession of nuclear weapons.[35] A former CIA chief of station in Tel Aviv believes that President Kennedy genuinely wanted, and was the last president who seriously tried, to stop Israel's acquisition of nuclear weapons, but that he got caught in an Israeli trap. This official believes that Kennedy offered the Israelis the Hawk missiles as an inducement to forego nuclear production. But "the Israelis were way ahead of us," he concludes. "They saw that if we were going to offer them arms to go easy on the bomb, once they had it, we were going to send them a lot more, for fear that they would use it."[36]

In relation to the development of a frame of reference that excluded Palestinians from policymaking considerations, this episode demonstrates how difficult it had become for any president who felt an affection for Israel or who felt he owed his election to Jewish voters to deny Israel what it wanted, even if this went counter to U.S. strategic interests. In this atmosphere, giving the Palestinian or Arab viewpoint on any question having to do with Israel an equal hearing was out of the question.

Shortly after Johnson took office after Kennedy's assassination in 1963, he told a visiting Israeli diplomat that Israel had lost a great friend. "But," he said, "you have found a better one." [37] Historians disagree about whether Johnson had an emotional commitment to Israel or was simply highly attuned to the domestic political value of winning the Jewish vote. As with many other presidents, past and future, the truth no doubt lay in some combination of these factors. But no one argues with the notion that Johnson advanced the U.S.-Israeli relationship to a new point. If Johnson's predecessors had shaped a policymaking frame of reference in which Israel was increasingly important and the Palestinians played no part at all, Johnson cast that frame of reference in concrete—achieving a new degree of warmth in relations with Israel, reaching new depths of hostility in relations with the Arab states, and ignoring the Palestinians so totally that he never even made a show of addressing the refugee problem.

Johnson counted a large number of Israelis and influential U.S. supporters of Israel among both his personal friends and his White House advisers. The number-two man at the Israeli embassy in Washington during the 1960s, Ephraim Evron, became a close friend and was a frequent guest at the LBJ Ranch in Texas. Abe Fortas, a Washington lawyer whom Johnson appointed to the Supreme Court; Arthur Goldberg, a Supreme Court justice whom Johnson named U.S. ambassador to the UN; Walt Rostow, Johnson's national security adviser; his brother Eugene Rostow, undersecretary for political affairs at the State Department; historian John Roche, a Johnson speechwriter; Ben Wattenberg, another speechwriter and Democratic party strategist; Harry McPherson, a special counsel who was given the "Jewish portfolio" midway through Johnson's term; banker Abraham Feinberg; and attorney and Universal Artists President Arthur Krim and his wife, Mathilde, a noted cancer researcher who was an Israeli citizen and a former member of the Irgun, the pre-state Israeli underground organization, were all ardent supporters of Israel and close enough to Johnson either personally or politically to have his ear on Arab-Israeli issues. [38]

Many of the pro-Israeli contacts went back to the early days of Johnson's political career in Washington in the late 1930s, when Franklin Roosevelt, taking a fancy to the younger man, sent Johnson around the country to broaden his acquaintance with politically important groups. Roosevelt sent an emissary to the New York Jewish community to tell them to "keep an eye on" Johnson and later sent Johnson himself to be introduced around. Johnson established lasting friendships there and campaign supporters who stayed with him into the 1960s.[39]

As a senator and as president, Johnson was always more interested in domestic than in foreign affairs, but early in Israel's existence he apparently felt it was incumbent on him as a Senate leader to learn something about the new state. In 1952, when he was Senate majority whip, he sought out an introduction to Eban and visited Eban's home for a discussion of Israel, hoping "to find out everything essential about Israel in the briefest possible time," in Eban's words. It is probably fair to say, in fact, that Johnson learned all he knew about the Middle East from the Israelis. As far as anyone knows, he never made the same effort to learn about the Arabs from the Arabs.[40]

All of these Israelis and Israeli supporters shaped Johnson's frame of reference on the Arab-Israeli conflict. The Rostows, for instance, were known for their pro-Israeli stance; although Walt Rostow's treatment of the Middle East was relatively evenhanded, both men clearly viewed the region and its problems from an Israeli perspective. After leaving government service, Eugene Rostow wrote extensively rationalizing the legality of Israeli occupation of the West Bank and Gaza and of Israeli settlements in the occupied territories.[41] During the critical period leading up to the June 1967 Arab-Israeli war, Johnson spent more time with Arthur and Mathilde Krim than he did with his formal advisers, and Mathilde Krim phoned him regularly and passed messages and documents to him during the crisis. She suggested policy statements for Johnson to read to the public during the war, and during a weekend at Camp David both Krims were among those who helped Johnson write a major speech spelling out U.S. policy in the aftermath of the war. Arthur Krim and Abe Feinberg spent hours with Johnson in 1968 trying to persuade him to respond favorably to an Israeli request for fifty F-4 Phantom aircraft. Justice Fortas served as an unofficial channel of communication between Johnson and the Israeli ambassador during the crisis period before the 1967 war; the Israelis knew Fortas was a confidant of Johnson, and it is believed that Johnson, knowing the justice's close ties to Israel, asked him to be an unofficial intermediary. Goldberg, often in close coordination with the Israeli embassy, shaped much of U.S. policy at the UN after the 1967 war—policy that has defined the U.S. approach to peace negotiations ever since—because Secretary of State Dean Rusk was deeply involved with Vietnam.[42]

The views of Eugene Rostow, laid out in some detail in several articles after he left office, provide an illustration of what the scholar Malcolm Kerr meant when he said that the Palestinians' dispossession had become an "unrecognizable episode" even among well-informed Americans. Rostow's perspective, which is so Israel-centered that it fails even to acknowledge the existence of Palestinians, is presumably the perspective that he gave Johnson in the 1960s. In one symposium in 1976, Rostow managed to describe the British Mandate and the 1948 war without ever mentioning the Arabs of Palestine or their exodus. He criticized the United States for not "requiring the Arab nations to make peace with Israel" after 1948; this failure, he contended, had allowed the Arabs to continue to dream of destroying Israel. By ignoring the Palestinian factor altogether, Rostow was able to portray Arab hostility to Israel as wholly unreasoned—not as a reaction to the Palestinians' dispossession but as a perverse belief that the mere existence of Israel was "an aggression against Arab rights."[43] Rostow's later writings propounding the legality of Israeli settlements in the occupied territories, which apparently influenced the views of later presidents, particularly Ronald Reagan, were premised on the notion that there was not a distinct Palestinian Arab people with any rights in Palestine.[44]

Johnson was not so rigidly pro-Israeli that he was not open to other views. George Ball, for instance, was among his wide circle of informal advisers. Ball had served as undersecretary of state, was known for his strong opposition to U.S. involvement in Vietnam, and was soon to become a vocal critic of Israel. Johnson's decision-making process was notable, in fact, for the wide-ranging discussions with friends and advisers that shaped it, and he was open to bureaucratic, congressional, and interest-group pressures. During one critical meeting at the White House on U.S. strategy in the period leading up to the 1967 war, Johnson called together more than a dozen cabinet members and formal and informal advisers and asked their views individually on Israeli and Arab capabilities and the best U.S. course of action.[45]

Johnson's affection for Israel also did not always produce absolutely pro-Israeli policies. The 1967 war is a case in point. In mid-May 1967, when Egypt's President Nasser moved Egyptian troops into the Sinai Peninsula and demanded the departure of the UN force that had been stationed there since the 1956 Suez war, and a week later, when he blockaded the Strait of Tiran at the mouth of the Gulf of Aqaba, which blocked Israel's access to its port at Eilat, Johnson's primary concern was not to relieve the threat to Israel but to avoid involving the United States, already mired in Vietnam, in a war that might involve a confrontation with the Soviet Union. Johnson has been criticized by supporters of Israel for his failure throughout the crisis to take a forceful stand in support of Israel. The Israelis did not have much doubt that they would prevail in a war with the Arabs, and the U.S. intelligence community was unanimous in the view that Israel would need only a week to ten days, or maybe even less, to "whip hell out of" the Arabs, as Johnson told Israeli Foreign Minister Eban. But Johnson nonetheless feared that the United States would be called on to intervene if by some chance Israel got into trouble. As a result, he would not commit the United States to any course, such as guaranteeing free passage for Israeli shipping, that might have to be backed up by U.S. military force. He also tried, although not hard, to discourage Israel from launching a preemptive strike, which it ultimately did anyway on June 5.[46]

But it would be incorrect to conclude that Johnson-era Middle East policy was not formed within an Israel-centered frame of reference that essentially ignored the Arab and particularly the Palestinian perspective simply because Johnson sometimes listened to advisers who did not favor Israel's position or because he put U.S. interests ahead of Israeli interests. Some scholars contend that although Johnson was surrounded by strongly pro-Israeli advisers and aides, their sentimental attachment to Israel was usually irrelevant to policy because they were not involved with foreign affairs.[47] But this argument is unconvincing for several reasons. With close foreign-policy advisers like the Rostows, the fact that other pro-Israeli aides might have had responsibilities outside the foreign policy arena is of little significance. Moreover, the influence people like Fortas and the Krims had on Johnson's thinking in the kind of friendly, informal setting where they often saw him—at the LBJ Ranch, for instance, where they could talk about Israel in emotional, human terms and not in hard policy terms—could be far more profound than the influence of formal advisers.

This argument misses the point in any case, the point being that because he was himself so much attached to Israel and had so closely surrounded himself with people who were deeply attached, Johnson took the Israeli perspective into account in all policy decisions on the Middle East throughout his administration, even if his decisions were ultimately not always pro-Israeli, whereas he rarely even recognized the existence of an Arab or particularly a Palestinian perspective. With a more open and inclusive frame of reference, Johnson would not, for instance, have thought it necessary as Senate majority whip to learn as much as possible about Israel while making no similar effort to learn about the Arabs. Nor would he in the three weeks leading up to the 1967 war have consulted with Israeli officials, personally or through designated intermediaries, on at least a daily basis and sometimes more, while maintaining little contact with Arab officials.

Johnson did not like Arabs, it seems clear, and he felt none of the affinity for these culturally different peoples that he did for Israelis. He regarded Arabs and their lives as alien to his own. Arabs lived in "that ancient land of the camel, the date, and the palm," as he once described the Arab world in a toast to Jordanian King Hussein. Israel, by contrast, was a modern nation, a land of pioneers who had brought water and irrigation projects to the desert as he had done on the Pedernales River in Texas. As one scholar has noted, Johnson tended to see Israel's struggle against Arabs as the modern-day equivalent of Texas's struggle with the Mexicans.[48] It may have been part politics, but it was also part genuine emotion, when Johnson told a B'nai B'rith convention in 1968 that he shared the delegates' deep ties with the land and people of Israel, "for my Christian faith sprang from yours. The Bible stories are woven into my childhood memories as the gallant struggle of modern Jews to be free of persecution is also woven into our souls."[49] It was also only partly political when Johnson's minority affairs adviser Harry McPherson told a presidential biographer that he had always felt that "some place in Lyndon Johnson's blood there are a great many Jewish corpuscles."[50] Nothing Arab was woven into Johnson's soul, and there were no Arab corpuscles anywhere in his blood.

Dealing with Egypt's Nasser did not improve Johnson's outlook on Arabs. Having seen the failure of the Eisenhower and Kennedy attempts to deal with nationalist governments in the Third World, and specifically with Nasser, Johnson turned away from attempting to befriend the Egyptian nationalist and before long developed a strong hostility toward him. One Middle East scholar has said that doing business with Nasser was always like trying to change a tire on a moving automobile, and Johnson was not alone in having trouble with the erratic Egyptian. But Johnson was less patient than some of his predecessors and took deep umbrage at some of Nasser's insulting anti–United States rhetoric. The intense distrust that developed between the two men was inevitable given Johnson's known Israeli sympathies, Nasser's unpredictability, and both men's deep sensitivity to perceived slights.[51]

Johnson's hostility to Nasser was symptomatic of an indifference or outright antipathy to Arabs in general that pervaded political discourse throughout Washington—in Congress and even in parts of the bureaucracy—during his administration.[52] Not surprisingly, the administration's indifference to the Palestinians was virtually complete. Unlike the three previous administrations, this one devoted no time or energy at all to resettlement or repatriation plans for the Palestinian refugees. Johnson's own lack of concern about the Palestinians or their political grievances, which mirrored the attitude of most of the administration and the country, is reflected in this lengthy dismissal in his 1971 memoirs:

> I was aware of the deep resentment Arab leaders felt over Israel's emergence as a nation-state. I knew that many Arab refugees in the area still had not been absorbed into community life. But I also knew that various Arab leaders had used the issue of Israel and the tragic plight of the refugees to advance personal ambitions and to achieve the dominance of Arab radicals over Arab moderates. I knew that resentment and bitter memories, handed down from generation to generation, could only endanger all those who lived in the Middle East. I was convinced that there could be no satisfactory future for the Middle East until the leaders and the peoples of the area turned away from the past, accepted Israel as a reality, and began working together to build modern societies, unhampered by old quarrels, bitterness, and enmity.[53]

Johnson's view betrays a misunderstanding of how and why the Arab-Israeli conflict originated. Although he was correct enough that Arab leaders had often used the Palestinian cause to advance their personal ambitions, the "deep resentment" of which he spoke arose not from the mere fact of Israel's emergence as a nation but from the Palestinians' dispossession. Asking the Palestinians and their champions among the Arab states simply to turn "away from the past" and give up old quarrels failed to address the reason for the quarrel and treated one side of the quarrel as having no merit.

Given the general frame of reference that defined discourse on the Palestinian issue in this period, Johnson's attitude is hardly surprising. By the mid-1960s, the Palestinians had drifted so far into the political background that virtually no one regarded them as a political factor of any consequence. Even Egypt, its major attention taken up with an inter-Arab war in Yemen, was uninterested in pursuing the Palestinian issue and had informally agreed with the United States that the problem was, in the term used by officials at the time, "in the icebox."[54]

As a result, few in the United States noticed or attached much significance when the Palestinians, provoked into action by years of Arab, Israeli, and U.S. complacency, began in the late 1950s and early 1960s to organize themselves along political and military lines. The Palestine Liberation Organization (PLO) was formed more or less by fiat at an Arab summit in 1964 by Egypt and several other Arab states whose primary objective was to co-opt the Palestinian movement and prevent guerrilla groups from drawing the Arab states into war with Israel. Because the PLO was regarded as—and indeed was, in its early days—a diplomatic tool of Egypt and the other Arab states, the United States dismissed the organization's importance. At the same time, policymakers also seemed unaware of the significance of the growth of a Palestinian guerrilla organization, called Fatah and led by Yasir Arafat, that was propounding a theory of armed struggle to liberate Palestine. Fatah and several other nascent Palestinian guerrilla groups began in the early 1960s to conduct cross-border operations against Israel from bases in Syria, Lebanon, and, despite King Hussein's efforts to suppress them, Jordan. Although the United States recognized that these groups' intensified guerrilla activity played a role in the Arab-Israeli tensions that ultimately led to war in June 1967, policymakers did not attach much long-term political importance to this Palestinian activity.[55]

As a university student in Cairo in the early 1950s, Yasir Arafat had begun with several fellow students to shape the Palestinian Students' Union into a political organization based on the philosophy that Palestinians should rely on their own resources and focus exclusively on the question of Palestine rather than allow the other Arabs to use the Palestinian cause as a rallying point for their own interests. This young group eventually became the leadership of Fatah. As the years went on, Arafat and his colleagues joined with other emerging Palestinian groups and formed a network throughout the Palestinian exile community. Fatah had been organized by the early 1960s, dedicated to liberating Palestine through armed struggle and political self-reliance. Within four years of the PLO's creation, Arafat and his Fatah organization had taken over its leadership and transformed it into an umbrella organization for several Palestinian groups. Whatever its shortcomings, the new PLO as reorganized in 1968 was generally independent of the Arab states and spoke more or less faithfully for most Palestinians throughout the world.[56]

The United States failed to anticipate these developments. In its tendency to shape Middle East policy in a frame of reference centered on Israel, the United States understood little about Palestinian concerns and aspirations and therefore had readily gone along with the impulse to put the Palestinian problem "in the icebox." U.S. officials also clung to what some have called "the myth of Arabism" even after its demise. Nasser's pan-Arabism, which had been a powerful force in Arab politics in the 1950s and early 1960s, had gained a large following among Palestinians attracted to Nasser's revolutionary ideas and seeking the kind of widespread support that a unified Arab effort behind their cause would provide. Pan-Arabism was clearly shown to be an empty force during the 1967 war, however, and as Palestinians increasingly began to look to their own resources, the ideology lost its appeal for all except the most leftist Palestinian groups. Yet a belief in the continued vitality of a pan-Arabism that enveloped the Palestinians in an Arabwide nationalism had the advantage for Israel and the United States of allowing them still to ignore the Palestinian problem; as long as the Palestinians' separate existence could be denied, Israel had no legitimate challenger to its claim to Palestine. Recognizing the death of pan-Arabism would have meant acknowledging that Palestinians had no other identity except as Palestinians and that they could not find a solution to their problem as part of the broader Arab world.[57] Few U.S. policymakers in the late 1960s understood or wanted to face the demise of pan-Arabism.

The policy that emerged in the immediate aftermath of the 1967 war was to determine U.S. attitudes and policy for the next quarter century. It was a policy in large measure inspired by Israel, and it took Israel's concerns into account without paying heed to the Palestinians. Within hours after the war began and it had become clear that Israel would win handily, Johnson's friends and advisers, including Mathilde Krim, who spoke with Johnson frequently during the war and helped shape his policy statements afterward, began talking to him about postwar arrangements and the shape of the peace that should emerge. The tack they took, which Johnson fully accepted, was to insist on what they were calling a "real, guaranteed, meaningful peace" and to demand that Israel not be forced to withdraw from the territories it had captured—the entire Sinai Peninsula, the Golan Heights, and the West Bank and Gaza Strip—except in exchange for this kind of full and permanent peace. Israel's supporters felt that Israel had been betrayed after the 1956 war, when President Eisenhower had forced the Israelis to withdraw from the Sinai without any assurance of a peace agreement with Egypt. Johnson himself had publicly opposed Eisenhower's action and was determined not to repeat it.[58]

The United States did not endorse permanent Israeli control of the occupied territories, but the notion that the territories should be returned to the Arabs only in exchange for an end to Arab belligerency and full peace became the basis for all future U.S. policy. It was the basis for UN Resolution 242, passed in November 1967, which has formed the foundation for U.S. policy ever since. The resolution called for Israeli withdrawal "from territories occupied in the recent conflict," although the extent of the territory was not spelled out;[59] it also required termination of all belligerency, respect for the sovereignty and territorial integrity of all states in the area, and acknowledgment of the right of all states to live in peace within secure and recognized borders. The resolution called for a just settlement of the refugee problem but did not mention the Palestinians by name or treat them in a political context.

Although Resolution 242 was put forth as a way to achieve the kind of genuine peace that had been missing since Israel's creation, Johnson and his advisers apparently did not recognize that resolving the territorial questions arising from the 1967 war would not resolve or even address the real problem that had existed since Israel's creation, which was the displacement of the Palestinians and a smoldering Palestinian nationalism. Israel's capture of additional territory had dramatically upped the ante in the Arab-Israeli conflict, and the Israelis clearly hoped that their demonstration of military superiority would force the Arab states to sue for peace. But because they ignored the Palestinian perspective, U.S. officials did not recognize that the Palestinians were upping the ante as well. In the wake of the 1967 war, in the words of scholar Mark Tessler, the Palestinians sought to "reestablish a proper and historically accurate understanding of the conflict," making it clear that the essence of the Arab-Israeli problem was the struggle between Palestinian nationalism and Zionism and emphasizing that they were a nation in need of a political solution, not a collection of refugees with only humanitarian needs.[60]

From the beginning, the United States had not recognized that Israel's main problem had always been with the Palestinians, not primarily with the Arab states. A "just settlement of the refugee problem," the formulation established in Resolution 242, would not accomplish the real peace Israel sought; returning the Sinai to Egypt or the West Bank to Jordan would not resolve the principal issue. It would be almost another decade before the United States would begin to acknowledge, although reluctantly even then, that the Palestinian issue was the heart of the Arab-Israeli conflict.

The 1961 trial in Israel of Nazi war criminal Adolf Eichmann, mastermind of the Nazis' "final solution" for the Jews, had a profound and lasting impact on the U.S. public; it both generated sympathy for Jews and Israel and demonized Arabs, who were increasingly associated with Hitler and his murderous schemes. The horrors of the Holocaust had been well publicized in the immediate aftermath of World War II and the discovery of the Nazi death camps, but the world was soon diverted from intense concentration on these events by other pressing developments—the reconstruction of Europe, the looming Cold War, the Korean War, and other manifestations of rising East-West tensions around the world. Discussion of the Holocaust was minimized even in Israel, where self-sufficiency and fighting for survival had become so important that the failure of Europe's Jews to fight Hitler's machine was often regarded as shameful.[61]

Remembrance of the Holocaust was suppressed even by Jewish intellectuals and writers, "as if the pain was too great and the historical events too close," as if the grief aroused would be overwhelming and disorienting. It required an extended period of rumination and collective introspection before the horrors could be confronted and the Holocaust's meaning dealt with head on. The silence began to be broken in the late 1950s, when Elie Wiesel, probably the most prolific and widely read intellectual commentator on the Holocaust, began writing. Other intellectuals and theologians in the United States such as Emil Fackenheim followed in the early 1960s.[62] Before long, the Holocaust began to be publicized in popularized versions such as *Exodus* and other books, movies, and television productions.

But the Eichmann trial, more than any previous event, brought the Holocaust to the fore as a trauma that had to be discussed and dealt with by Jews and non-Jews throughout the world, for the trial served to redeem Jewish powerlessness by showing that a Jewish state could avenge Jewish suffering. The eight months of the trial, followed by Eichmann's execution in May 1962, opened the floodgates. Press coverage of the trial and the atrocities it revealed was intense, in Israel and throughout the world. In response to one poll in the United States, 30 percent of Americans said they had become more sympathetic to Israel and Jews following publicity surrounding the Eichmann trial.[63] Of even more importance than retribution against Eichmann himself, Eban has said, was the "electrifying" effect of the trial on world opinion and on the generation of Israelis born after the Holocaust. Unimaginable horrors were exposed day after day during the trial, and "a sharp light was thrown on the role of the Jewish people as history's most poignant victim." [64] The world and the U.S. public came to know and understand the centrality of the Holocaust to Jewish experience and to Israel's struggle for existence.

In the zero-sum atmosphere in which Israel and the Arabs and Palestinians were viewed in the United States in this period, the deeper sympathy aroused for Israel produced a deeper aversion for Arabs, and in the public consciousness Arabs became, in a kind of continuum, the ones playing Hitler's role by trying to exterminate Israel. This connection was made during the Eichmann trial, when the Israeli prosecutor submitted documents showing that the former Mufti of Jerusalem, Haj Amin al-Husseini, and other Arabs had opposed plans to rescue the Jews. The prosecutor also tried to establish that Eichmann and the Mufti had had "firm links." All that could be determined was that they had met once, possibly in Eichmann's office, possibly at a social event, but for all intents and purposes the connection had been made indelibly. Even today, the Israeli Holocaust museum at Yad Vashem has a display showing the Mufti with Nazi officials, leading the visitor to conclude that there is little difference between Palestinian enmity toward Israel and Nazi plans to destroy the Jews.[65]

This supposed continuity between Nazis and Arabs found full expression in the lead-up to the 1967 war, when many Israelis and many Americans feared that Israel was about to experience another Holocaust. In fact, the *threat* of extermination was never real, and Israeli and U.S. leaders knew it, but, as one Israeli writer has noted, the *fear* of extermination that Israelis felt was real. All over Israel, "one heard and read about the danger that the Arabs were about to 'exterminate Israel.' The phrase had no precise meaning, but everyone used it: No one said that the Arab armies would 'conquer' Israel or that they would 'destroy' its cities, not even that they would kill its inhabitants. They said that the Arabs would 'exterminate Israel.'" Israeli newspapers continually identified Nasser with Hitler.[66]

Israel's swift victory in 1967 was as electrifying in its own way in the United States as the Eichmann trial had been. If *Exodus* had created for millions of ordinary Americans an image of courageous Israeli pioneers fighting for survival against Arab hordes, and the Eichmann trial and the fearful run-up to the war had reminded Americans of the grave dangers Jews had always faced, the war produced the real thing—not fictional heroes but flesh-and-blood supermen, still facing grave danger, who had proved, rather stunningly, that this time they could defeat Hitler.

For U.S. Jews, the experience was often intense, exposing a bond and an identification with Israel that many had not known they felt. Well-known U.S. rabbi Arthur Hertzberg wrote in the aftermath of the war that many U.S. Jews "would never have believed that grave danger to Israel could dominate their thoughts and emotions to the exclusion of all else." The fear for Israel, capped by the victory, produced a unity and solidarity with each other and with Israel that came as a surprise to many Jews. Many who had forgotten their Jewishness felt a new sense of identity. Young Jews who knew nothing firsthand about the Holocaust felt a shared danger that brought the Holocaust to life, as well as a shared sense of triumph that gave them a collective identity for the first time.[67]

The solidarity and sense of identity with Israel that the war evoked in U.S. Jews was shared on a different level by vast numbers of non-Jewish Americans. Israel became the hero of the United States; probably, because the United States was then mired in Vietnam, Israelis provided a kind of

surrogate for the heroism and military exploits Americans could not admire in their own military. Polls showed that sympathy for Israel surged
to 55 percent, while sympathy for the Arabs, never high in any case, fell
to near zero.[68] For the media, the Israeli victory made good copy and extremely good pictures. Photos on the cover of *Life* magazine of smiling
young Israeli soldiers at the Western Wall in Jerusalem or the Suez Canal
helped Americans share the flush of Israel's victory. In fact, the war brought
about a revolution in media coverage of the Middle East. Neither the 1948
nor the 1956 Arab-Israeli war had been covered by television, but the networks sent large numbers of people to Israel in 1967 and covered the war
intensively. The number of foreign correspondents in what became permanent bureaus in Israel, from all media and all countries, soared to almost
four hundred after the 1967 war—a number that in succeeding years would
triple or quadruple or more during crisis periods.[69]

On a more intellectual level, the Eichmann trial and the 1967 war
brought forth from Jewish thinkers a philosophy, constituting a response
to the Holocaust and Jewish suffering, that became central to Jewish thinking. This so-called Holocaust theology, whose principal spokespeople were
intellectuals and theologians like Wiesel, Fackenheim, and Irving Greenberg, included among its themes the notion that the Holocaust, now after
years of silence acknowledged to be the defining experience of Jewish existence, taught the lesson that Jews must have enough power that it would be
impossible to inflict such suffering on them ever again; a strong Israel was
the manifestation of that empowerment. Another principal tenet of Holocaust theology was that Jews had been innocent victims in Europe ("history's most poignant victim," per Eban) and were innocent still as they tried
to forestall another catastrophe inflicted by another predator. Here again,
the idea emerges that Arabs were modern-day Nazis. "In this formulation,"
notes Jewish scholar Marc Ellis, "the transference of European history to
the Middle East is complete; insofar as Palestinian Arabs and the Arab
world in general attempt to thwart Jewish empowerment in Israel, they
symbolize to Holocaust theologians the continuity of the Nazi drama."[70]

It began to be common to attribute Palestinian enmity toward Israel
to anti-Semitism. One typical remark came from theologian Emil Fackenheim. Observing that Palestinian hostility to the Jewish "invaders" in
Palestine was initially understandable, Fackenheim said one had to wonder
whether, "had these invaders not been Jews, [Palestinian] hostility . . .
would have remained implacable." Indeed, he went on, "except in the context of Muslim and . . . Arab anti-Jewish attitudes, Arab policies toward Israel would appear to be unintelligible."[71] (This argument ignores the fact

that the Palestinians also opposed the British "invaders" in Palestine, who were not Jews. Moreover, the implacability of Palestinian hostility to Israel is explainable by the implacability and irreversibility of the Palestinians' displacement.)

Ordinary Americans, even ordinary U.S. Jews, did not read these Jewish philosophers and were not consciously aware of the theology they propounded or the criticism of the Arabs. But, to the extent that any intellectual helps mold and define community thought, and to the extent that the Holocaust theologians articulated a thought process that was being put forth in a less erudite way by *Exodus* and *Life* magazine and media paeans to Israel's accomplishments, these thinkers defined and refined a frame of reference that had always juxtaposed Israelis in white hats to Palestinians in black hats, with few shades of gray, and that now showed Israel in heroic raiment and Palestinians in brown shirts with swastikas. .

This transference of Nazi motives to the Palestinians began to be felt by individual Palestinians in the United States after the 1967 war. Needless to say, the feeling of solidarity with Israel that the war aroused in so many Americans completely excluded the Palestinians, but, more than that, many Palestinian Americans began to experience hostility from previously neutral Americans. One Palestinian American scholar who came to the United States as a student in the 1950s recalls being shocked at the degree of partisanship that Americans demonstrated during and after the war. He felt that the attitude throughout the United States—in the government, in the media, and among individuals—was that "we Americans beat out these Arabs, via Israel." The feeling he encountered was not merely pro-Israeli; it was as if "it was a personal victory for America." He was shaken and startled by the reaction and recalls wondering, "Why do they feel that we Palestinians and the Arabs are their enemies?"[72]

By the late 1960s, Israel and the United States had redefined Palestinian enmity toward Israel. No longer seen as harmless refugees, the Palestinians had become predators in the popular imagination—largely because of the image portrayed by U.S. and Israeli writers and moviemakers, and even before the Palestinians had begun to turn to terrorism. It would be an exaggeration to say that most policymakers consciously shared this popular perception of Palestinians and Arabs in general as latter-day Nazis, but the widespread popular hostility could not help but have some impact on a group of policymakers whose top levels already felt so strongly connected to Israel.

More than two hundred thousand Palestinians, fleeing Israeli forces advancing on the West Bank and the Gaza Strip, became refugees during the 1967 war; a large proportion of these, perhaps almost half, were already refugees from 1948 now fleeing for a second time.[73] Few in the United States, either inside or outside the government, paid much heed. Throughout the decade and a half of the Eisenhower, Kennedy, and Johnson administrations, the United States had been so unconcerned with the Palestinians as a policy issue and a political problem that more refugees aroused little interest. Nor did anyone pay much attention to the implications of another, far more significant number: the one and a quarter million Palestinians whom Israel now ruled over after occupying the West Bank and Gaza. The question of who ruled over Palestinians not thought to have a political identity in any case was of little concern.

But 1967 had created many new realities. First and foremost, the fact that Israel now exercised control over more than a million Palestinians meant that, no matter how they might try, Israel and the United States would not be able to ignore the Palestinians as a political reality for long. Second, the occupation awakened the Palestinians to their own situation. Many Palestinian intellectuals date their activism to the shock of 1967. The same shock attracted many more young Palestinians to paramilitary organizations like Yasir Arafat's Fatah, and these groups were emboldened to undertake more cross-border raids from neighboring Arab countries. The success of many of these raids, and in particular the strong resistance of Fatah's fighters to an Israeli attack on a guerrilla base in the Jordanian village of Karameh in March 1968, instilled great pride in the Palestinians and raised their political consciousness even further. Thousands of new recruits signed up to join Palestinian guerrilla organizations after the Karameh battle, swamping commando training facilities.[74]

In the aftermath of the Arab states' humiliating defeat the previous June, the Karameh incident focused attention on Palestinian fighters as the only Arabs attempting to stand up to Israel and able to acquit themselves reasonably well. Within four months after the Karameh watershed, Arafat and Fatah and the contingent of Palestinian activists who supported armed struggle against Israel and independence from the Arab states had taken control of the PLO. The Palestinian resistance movement now became a factor of considerable significance in Middle East politics. The PLO made political gains that would prove to be irreversible and, by forcefully articulating a political agenda for the Palestinians, fundamentally altered the dynamics of the Arab-Israeli conflict.[75]

At the same time as the Palestinians were becoming more active and were beginning to push themselves forward as a political factor, the United States was moving closer to Israel. U.S. policymakers, more inclined than ever before to view the Middle East through an Israeli prism, were consequently also more inclined to ignore the Palestinians. The point had been reached when more than the pro forma pledge to search for a just solution of the "Arab refugee" problem was required, but it would be another decade—one filled with terrorism and another major war—before the United States would recognize this reality.

6 Richard Nixon and Gerald Ford

An Unrecognizable Episode

President Richard Nixon came to office in 1969 intending to pursue an impartial policy toward the Arab-Israeli conflict, but he had no interest in, and knew little about, the Palestinian situation or its political ramifications. When Nixon was forced to resign the presidency following the Watergate scandal over five years later, in August 1974, the Palestinians had still apparently not made much of an impression on him, although they had begun to thrust themselves on the world stage by launching a campaign of international terrorism and sparking a civil war in Jordan. Neither Secretary of State William Rogers nor National Security Adviser Henry Kissinger was any better informed or any more deeply interested in the Palestinians than Nixon himself when the Nixon administration took office. Kissinger, who became secretary of state in 1973 and remained in that position when Gerald Ford succeeded Nixon, did become keenly aware of the Palestinians and the centrality of their role in the Arab-Israeli peace process, but he spent much of his last three years in office trying to undermine their growing political strength and ignore them as a political factor in peace negotiations.

Disregard for all Arabs, including the Palestinians, was inevitable in the atmosphere prevailing after the 1967 war. The fiery rhetoric of militant Arabs and their lurid threats against Israel had cast them as pariahs, as had the belligerent declaration of the Arab heads of state shortly after the war that there would be no recognition of Israel, no negotiations, and no peace agreement. The fact that six Arab states broke off diplomatic relations with the United States during the war, as well as their increasing alliance with the Soviet Union, the Cold War enemy, increased the Arabs' isolation from Americans and the sense that they were all alien. The Palestinians' resort to terrorism in the late 1960s added greatly to this alienation. At a time when popular support for Israel was exploding, the Arabs had clearly, in the minds of Americans, placed themselves on the wrong side.

Nixon's and Kissinger's policymaking frame of reference was shaped pri-marily around the Soviet Union and the question of how each policy step would affect Cold War tensions; within this framework, given the wide-spread pro-Israeli and anti-Arab sentiment in the late 1960s and early 1970s, Israel naturally maintained its paramount place. The United States was unable to look at the Middle East except from a vantage point, for the most part rigid and unnuanced, that viewed Arabs as pro-Soviet radicals who wanted Israel destroyed.

Perceptions changed markedly after the 1973 war, when the United States began dealing directly with Egyptian President Anwar Sadat and Syrian President Hafiz al-Asad and the media began conveying to the U.S. public a somewhat more favorable image of Arabs. Increased press interest in the Middle East also brought a slightly better, although limited, under-standing of the Palestinians. U.S. policymakers themselves gradually be-came aware of the political nature of the Palestinian issue and its centrality to the Arab-Israeli conflict. But domestic political constraints prevented the United States from seriously addressing the issue, and by the end of the Nixon-Ford-Kissinger era a new body of assumptions, having to do with the unacceptability of the PLO, had arisen to constrain policymaking flexi-bility. Although it became more acceptable to talk about the Palestinian people's needs, U.S. policymaking horizons remained limited by the refusal to deal with the PLO, and this refusal came to form a new blind spot within the frame of reference.

Nixon and Kissinger were foreign-policy globalists, guided by a single im-pulse: to thwart Soviet goals and in the East-West tug of war always to maintain a strategic and diplomatic advantage over the Soviets. All U.S. policy moves with regard to the Middle East throughout Nixon's term, and throughout the term of Ford, who was carefully tutored and guided in his foreign policymaking by Kissinger, were motivated primarily by this over-riding goal.

In the Middle East, Nixon and Kissinger initially approached their pri-mary goal via differing routes but, given their common global political in-terest, the differences were ultimately ones only of nuance. As a private citi-zen, Nixon had written to Secretary of State Dean Rusk during the 1967 war observing that the Soviet Union had blocked all previous attempts to find a peaceful solution and would continue to do so, extending its influence in the Arab world, unless the United States was able in the aftermath of the war to demonstrate that its own interest in peace between the Arabs and Israel was impartial. He came to office in 1969 believing the Arab world had aligned itself with Moscow because the United States had not been impartial, and he espoused "evenhandedness."[1] Kissinger, however, believed that the way to combat the Soviets in the Middle East was to strengthen U.S. allies while weakening Soviet allies and undermining their confidence in the Soviets. This belief meant never accommodating those Arabs who were Soviet friends, particularly not at the cost of exerting pressure on a U.S. ally, Israel. It meant guaranteeing Israel's security by maintaining Israeli military superiority over the Arabs. And it meant frustrating Soviet efforts to satisfy the Arabs' diplomatic demands, always demonstrating that the Soviets were unable to produce diplomatic progress. Ultimately, because Nixon was far more concerned with thwarting Soviet aims than with favoring or not favoring one side or the other in the Middle East, he came over to Kissinger's strategy for weakening Soviet influence.[2]

Throughout the first two to three years of Nixon's first term, Middle East policymaking was dominated by sharp tension between the Nixon-Kissinger globalist strategy centered on defeating the Soviets and a regionalist strategy pursued by the State Department under Secretary of State Rogers; the regionalist approach saw events in the Middle East as driven primarily by local factors rather than as inspired by the Soviet Union.[3]

According to the globalist approach, the issues involved in the Arab-Israeli conflict were less important than the impact of the conflict on U.S.-Soviet competition. Kissinger had no appreciation for the regional nature of the conflict, according to former Ambassador Richard Parker, until almost five years into his tenure, when he went to the Middle East in the wake of the 1973 war and finally met some Arab leaders. Indeed, in his first few years in office Kissinger advocated that the United States specifically avoid any serious effort to resolve the conflict, in the belief that stalemate was in the U.S. interest because it would frustrate the radical Arabs and the Soviets.[4]

The State Department's regionalists, however, believed that conflict in the Middle East had local causes unrelated to the Soviet Union and that the Arabs had turned to the Soviets chiefly because the United States was perceived to be totally pro-Israeli. The Soviets could and did exploit tensions to gain advantage, and for that reason the United States should work to resolve the underlying disputes. Deadlock, in the State Department view, only increased the possibility that the U.S. position in the Arab world would deteriorate further.[5]

This fundamental divergence of strategic outlook prevailed in uneasy balance throughout the first two years of Nixon's term. In establishing the division of responsibilities for foreign policymaking in his administration, Nixon initially gave responsibility for shaping Middle East policy to the State Department, while preserving direct White House responsibility over most other major issues by assigning them to Kissinger as national security adviser. There were several reasons for assigning primary responsibility for the Middle East to the State Department: initially desirous of establishing better relations with the Arab states, Nixon thought that Kissinger's Jewishness might stand in the way; he also feared that because the Arab-Israeli conflict was so intractable any U.S. initiatives would fail and that failure should be kept as far away from the White House as possible.[6]

As a result, Secretary of State Rogers and the regionalists under him enjoyed a free hand for a while to devise strategies while Kissinger chafed and maneuvered in the background to undercut them. One of these initiatives was the Rogers Plan of 1969, which called for Israeli withdrawal to the borders existing before the 1967 war, with only "minor adjustments." Because of his own initial ambivalence about the best way to combat Soviet influence, Nixon let the State Department have its head in putting forth the plan as a signal to the Arabs, but he also privately signaled the Israelis, as did Kissinger separately, that the United States did not wholeheartedly support the initiative.[7]

In the kind of globalist perspective from which Nixon and Kissinger approached foreign policy, every local crisis took on the aspects of a global confrontation and tended to be perceived as a test of strength between the United States and the Soviet Union, even if the Soviets were not involved. This outlook prevailed during the Jordanian civil war in September 1970. This crisis was the Nixon administration's first encounter with the Palestinians, but because Nixon and Kissinger were focused on the Soviet angle and uninterested in anything about the Arabs except their perceived radicalism or moderation, neither man recognized the regional causes of the Jordanian conflict or the significance of the Palestinians' emergence as a political factor in the Arab-Israeli equation.

Following the 1967 war and the striking performance of Palestinian armed groups against Israeli forces in the March 1968 battle of Karameh, the numbers of armed Palestinian guerrilla groups, called *fedayeen* (meaning "self-sacrificers"), had grown dramatically, as had the numbers of cross-border raids into Israel. Arafat's organization Fatah continued to be the largest *fedayeen* group, but several other groups—some beholden to one or another Arab state, most independent; some Marxist, most not—emerged after 1967. Each had its own following among Palestinian civilians, particularly in refugee camps; each had its own armed group. Among the best known of these new groups were the Marxist-oriented Popular Front for the Liberation of Palestine (PFLP), led by George Habash and Wadi Haddad. For the most part, the *fedayeen* used Jordan as a base of operations, and as they gained in strength and boldness, they began increasingly to act like a state within a state, challenging King Hussein's authority and taking physical control of parts of Jordan, including parts of the capital, Amman. At least two assassination attempts were made against Hussein, and some of the radical *fedayeen* groups, particularly the PFLP, were calling for the overthrow of Hussein and the Hashemite monarchy.[8]

After sporadic fighting between *fedayeen* and the Jordanian army in mid-1970, the crisis came to a head in September when the PFLP hijacked four international airliners, blew up one in Cairo after removing the passengers, and flew the other three to an abandoned airfield controlled by the PFLP in a remote area of the Jordanian desert. The PFLP had already burst on the international scene by hijacking an Israeli El Al airliner in December 1968. After holding the passengers from the three airliners hostage for several days, the hijackers released them and destroyed these three planes as well. The PFLP's stated objective was to force Israel to free *fedayeen* prisoners, but it also hoped to provoke a full-scale confrontation with Jordan's army—a confrontation it expected the *fedayeen* to win with the help of Syrian and Iraqi forces. The Jordanian army struck against the *fedayeen* a week after the hijackings, but the situation soon moved beyond a pure civil war. Within a few days, Syrian tanks crossed the border into northern Jordan to aid the *fedayeen*, and King Hussein, fearing that his military could not fight off a Syrian invasion, asked for U.S. and Israeli help. Israel prepared a plan for air strikes and ground intervention against the Syrians, but intervention proved unnecessary when Syria withdrew the tanks following an air strike by the Jordanian air force.[9]

Although there was never good evidence that the Soviet Union was involved in the Jordan confrontation, Nixon and Kissinger were convinced otherwise and saw the crisis purely as a face-down with Moscow and not as what it was—an indication of festering Palestinian discontent after two decades of statelessness and dislocation. Both men believed that Soviet incitement of the Palestinians had caused the crisis in Jordan and that the Soviets were behind Syria's moves against its neighbor.[10] In fact, all evidence indicates the contrary. The Soviets had not established a relationship with the *fedayeen* or the PLO at this point; they had no particular reason for overthrowing Hussein; and when Syrian tanks moved toward Jordan, they warned against intervention and urged restraint on all concerned in *démarches* to Syria and Egypt. Former Ambassador Talcott Seelye, who headed the State Department's special task force during the crisis, has characterized as "pure nonsense" any suggestion that the Soviets were involved or that the United States forced them to back down.[11]

Nixon and Kissinger were products of the times in their thinking on the Arab-Israeli conflict, their views shaped by the conventional wisdom about Israelis versus Arabs and by their global perspective. The Soviet-centered frame of reference that guided their thinking on Middle East issues was of necessity focused on Israel rather than the Arabs. A strategy that had as one of its essential elements guaranteeing Israel's security in order to thwart the Soviets could not, perforce, view the Arab-Israeli conflict from an Arab perspective and certainly not from a Palestinian perspective. In a globalist framework, Arabs were one-dimensional, either "radicals" or "moderates" according to how much they threatened Israel and how much military equipment they obtained from the Soviets. Globalist policymakers saw no nuances in the Arab position or in Arab thinking. Arab grievances, the root causes of their enmity toward Israel, the reasons for their ties to Moscow were of little or no interest to a United States concerned at this point almost exclusively with broad strategic questions. Moreover, when they did address the Middle East, policymakers tended to see only the situation created by Israel's 1967 victory. Resolving the new issues raised by Israel's occupation of vast stretches of Arab territory became the priority task, tending to push the Palestinians' original grievances even farther to the background.

Nixon and Kissinger themselves knew virtually nothing about the Arabs when Nixon's term began and even less about the Palestinians. Nixon had been in the Middle East during and shortly after the 1967 war and had gained some understanding of the depth of Arab feeling about Israel and about the United States as Israel's supporter, but because his overriding interest was in frustrating Soviet advances, he had little interest in the origins of the conflict or any of its intricacies. He tended to accept unquestioningly most of the conventional wisdom about the conflict. In describing the 1970 Jordanian crisis in his memoirs, for instance, he recalled that he had feared that the United States would be drawn in because the United States "could not stand idly by and watch Israel being driven into the sea." [12] The notion that Israel was in danger of being driven into the sea had become such a standard part of the rhetoric that Nixon seems to have used it unthinkingly, for Israel was not in danger during the 1970 crisis.

Nixon could and did criticize Israel. His memoirs referred more than once to Israel's "total intransigence" in the wake of its 1967 victory toward negotiating a withdrawal from the territories it had occupied, and he was openly critical about the pressures of the pro-Israel lobby. Having received only about 15 percent of the Jewish vote in 1968, he clearly had no sense of indebtedness or obligation to the lobby or the Jewish community. Eban says he rarely heard Nixon say a "sentimental word about our country and its cause." [13] But Nixon clearly had high regard for the Israelis. He admired their patriotism and liked the fact that they showed what he called "guts" and "moxie." He often used florid language that was anti-Semitic or bordered on it, but by most personal accounts he was not anti-Semitic, and he was quite comfortable with the several Jews among his close advisers. In addition to Kissinger, these included Leonard Garment, a high-ranking domestic adviser; speechwriter William Safire; Max Fisher, a prominent Republican contributor and a chief connection to the Jewish community; and Rita Hauser, the U.S. delegate to the UN Human Rights Commission.[14]

Nixon may not have been sentimental about the U.S.-Israeli relationship, but it was clearly in his mind a strategic tie invaluable to U.S. global interests. Israel fit perfectly into his global frame of reference because it was on the correct side of the radical-moderate divide. U.S. interests, Nixon wrote in a 1970 memorandum to Kissinger, "are basically pro-freedom and not just pro-Israel because of the Jewish vote. We are *for* Israel because Israel in our view is the only state in the Mideast which is *pro*-freedom and an effective opponent to Soviet expansion." [15]

Nixon thought of the Arabs according to the rote formulas current throughout the United States. In his 1978 memoirs he recalled having traveled to Egypt as a private citizen in 1963 and meeting Egyptian President Nasser. Although he indicated that he was surprised at Nasser's dignity and quiet manner in private, he could think of no reason for the Egyptian's enmity toward Israel other than "his blind intolerance of the Jews." [16] Any notion that the Arab position on Israel had something to do with the displacement of the Palestinians had long since been forgotten by Nixon as by the rest of the country. Palestinians thus generally appeared to him not as a people with a political grievance nor even the way they had appeared for the previous two decades as refugees but, because they had set out on a path of international terrorism and revolution, as radicals doing the Soviets' business. Palestinians had a functional status in Nixon's mind but little more. He did not think enough about them to mention them more than twice in his 1,100-page memoir, published four years after he left office, and then his reference was to the Palestinians as guerrillas or extremists, not as a distinct people.

Palestinians were not real for Kissinger either—nor were most other Arabs until he began shuttling around the Arab world in the aftermath of the 1973 war. Before he came to Washington in 1969, Kissinger had never visited an Arab country and knew so little about the Arab-Israeli conflict that he thought his leg was being pulled when shortly after taking office he first heard the phrase "a just and lasting peace within secure and recognized borders," one of the central elements of UN Resolution 242, which the United States regarded as the basis for an Arab-Israeli peace settlement.[17]

Israel was a different matter entirely for Kissinger. He did not hesitate to pressure Israel hard during negotiations over the several disengagement agreements with Egypt and Syria after the 1973 war, which won him opprobrium from Israeli supporters in the United States and more than once occasioned anti-Kissinger demonstrations by Israeli hard-liners in Jerusalem. But Israel for Kissinger was a vividly personal cause. Aides have described him in his dealings with the Arabs and Israel as "objective but not detached." He was proud to be a Jew, had a strong sense that Jews and Israelis were "his people," and is said to have been anguished by the attacks on him from the Jewish community during the negotiations. Associates say he dealt with the Israelis less as a statesman than as a friend and adviser, sharing his insights and analysis with them, and he sincerely felt that the concessions he asked of Israel would make Israel and Jewry prosper.[18]

One scholar has observed that Kissinger's long two-volume memoirs contain virtually no reference to the issues themselves—"no review of history, no effort to assess the competing claims and myths of the parties, no probing of their psyches, no analysis of their strategic conceptions."[19] Kissinger's superficial knowledge of the issues was evident in this description of the origins of the Arab-Israeli conflict from his memoirs:

> The movements of Zionism and Arab nationalism, to be sure, were spawned in the late 1800s but they were not directed against each other. Only when the centuries of Ottoman rule had given way to the British Mandate, and the prospect of self-determination for Palestine emerged, did the Arab and the Jew, after having coexisted peacefully for generations, begin their mortal struggle over the political future of this land.

The modern era, which gave birth to this communal conflict, then bestowed all its malevolent possibilities upon it. The Nazi holocaust added moral urgency to the quest for a Jewish state. But no sooner was it established and blessed by the international community in 1948 than it was forced to defend its independence against Arab neighbors who did not see why they should make sacrifices to atone for European iniquities in which they had had no part.[20]

This is a striking example of the observation by the late scholar Malcolm Kerr that even among sophisticated Americans the Palestinians' displacement had become an unrecognizable episode. Kissinger showed a rare understanding here that the conflict grew out of nationalism and had not, as was the common wisdom, been going on for centuries or millennia. He also indicated an understanding of the Arabs' resentment at having to "make sacrifices" for Israel's benefit, but his description omitted other essential ingredients in the Palestinian story—including, most strikingly, any mention of the Palestinians themselves or their displacement. The conflict according to Kissinger grew mysteriously out of an inchoate malevolence in the modern era. His analysis is a demonstration of the extent to which Palestinians had ceased, in the public mind and in policymaker perceptions as well, to be a part of their own story.

The 1970 Jordanian crisis should have been a signal to the United States that although the *fedayeen* had been defeated for the moment, the Palestinians and the Palestinian problem could no longer be ignored. But in their sense of triumph about what appeared to be a clear-cut victory by moderates over radicals and Soviet proxies, Nixon and Kissinger hardly noticed the implications of the Palestinians' defeat. Within the administration, those who had argued that the conflict had local causes and needed to be addressed at its source lost influence. Kissinger increasingly consolidated his hold on Middle East policymaking, undercutting the State Department and Secretary of State Rogers, and Nixon was won over to the Kissinger strategy of what one scholar calls "standstill diplomacy"— strengthening Israel while deliberately frustrating Arab hopes for diplomatic progress.[21]

The Jordanian crisis was a watershed in U.S.-Israeli relations, establishing Israel as a strategic asset by virtue of its readiness to intervene at U.S. request and seeming to confirm the correctness of Kissinger's belief that a strong Israel was in the interest of the United States. Before the crisis, the United States had extended military credits to Israel for the fiscal years

1968, 1969, and 1970 in the amounts of $25 million, $85 million, and $30 million, respectively, whereas in the three years following the crisis—fiscal years 1971–1973—military credits increased by a multiple of almost ten, reaching $545 million, $300 million, and $307.5 million, respectively. Military aid during the October 1973 war increased the total during fiscal 1974 exponentially again, to $2.2 billion. The United States had delayed responding to Israel's requests for Phantom jets and other sophisticated aircraft throughout 1969 and most of 1970 in the belief, pressed by the State Department and initially supported by Nixon, that Israel already enjoyed military superiority and would be less inclined to make territorial concessions for peace if strengthened further. One month after the Jordanian crisis, in October 1970, however, President Nixon approved a $90 million arms package for Israel and sought a $500 million supplemental appropriation for the current fiscal year to cover arms expenditures. In December 1971 during a visit to Washington by Israeli Prime Minister Golda Meir, the United States signed the first long-term arms deal with Israel, agreeing to provide new Phantom and Skyhawk aircraft over a three-year period and thus avoiding repeated haggling and supply disruptions whenever short-term agreements expired.[22]

By this point the United States had long since ceased objecting to Israel's possession of nuclear weapons. Indeed, although Israeli officials never acknowledged Israel's capability to the United States, the implicit knowledge throughout the U.S. government came to be another point of shared intimacy, a kind of conspiracy of silence. Nixon and Kissinger believed that the spread of nuclear weapons was inevitable and not something the United States should oppose. They disdained the Nuclear Nonproliferation Treaty and decided early on not to press any nation to sign it. Former National Security Council staffer Morton Halperin remembers that Kissinger saw nothing wrong with the Israelis having nuclear weapons and winked at reports that in 1969 Israel stole weapons-grade uranium from a plant in Pennsylvania. It was common knowledge at the White House, according to Halperin, that Kissinger had no qualms about Israel making nuclear weapons or stealing the material to do so.[23]

In the period following the Jordanian crisis, when the United States opened the arms pipeline to Israel, the administration also gave Israel several diplomatic assurances that amounted to making the United States and Israel diplomatic partners. In response to Israeli requests, Nixon promised in 1971 not to press Israel to withdraw to the borders existing before the 1967 war, not to force Israel to participate in negotiations for a comprehensive peace settlement but to concentrate only on small incremental steps in the peace process, not to force Israel to accept the Arab version of a refugee settlement, and in general not to be a party to any peace settlement that Israel felt would endanger its security.[24] Israel also sought assurances that the United States would veto any anti-Israeli resolution in the UN Security Council. Although Nixon refused to give such an assurance in a formal way, in fact the United States used only its second veto ever in September 1972 on a resolution condemning Israeli attacks in Lebanon and Syria and in the next twenty-five years cast vetoes more than thirty times on Middle East issues, usually to protect Israel.[25]

The closer alliance with Israel brought out a tension between two schools of thought within the Nixon administration over whether the alliance was truly of strategic benefit to the United States or was only of sentimental value because Americans felt affection for Israel and a moral obligation to preserve its existence. Those in the first school, which tended to include policy globalists and politicians responsive to outside political pressures, generally saw Israel as an essential barrier to Soviet penetration of the Middle East. The other school, usually including regionalists and nonpolitical careerists in the bureaucracy, saw the alliance as nonstrategic and dictated primarily by U.S. affinity with Israel. Seen in this light, Israel could be a burden rather than an asset and, instead of serving as a block to Soviet penetration, was a cause of increased Soviet influence because the Arabs might be much less influenced by the Soviets were it not for the fact that the United States supported Israel.[26]

Although Kissinger used both arguments when it suited his purposes— occasionally arguing, for instance, that Israel was not a strategic asset and that the attachment was only a sentimental one, presumably in order to justify withholding aid when he wanted concessions from Israel—his basic position was the globalist one that Israel's military superiority served U.S. Cold War interests. The corollary to the argument between these two perspectives was the conflict over whether providing more arms to Israel made it more or less ready to make concessions toward a peace settlement. Although he was not averse to occasionally exerting pressure on Israel as a tactic, Kissinger's basic belief was that withholding arms would make Israel feel insecure and therefore intransigent and would raise Arab hopes, and he had argued from the beginning against the Nixon–State Department inclination to withhold arms in the hope of inducing flexibility. In 1970 he won his point.

Another inescapable corollary of making Israel a military and diplomatic partner was that the Arab and particularly the Palestinian point of view could never be taken into account equally with Israel's when the United States made policy on the Arab-Israeli conflict. Although this had been the case from the beginning, the new reality of long-term military-aid agreements and explicit pledges effectively giving Israel a diplomatic veto over aspects of U.S. policy introduced a formality that had not existed previously. The Israel-centered frame of reference in which policy had always been made had now become a matter of formal agreement.

The events of 1970 induced in the United States a kind of diplomatic torpor with regard to the Middle East that Kissinger believed was good strategy. The administration tended to look only at the surface, and it assumed that all was right with the world: U.S. ally Israel had seemed to prove its worth as a barrier against the Soviets; Jordan's King Hussein, another ally, was safe; the radicals and Soviet proxies had been put down; the Soviets were quiescent; peace, or at least a condition of no war, prevailed. In fact, however, the United States was allowing its perceptions to be guided by its desires, seeing only what it wanted to see. After a major war in 1967, a drawn-out war of attrition along the Suez Canal in 1969 and 1970, and a serious flare-up in Jordan, all of which threatened to draw the United States and the Soviet Union into direct conflict, the administration so wanted the relative quiet that characterized the status quo from 1971 to 1973 to continue that it let wishful thinking form the basis of its policy.

Kissinger in fact has acknowledged in retrospect that the United States misjudged the situation in many respects, noting in his memoirs that he underestimated Egyptian President Sadat, missed the significance of Sadat's February 1971 proposal for an interim agreement with Israel along the Suez Canal—which ultimately proved to be a model for the Sinai disengagement agreement signed following the October 1973 war—and failed to respond to Sadat's expulsion of fifteen thousand Soviet advisers in 1972.[27] In its pursuit of stability, the administration failed to recognize that just beneath the surface frustrations were mounting in Egypt and Syria and among the Palestinians—were mounting in fact in direct proportion to the warmth of the U.S.-Israeli relationship.[28]

The October 1973 war, launched by Egypt and Syria in a coordinated surprise assault on Israeli forces in the Sinai Peninsula and the Golan Heights in the hope of retrieving those territories from Israeli occupation, shattered the complacency that had characterized U.S. and Israeli policy for the previous three years. The war set in motion an intense diplomatic process that would focus U.S. foreign policy on the Middle East for the remainder of Nixon's period in office and throughout Gerald Ford's, and that would culminate, more than five years later, in an Israeli-Egyptian peace treaty.

The strongly pro-Israeli mood in the country had a profound impact on the mood and the decisions of policymakers. Senator Henry Jackson, one of Israel's best friends in Congress during his several terms in the House and Senate, was asked in the 1970s whether the pro-Israel lobby was "taking over" Congress. He scoffed at this notion, saying, "These people don't understand. They refuse to realize that the *American people* support Israel. Americans, whether Gentile or Jew, respect competence. They like the idea that we are on the side which seems to know what it's doing."[29]

Jackson conveyed an accurate picture of U.S. popular support for Israel in this period. Since 1967, Americans had been taking sides in a much more definite way. Israel was perceived to be with the United States on the side of right and justice; Arabs were enemies of the United States, as they were of Israel. A poll taken in 1975, in which respondents were asked to indicate whether various value-laden words applied more to Israelis or to Arabs, indicated overwhelmingly that Americans thought of Israelis as possessing good qualities and Arabs as exhibiting bad qualities. Respondents applied virtually all positive characteristics—"peaceful," "honest," "friendly," "moderate"— to Israelis rather than to Arabs by margins of six or seven to one. Unfavorable terms—"backward," "greedy," "barbaric"—were applied to Arabs by similar margins. Perhaps most telling, 50 percent of all respondents assigned the phrase "like Americans" to Israelis, only 5 percent to Arabs.[30]

Policymakers do not always make policy on the basis of polls, but they are certainly aware of the pulse of popular opinion and often share it. The sentiment that such polls reflect creates an atmosphere that inevitably does have an impact on policymaking. In direct impact, the actions of organized lobby groups have a greater influence, but the pressures of public opinion and of lobbies are so intertwined that it is impossible to measure where one leaves off and the other begins. In the case of the Arab-Israeli conflict in the 1970s, the two dovetailed fairly closely, the pro-Israel lobby simply giving shape and direction to the public's pro-Israeli feelings and acting as a conduit to communicate those feelings to Congress and the administration. As it happened, public opinion and the lobby both also dovetailed in a broad sense with the Israel-first policy pursued by Nixon and Kissinger for strategic reasons.

The pro-Israel lobby gained a great deal in strength throughout the early to mid-1970s, and its impact on policymaking, at least in always reminding the administration of Israel's interests and trying to keep it on a rigidly straight and narrow pro-Israeli path, was considerable. The principal pro-Israel lobby group, AIPAC, for instance, opened the 1970s with a burst of energy by bringing fourteen hundred Jewish leaders from thirty-one states to Washington in January 1970 to protest the Rogers Plan. The lobbyists were able to see 250 congressmen, almost half the entire Congress.[31] In this instance, Nixon and Kissinger needed no inducement to ignore the State Department plan, but the knowledge that pro-Israeli activists could mobilize such a sizable force to dramatize their point was a lesson for the future for the administration.

Probably as important as lobbying on specific policy issues, and perhaps more important, were the educational efforts of organized Israeli supporters. AIPAC, for instance, maintained a steady information campaign for the benefit of Congress, the administration, and whoever among the public was interested. A publication called *Myths and Facts*, which gives the Israeli perspective on the Arab-Israeli conflict, went through six editions and 750,000 copies between 1964 and 1980. By the early 1970s, a regular newsletter published by AIPAC, the *Near East Report*, had a circulation of thirty thousand, including among congressmen and senators.[32]

Some organizations were formed specifically as educational groups. JINSA, the Jewish Institute for National Security Affairs, was organized after the 1973 war specifically to keep the issue of Israel's security and its contribution to U.S. security interests always before U.S. defense officials. Galvanized by the fear that Israel's very existence was on the line during the 1973 war and that it was saved only by a massive U.S. resupply effort, several prominent U.S. Jews maintained contact with Pentagon officials throughout the war and established JINSA afterward to institutionalize the contact. JINSA's sole objective, by its own account, is to shape a frame of reference focused on Israel and on what one official has called the "strategic symbiosis" between Israel and the U.S. JINSA is not interested in lobbying, one organization leader has said, "but in *shaping thought*." Many of JINSA's leading members moved to influential positions within the government, in the State and Defense Departments and the National Security Council staff,[33] where they played a key role in shaping policymaker thinking.

The dovetailing of public support for Israel and lobby activism on behalf of Israel in the early 1970s had an impact on policymaking as much in an indirect and implicit way as in a direct way. Public and lobby interest in Israel and concern for its security had tended increasingly over the years, but particularly after 1967, to define boundaries around policymaking that the administration felt it could not go beyond. This kind of unspoken pressure tends to make policymakers shape their decisions in anticipation of direct pressure that in the end may never have to be exerted. It also helps establish or maintain a mind-set centered on Israel by always keeping Israel and its concerns before policymakers. The kind of institutional tie that pro-Israeli organizations like JINSA established with government agencies in the 1970s had a powerful indirect influence on policymaker thinking. One student of Washington lobbying describes the modus operandi: activists like JINSA's "don't actually go into someone's office and ask them to do this or that. Instead, they make friends with them, suggest ideas, 'educate' them, and hope they'll make decisions in keeping with JINSA's philosophy." [34] In the absence of any similar pressures on behalf of the Arabs, and given the strong popular support for Israel throughout the country, policymakers generally had no other philosophy to guide them.

Although the Palestinians precipitated the 1970 confrontation in Jordan, the crisis reinforced the U.S. tendency to ignore the Palestinians. Their emergence as a political force was a considerable complication for U.S. policymakers, whose frame of reference remained so centered on Israel and so accustomed to a one-dimensional image of Palestinians that a sudden major shift in focus was all but impossible. Kissinger dealt with the Palestinians throughout his next six years in office as if they would quietly disappear if ignored.

Some in the State Department apparently hoped immediately after the crisis to deal more directly with the Palestinian issue but, with Kissinger enjoying increased influence in setting Middle East priorities and State itself engaged in an ultimately unproductive initiative toward Israel and Egypt, the impulse came to naught. [35] Over the next three years, during the period of Kissinger's "standstill diplomacy," the administration did not deal with the Palestinian issue at all, even as a refugee problem. [36] It was an easy issue to ignore in these years. The Jordanian civil war and the Palestinian resort to terrorism against Israeli, U.S., and international targets in the late 1960s and early 1970s had appeared to prove the correctness of the Nixon-Kissinger view that Palestinians were radicals, but in defeat after the Jordan insurrection, the Palestinians seemed not to be an issue with which the United States needed to be concerned. Even terrorism was not a major issue, in the sense that it did not require a major focus by senior policymakers or a major shift in policymaker attention. In their assumption that all Palestinian actions were Soviet-inspired, policymakers saw no need to look at Palestinians in another dimension or to look beneath the surface to discover whether any grievances underlay the terrorist acts or how Palestinian anger might be reconciled with Israel's existence.

In the wake of the 1973 war, any serious diplomatic effort to resolve the Arab-Israeli crisis inevitably had to involve the Palestinians in some way, but the United States devoted considerable effort over the several years following the war to finding ways to skirt the issue and, in assurances made to Israel, bound itself to restrictions that severely limited its diplomatic flexibility. The reasons devised now for avoiding the Palestinian issue—that Palestinians were unchangeably radical, natural terrorists bent uncompromisingly on Israel's destruction; that the PLO itself was radical; that any indication of moderation was insincere and designed to deceive—came to constitute a new set of assumptions and a new mind-set.

It is interesting to trace the growing awareness of the Palestinian issue—and the growing tendency to deal with it by denying it—in the commitments the United States made to Israel as the negotiating process began to unfold following the 1973 war. Israeli Prime Minister Meir had made her now well-known comment that there was no such thing as Palestinians during an interview published in the London *Sunday Times* in 1969. "It was not as though there was a Palestinian people in Palestine considering itself as a Palestinian people," she had declared.[37] But two years later, when she sought diplomatic assurances from the United States, the Palestinian issue clearly had not concerned her enough to demand assurances on that score. By December 1973, when the United States and the Soviet Union were making arrangements for the opening of the Geneva peace conference that followed the 1973 war, alarm bells had begun to ring in Israel. Clearly more concerned than Kissinger about the likelihood that a peace process would inevitably come around to dealing with the Palestinians, Israel balked at attending the Geneva conference when the initial draft of the joint U.S.-Soviet letter of invitation stated that the question of future Palestinian participation would be discussed during the first stage of the conference. To accommodate Israel, Kissinger negotiated watered down wording in the invitation that excluded any specific mention of the Palestinians. He also gave the Israelis a secret memorandum of understanding promising explicitly that no other parties would be invited to future meetings at Geneva without the agreement of the initial participants, thus giving Israel a veto on Palestinian participation.[38]

Israel's demands on the United States became more insistent. At Israeli request, the United States committed itself further in the aftermath of the war not to be a party to any effort to interpret UN Resolution 242 in a way that would alter "the character of the State of Israel"—meaning that the United States would oppose any attempt to resolve the Palestinian refugee problem by means of a massive repatriation of Palestinians to Israel.[39]

PLO Chairman Arafat made at least four overtures to the United States in the form of private messages shortly before and during the 1973 war, indicating acceptance of Israel and a desire to participate in peace negotiations, but the United States rebuffed the overtures, both because Arafat threatened Jordan and more fundamentally because Kissinger assumed the PLO to be unrepentantly radical. Ignoring the significance of this first Palestinian indication of a willingness to coexist with Israel, making no effort to see whether the PLO could be argued out of whatever designs it had on Jordan, and assuming that a PLO-run Palestinian state was "certain to be" irredentist and incapable of maintaining any moderate stance, Kissinger sent what he calls in his memoirs "a nothing message" in response to the first PLO overture in August 1973, ignored a second and a third, and finally responded to a fourth message sent during the war, but then only as a tactic to keep the Palestinians quiet. Kissinger feared that the PLO could disrupt the nascent peace process begun after the war, so in the hope of putting the PLO "on its best behavior," he sent an emissary in November 1973 to meet with an official of the PLO and listen to, but not negotiate over, its proposals. The emissary was General Vernon Walters, then deputy director of the CIA, who had previously assisted with Kissinger's secret negotiations with North Vietnam.[40]

Kissinger's objective was not seriously to probe the PLO position but simply to keep the PLO quiescent while he made a first exploratory postwar visit to Egypt. During the meeting with Walters, Arafat agreed, through his emissary, to halt terrorist attacks by Fatah on U.S. and other Western targets.[41] Although Arafat clearly hoped for some kind of recognition and some diplomatic progress in return for his efforts to protect Americans overseas, nothing political came of the contacts with the United States. One more meeting occurred in 1974 with Walters, who again had only a listening brief, but no political progress was made,[42] largely because the United States wanted no progress.

Kissinger appears to have been somewhat nonplussed by the emergence of the Palestinian issue as a political question that might require U.S. attention and of the PLO as an organization that might be prepared to show some political moderation. "It is important to recall how the PLO appeared at that time," he wrote much later in his memoirs, by way of explaining his consternation at having to deal with the issue. In 1973, he said, the Palestinians "were still treated as refugees in the UN, as terrorists in the United States and Western Europe, as an opportunity by the Soviets, and as simultaneous inspiration and nuisance by the Arab world." Everyone showed "extraordinary ambivalence" in their approach to the Palestinians.[43] This passage perfectly describes the shape of the U.S. and international mindset at the time and explains why Kissinger seems to have had difficulty shifting his thinking to encompass the notion of Palestinians as legitimate claimants to any part of old Palestine.

The PLO's emergence was, of all Israel's nightmares, the most elemental, as Kissinger has observed;[44] it posed a psychological and an existential challenge although not necessarily a physical threat to Israel. The possibility that a group claiming all or any part of Palestine might gain legitimacy was so nightmarish for Israelis that few in Israel or in the United States could—or would—conceive of it. Thus, any thought of the PLO as a legitimate organization and any thought that it might have qualities that would tend to enhance its legitimacy, such as political moderation or flexibility, tended to be generally excluded from the frame of reference.

Arafat's overtures worried Kissinger enough that he believed something had to be done to ensure that the Palestinians were bypassed. His hope was for some sort of agreement on the Jordanian front that would result in an Israeli pullback from small areas of the West Bank and a reassertion of Jordanian administrative control. The longer an agreement to resolve Israel's occupation of the West Bank was delayed, he believed, "the more inexorable the growth of the political status and weight of the PLO."[45] In discussions in Israel in early 1974, he argued the need for an Israeli-Jordanian agreement by noting that Israel had a choice between dealing with Jordan immediately or facing the PLO later. His own concern was not for any of the particulars of such an agreement but for working out a strategy to foreclose the issue before the PLO was strong enough to force its way in.[46]

Kissinger was probably naïve to believe that the PLO could be shut out for long under any circumstances, but he was correct in believing that if a deal were not negotiated with Jordan soon, Jordan itself would be shut out. After the attempt to forge an Israeli-Jordanian agreement failed in the summer of 1974, leaders of the Arab states, meeting at a summit in Rabat, Morocco, in October, endorsed the PLO as the "sole legitimate representative" of the Palestinian people, meaning that the Arab states no longer recognized Jordan's right to resume control of the West Bank or any part of it that might be removed from Israeli occupation. This decision was a turning point, for it thrust the Palestinians forward as the key issue in the Arab-

Israeli conflict, giving them and the PLO a legitimacy neither had previously enjoyed, even from the Arab states, and focusing attention on the political nature of the Palestinian issue.[47]

A month later, Arafat was invited to speak at the UN in New York, where his now well-known plea—"I have come to you bearing an olive branch and the freedom fighter's gun. Do not let the olive branch fall from my hand"—was widely acknowledged outside the United States to be conciliatory. The Palestinians were making their mark on the international community. Within days of Arafat's speech, the UN gave the PLO observer status, and the General Assembly passed a resolution affirming the "inalienable rights" of the Palestinian people, including their right to self-determination and to national independence and sovereignty—strong evidence of the PLO's diplomatic success in putting across to the world a sense of the centrality of the Palestinian problem.[48]

The United States was not convinced, however. Reacting to Arafat's UN speech, the United States carefully ignored his olive branch, concentrating on the revolver he carried on his hip and denouncing his failure to make an explicit overture to Israel. Kissinger, disturbed that Arafat had called for the establishment of a democratic secular state in Palestine in which Jews and Arabs would live together, dismissed the speech in a press interview two days later. "Our reading of it," he said, "is that it called for a state which really did not include the existence of Israel and therefore was dealing with a successor state, and we do not consider this a particularly moderate position."[49] Nor did the U.S. press, which generally ignored the speech's conciliatory aspects and interpreted it as an attack on Israel.[50]

Arafat expressed chagrin that what he intended as an appeal for reconciliation was disdained in Israel and the United States. In meetings with Senators George McGovern and Howard Baker in March and April 1975, respectively, Arafat pointed out that the Palestine National Council, the PLO's legislative arm, had taken a "bold" and "realistic" step the previous June by formally deciding to establish a Palestinian "national authority" over any occupied territory relinquished by Israel, meaning that the Palestinians would accept sovereignty over a limited territory. Asked specifically whether the PLO's position meant that it accepted Israel within the 1967 borders, would settle for a state limited to the West Bank and Gaza, and would agree to mutual recognition, Arafat said "yes." He disavowed any Palestinian intention to destroy Israel and said that the goal of a democratic secular state was a long-term vision of a day when the Jewish and the Palestinian people would live together. Senator Baker later asked Saudi Crown Prince Fahd if he thought Arafat had the personal capacity to change from a guerrilla leader to a responsible government leader. Fahd responded that the transition would be "almost automatic" and that if the United States extended its hand to Arafat and cultivated him, his position among the Palestinians would be so strengthened that extremist Palestinian factions would "wither on the vine."[51]

Several months later, in September 1975, as part of Sinai II, the second disengagement agreement between Israel and Egypt, Israel demanded and received from the United States a commitment on the Palestinian issue that was to tie U.S. hands in the negotiating process for almost the next decade and a half. In a separate memorandum of understanding given to Israel when the disengagement agreement was concluded, the United States agreed that it would "not recognize or negotiate with the Palestine Liberation Organization so long as the Palestine Liberation Organization does not recognize Israel's right to exist and does not accept Security Council Resolutions 242 and 338." (Resolution 338 brought the 1973 war to an end and called for the start of peace negotiations on the basis of Resolution 242.)

This pledge allowed the United States some flexibility; administration spokesmen, including those directly involved in negotiating the memorandum of understanding, have noted that, in forswearing formal negotiations with the PLO, the United States deliberately left the door open for less formal exchanges of views with the organization, for instance in order to work out understandings with it about its participation in peace negotiations. Nonetheless, as Harold Saunders, who was deputy assistant secretary of state at the time and closely involved in the negotiations, has acknowledged, there were political constraints against using whatever flexibility the United States had allowed itself, and in fact the pledge constituted a rare self-limitation on U.S. foreign-policy autonomy. It conveyed the idea— to the Arabs, to the international community, to the U.S. public, and, of course, to Israel—that this sector of U.S. foreign policy was subject to Israeli guidance.[52] The pledge had a psychological impact as well, for it gave Israel and its supporters a handle for strenuous opposition to any move that even hinted at an overture to the Palestinians, and this threatened opposition proved to be inhibiting to policymakers disinclined to take on an irate pro-Israel lobby.

The commitment, moreover, established a mind-set that cast the Palestinians as radical and intransigent for not accepting the UN resolutions and not recognizing Israel's right to exist, even though both were unusual demands. The Palestinians had always felt that they could not endorse Resolution 242 because it did not deal with them in a political context, making no mention of Palestinians except as refugees and even then not by name.

The demand that the PLO recognize Israel's right to exist was also out of the ordinary, for specific recognition of a nation's "right" to exist, rather than simply of its existence, had not been a requirement of diplomatic discourse for any other nation or entity. Although many Palestinians were ready by this point to accept Israel's existence as a reality that could no longer be denied, most Palestinians felt that specifically recognizing its "right" to exist—that is, its moral legitimacy—was psychologically unacceptable because this would mean recognizing Israel's right to have displaced the Palestinians. These were nuances that most in the policymaking community seem not to have noticed.

Some of Kissinger's aides have said that he did recognize that the United States would sooner or later have to face the issue of Palestinian control over the West Bank.[53] Other scholars give him less credit, believing he had a blind spot where the Palestinians were concerned because he continually put off the necessity of dealing with the issue in the hope that some way around it would appear.[54] Whatever may have been going on in Kissinger's head in terms of recognizing the inevitability of dealing with the Palestinian issue, he gave no outward sign, either in his decisions while in office or in his later memoirs, that this recognition had dawned on him. Deliberately foreclosing U.S. options on negotiating with the PLO was part of his blind spot.

Ford, who was in office throughout the maneuvering over the possibility of a West Bank disengagement agreement and the negotiations for Sinai II that produced the pledge not to negotiate with the PLO, was even more inclined to deny the significance of the Palestinian issue. Although he presided over one of the most critical periods in U.S. decision making on the issue, a period in which the Palestinians clearly emerged as a factor to be considered in any Arab-Israeli peace process and in which the United States was making pivotal decisions on whether and how to deal with the issue, Ford did not discuss the Palestinians anywhere in his 1979 memoirs. In a curious denial of all aspects of the issue, he failed in the memoirs even to make any mention of the Palestinians in connection with his discussion of possible West Bank negotiations—a treatment that was itself surprisingly brief. As late as 1979, Ford acted, to a greater extent than most policymakers, as though the Palestinians did not exist.[55]

Ford was not an experienced foreign-policy strategist; he had been a politician all his life and was heavily influenced by what was politically feasible. His instincts were political rather than policy-oriented, and he learned most of what he knew about foreign policy from Kissinger. Ford had had virtually no contact with Arabs and had little knowledge of the Arab perspective on Arab-Israeli issues, his exposure in U.S. politics having been almost entirely to the Jewish and Israeli perspective.[56] His relative lack of sophistication in foreign affairs, however, does not adequately explain his denial of the Palestinian problem when he later wrote his memoirs. The first year or more after Ford took office in August 1974 marked a radical change in the international acceptability of the PLO and the Palestinians. The Rabat Arab summit decision in October 1974 to declare the PLO the sole legitimate representative of the Palestinian people was only the first indication of a new Palestinian prominence. This decision was followed only a month later by Arafat's speech at the UN. The fact that Ford did not mention any of these developments in his memoirs says as much about how unimportant a part of anyone's frame of reference the Palestinians were as it does about the superficial nature of Ford's engagement in foreign-policy issues.

Ford quickly learned how politically dangerous the Middle East minefield was. He angered Israel's supporters when in March 1975, believing that Israeli inflexibility had caused the breakdown of Kissinger's attempt to negotiate a second Israeli-Egyptian disengagement agreement, he announced that the United States would reassess its policy toward Israel and would suspend new military and economic aid agreements with Israel while the reassessment proceeded. The reassessment went on for three months, but, principally because of heavy pressure from the pro-Israel lobby and Israel's supporters in Congress, it resulted in no policy changes either toward Israel or in the direction peace negotiations were taking.

Ford was chagrined to find that, despite his career-long friendship with Israel, several leaders of the Jewish community labeled him anti-Israeli and even anti-Semitic for suggesting that Israel owed the United States some quid pro quo, in the form of diplomatic flexibility, in return for U.S. assistance in maintaining Israeli military superiority. Ford was further disconcerted when in the midst of the reassessment seventy-six senators signed a letter urging him to "be responsive" to Israel's request for $2.59 billion in military and economic aid. Recognizing, he said in his memoirs, that the letter was inspired by Israel, Ford admitted that he was "really bugged" by the influence the missive demonstrated. Because of the letter, "the Israelis didn't want to budge. So confident were they that those seventy-six Senators would support them no matter what they did, they refused to suggest any new ideas for peace."[57]

The letter did indeed demonstrate that it would be extremely difficult politically for the United States to change course in either the peace process or its relations with Israel. The reassessment was quietly wrapped up with no change in policy. Aid to Israel was resumed. The nearly unanimous advice Kissinger had received during a round of meetings with outside experts to pursue a comprehensive peace settlement that would address all Arab-Israeli issues was shelved in favor of continuing with the step-by-step, agreement-by-agreement process that he had thus far been pursuing and that Israel favored. As a result, Kissinger tried again in September 1975 for a second Israeli-Egyptian disengagement agreement, concluding the Sinai II agreement with its separate codicils calling for new arms agreements with Israel and no negotiations with the PLO.

The reassessment process provided an example not only of the critical role domestic political pressures play in shaping policy but also of how policy might be made but is usually not. Kissinger's consultations with a wide range of academics, prominent foreign-policy and cabinet figures from past administrations, U.S. ambassadors in the Middle East, and his own aides, intended primarily to discuss future options in the negotiating process, were a rare example of senior policymakers going outside their own tight circle of advisers. Among former policymakers, Kissinger's interlocutors included Dean Rusk, McGeorge Bundy, George Ball, Douglas Dillon, Cyrus Vance, George Shultz, Robert McNamara, David Bruce, Peter Peterson, John McCloy, William Scranton, Averell Harriman, and Charles Yost. His consultations with academics included talks with Zbigniew Brzezinski, Malcolm Kerr, and Nadav Safran. Ford himself met with prominent supporters as well as critics of Israel—including Eugene Rostow and Arthur Goldberg among the supporters and William Fulbright and George Ball among the critics. Ford also met with a group of Arab Americans, the first president ever to do so.[58]

Although the weight of the advice from these consultations was to return to the Geneva conference to pursue a comprehensive settlement on all fronts that would include Israeli withdrawal more or less to the 1967 borders and strong security guarantees for Israel, the Israelis strongly objected to this approach, and pressures from Israeli supporters caused it to be dropped. Kissinger's State Department Middle East specialists advised him unanimously that an attempt to pursue comprehensive negotiations could not possibly survive the assault of Israeli supporters, the letter from the seventy-six senators being a case in point. Both Kissinger and Ford feared in any case that this option involved such complex issues that it would produce only stalemate.[59]

What is interesting about this exercise is, first, that it was undertaken at all, that an administration made such an unusual effort to look beyond its own restricted perspective and solicit ideas and advice from experts not so constrained by political pressures and the minutiae that can often limit the vision of policymakers; and, second, that pressures from Israel and the pro-Israel lobby were so intense as to foreclose the option most heavily favored by the outside experts. It is a moot point whether the administration would have been able to withstand the further pressures that surely would have been brought had the Geneva conference option been pursued regardless. The point is that no one in the administration thought it safe to try.

The notion of a role for the Palestinians in peace negotiations did not figure in these consultations.[60] Senator Fulbright may have raised the issue in his meetings with Ford; he had spoken as early as 1970 of the need to involve the Palestinians, noting in a speech on the Senate floor that they had been done a great historical injustice and were entitled to some form of self-determination, although they could not expect to do an equal injustice to Israel by driving Israelis from their land.[61] But if he raised the issue at all, he did not press it, and few of the other experts consulted had yet even focused on the Palestinian issue. Journalist Edward Sheehan sat in on Kissinger's meeting with several academics during the reassessment and himself asked Kissinger what plans he had for the Palestinians. "Do you want to start a revolution in the United States?" was Kissinger's curt dismissal of the issue. Sheehan says he left the meeting wondering what the point was of having a U.S. plan for peace if Kissinger intended to exclude both the Palestinians and the Soviets.[62]

This, of course, was part of Kissinger's fundamental dilemma, what has been called his blind spot, with regard to the Palestinians: how he could pursue a peace plan, whether a comprehensive plan that would tackle all issues at once or a step-by-step process that would ultimately have to confront all issues in some sort of progression, without recognizing and dealing with the core of the Arab-Israeli conflict. Kissinger was not unaware of the centrality of the Palestinian issue, but he made policy as though it would somehow go away. Throughout his shuttle diplomacy in 1974 and 1975, Egyptian President Sadat and Syrian President Asad constantly raised the subject of the Palestinians, arguing that the core of the conflict was not Soviet Cold War machinations or baseless Arab enmity toward Israel, but the Palestinian problem.[63] But Kissinger did not want to or know how to address the issue.

With no other options in mind, he allowed a trial balloon to be floated in November 1975 that would prove to be of no policy import at the time but was symbolically of great significance. In prepared testimony before the Middle East Subcommittee of the House Foreign Affairs Committee, which was holding hearings on the Palestinian problem,[64] Deputy Assistant Secretary of State Saunders stated that "in many ways" the Palestinian problem was the "heart" of the Arab-Israeli conflict and that final resolution of the conflict would not be possible until a just and permanent status was defined for the Palestinians. They regarded themselves as having their own identity, Saunders noted; they desired a voice in determining their political status, and they were a political factor which must be dealt with if peace were to be achieved. Noting that the PLO had given some indications that Palestinians might be ready to coexist in a Palestinian state alongside Israel, Saunders suggested that some sort of diplomatic process might be initiated to determine more clearly what Palestinian interests and objectives were.[65]

The statement, which came to be known as the Saunders Document, was worded extremely cautiously. The novelty of the U.S. government taking a position on the Palestinians that defined the issue in a political context is indicated by the hesitancy with which Saunders even recited their name, referring to them as "the Arab peoples who consider themselves Palestinians." His reference to the Palestinians' sense of identity as a people was carefully couched in terms that put this idea forth as a Palestinian, but not necessarily a U.S., belief. Saunders also carefully committed the United States to nothing in regard to the inclusion of the Palestinians in the negotiating process. Because this hearing came only two months after the United States had pledged not to negotiate with the PLO unless it made certain precisely defined concessions, he said that the next step should be an effort to elicit a "reasonable definition of Palestinian interests," only after which might negotiation on Palestinian aspects of the conflict be started. He specifically noted that because the PLO had not recognized the existence of Israel or explicitly stated a willingness to negotiate peace with Israel, "we do not at this point have the framework for a negotiation involving the PLO." Saunders himself has said that the statement presented a problem, not a new policy. As the lowest ranking of those who could have been sent to give the testimony, he was chosen specifically so that it would appear analytical rather than political or policy-related.[66]

Ignoring the tentative nature of the statement and interpreting it as a crack in the solid front against dealing with the Palestinian issue, Israel and its U.S. supporters reacted angrily. Kissinger himself had carefully checked and revised the wording in the document before Saunders delivered it and is reported to have cleared it with President Ford, but as soon as the outcry against the testimony surfaced, he publicly dismissed it as an "academic exercise," without trying to defend or justify it.[67]

The Saunders Document was a milestone in U.S. Middle East policy, even though it was officially repudiated and made no difference in policy at the time. In most ways it was almost three decades late, a recognition of the origins of the conflict that the United States had not acknowledged since 1948. But in many ways it was before its time; as is evident from Israel's anger and Kissinger's reaction, few in the United States or in Israel were yet ready to recognize the "unrecognizable episode" and accept the necessity of dealing with the Palestinians, so enduring was the established frame of reference. It took a policymaker of unusual insight to look beyond the conventional wisdom; Saunders, whom Middle East scholar William Quandt has praised for his analytical skill and his "sense of the human dimensions" of the Arab-Israeli conflict, fit this bill.[68]

Saunders's statement was intended to signal that after the second Israeli-Egyptian disengagement agreement, Sinai II, the necessary next step was to address the Jordanian and Syrian fronts, where the Palestinian issue would have to be on the agenda. More than that, by acknowledging the Palestinians' own sense of political identity, the statement signaled the first U.S. awareness that the Palestinian issue had a political context. Despite Kissinger's disavowal of the Saunders Document, policymakers did spend 1976—a year that Saunders calls a "down year" in policymaking terms because of the presidential election—attempting to learn more about the Palestinian question, particularly studying land use in the occupied West Bank and Gaza. Although Ford was not reelected, this material constituted a body of analysis for the Carter administration, in which many of the State Department's principal Middle East policymakers continued in key roles.[69]

Recognition of the centrality of the Palestinian issue dawned earlier in some circles outside the government than it did among policymakers, although the dawning was extremely limited and slow. Some few others in Congress followed Senator Fulbright's 1970 speech in the Senate about the historic injustice done to the Palestinians with similar statements, but their impact was minimal. In 1971, Indiana Democrat Lee Hamilton gave a speech in the House saying the Palestinians needed political, humanitarian, and economic justice. He advocated self-determination for the Palestinians in the form of either an independent state on the West Bank, a semi-autonomous entity connected to Jordan, or full union with Jordan.[70] For the times, these statements showed remarkable understanding of the true nature of the Arab-Israeli conflict, but they were so much outside the prevailing frame of reference that they had little impact on policymaking.

A few isolated voices in the media also began to notice the Palestinians in these early years. The outlook of these individuals and their experiences with others in the media provide an insight into the closed mindset that then prevailed. Foreign correspondent and syndicated columnist Georgie Anne Geyer has described a personal awakening that is revealing. She visited the Middle East for the first time in 1969. "I soon became shocked at myself," she has said, "over my own lack of knowledge and about my prejudice against Arabs." She feels she was prejudiced before the trip because she had never known any Arabs and "had been exposed to highly prejudicial writing about them." Meeting Arabs proved to be an enlightening encounter for her. "For the fair-minded journalist," she notes, "the Middle East involves a special confrontation—a confrontation with oneself and one's previous prejudices."[71]

Once she had had her own enlightenment, Geyer found it extremely difficult to get the Arab and Palestinian perspective across in the media. She said Americans generally received a distorted picture of Arabs:

> I became appalled at the unfairness of the picture presented in the American press of the "dirty street Arab," or the Arab with the knife in his teeth, or the fat and lazy desert shaykh. The cartoonists were and are particularly culpable on this, although the Arab terrorists give them quite enough fodder. Nevertheless, what one saw in the American press at that time, because of a combination of liking for Israel, emotional reaction to the Holocaust, and the limited nature of Arab efforts to present their position, was one of the most grotesque characterizations in journalistic history. The kind of prejudice that would not have been permitted with regard to any other subject was a daily phenomenon when it came to reporting on the Arab world.[72]

A few other media correspondents experienced the kind of perceptual change that hit Geyer after visiting the Middle East; however, before the 1973 war, which brought an exponential increase in U.S. public interest in the Middle East, media interest in and knowledge of the area and specifically of the Palestinians remained extremely limited. ABC correspondents Peter Jennings and Barrie Dunsmore produced a documentary on the Palestinians in 1970 specifically intended, according to Dunsmore, to refute the general public image of Palestinians as "ragged refugees" and to show that they "had developed into a very important influence in the Arab world."[73] Until after the 1973 war, however, this sort of coverage remained quite an unusual, pioneering undertaking.

The war, the Arab oil embargo that accompanied it, and Kissinger's shuttle diplomacy all opened up the Middle East to the U.S. media. Vietnam was winding down as a focus of foreign-policy attention; for the first time

U.S. interests were directly affected by an Arab-Israeli war because of the oil embargo; and also for the first time the United States was directly and deeply involved in Middle East diplomacy. Fourteen reporters accompanied Kissinger on his shuttles from Israel to Egypt to Syria, and they spent a great deal of time in the Middle East, meeting people on both sides of the conflict.[74] Inevitably, these reporters, like Geyer, learned about the Palestinian problem and about the Palestinians themselves, and an increased awareness of the Palestinians seeped through to the U.S. public. Also inevitably, a few reporters, through questions at press briefings and the like, kept the Palestinian problem before policymakers, adding, however slightly, to the pressure Kissinger received on this issue from the Arab leaders he dealt with. The process was extremely slow; public opinion remained overwhelmingly pro-Israeli, and the pro-Israel lobby continued to have a significant impact on policy formulation as well as on public opinion. But this was the first stage in altering a public mind-set that had excluded the Palestinians from consideration for a quarter century.

The Arabs themselves played a considerable part, in diverse ways and in both a positive and a negative sense, in shaping U.S. perceptions about the Arab-Israeli conflict. On the negative side, until the mid-1970s most Arab states, and the Palestinians as well, created such difficulties for journalists and imposed such severe restrictions that reporting from the Arab world was extremely difficult. For instance, during the 1967 war—the first Arab-Israeli war covered by television—virtually no reporting was done from Arab countries because they made it so difficult. ABC News had correspondents in both Cairo and Beirut, but their access was so limited that they could do little. The correspondents in Cairo were jailed and deported. As a result, all on-the-scene reporting in 1967 was done from Israel, which has always been hospitable to journalists. When Jennings and Dunsmore were filming their 1970 documentary on the Palestinians, they were arrested three times in various Arab countries. The Palestinians themselves harassed them constantly, even destroying film, in an apparent attempt to sabotage what they feared would not be a fair story.[75]

The atmosphere for reporters in the Arab world improved considerably after the 1973 war, although the degree of access journalists could count on varied from country to country and often from one period to the next. Criticism, to which many Arab states were extremely sensitive, often assured that a journalist's access was cut off, whereas journalists who pandered to the Arabs or to a particular Arab country were given red-carpet treatment. Geyer found that, notwithstanding some untoward incidents like the Jennings-Dunsmore experience, the Palestinians were the best public-relations people in the Arab world. During her 1969 trip, the Palestinian leadership gave her ready access to Arafat and other leading PLO figures, and she was able to maintain the contacts in later years. Geyer did have difficulty, however, with what she characterized as a cultural gap, largely involving rhetoric and a tendency to declaim rather than give information. She recounts an instance in 1978 when she went to the West Bank to do research on Israel's occupation practices. She was seeking information on such things as confiscation of Palestinian land, water issues, expulsion of Palestinian inhabitants, and prisoners, but when she met with a Palestinian mayor, he ranted for two hours, repeating the historic injustices done to the Palestinians but not giving her hard information.[76]

Egyptian President Sadat made considerable public-relations gains in the United States for all Arabs in the years after the 1973 war by not delivering bombast. Virtually unknown by the U.S. public and disdained by U.S. policymakers as an ineffectual leader before the war, Sadat turned out to be a particularly appealing figure. He made himself accessible to journalists, who returned the favor by giving him a great deal of air time in the United States, and the relatively measured terms in which he spoke brought a new image of Arabs to a large segment of the informed U.S. public. He was able to put across the Arab point of view in a way that had never been done before, and although he won opprobrium in the Arab world for concentrating too heavily on Egypt's interests at the expense of the interests of other Arabs, in the United States all Arabs, including the Palestinians, benefited from the image he presented of Arabs as personable, reasonable, and, all in all, not wholly unlike Americans.

It is important to examine the quality of the Palestinian image in this period, for it was double-edged. For two decades after Israel's creation, there was no "Palestinian image." The Palestinian people were largely forgotten. Without a state, a leadership, or an army, and facing a conscious attempt by Israel to forget them, they were unable to remind the world of their existence until they undertook a campaign of terrorism. The small-scale cross-border raids that continued throughout the 1950s and 1960s had accomplished little of significance militarily or psychologically. They had raised tensions, sometimes enough to spark full-scale warfare between Israel and the Arab states, but the Palestinian ingredient was always more or less unrecognized. Hijackings of international airliners, terrorist attacks on Israeli targets inside and outside Israel, and attacks on U.S. targets such as the murder of two diplomats in Khartoum, Sudan, in March 1973 finally brought the name *Palestinian* to the world's consciousness.

Not, of course, favorably. The word *terrorist* was automatically associated with *Palestinian*, the two becoming synonymous in the minds of probably most Americans. This connection tended to continue to divert attention from the central political issues and gave Israel and its supporters a justification for strong opposition to any effort to address the problem seriously or to deal with the PLO. The terrorist image lingered for decades, well beyond the start of peace negotiations between Israel and the PLO in the mid-1990s and long after the PLO had ceased terrorist operations and publicly renounced terrorism. The widespread public revulsion against PLO Chairman Arafat himself, who came to be the embodiment of terrorism for many Americans, also lingered.

Paradoxically, however, the impact of the upsurge of Palestinian terrorism in the late 1960s and early 1970s was not wholly negative. As one scholar has noted, the Palestinians needed publicity for their plight, and terrorism became a "form of mass communication."[77] Some concept of the Palestinians as a people and a national entity did filter out along with the negative image. Journalists who covered terrorist incidents and their aftermath gradually gained a broader picture of the Palestinians in the course of their reporting and conveyed it to audiences. Policymakers who dealt increasingly with Arab leaders also began to get a less one-dimensional impression of the Palestinians. Had terrorism not brought a measure of international notoriety to the Palestinians, the Arab states would most likely not have focused negotiating authority on the PLO by declaring it the sole legitimate representative of the Palestinians in 1974, the UN would most likely not have invited Arafat to plead the Palestinian case before the General Assembly in November 1974, and the United States would most likely not have come around to the position enunciated in the Saunders Document in 1975, recognizing the centrality of the Palestinian issue to the Arab-Israeli conflict.

Former Deputy Mayor of Jerusalem Meron Benvenisti has observed that Israelis could not abide the notion of a symmetry between their own claims to Palestine and those of the Palestinians. "Israelis have a profound feeling," he said, "that once they accept the symmetry that the other side is also a legitimate national movement, then their own feeling about their own right and legitimacy will be dimmed."[78] As the Palestinians began to come out of their long limbo in the 1970s, this fear of symmetry—what Kissinger described as Israel's most elemental nightmare— dictated the reaction of Israel and, in its Israel-centered perspective, of most of the United States. The Palestinians threatened not Israel's physical security but its peace of mind and its sense of legitimacy. In reaction, the Israelis and their supporters in the United States began a distinct effort to undermine any Palestinian national claims and to delegitimize the PLO as the Palestinians' political representative. New boundaries were drawn around thinking on the issue, and the frame of reference took on new aspects.

By the mid-1970s, the frame of reference on the Arab-Israeli question had for so long ignored the Palestinians as a political factor and the tentative efforts to recognize them were still so occasional that a substantial mental shift was required to focus thought on the Palestinians in the first place; recall the senator who as late as the 1980s asked where on earth the Palestinians had come from to begin with. Those who made the mental shift encountered strong resistance. In the United States, a country generally ignorant of Palestinian grievances or the origins of the conflict, it was relatively easy for Israeli supporters, picking up the dark images of Arabs that had prevailed for a century or more and linking them with the vivid evidence of Palestinian terrorism, to portray the Palestinians, and particularly the PLO, as irredeemably evil and a threat to the existence of Israel.

More subtle arguments were designed to undermine any national Palestinian claim and to "prove" that, no matter how deserving the Palestinians might appear to be, in fact they had no real basis for their claim. The prominent and respected Middle East scholar Bernard Lewis, for instance, published a lengthy article in the magazine *Commentary* in January 1975 arguing against the Palestinian case in scholarly terms. Palestine had never had precise borders until the British Mandate was established, Lewis argued; Palestinians had considered themselves Syrians during Ottoman times or part of the whole Arab nation and had only recently begun to call themselves Palestinians; Palestinians had no sense of separate nationality when they were first dispersed; the Arab states, particularly Jordan, were themselves doubtful about the wisdom of establishing a Palestinian national entity; and so on. Lewis's arguments were so sophisticated that the reader tended not to notice that some—for instance, the assertion that Palestinians had no separate sense of national identity—were wrong and that most others were beside the point or—like the lack of precise borders or precise name—applied equally to Israel before its establishment as a state.[79]

Because the PLO was so widely portrayed as radical—"a nest of terrorists," according to Lewis[80]—moderation became a catchword, something much to be desired but seemingly never exhibited by Palestinians. In the view of Hisham Sharabi, a leading Palestinian intellectual living in the United States since the 1940s, the difference between Palestinian moderation and Israeli moderation has always lain primarily in the desire of the Palestinians to remember and of the Israelis to forget. "I know moderation through direct experience," Sharabi has written ironically. "Like many Palestinians in the United States, I had to be 'moderate' to be heard, that is, to be allowed to tell our side of the story. . . . This meant, above all, restricting our discourse to the practicalities of the present and always refraining from dredging up the past. What was the point in talking about 1948, about the dispossession, expulsion, exile, and suffering of the Palestinians, when Jews could talk about the Holocaust?"[81]

As peace negotiations proceeded after the 1973 war and contacts with Arab leaders became a regular thing, U.S. policymakers were increasingly made aware of the centrality of the Palestinian issue, but the possibility of a change in policy was stymied both by the limited, Israel-centered perspective from which senior policymakers themselves approached the issue and by the kind of intense lobby pressure that could mobilize three-quarters of the Senate on behalf of Israel. The Saunders Document had a considerable impact in removing the blinders that had always formed the context for policymaking on the Middle East; both within and outside the government, Palestinians who had been thought of only as refugees, as *fedayeen*, or as terrorists would now to a much greater extent be seen as "a people" with a collective identity and collective interests. But, at the time, this was only a small step.

It cannot be known with certainty whether the United States might have been able to begin a negotiating process involving the Palestinian issue if it had gone farther at the time—if it had followed up on overtures from the PLO and tried to establish a dialogue, if it had not agreed to impose a gag on itself about negotiating with the PLO. But there is every reason to believe that a determined effort to start a negotiation between Israel and the Palestinians might have produced in the mid- to late 1970s a peace process no worse, and perhaps somewhat better, than what was finally begun in the 1990s after thousands had died, particularly on the Palestinian side, during the intervening two decades. Some U.S. policymakers believe that the bloodshed of the October 1973 war could have been avoided if the United States had marshaled the same intense diplomatic effort in 1971 or early 1973 that it did after the war.[82]

The diplomatic straitjacket in which the United States placed itself in

1975 concerning contacts with the PLO, however, restricted policymaking for some time to come. The new U.S. blind spot concerned the PLO. The new ingredient in the conventional wisdom was the idea that the PLO did not truly represent the Palestinians and that if only it could be bypassed, some solution could be achieved for the Palestinians. For another fifteen years or more, despite efforts by Jimmy Carter to alter the conventional thinking, this became the easy way to avoid seriously addressing the Palestinian issue.

7 Jimmy Carter
Making a Difference

Jimmy Carter changed the vocabulary of the Palestinian-Israeli conflict in
the United States and to a great extent changed the frame of reference for
the Palestinian issue. By broaching the notion of giving the Palestinians a
homeland, by trying to deal with the PLO, by recognizing the Palestinians
as a critical factor in any peace settlement and attempting to involve them
in the peace process, Carter overturned assumptions and misconceptions
that had been current for decades about the Palestinians' unimportance
and in a real sense took U.S. policy out of the old constricting framework
around thinking on the Palestinian problem. Carter was a rarity among
U.S. presidents dealing with the Arab-Israeli problem. More than any president before or since, he made an imaginative, good-faith effort to involve
the Palestinians in negotiations throughout 1977, confronting Israel's objections, trying to face down opposition from within the United States, attempting different alternatives and new ideas when initial proposals were
rejected, and persisting even when obstacles loomed.

He was ultimately defeated, however, by the persistence of a frame of
reference that continued, despite his serious efforts to alter it, to center on
Israel and Israel's concerns and to ignore or consciously discard the Palestinian perspective. Although he successfully negotiated an Israeli-Egyptian
peace treaty, electoral politics ultimately undermined Carter's attempts to
bring the Palestinians into the process. No U.S. president except Eisenhower
has won an election while putting heavy pressure on Israel, and Carter, already in political trouble and losing popularity for a variety of other reasons, simply did not in the second half of his term have the political capital
to expend on a serious effort to oppose Israel's desire to keep the Palestinians out of peace talks. In the end, Carter's efforts to begin a serious peace
process that would involve the Palestinians fell victim to an enduring frame

of reference that held Israel's concerns to be paramount and the Palestinian perspective to be unimportant or even pernicious.

Carter knew little about the Middle East when he was elected in 1976, and what he did know came from an Israeli perspective. He had been to Israel once on an extensive tour provided by the Israeli government while he was governor of Georgia but had never visited an Arab country or met an Arab leader. A devout Southern Baptist, Carter was steeped in the Bible and appreciated the idea of Jewish restoration in Palestine. He also believed that the Holocaust had given Jews the right to a homeland, something he considered "compatible with the teachings of the Bible, hence ordained by God." For moral and religious reasons, as well as from what he calls a sense of responsibility for ensuring Israel's ability to defend itself, he regarded his commitment to Israeli security as unshakable. Yet Carter was quite different from his predecessors in his desire, from the beginning, to explore new ideas and venture into new diplomatic territory and in his perception that a secure and stable Middle East peace would require what he called a "broader perspective."[1] That expanded perspective encompassed the Arab and the Palestinian viewpoint. As one of his principal foreign-policy aides, former Assistant Secretary of State Harold Saunders, has noted, Carter came to office, almost alone among presidents, knowing there were two sides to the Arab-Israeli conflict.[2]

Multiple factors account for Carter's new approach. He was highly intellectual, a quick study, and a voracious reader—described by some aides as probably the smartest president ever in terms of sheer brain power—and in the months of transition between his election and the inauguration and into the first months of his presidency, he read extensively about the Middle East, learning what he knew in this early period from books rather than from dealing with people. He was a problem solver, taking special pleasure, according to his aides, in tackling and doggedly pursuing problems others had been unable to solve. He often approached a problem, in fact, simply because it was a challenge and acted, sometimes with a trace of righteousness, as though others would have no choice but to follow him because he was doing what was right.

Although not an evangelical Christian, Carter was and is an idealist, and in his public life both during and since his presidency he has demonstrated a missionary zeal about trying to make a difference in the world. In the mid-1990s, following a series of private interventions in Bosnia, North Korea, and Haiti, Carter told an interviewer that he had "one life and one chance to make it count for something." His faith, he said, "demands—and this is not optional—my faith *demands* that I do whatever I can, wherever I can, whenever I can, for as long as I can with whatever I have to try to make a difference."[3] Carter's sense of mission took him into areas of diplomacy that others might have shunned as too risky.

He was not a politician in the usual sense, not inclined toward the kind of deal making and maneuvering that is usually the stuff of politics in Washington, and, in the early months of his presidency and during his personal diplomacy in the 1990s, he was essentially oblivious to the criticism his policies and actions generated. Carter was genuinely impatient with diplomatic formulas, and more than once in the first few months of his presidency he broke the bonds of the old frame of reference on the Palestinian issue, almost without realizing the consternation and dismay his statements and actions caused Israel and Israeli supporters in the United States. This style led some to regard him as politically naïve and a loose cannon, but in fact his actions, if not specifically planned, were the deliberate acts of a man who knew his mind and was irritated with the limitations of diplomatic language. Carter was as unsympathetic toward the Arabs' rigidity, particularly their refusal to make peace with Israel, as he was toward Israeli and U.S. blinders, especially the refusal to accept the existence of the Palestinians and the PLO. He consistently trampled on the diplomatic conventions by using the words *Palestinians* and *PLO* interchangeably,[4] and he spoke openly of the need to guarantee Palestinian "rights" in any peace settlement.

Carter's statement on the Palestinians' need for a homeland, made at a town meeting in Clinton, Massachusetts, on March 16, 1977, indicated a break with the conventional wisdom that the Palestinian-Israeli conflict arose from nothing more than Palestinian hostility to the notion of having Jews in their midst. Noting that the need to deal with the Palestinian problem should be one of the basic principles of U.S. Middle East policy, Carter observed that the Palestinians "claim up 'til this moment that Israel has no right to be there, that the land belongs to the Palestinians, and they've never yet given up their publicly professed commitment to destroy Israel. This has to be overcome. There has to be a homeland provided for the Palestinian refugees who have suffered for many, many years." Carter's statement, which had not been suggested by or cleared with his aides and on his explicit instructions was never disavowed or clarified,[5] indicated that he was able to go beyond the conventional wisdom to an understanding that the reason for the Palestinians' hostility lay with the fact that they had been displaced and no longer had a homeland. In 1977, this depth of insight was rare.

With regard to Middle East negotiations in the 1970s as with other diplomatic interventions in the 1990s, Carter took the attitude that a solution to any problem can be found only by negotiating with all concerned, however much they may be regarded as outside the pale. In much of his freelance diplomacy after leaving office, Carter dealt with leaders and rebels whom much of the world regarded as odious because he believed these were the leaders whose cooperation was necessary to achieve a solution. He never shared the widespread U.S. abhorrence for negotiating with the PLO because it had committed terrorist acts. He deplored terrorism but believed that because the Palestinians had to be involved in negotiations and the PLO was the only organization representing them, negotiations with the PLO were absolutely necessary. "I'll talk with anybody who wants to talk about peace," Carter has said.[6]

Human rights was a major theme of Carter's administration and a strong factor in his interest in the Palestinian issue. Harold Saunders observes that Carter had a keen sense that the rest of the world saw the United States as a bastion of freedom and cared far less about U.S. nuclear strength than it did about its dedication to human rights and to the values embodied in the Bill of Rights. Carter employed this commitment to individual freedom and human rights in the South, where, heavily influenced by his mother, he was a strong opponent of segregation. He was able, Saunders says, to see the "human root" of people, and in office he tended to compare Palestinians to blacks, seeing them as another disenfranchised people.[7] William Quandt, who was the director of Middle East affairs on the National Security Council staff under Carter, recalls that when people told Carter that the Palestinian-Israeli situation was hopeless and that it was a kind of primordial conflict that had been going on for centuries and would never be resolved, Carter responded by likening it to the situation of blacks in the South and the rise of integration; you did not necessarily have to change people's hearts, Carter seemed to think, but it was possible to change their behavior, which could be done in the Middle East as well as in the United States.[8]

Although Carter never defined, either at the time or later, exactly what he meant when he called for a homeland for the Palestinians,[9] he was concerned primarily to ensure that Palestinians had the kind of universal rights that peoples everywhere were entitled to: the right to vote, the right to meet and debate issues, the right to own property free of the fear of confiscation, and the right to be free of military rule. He seems not to have cared about precisely how these rights would be guaranteed and never favored creation of an independent Palestinian state, but he generally favored a Jordanian-Palestinian confederation of some sort and an end to Israeli occupation. He speaks frankly in his memoirs of Israel's "continued deprivation of Palestinian rights" as "indefensible" and in violation of basic Israeli and U.S. moral and ethical principles.[10]

Carter's interest in the Middle East was in all respects intellectual rather than emotional or personal. He was not a warm person and felt no particular warmth toward either Israelis or Palestinians. He has been described as a man who only rarely revealed himself, with a cold demeanor and little sense of humor.[11] Samuel Lewis, who was U.S. ambassador to Israel from 1977 to 1985, has noted that although Carter could debate the legal interpretation of treaties with Israeli lawyers and biblical history with Israeli religious scholars, he had little "understanding" of Jews, especially of "the Holocaust-scarred generation" that still led Israel during Carter's presidency.[12] Lewis's observation is revealing for the indication it gives of the general public's expectations of policymakers in the framework within which they had to operate. One gathers from his remarks that "understanding" for Jews and empathy for Jewish feelings about the Holocaust were expected in a president dealing with the Arab-Israeli conflict. A similar empathy for Palestinian feelings about their own plight and their view of the origins of the conflict was, however, not expected and not part of the frame of reference.[13]

Lewis's observations also aptly describe Carter's cerebral nature and approach to problem solving. All Carter's aides comment on his easy absorption of massive amounts of written material and his quick grasp of a situation, although some believe that in his concentration on detail he sometimes lost sight of the larger picture. Carter knew the Middle East reasonably well from an academic standpoint by the time he began dealing with it officially and meeting personally with Middle East leaders. Even Carter's interest in human rights was more intellectual than emotional—the idealist's commitment to fair play, at least on the books, without the crusader's sense of involvement. He certainly never had an emotional connection with the Palestinians or the Palestinian cause, and, despite his belief that they deserved a fair deal, his concern seems to have had little human content. He never met a Palestinian until after he had left office. Saunders recalls that after Carter made a trip to the Middle East as a private citizen in 1983 and met with Palestinians for the first time, he told Saunders that he had always previously dismissed what Saunders and Quandt told him about the Palestinians as the "experts' view"—the advocacy of Arabists for the Arab viewpoint—but that after meeting with Palestinians he had discovered that they were right.[14]

Carter himself has given an interesting account of his first encounter with Palestinians, describing how much his eyes were opened during the 1983 trip by seeing how Palestinians lived and were treated in the West Bank and Gaza under Israel's occupation and by hearing the Palestinian perspective on the conflict directly from Palestinians. The allegiance to the PLO among Palestinians from all walks of life apparently surprised Carter, as did the national content of what he heard from and about the PLO. He recalls startling a group of PLO officials by having to ask them what the PLO's purposes were and, when handed a leaflet describing the PLO as the national liberation movement of the Palestinians, he was struck by how many times the word *national* appeared in a short statement.[15]

Carter's surprise at learning, years after leaving office, that the Palestinians had strong national aspirations is an indication of how little he knew about the Palestinians, despite his advocacy of their rights. Although he undoubtedly did not feel strongly one way or the other about the merits of establishing an independent Palestinian state, he had always publicly opposed it, most likely for political reasons.[16] This position may have obscured the Palestinians' national aspirations from his field of vision; clearly, trying to assure Palestinian civil and human rights was his primary concern. Whatever the case, it is clear that even Carter, unfettered though he generally was by the constraints of the usual mind-set about Palestinian-Israeli issues, did not completely overcome a frame of reference in which Palestinians had always played no part.

If Carter himself was unusual for the attention he paid to the Palestinian issue, the foreign-policy team he assembled was itself unique in its innovative approach to the Arab-Israeli conflict and its desire to move beyond the strictures that had always bound Middle East policymaking. Carter's collegial approach to the decision process gave these policymakers a degree of input that was highly unusual. Although he kept tight hold on the reins of policymaking, he enjoyed, and he learned from, frequent freewheeling discussions on policy issues with a wide circle of advisers. He held weekly breakfast meetings with Vice President Walter Mondale, Secretary of State Cyrus Vance, National Security Adviser Zbigniew Brzezinski, and, in later years, Secretary of Defense Harold Brown. There were also frequent ad hoc meetings to discuss particular issues and occasionally more formal National

Security Council meetings with a broader attendance—altogether constituting one of the most centralized but also wide-ranging decision-making processes of any presidential administration. On the Middle East, Carter's policy team, which has been called more cohesive and coherent than any other in recent history, included not only top-level policymakers but senior members of the bureaucracy who had worked on the region for years and career ambassadors in the key Middle East capitals, all of whom worked well together and were given real input.[17]

As national security adviser, Brzezinski had the most frequent contact with Carter on foreign-policy issues, meeting with him alone each morning for a national security briefing. Brzezinski's access gave him a unique opportunity to tutor Carter, the foreign-policy neophyte. The two men had known each other for several years, and Brzezinski had advised Carter on foreign policy during the campaign. Although Carter was so quick to grasp the intricacies of a situation and so much inclined to listen to a variety of viewpoints that no one person had a deep influence on his thinking, Brzezinski had a considerable impact on policy by virtue of his ability to direct Carter's attention to an issue or suggest a policy emphasis. Carter always maintained a personal distance from Brzezinski, but he apparently enjoyed holding broad conceptual and strategic discussions with this key aide early in his presidency.[18]

On Middle East issues, Secretary of State Vance took the lead to a greater extent than Brzezinski, whose primary expertise was in Soviet affairs, but Brzezinski came to office with a known viewpoint on many Middle East issues, including the Palestinians, that was more clearly formulated and more progressive than either Carter's or Vance's. An early admirer of the Irgun, the pre-state Zionist underground and terrorist organization run by Menachem Begin, Brzezinski had visited Israel in 1976 and specifically sought out Begin, then an opposition leader, for what Brzezinski regarded as a meaningful meeting with a fabled hero. Brzezinski was able, however, to put aside hero worship—his later prickly dealings with Begin when Begin became prime minister made doing so easier—and came to the unusual conclusion during his travels through Israel that acquiring land could not give Israel total security, especially if by so doing Israel increased Arab hostility. In office, Brzezinski unsuccessfully pushed the idea that security and sovereignty should be decoupled, attempting to ensure Israel's security not by extending sovereignty but by extending its security lines beyond formal sovereign borders.[19]

The interesting aspect of Brzezinski's idea was less its actual merits than the innovativeness it demonstrated and the willingness he showed to move beyond the limits of the conventional wisdom on the sacrosanct issue of Israel's security. Brzezinski was taken with the similarity between the Palestinian-Israeli situation and the French-Algerian situation. He had read extensively on the independence struggle in Algeria, in policy meetings frequently citing British historian Alistair Horne's 1977 book *A Savage War of Peace* as an object lesson for Middle East policymakers. He saw the PLO and Algeria's FLN as similar organizations.[20]

Brzezinski had also left a paper trail that clearly indicates his innovative views on the Palestinian issue. In 1975, he coauthored an article in *Foreign Policy* concluding that the central problem in the conflict, the Palestinian issue, could no longer reasonably be avoided and advocating establishment of an independent Palestinian state in the West Bank and Gaza. Assuming that such a state would almost certainly be PLO-dominated, the authors predicted that it would be so "inextricably bound" to Israel geographically and economically that it would have to cooperate and live peacefully.[21]

Brzezinski had also been among the drafters of a report advocating that any administration elected in 1976 should pursue a comprehensive approach to achieving a Middle East peace. Published by the Brookings Institution in Washington in December 1975 and authored by a study group made up of several foreign-policy and Middle East experts who had met over the previous year, the report urged that the negotiating process move beyond the step-by-step approach that had so far been the norm to a comprehensive approach that would attempt to resolve all issues at a multilateral peace conference. Among the elements the report considered essential to a stable peace were Israeli withdrawal in agreed stages to the borders existing before the June 1967 war, with no more than minor modifications, and Palestinian self-determination in the form either of an independent Palestinian state or of an entity federated with Jordan, provided the Palestinians accepted the sovereignty and integrity of Israel.[22]

William Quandt, a University of Pennsylvania professor and Middle East expert who had been among the authors of the report and was appointed by Brzezinski to direct Middle East affairs on the National Security Council staff, believes it would be an exaggeration to say that the Brookings report served as a blueprint for early Carter-administration policies. But the report certainly played some part in shaping administration thinking. The appointment of two of its authors, Brzezinski and Quandt, to the National Security Council staff was a clear indication at least that Carter was open to the policies it espoused. The report also found a receptive audience within the government among those involved in the peace process. Saunders, who had been deputy assistant secretary of state for Near Eastern affairs in the Ford administration and stayed on in the Carter administration, eventually becoming assistant secretary, has described the Brookings report as stating openly what those in government could not say about the need for a comprehensive solution that would involve the Palestinians.[23]

The Carter team quickly aroused the concern of Israeli supporters in the United States. Even before the inauguration, Brzezinski, who had himself come under attack as an anti-Semite for his earlier writings and his association with the Brookings report, began to receive complaints from pro-Israeli lobbyists and congressmen about his appointment of Quandt. Florida Senator Richard Stone, one of Israel's most vocal supporters in the Senate, came to Brzezinski the day after the inauguration with a list, topped by Quandt's name, of allegedly anti-Israeli personnel whom he wanted dismissed. Brzezinski rejected the complaints, but they persisted throughout Quandt's two years on the National Security Council staff.[24]

Vance has been characterized as a legalist, less theoretical and innovative than Brzezinski, but also as an idealist who shared Carter's interest in human rights and was highly respected for his own honesty and integrity. According to those who worked with him, he was extremely fair-minded, and he more than anyone else who dealt with both Arabs and Israelis during the Carter years was able to retain the confidence of both sides. Vance had a clear foreign-policy viewpoint and knew the Middle East well from the beginning. According to Saunders, when Vance was preparing for his first trip to the Middle East only weeks after he took office, he needed none of the in-depth tutorials usually given to officials in a new administration. Operating from the perspective of a regionalist who believed that U.S. policy in the 1960s and 1970s had been too much oriented toward the Cold War at the expense of Third World problems and having had extensive experience as a negotiator and mediator working on the Cyprus conflict and the Vietnam peace talks, he was convinced that even the most intractable problems had to be dealt with in some fashion.[25]

Accordingly, he believed that a serious effort should be made to resolve the Palestinian issue. Like others on the Carter team, Vance had no qualms about dealing with the PLO, recognizing it as a representative organization that would have to be accepted if the Palestinian issue was to be tackled. He chafed under the pledge Kissinger had made to Israel in 1975 not to negotiate with the PLO until it accepted UN Resolution 242—a commitment he felt restricted U.S. flexibility at a time when the Palestinian question had become pivotal. Because he believed that the Palestinians had been "ejected from their homes" in 1948, as he put it in his memoirs, he agreed with Carter that the Palestinian issue was the central human-rights issue of the

Middle East and believed that peace could be achieved only if the Palestinians gained some form of self-determination.

Carter's White House team was not universally with him on his Middle East and Palestinian policy. Vice President Mondale and his long-time aide David Aaron, who became Brzezinski's deputy on the National Security Council staff, had long been vocal friends of Israel and generally opposed efforts to exert pressure on the Israelis. During the first year or more, when there was no direct political risk, Mondale was supportive of Carter's initiatives, even to the point of being willing to use aid to Israel as a lever against Prime Minister Begin's hard-line stance. By the middle of 1978, however, with congressional elections nearing and the presidential campaign soon to begin, Mondale began to advocate what Brzezinski has called a passive posture "tilted in favor of the Israelis." Apparently believing that Carter's confrontational relationship with Begin would seriously damage Carter's and the Democratic Party's political prospects, Mondale had sharp disagreements with Vance, Brzezinski, and Quandt over policies and language he deemed too critical of Israel. Brzezinski has observed that whereas Carter almost never thought of the impact of foreign policy on domestic politics, Mondale rarely considered foreign policy in any other terms.[26]

Other White House officials, particularly domestic adviser Stuart Eizenstat, were also highly politically attuned and used their positions to press for policies that were friendlier to Israel and therefore safer politically. Eizenstat frequently acted as a conduit for passing policy suggestions and requests for increased aid from the Israeli embassy and from AIPAC to the White House. In 1978, for example, at AIPAC's suggestion, Eizenstat proposed that the United States supply Israel with technical data on the F-18 aircraft in order to "help break the ice" with Israel. The information was released to the Israelis.[27]

There were other domestic advisers of a pro-Israeli bent in Carter's White House. These included White House counsel Robert Lipshutz; Edward Sanders, a pro-Israeli activist appointed in mid-1978 as an adviser on Middle East affairs; and Alfred Moses, a Washington attorney who succeeded Sanders in 1980. These advisers lobbied throughout Carter's term for increased aid to Israel, against pressure on Israel and any position that would promote Palestinian interests, and in general for a lower diplomatic profile for Carter and the United States in the negotiating process. After the Camp David agreement and the Egyptian-Israeli peace treaty, when Carter pulled back from activism in Middle East affairs, he appointed two special Middle East envoys, Democratic Party leader Robert Strauss and later negotiator Sol Linowitz, who were both supporters of Israel. Strauss in particular, who as a party politician performed his duties with a close eye to their impact on domestic politics and Carter's reelection chances, made it clear to Carter that any pressure exerted on Israel would be damaging politically.[28]

Quandt observed in *Camp David*, his thoughtful study of the political and diplomatic process involved in negotiating the Camp David accords, that there are always serious political limits on any president's power to make Middle East policy, and all presidents must function within boundaries set by the electoral cycle.[29] No presidential experience with the Middle East better illustrates this theory than Carter's. Carter surprised everyone with his willingness to flout the conventions on the Palestinian issue. He said things about Palestinians, about the relevance of their history and the legitimacy of their grievances, that no policymaker had said publicly before. But Carter met a stone wall—a wall erected by Israeli supporters in the United States and by Israel itself under the leadership of Begin, who took office only months after Carter himself did. Begin was to this point the Israeli prime minister most determined not simply to ignore the Palestinians but actively to thwart Palestinian aspirations and pursue the extension of Israeli sovereignty over the remaining parts of Palestine in the West Bank and Gaza. The sound defeat of all Carter's efforts for the Palestinians, from the vision of a homeland to the plans for autonomy framed by the Camp David accords, provides striking evidence of the extent to which conventional wisdom can dictate policy.

Guardians of the frame of reference began to go after Carter almost immediately. In the belief that Carter enjoyed maximum leverage during his first year and that rapid movement was vital, the new administration made the Middle East a priority. The new national security team had met informally before the inauguration and decided then to send Vance to the area for preliminary talks with Arab and Israeli leaders in February. The need to address the Palestinian issue was at the top of Vance's agenda in each of the countries he visited. He took the position that the Palestinian problem was the essence of the Arab-Israeli conflict and that, without its resolution, there could be no peace and ultimately no security for Israel.[30]

This approach unnerved Israel and its U.S. supporters. Prime Minister Yitzhak Rabin immediately bristled at the notion of taking the Palestinian issue into account. He made it clear to Vance that Israel would never accept an independent Palestinian state in the West Bank and Gaza because, he believed, the real Arab aim continued to be the destruction of Israel. The following month, during a visit by Rabin to the United States, which went badly and which Carter termed "a particularly unpleasant surprise," Rabin made it clear that Israel would not attend a reconvened Geneva conference if the PLO or other representative of the Palestinians was there, and he was unreceptive to Carter's desire to explore new ideas and new approaches to the peace-making process.[31]

Inside the United States, Israel's supporters immediately began to put intensive pressure on Carter. In the zero-sum context in which Palestinian-Israeli issues were usually viewed, any attempt to recognize the existence of a separate Palestinian people, much less take them into account in the negotiating process, appeared directly hostile to Israel. As a result, pressure from the pro-Israel lobby went beyond simply supporting Israel and took on an anti-Palestinian tone. AIPAC and other pro-Israeli groups and individuals sent Carter and White House aides a steady stream of anti-Palestinian letters and literature. After Carter's March 1977 statement calling for a Palestinian homeland, AIPAC mobilized a heavy lobbying effort with Congress and the White House opposing any such thought. Congressional pressure against Carter's gestures toward the Palestinians was intense.[32]

It did not ease Carter's relationship with Israel or the U.S. Jewish community that, quite by happenstance, he got along well with most of the Arab leaders he dealt with but took an instant dislike to Rabin and, following his election in May 1977, to Begin. Carter's liking for Egyptian President Anwar Sadat was immediate and intense. Carter himself said that on the day he first met Sadat in April 1977 "a shining light burst on the Middle East scene for me." According to Carter's aides, the two men formed a deep rapport, and Carter identified closely with Sadat, regarding him as "family" in the southern sense. The president also got along well with and respected Jordan's King Hussein and Syria's President Hafiz al-Asad, both of whom he met within the first few months of his presidency. By contrast, his first meetings with the Israeli leadership went badly. Carter and Rabin rubbed each other the wrong way personally and substantively, and although Carter's first meeting with Begin in July 1977 was congenial, the two were soon at loggerheads over U.S. interest in the Palestinians and Begin's large-scale construction of Israeli settlements in the West Bank.[33]

Carter's personal reactions to the two Israelis were undoubtedly influenced by the contrast between their opposition to his search for a new approach to the peace process and the Arabs' support. Carter and his team found the Arabs to be ready at this point to discuss conciliatory moves, which put Carter in direct confrontation with Israel's leaders. Vance recalls in his memoirs that in the early days the administration put the burden for stalling movement in the peace process on Israel. "The hope for a just and durable peace," he wrote, "ultimately rested on the capacity of the Israeli political leadership to resolve its internal divisions and atavistic fears and mistrust of the Arabs." [34] This approach, with its demand for a fundamental change of outlook by Israel, was so far outside the prevailing frame of reference that conflict on a deeply personal level between Israeli and U.S. leaders was inevitable.

Begin's determination to build Jewish settlements in the occupied West Bank and Gaza became a particular point of contention between the Carter administration and Israel. Conflict began only days after Begin's return home from his first trip to Washington, when the Israeli government gave formal approval to three existing West Bank settlements. Carter and his foreign-policy team regarded the construction of settlements as a kind of "creeping annexation," in the words of Vance, and Carter made clear to Begin during his initial visit the U.S. belief that settlements violated international law. Continued settlement activity, he told Begin, sent the message that Israel intended a permanent military occupation and virtually foreclosed the possibility even of convening a peace conference. [35] The United States publicly reacted to Begin's move by formally terming the settlements illegal under international law, which was to be the consistent U.S. position throughout Carter's administration.

In retrospect, it was clear quite early on that the interpretation Begin and his Likud Party put on UN Resolution 242 would also put Israel and the Carter administration at odds, although Begin dodged and weaved around the issue enough that it was some time before Carter was clear on the Israeli leader's position and clear that he had no intention of moderating it. From 1967, when Resolution 242 was adopted, the United States and the international community had interpreted its withdrawal clause, calling for "withdrawal of Israeli armed forces from territories occupied in the recent conflict," to mean virtually complete withdrawal from all fronts on which Israel had captured territory—the West Bank and Gaza, as well as the Sinai Peninsula and the Golan Heights. Begin and the Likud, however, interpreted the resolution as not applicable to all fronts, and as became clear later, they specifically excluded the West Bank and Gaza. During his initial meeting with Carter, even though he said he would accept no "foreign sovereignty" over the West Bank, Begin misled Carter by expressing his acceptance of 242. The U.S. team, hearing what it wanted to hear from Begin and unaccustomed to men of his strong ideological convictions, concluded that it had secured the Israeli's agreement to the principle of withdrawal on all fronts and glossed over his remark about no foreign sovereignty, putting it down to maximalist rhetoric without realizing how serious he was.[36]

This would not be the last time U.S. policymakers were misled by their hopes and expectations into underestimating the deep resolve and ideological commitment of Israel's Likud leaders. In the concurrent ascendancy of Carter in the United States and Begin in Israel, the first U.S. president to recognize the Palestinian stake in the conflict over Palestine confronted the first Israeli prime minister, although not the last, absolutely determined never to cede an inch of territory in what remained of old Palestine or make concessions to the Palestinians in any way. Such Israeli determination did not fit with U.S. assumptions about Israel. Most U.S. policymakers could not conceive that Israel's hard-line right wing had different goals in the Middle East than the United States did and that it saw peace differently. It was some time—well into and past the Camp David process—before Carter absorbed the fact that Begin's hard stand was not negotiable, that he never had any intention of accommodating the United States by willingly ceasing construction of Israeli settlements, relinquishing territory in the West Bank or Gaza, or recognizing the existence of a Palestinian people or the legitimacy of their claims. Begin, however, had a clear view from the beginning of what he could get away with. The story is told that after Carter emphasized the U.S. objection to Israeli settlement activity during Begin's first visit, Israeli embassy officials asked Begin what he intended to do. He would build the settlements anyway, he responded, predicting that the Americans would be irked for six months and then would revert to normal.[37]

Begin's electoral victory, against all predictions, in May 1977 had sent shock waves through the United States. He was completely unlike the usual images of Israel and Israelis. Editorial writers called him an extremist; the *New York Times* editorialized that Israeli politics were dangerously "out of sync." U.S. Jews were uneasy about Begin's past as leader of the pre-state Irgun and uncomfortable with his vision of a "Greater Israel," which saw the West Bank as irrevocably a Jewish land divinely bestowed. Charges that Israel was colonialist for ruling over another people in the occupied territories, as well as comparisons of Israel to South Africa, began to be heard.[38] Many in the U.S. Jewish community and many political leaders who had always been strong supporters of Israel were initially disconcerted by Begin's hard line and urged Carter to stand firm in his intention to pursue a comprehensive peace settlement. Vice President Mondale, former Supreme Court Justice and UN Ambassador Arthur Goldberg, Senator Hubert

Humphrey, and other Democratic congressional leaders supported Carter at this point and urged him to confront Begin aggressively.[39]

But if U.S. Jews were chagrined at first by Begin and his hard-line stance, they quickly adapted, and the little support Carter initially enjoyed dissipated, proving no match for the intensive lobbying campaign launched against him. The story of the U.S. Jewish community's rallying around Begin is, in fact, the story of the frame of reference, of the enduring nature of the mind-set that essentially approved of almost any Israeli policy and Israeli leader because the United States could not *not* support Israel. And because support for Israel had always been a zero-sum equation in regard to the Palestinian issue, there was ultimately no way to accommodate both Begin and the Palestinians in the frame of reference.

Within a brief time, U.S. public opinion was able to embrace Begin. The support of Reform Jewish leader Rabbi Alexander Schindler, a relative "dove" on Israel's occupation of the West Bank and Gaza then serving as chairman of the Conference of Presidents of Major American Jewish Organizations, was decisive. Schindler was initially concerned about Begin's rightist politics and says he hoped at the time that being in office would move Begin away from the extreme end of the political spectrum. As the leader of the U.S. Jewish community, Schindler saw his alternatives as either openly supporting Begin despite his misgivings or criticizing him and thereby encouraging the "pro-Arab Carterites" to "abandon" Israel. Ultimately, Schindler swallowed his objections to Begin's hawkish position and openly endorsed him. Likud party leaders considered Schindler's support a "big break" in maintaining U.S. support.[40]

With Schindler's endorsement, the battle was engaged between Carter and his foreign-policy team on one side, perceived to be a hotbed of pro-Arab sympathy, and, on the other side, those who saw virtually any criticism of any aspect of Israel as a danger to its existence. The battle was often intense. In one week in June 1977, just after Begin's election, the White House received a thousand letters concerning the Middle East, 90 percent of which were critical of Carter's policy.[41] Brzezinski came under particular attack for allegedly being anti-Israeli.[42]

Many Jewish community leaders remained uneasy about Begin's "Greater Israel" policies, including particularly his settlements policy, but the general decision to circle the wagons around the Israeli leader had the effect of silencing criticism. One survey of U.S. Jewish leaders in early 1978 revealed that by three to one they wanted Israel to be more moderate, but the results were never published because they were thought to be too embarrassing for Begin. The 1977 annual report of Schindler's Conference of Presidents stated clearly its belief that public dissent gave aid and comfort to the enemy and weakened Jewish unity, which was essential for Israeli security.[43]

Two forces were working against each other at this point. On the one hand, Carter's belief that the Palestinian problem had to be dealt with as part of the peace process, as well as his interest in human rights, called increased attention both to the Palestinians themselves and to Israel's policy toward the West Bank and Gaza and its treatment of Palestinians in these territories. On the other hand, Israel's U.S. supporters, determined to maintain solidarity with Israel and seeing increased attention to the Palestinians as a direct threat to Israel's interests as enunciated by Begin, made a concerted effort to undermine the Palestinian role in the peace process and to deflect criticism of Israel's occupation practices. The conscious decision to rally around Begin and mute criticism of his policies effectively tightened the parameters around acceptable public discussion. The frame of reference for public discourse remained Israel-centered, and a kind of pall was cast on serious discourse about the Palestinian-Israeli conflict.

Some topics were placed off limits altogether, much as the Palestinian situation had always been. One example of a subject not discussed was Begin's past. Immediately after his election, CBS News referred to Begin as an ex-terrorist because of his leadership of the Irgun, the organization responsible for the 1946 bombing of the King David Hotel, the 1948 massacre at the Palestinian village of Deir Yassin, and other bombings of civilian targets in the years before Israel's establishment. In the early years neither Begin himself nor Israel's U.S. friends had hesitated to use the term, but Begin objected to it from CBS News and demanded an apology, which was immediately issued.[44] From that time forward, it became generally unacceptable to use the word with respect to either Begin or his successor Yitzhak Shamir, whose pre-state underground organization, the Stern Gang, had also committed acts of terrorism.

Another issue raised and quickly quieted was Israel's human-rights record in the occupied territories. After the *London Times* issued a report in 1977, not repeated in the United States, citing what it called a "widespread and systematic" pattern of torture of Palestinian prisoners in the occupied territories by Israeli police and military, the U.S. State Department touched on the issue in its 1978 annual report on human rights around the world. Noting cautiously that it saw no evidence of a systematic policy of torture, the State Department concluded that there had been documented reports of the use of "extreme physical and psychological pressures" during interrogation. The following year, State noted, again circumspectly, that reports of torture and brutality by Israelis were so numerous that they could not be ignored. Information obtained and publicized by the *Washington Post* in early 1979 indicated that the U.S. consulate general in Jerusalem believed the evidence of physical mistreatment of prisoners was strong enough to indicate that a systematic pattern of torture existed.[45]

Israel denied any use of torture and denounced the *Post* for "dishonest, libelous and utterly false" reporting. The outcry within the United States was intense. Jewish organizations dismissed the charges of torture and accused the *Post* of joining a left-wing extremist campaign against Israel. Public commentary shifted from the accuracy of the charges to the propriety of raising them. The *New York Times* editorialized that the State Department had in its 1979 report engaged in "clumsy public relations" by "attracting unfair attention to some alleged lapses." The *Times* wondered, "Why rile the Israelis again?"[46] This question could have been asked only in a context where the focus was on the perspective of one side. Although evidence of Israeli use of torture against Palestinian prisoners continued to be reported for years by human-rights groups such as Amnesty International and Middle East Watch, the reports were generally ignored until an Israeli commission, the Landau Commission, found in November 1987 that Israel's internal security service, Shin Bet, had been conducting systematic torture to gain confessions from Palestinian prisoners and had, as a matter of policy, been lying in court about how the confessions were obtained.[47]

By the late 1970s, the U.S. public had adjusted—adjusted to Israel under a hard-line leader, ignored what was most difficult to swallow such as the evidence of torture, and continued to support Israel because it had always done so before. Public opinion polls showed little decrease in 1977 or 1978 from the consistent sympathy levels of 45 to 50 percent that they had shown for Israel throughout most of the previous decade. There was some increased sympathy for the Arabs, thanks primarily to the increased popularity of Egyptian President Sadat and perhaps in small measure to Carter's attention to the Palestinians, but sympathy levels for Israel remained higher than those for the Arabs by four to one.[48]

Support for Israel in Congress also did not slacken; nor did interest in the Palestinians pick up. The story is told by two Israeli journalists that when Moshe Arens, then chairman of the Knesset Foreign Affairs Committee, came to Washington in late 1977, the pro-Israeli staffers on the Senate Foreign Relations Committee were deeply worried that because he was a rightist he would "blow it" when he met with senators on the committee, most of whom, although pro-Israeli, were accustomed to Labor's more flexible position. Arens began with an uncompromising defense of why Israel had to retain control over the occupied territories and within minutes, to the pleasant surprise of anxious staffers, had won over the senators. At the end of the presentation, committee Chairman John Sparkman said to Arens, who was raised in the United States and speaks unaccented English, "Son, you're wonderful! You speak American!" The inescapable conclusion is that the senators cared more about Arens's style than about the substance of his remarks.[49] The new reality of Israel's hard-line policy, which was directly opposed to the notion of the centrality of the Palestinian issue and came just when the importance of the Palestinians was beginning to be recognized, clearly did not significantly alter the basic outlines of the frame of reference.

During the first year of the Carter administration Israel introduced and began seriously to press the notion that it was a strategic asset to the United States and a vital ally on whom Washington had to rely in the Cold War struggle with the Soviet Union. Although not a wholly new concept, the notion as now promoted was designed specifically to strengthen U.S. sympathy for and attachment to Israel. Begin raised the issue of Israel's strategic importance during his first meeting with Carter in July 1977. When Begin presented Carter with a lengthy document enumerating the strategic benefits of alliance with Israel—from masses of captured Soviet equipment turned over to the United States for analysis, to Israel's key geographic location, to its position as a check on a flare-up of Arab radicalism—he was making the point that aid to Israel was not charity but a sound investment that ultimately returned strategic value to the United States. Begin, a proud and suspicious man, fundamentally distrusted the moral commitment of the United States to Israel. Fearing that changing views might eventually cause the United States to abandon Israel as it had Taiwan, he believed that by demonstrating its strategic indispensability Israel would not have to rely on U.S. good will but would put the United States in Israel's debt.[50]

Carter did not pay more than lip service to the notion of strategic cooperation with Israel, but Israel and its supporters latched onto and continually promoted the idea.[51] It slowly became part of the body of U.S. assumptions about Israel—a basic tenet of the U.S. mind-set and one more factor in tilting the frame of reference toward the Israeli perspective. In a framework in which Israel was vital to U.S. strategic interests, any moral demands being newly placed on the conscience of Americans by the increasing awareness of the Palestinians' situation and of Israel's occupation practices had to take second place. In purely pragmatic terms, the Palestinians could not compete for attention with an Israel that helped protect U.S. national security.

In August 1977, just before Secretary of State Vance was to leave on another trip through the Middle East to attempt to work out a formula for Palestinian participation in the peace process, Carter received a private message from Arafat indicating that the PLO was prepared to live in peace with Israel and would make public and private commitments to that effect if the United States would commit itself to establishment of an independent Palestinian state, which could be linked to Jordan. Carter responded to Arafat's overture by promising that his administration would open a dialogue with the PLO if it would meet the minimum requirements of the Kissinger Sinai II pledge—acceptance of UN Resolution 242 and recognition of Israel's right to exist.[52] This overture began a two-month effort, unsuccessful in the end, to devise some formula to facilitate U.S.-PLO negotiations.

The PLO had been moving toward a more moderate stance over the previous few months. In March 1977, presumably in response to Carter's "homeland" statement, the PLO's legislative arm, the Palestine National Council (PNC), had adopted a resolution pledging to accept independence in a territory limited to the West Bank and Gaza. A new PLO Executive Committee excluding representatives of the "rejection front," which rejected coexistence with Israel, was also elected at this PNC session.[53] The PNC resolution moved well beyond previous positions and represented a victory for elements within the PLO— Arafat, his Fatah organization, and the nationalist mainstream in the West Bank and Gaza—who advocated pursuing Palestinian goals by political means rather than through military action. According to some analysts, the new stance indicated that for these mainstream elements the longstanding goal of establishing a democratic, secular state in all of Palestine had begun to be viewed as a distant and probably unrealizable goal.[54]

The Sinai II commitment would prove to be a major impediment to progress on Arafat's initiative. Although there is some question whether Carter was bound by the pledge,[55] he and Vance took it as a binding commitment, in part for domestic political reasons, in part in the hope of pressuring the PLO into accepting Resolution 242 in modified form.[56] Vance, in fact, interpreted the commitment so strictly that he would not permit any direct U.S. contacts with the PLO at all, even though the addendum to Sinai II had deliberately been written so as not to prohibit informal, exploratory exchanges, only formal negotiations.[57] Whatever the Carter administration's legal obligations, in the end U.S. adherence to the letter of the commitment curtailed what might have been fruitful contacts with the PLO. One scholar has noted that Arafat and other PLO leaders came close to reciting the precise words that the United States demanded, saying them by euphemism, by indirection, and explicitly through intermediaries. But at the time they were politically unable to pronounce the exact formula demanded by the United States explicitly and publicly without obtaining reciprocal Israeli concessions. The PLO regarded recognition of Israel's "right" to exist— and thus of Israel's right to sovereignty in Palestine—as its last bargaining card, which the Palestinians could not relinquish without receiving recognition of their own right to self-determination and independent statehood in Palestine. From the Palestinian perspective, what the United States was offering—a promise to open a formal U.S.-PLO dialogue, but no promise of Israeli-PLO dialogue and no commitment to Israeli concessions—was inadequate in return for such a major Palestinian concession.[58]

During his Middle East trip, at stops in Egypt, Syria, Jordan, and Saudi Arabia, Vance carried on a running negotiation with the PLO, conducted indirectly through the various Arab leaders, over the kind of statement the Palestinians would be willing to make with regard to Resolution 242. At one point, Vance proposed, through Saudi King Khalid, that the PLO issue a statement accepting Resolution 242 "with the reservation that it considers that the resolution does not make adequate reference to the question of the Palestinians since it fails to make any reference to a homeland for the Palestinian people." An additional sentence—"It is recognized that the language of Resolution 242 relates to the right of all states in the Middle East to live in peace"—would satisfy the U.S. demand for PLO recognition of Israel's right to exist. Asked by King Khalid if the United States would assure that the Palestinians would obtain a homeland in the West Bank if the PLO accepted this language, Vance replied that while this was the U.S. goal, it could not be guaranteed.[59]

Because the PLO could not talk directly with the United States, it received mixed signals from the various Arab intermediaries. The Egyptians first conveyed the impression that the United States had promised to recognize the PLO and invite it to a Geneva peace conference in return for accepting the statement, but the Saudis, conveying accurately the more limited intentions, reported that Washington would agree only to open a dialogue with the PLO, not necessarily invite it to a peace conference, in exchange for PLO acceptance of Resolution 242. The Saudis thus gave the impression that the United States had hardened its position.

The Arab leaders also conveyed to Arafat a tentative plan suggested by Vance to establish a trusteeship, administered jointly by Israel and Jordan, for the West Bank and Gaza—the purpose being, in Vance's words, to allow the Palestinians to "demonstrate whether they were prepared to govern themselves and live peacefully with Israel." Strenuously objecting to the paternalistic aspect of this proposal and angered that all they could expect in return for their concession was a dialogue with the United States, not necessarily inclusion in the peace process, the PLO Executive Committee voted to reject Vance's proposed language.[60]

The concept embodied in Vance's trusteeship proposal of a transitional arrangement for the West Bank and Gaza was later incorporated into the Camp David accords and thereafter became part of the conventional wisdom on how to deal with these territories and with the Palestinian problem as a whole.[61] Future administrations always included some sort of transitional arrangement in their peace proposals. Although Vance's principal intent was to devise a compromise formula that might be acceptable to both Israelis and Palestinians, the notion of trusteeship or some other transitional arrangement was in fact a holdover from the old days, incorporating the nineteenth-century assumption that Arabs were not ready for self-government, as well as the modern, post-1948 assumption that any independent Palestinian state would, almost by definition, be radical. The idea was that because Israel feared Palestinian radicalism—a fear both Carter and Vance said they shared with regard to permitting establishment of an independent Palestinian state—the Palestinians had to pass through a transitional phase in which they would prove themselves before any thought could be given to self-determination or independence. Despite the genuinely evenhanded approach that Vance and the Carter team were taking in this period, there was an element of the Israel-centric to the proposal, for similar proof of its desire to live in peace with Palestinians was not demanded of Israel.

Shortly after the August contacts on Resolution 242 floundered, Arafat again approached the United States through an intermediary, indicating that the PLO would accept the resolution if the United States made certain private commitments about the PLO's role in future negotiations. The United States sent educator Landrum Bolling to meet with Arafat and convey the message that if the PLO accepted Resolution 242 with a statement of reservation about its failure to address the Palestinian question, the United States would talk to the PLO but could not make additional promises.[62]

At this point, the political problems of both Carter and Arafat collided with each other. Carter was under intense domestic pressure for even attempting to deal with the Palestinian issue, and although he probably need not in fact have been so rigid in requiring the PLO's exact compliance with the Sinai II pledge, he clearly felt at a minimum that the political pressures on him were such that he could not flout it. Arafat was under heavy pressure as well, both from within the PLO and from some Arab states. He was as rigid in his own way as Carter was; the language proposed by the United States on accepting "the rights of all states in the Middle East to live in peace," for instance, skirted the issue of directly recognizing Israel's "right" to exist and might therefore have been acceptable to the Palestinians. But many PLO members were still fearful of giving up the Palestinians' ultimate concession without assurance of statehood. In addition, some Arab states, particularly Syria, saw their ability to speak for the Palestinians as a point of leverage and were unwilling to have the United States deal with the PLO. As a result, under Arab pressure to reject the compromise conveyed by Bolling, the PLO Central Committee met in September and again rebuffed the United States.[63]

Carter and others in the administration, particularly Brzezinski, grew increasingly impatient with the PLO following this unsuccessful round.[64] The administration continued efforts in the fall of 1977, through a series of intricate and complex negotiations with both Arabs and Israelis, to organize a comprehensive peace conference and resolve the question of Palestinian representation at Geneva without attempting to obtain PLO acceptance of Resolution 242. Vance pursued a proposal for a unified Arab delegation as a way to include the Palestinians. But obstacles arose at every turn from both Israel and the Arab states.[65] Finally, Egyptian President Sadat's trip to Jerusalem in November, undertaken without prior consultation with the United States, took control of events out of Carter's hands for the time being and changed the direction of the peace process. From this point on, as negotiations between Egypt and Israel continued into 1978, leading to the Camp David accords in September and the Egyptian-Israeli peace treaty in March 1979, Carter always considered efforts to resolve the Palestinian problem as subordinate to bilateral Egyptian-Israeli issues.

When the PLO joined with other Arabs in denouncing Sadat's trip to Jerusalem and, along with the Arab states, rejected an invitation by Sadat to attend a preliminary peace conference in Cairo, Carter lashed out, angrily charging at a press conference that the PLO had been "completely negative" and "had not been cooperative at all" despite his and Sadat's efforts to include the organization in the negotiating process. During an interview with *Paris Match* shortly afterward, Brzezinski, contending that the United States had done everything it could to draw the PLO into the peace process, made his well known "bye-bye PLO" statement.[66] The disagreement between the United States and the PLO fundamentally came down to a difference over self-determination for the Palestinians. As noted, Carter, like all presidents and policymakers before him, had grown up politically with the notion that a Palestinian state would be radical and unstable, and, despite his understanding of the Palestinians, his frame of reference did not extend to placing the solution to the problem in a national context. For the Palestinians, however, there could be no other solution. Having altered the original maximum goal of pushing Israel out of Palestine and establishing a "democratic, secular" state in which Jews and Palestinians would live together and having repeatedly communicated to the United States the PLO's readiness to live peacefully alongside an Israeli state, the PLO felt it could not now explicitly concede Israel's moral legitimacy without a U.S. guarantee of self-determination in the West Bank and Gaza. Realistically, no matter what concessions the PLO made, there was no hope of obtaining independence without such a U.S. guarantee. No government in Israel, Labor or Likud, would agree to it. Carter did not truly understand this Palestinian thinking.

He also did not fully understand inter-Arab political rivalries, particularly that for their own reasons Egypt, Syria, and Jordan all found it to be against their interests to permit the PLO a prominent role in peace negotiations and that each one therefore was attempting to undercut the Palestinian push for self-determination and U.S. sponsorship in the peace process. Sadat jealously guarded Egypt's preeminent place in the Arab world and did not want competition from the PLO; Syria's Asad viewed his ability to speak for the Palestinians as one of his few points of leverage, which he did not want to forfeit to the U.S.; Jordan's King Hussein, still feeling that his throne was threatened by the PLO and still desirous of reasserting Jordanian control over the West Bank, was completely opposed to Palestinian independence.

Carter mistook this inter-Arab political maneuvering for agreement with his own reasoning on the undesirability of a Palestinian state. He writes in his memoirs that, with the sole exception of Saudi Arabia— the only Arab state that in private conversations with him had supported Palestinian independence—all Arabs "could see that an independent nation in the heart of the Middle East might be a serious point of friction and a focus for radicalizing influence."[67] By thus projecting his own views onto the Arab states, Carter found an easy way out of the political difficulties he would have faced at home and with Israel had he supported self-determination for the Palestinians.

Carter's opposition to real self-determination led to the enunciation of an equivocal formulation that was to become a staple of administration policy on the issue. At a meeting with Sadat at Aswan, Egypt, in January 1978, using wording fashioned by his foreign-policy advisers, Carter spelled out his views on the requirements for a peace settlement. Among other things, he said, a solution must "enable the Palestinians to participate in the determination of their own future." [68] The statement, which became known as the Aswan formula and was later incorporated into the Camp David accords, was one of those diplomatic ambiguities that are so highly interpretable that they satisfy virtually everyone—except in this instance the Palestinians themselves. The Carter team was attempting to come as near to advocating Palestinian self-determination as was possible without using the term. The Egyptians reacted with pleasure at having obtained what one journalist called the concept of self-determination without the actual term; Begin, seeing exactly the reverse, was pleased to note that Carter had avoided granting the Palestinians self-determination. Only the Palestinians—on whom the anomaly of being accorded the right to "participate in" but not to "make" the determination of their own future was not lost—were displeased. [69]

Throughout this period, Carter was under intense domestic political pressure. He was deeply frustrated, from the earliest months of his presidency, by the heavy pressures exerted against him whenever he even referred to Palestinian rights; as Quandt has observed, Carter found that the "constraints of the American political system came into play whenever he tried to deal with the Palestinian question." As early as the fall of 1977, Quandt says, Carter tired of "the role of public advocate of controversial ideas" and began simply to say less in public, leaving the diplomatic moves to the State Department. [70]

This chapter in Carter's Middle East policymaking, showing the tension between his own inclinations and the demands of the guardians of the conventional wisdom, is one of the most intriguing in Carter-era diplomacy. It demonstrates how powerful the conventional wisdom on Israel and the Palestinian-Israeli conflict was as a determiner of policy, for it ultimately caused Carter to drop his efforts on behalf of the Palestinians. Although he was angered and frustrated as much or more by Israel's refusal to deal with the Palestinian issue as by the Palestinians' failure to make the concessions he felt were necessary for a dialogue with the United States, it was simpler and more politically expedient in the end to vent his frustration on the Palestinians.

The irony is that Carter of all presidents wanted to move ahead with the Palestinians, and it might be speculated that had he better understood the Palestinian position and the root of Palestinian grievances, he would probably have been able to.[71] But his personal frame of reference, although remarkably open to the Palestinian perspective, remained limited. Because even he did not see the Palestinians as equal partners in any negotiation and did not focus on the need for some reciprocity if any peace process was to be successful, neither he nor virtually anyone else in the country recognized the futility of demanding concessions of the Palestinians that were not also demanded of Israel. As a result, the conventional wisdom throughout the country came increasingly to center on the PLO as unremittingly radical and inflexible and as bent blindly on Israel's destruction.

The contrast with the latest hero, Sadat, and his willingness to recognize and make peace with Israel made the Palestinians appear all the more radical and unbending, although in fact Egypt's conflict with Israel involved a different set of issues altogether. Sadat was as uncompromising on Egypt's basic issues as the Palestinians were on theirs, but because recognition of Israel's right to exist was not a fundamental issue for Egypt as it was for the Palestinians—because it was not an issue that went to the core of Egypt's own existence—this was a relatively easy concession for Sadat. Few in the United States focused on this distinction, and so, because Sadat had recognized Israel, the Palestinians' refusal to do the same came across as stubborn intransigence. Furthermore, because the issues were different and precisely because they did not involve existential questions, Egypt could reasonably demand true reciprocity from Israel and ultimately obtained it, which, in the circumstances, was beyond the realm of possibility for the Palestinians.

As 1978 proceeded, with round after round of U.S.-mediated Egyptian-Israeli talks, leading finally to the Camp David accords in September, prospects for a meaningful resolution of the Palestinian problem grew increasingly dim. During a meeting with Carter in Washington in December 1977, Begin had presented a plan for "home rule" for West Bank and Gaza Palestinians that was ultimately to become the basis for the autonomy proposed for the Palestinians in the Camp David accords. Carter and Vance recognized Begin's presentation of the plan, which did not provide for Israeli withdrawal or sovereignty for the Palestinians, for what it was—a tactic to avoid withdrawing and reaching an equitable solution to the Palestinian problem. But others in the administration, particularly Brzezinski, saw in the plan aspects of the transitional arrangement first proposed by Vance, and it was ultimately incorporated in the Camp David accords.[72]

Thus, by early 1978, the administration's original concept of working toward a comprehensive peace settlement that included resolution of the Palestinian problem had been markedly scaled back to achieving an agreement only between Egypt and Israel along with an as yet undefined transitional arrangement for the West Bank and Gaza. Talks with the PLO were no longer on the agenda, nor was the notion of having the Palestinians present at peace negotiations.[73] As Carter and his foreign-policy team worked on bringing Egypt and Israel together on bilateral issues, they attempted to ensure that any accord would be linked to future progress on an agreement regarding the Palestinians, but virtually all the original game plan had been given up.

The National Security Council Middle East director, Quandt, sent Brzezinski a memorandum in May 1978 noting that in response to Israel's demands the United States had already adjusted its position downward to such an extent that the only hope for obtaining any agreement on the West Bank and Gaza lay in the forlorn possibility that Begin would commit Israel at least conditionally to eventual withdrawal from the West Bank. Quandt bluntly detailed U.S. concessions:

—We have come out strongly against an independent Palestinian state and have relegated the PLO to obscurity. We no longer even speak of a Palestinian homeland.

—We have publicly stated that 242 does allow for border changes, and have dropped our emphasis on only "minor modifications" in deference to Begin's sensibilities.

—We have spoken of an Israeli military presence in the West Bank/Gaza for an interim period and beyond, which the Israelis have viewed as endorsement of a permanent military presence, to the acute embarrassment of the Egyptians, Jordanians, and Saudis.

—We have left the strong impression that Israel will remain in control of a unified city of Jerusalem; will have a veto over the return of refugees; and will be able to keep existing settlements in the West Bank.

—We have suggested to Israel a bilateral mutual security treaty and have forsworn the use of military and economic aid as a form of pressure.

—We have made it clear that Israeli withdrawal from the West Bank/Gaza would be conditional upon the achievement of full peace, security, and recognition.

What have we gotten in return from Begin? . . . The truth is that Begin has not moved an inch in his thinking on the West Bank/Gaza, in contrast to his rather forthcoming proposals on Sinai.[74]

Two events in early 1978 solidified public support for Israel and further thwarted Carter's efforts to press Israel for movement in the peace process. In February, the administration announced plans to sell Saudi Arabia sixty F-15 aircraft. The sale finally passed Congress in May, but the administration's fight with pro-Israeli forces was hard and politically costly. Vice President Mondale, whose reputation as a friend of Israel made him Carter's bellwether of U.S. Jewish sentiment, had been prepared before announcement of the proposed sale to support the notion of exerting pressure on Begin, believing that U.S. Jews did not support his no-withdrawal interpretation of Resolution 242 or his determination to build Israeli settlements in the occupied territories. The outcry in the Jewish community, however, against selling arms to Saudi Arabia, which was portrayed as directly threatening Israel's security, was so great that Mondale backed away from association with the idea of leaning on Israel.[75]

The second event that undermined Carter's efforts was a PLO terrorist attack against Israel in March that killed thirty-seven Israelis. A seaborne force launched from Lebanon seized an Israeli passenger bus on the coastal road. The attack was a serious setback for the Palestinian image in the United States. When in retaliation Israel launched a full-scale invasion of southern Lebanon designed to push PLO forces away from the border, Carter took a strong stance and supported a UN resolution calling for Israel's withdrawal and the establishment of a UN monitoring force. But the PLO attack, because it coincided with the debate over arms for Saudi Arabia, renewed sympathy for an imperiled Israel, again galvanized Israel's U.S. supporters against Carter's perceived pro-Arab tilt, and in general, as Vance noted to Carter at the time, refocused the attention of Israel's supporters from the peace process to concern for Israel's security.[76]

Carter had been worn down, reined in by the frame of reference, by the time of the Camp David summit so that, as Quandt has observed, the "temptation arose to aim for the attainable, not necessarily the preferred." Already looking toward the next presidential election campaign and under heavy domestic criticism for other policies as well as his Middle East policy, Carter decided to avoid further conflict with Begin and settle for whatever he could obtain from the Israeli leader without a confrontation. An Egyptian-Israeli peace agreement would win back some popular support. The U.S. public, he knew, would support anything he could get Begin and Sadat to agree to; he would be hailed for mediating, and the public, unconcerned about the details if Israel and Egypt agreed, would not lament if the Palestinians were left out. At this point, Carter himself, in desperate need of a success, was prepared to move ahead without the Palestinians and without linking an Egyptian-Israeli agreement to a broader resolution of the West Bank issue if that proved the only way to bring Begin along.[77]

The Camp David accords of September 1978 and the Egyptian-Israeli peace treaty of March 1979, which codified the accords, called for the establishment of autonomy for the Palestinian inhabitants of the West Bank and Gaza, enshrining the concepts of a transitional period and of giving Palestinians the right to "participate in" the determination of their future but not to decide it themselves. A period of autonomy would begin after a so-called self-governing authority or administrative council had been elected for the West Bank and Gaza; procedures for the elections were to be established by representatives of Israel, Egypt, and Jordan, with Palestinians participating as part of the Egyptian and Jordanian delegations. The period of autonomy would last for up to five years, during which Israel, Egypt, Jordan, and the elected Palestinian representatives would hold negotiations on the final status of the West Bank and Gaza.

The Israeli position prevailed on all critical issues regarding the West Bank and Gaza: withdrawal, the applicability of Resolution 242 to these territories, and Israeli settlements. The issues of withdrawal and the interpretation of 242 were left deliberately ambiguous; Begin agreed to "a withdrawal of Israeli armed forces" of unspecified size, during the interim period, but he made no commitment to eventual withdrawal from the occupied territories. To accommodate Begin's refusal to agree that Resolution 242 applied to the West Bank and Gaza, Carter and Sadat agreed to avoid linking any final-status issues to the resolution, so that the accords stipulated, pointlessly, that negotiations would be based on 242 but said nothing about basing a final agreement on the resolution. Begin won the day on settlements as well. Although the United States understood him to have agreed during the Camp David talks to freezing settlement construction throughout the autonomy negotiations and to ratifying this agreement through a letter to Carter separate from the accords, Begin contended that he agreed only to a three-month freeze, which is all he referred to in the letter to Carter. A month after Camp David he announced that West Bank settlements would be "thickened." The agreement was silent on such other key issues as future sovereignty of the territories, the status of Jerusalem, and the fate of Palestinian refugees and other Palestinian exiles.[78]

Despite U.S. and Egyptian efforts, in the end there was no linkage in the Camp David accords, or in the later peace treaty, between the agreement over the Sinai and resolution of the Palestinian issue. Indeed, nothing in the agreement precluded permanent Israeli control over the West Bank and Gaza. The Carter team had hoped that Israel, made vastly more secure by the peace treaty with Egypt, would feel confident enough to move forward on other fronts toward a comprehensive peace settlement and particularly toward an end of the West Bank/Gaza occupation and resolution of the Palestinian issue.[79] But Carter had not bargained on the depth of Israeli hostility, from the left as well as the right of Israel's political spectrum, to making territorial concessions to the Palestinians. Despite more than a year of close contact with Begin and repeated evidence of Begin's determination to retain and in fact to consolidate control over the West Bank and Gaza, Carter also did not fully grasp Begin's deep, spiritual commitment to a land he regarded as the sacred essence of the Jews' biblical heritage. Indeed, Carter did not fully comprehend that with the Palestinian question he had raised an issue that separated him altogether from Israel and its supporters. If he was unprepared for the depth of feeling on the Palestinian issue in Israel, he was perhaps even more unprepared for the similar intensity of feeling demonstrated by U.S. public opinion. Carter could not combat the solidarity shown for Begin's hard-line position, could not stand up to the fact that Americans rallied around Begin despite widespread misgivings among the public, in the press, and even in the U.S. Jewish community about his inflexibility on withdrawal and settlements. This solidarity shows the powerful constraints and the remarkable staying power of a mind-set.

Few Americans, including many policymakers, understood why Palestinians considered Camp David a humiliation. Although it is widely believed in the United States even today that Arafat and the PLO rejected the Camp David process because they remained bent on Israel's destruction, in fact the PLO let the United States know through indirect channels immediately after the accord was signed that it was seriously interested in exploring the meaning and implications of the agreement.[80] Few clarifications could be made, however, for the agreement did not commit Israel to any of the steps that would have brought an end to the occupation.

The Palestinians rejected Camp David not because they were intent on destroying Israel but because they believed the agreement gave them nothing. During an interview in October 1978, a month after Camp David, Arafat and other PLO leaders told Seth Tillman, a former staff member of the Senate Foreign Relations Committee, that the PLO was willing to accept a state limited to the West Bank and Gaza, existing alongside Israel, and had been trying since 1973 to establish a dialogue with the United States, but considered Camp David a betrayal. A month later, Representative Paul Findley, senior Republican on the House Middle East Subcommittee, met with Arafat and secured a commitment from the PLO leader to accept a Palestinian state in the West Bank and Gaza and, having obtained that, to grant Israel de facto recognition and renounce "any and all violent means to enlarge the territory of the [Palestinian] state." Although Findley believed that Arafat's pledges met the requirements of the Kissinger Sinai II commitment, the Carter administration did not react to either of these pledges or the earlier statements made to Tillman.[81]

Palestinians said they regarded Camp David's provision for self-rule as a "disgraceful" euphemism for continued occupation, and the Israelis gave them no reason to think otherwise. Israel never, for instance, stated which powers and responsibilities, if any, it would allow a self-governing authority to exercise.[82] Political scientist Ann Lesch interviewed numerous Palestinians in the West Bank and Gaza in the months before and after Camp David and found them to be strongly of the view that the autonomy plan, rather than benefiting the Palestinians, would ultimately legitimize the occupation and make the achievement of self-determination impossible. Palestinians did not believe that the administrative council envisioned in the autonomy plan could function as more than a figurehead and considered this part of the plan a humiliation. Many of Israel's own statements and actions, including continued settlement construction and assertions by cabinet members about future plans for the territories, made autonomy look to the Palestinians like "a trap that would lead to the incorporation of the territories into 'greater Israel.'"[83]

Palestinians questioned whether the United States would be able to enforce Israeli compliance with the agreement. Nicholas Veliotes, who was U.S. ambassador to Jordan during the Carter administration and tried to persuade King Hussein to accept the Camp David accords, believes the Palestinians backed away from the accords largely because of the U.S. inability to impose a meaningful freeze on Israeli settlement construction. The Palestinians regarded the accords as badly flawed in any case, Veliotes notes, and Begin's violation of the long-term freeze Carter thought he had achieved created the perception that Israel was "sticking it to the president"—a perception that undermined Veliotes's own and other diplomats' efforts to persuade the Arabs that Carter seriously intended to resolve the Palestinian problem.[84]

Quandt, who was closely involved in negotiating the agreement, has concluded that it might have been possible to attract Palestinians to the negotiating process if the United States had secured a real freeze on Israeli settlement construction; if the Palestinian self-governing body had been given control over land and water resources; if there had been hope that elections for the self-governing authority would be genuinely free and not encumbered by Israeli-imposed restrictions on who could and could not vote; or if Israel's military occupation authority had been abolished. The absence of any of these provisions tended to devalue the concept of autonomy in Palestinian eyes.[85] The Palestinians were also disturbed that there was no provision in the accords for refugee or exile return. With approximately twice as many Palestinians living outside the occupied territories as inside at the time, a self-governing authority elected only from the West Bank and Gaza could not represent true autonomy for all the Palestinian people. Few people understood the importance to the Palestinians of securing the right of all Palestinians to be represented in any peace negotiation and in any interim or final arrangement.

The most serious consequence of the Camp David accords from the Palestinian perspective was the absence of a link between the Sinai agreement and the West Bank issue. Despite the rhetoric and promises to the contrary, Egypt had made a separate peace with Israel, which relieved the pressure on Israel to move forward on the Palestinian issue.[86] Because Egypt was the strongest Arab country and the only one able to pose a significant military threat to Israel, its removal as a factor in the Arab-Israeli conflict seriously reduced the military and diplomatic leverage of all the other Arab parties and removed virtually all incentive for Israel to make concessions in the West Bank and Gaza or on any other front. Most analysts agree, moreover, that if Egypt had still been in a state of war with Israel and mobilized for combat in 1982, Israel would not have launched its invasion of Lebanon or at least would not have carried the attack to such lengths, moving as far north as Beirut and laying siege to the capital. Nor, most likely, would the United States have allowed the invasion to progress had there been the threat of general Arab-Israeli warfare and superpower involvement.[87]

The Palestinians' negative reaction to the Camp David agreement seemed to confirm for the U.S. public and even some policymakers one of the essential ingredients of the conventional wisdom—that Palestinians were unalterably radical. The question inevitably asked, even now, has always been why the Palestinians could not have done *something* differently—made more concessions, spoken in more conciliatory tones, agreed to go along with the Camp David process even though it proposed to decide their fate without their participation as equal negotiating partners.

The answer is that the PLO could certainly have made itself look more reasonable to Americans if it had agreed to accept Resolution 242 and recognize Israel's right to exist; at a minimum, the Palestinians could have made a better effort to explain their position to the public and to policymakers. But the next question has to be whether even the most conciliatory Palestinian position would have altered Israel's hard-line stance under Begin or enhanced Carter's ability to induce Israel to begin relinquishing control of the occupied territories—and the answer to that question is no. Palestinian conciliation would not have turned Begin into a dove, and, given the U.S. mind-set on Arab-Israeli issues, even the ultimate Palestinian concession would most likely not have brought about the public support Carter needed to confront Israel seriously.

Former Assistant Secretary of State Saunders has written that policymakers involved in the peace process found it difficult at the time to understand why Palestinians seemed to prefer to "drift" along while Israel steadily expanded its control over the West Bank rather than become involved in a process to halt that expansion. By U.S. logic, Saunders observes, it appeared preferable by far to accept the Camp David process, negotiate a self-governing authority for the West Bank and Gaza, and then negotiate a permanent relationship between Israel and a Palestinian political entity of some sort. This alternative, which would have given the Palestinians some form of elected self-government for the first time, seemed much better to many U.S. policymakers than continuing to live under Israeli military occupation.[88]

Palestinian logic led elsewhere however. The Palestinian perspective on the U.S. logic, as Saunders explained, was that by agreeing to negotiate on U.S. terms the Palestinians would have been being asked "to legitimize and perpetuate Israeli possession of land that they feel was once legitimately theirs, . . . an act of generosity that is virtually without historical example," and they would still be denied the recognition of their identity that would have come with U.S. and Israeli acceptance of the Palestinian right to self-determination.[89] Saunders's observations speak directly to the way in which a relatively closed frame of reference obscures vision and hinders policy innovation. Many U.S. policymakers at the time, despite their openness to the Palestinian viewpoint, were still so accustomed to viewing the conflict through an Israeli prism, as well as from a practical U.S. vantage point, that few appreciated the Palestinian perspective.

Whatever the official U.S. perception or understanding of the Palestinians, by the time the Egyptian-Israeli peace treaty was signed in March 1979 and the autonomy negotiations began between representatives of Egypt and Israel, Carter had had enough and was eager to back away. With a presidential reelection campaign approaching, he was no longer interested in trying to understand the Palestinians or confront Israel's solid bloc of support. During a difficult stage in the negotiations in February, before the treaty was signed, he had almost backed out of involvement in the peace process. Brzezinski and Carter's close friend and adviser Hamilton Jordan were telling Carter that they believed the Israelis were attempting, by being obstinate in the negotiations, to ensure that Carter was not reelected; Vice President Mondale was urging him to take a totally passive position and not press Begin at all, for fear of the political consequences if he did; and Carter was deeply discouraged that, as he told Brzezinski, much of the U.S. press portrayed him as anti-Israeli whenever he tried to move the parties toward concluding an agreement.[90]

Carter came out of his discouragement long enough to launch a strong initiative to conclude the treaty, but he pulled back immediately after the signing. Telling his aides that he needed a political shield at home, he appointed Democratic Party official Robert Strauss as special Middle East negotiator. Brzezinski recalls that at the first meeting Strauss attended with Carter and his aides to review Middle East policy in May 1979 Carter conveyed as clearly as he could a total disinterest in any further discussion of Middle East strategy. Strauss did act as a shield for Carter, continually warning the president about the negative political consequences of exerting any pressure on Israel, and he soon became discouraged himself with the difficult politics of the job and resigned within six months to head Carter's reelection effort.[91] He was replaced by another political shield. Attorney Sol Linowitz, who had negotiated the Panama Canal treaty, had no experience with Middle East issues but was a strong supporter of Israel.

The Iranian hostage crisis, which arose when the regime of the Ayatollah Khomeini in Iran seized the U.S. embassy in Tehran in November 1979 and held diplomats hostage, obviated any expectation that Carter would turn his energies back to the Arab-Israeli situation during the last year of his presidency. Vance continued a lonely effort to involve the Palestinians in the peace process, but he too was ultimately defeated by domestic politics.[92] He gradually lost influence to more politically attuned aides and finally lost Carter's ear altogether when in March 1980 he approved a U.S. vote in favor of a UN Security Council resolution on the Palestinians that Washington later disavowed. The administration had decided to vote for the resolution if wording on Jerusalem that was deemed objectionable was removed, and after the resolution was modified, Vance instructed the UN ambassador to vote for it. In the event, the resolution contained several politically sensitive references to Jerusalem and called for dismantling Israeli settlements in the occupied territories. Under pressure from Mondale and Carter's political aides, Vance was forced to issue a public retraction. The incident, occurring in an election year, came at a particularly sensitive time. Mondale was urging Carter to repudiate his opposition to Israeli settlements in time for the New York primary, in which Carter was being opposed for the Democratic Party nomination by Massachusetts Senator Ted Kennedy. The primary occurred shortly after Vance's retraction, and Carter lost, the Jewish vote going heavily to Kennedy. White House political aides blamed Vance.[93] Already deeply discouraged, Vance resigned shortly thereafter after unsuccessfully recommending against a mission, which ultimately failed, to rescue the hostages in Iran.

Vance was not the only U.S. official to run afoul of Israel's supporters in the United States over the Palestinian issue. In July 1979, during discussions at the UN about a possible resolution to amend Resolution 242 to make it more palatable to the Palestinians, UN Ambassador Andrew Young, then serving as head of the Security Council, met with the PLO's UN delegate to see if wording could be found to satisfy the PLO. Although in fact Kissinger's 1975 Sinai II pledge had not forbidden exploratory talks with the PLO, Young's meeting caused such an outcry from the U.S. Jewish community at an already politically sensitive time, and he had so angered Carter and Vance by not informing them of the meeting, that he was forced to resign. Not for the first or the last time, the constraints that the Sinai II commitment had imposed on policymaking thwarted what might have been a promising initiative. Both the Young incident and the UN vote in 1980, by making Carter appear fumbling and inept, greatly diminished his credibility as a leader and policy innovator.

Autonomy negotiations between Egypt and Israel—Jordan having refused to participate—continued throughout the remainder of the Carter administration with the mediation efforts of Linowitz. By the end of Carter's term, Linowitz felt he had made substantial progress in negotiating the terms of autonomy, but in fact agreement had not been reached, and was not near, on the most critical issues. There was no agreement on halting construction of Israeli settlements, none on whether the approximately one hundred thousand Palestinians resident in East Jerusalem could participate in elections for the self-governing authority—which Israel wanted to prevent—and none on future control of water and land resources. The fundamental objectives of Israel and of Egypt, acting on behalf of the Palestinians, were widely divergent. Israel, concerned to prevent the self-governing authority from ultimately becoming a state, worked to limit the authority's jurisdiction to administrative matters, handled under the continued control of the Israeli military government, and to restrict autonomy to the inhabitants of the occupied territories rather than to the land. Egypt, however, wanted legislative and executive authority for the self-governing body and autonomy for the land as well as the inhabitants. Despite Linowitz's optimism, the negotiations accomplished little on the issues of greatest importance to the Palestinians.[94]

Samuel Lewis, who served throughout Carter's term as U.S. ambassador to Israel, has said that despite the great tension in the U.S.-Israeli relationship over Israel's West Bank policy during the Carter years, the interests of the two countries basically coincided. "We were trying to help Israel make peace," he says; the only argument was over tactics.[95] Lewis's observation goes to the heart of the issue of making policy within the constraints of a frame of reference focused on one side in an international dispute. Despite Carter's efforts on behalf of the Palestinians, in the end most Americans viewed the issue as one of helping Israel make peace, not helping the Palestinians or the Arabs, or even Israel *and* the Arabs, make peace. In the end, the United States did not act as an impartial mediator between two equal parties in a negotiation. In negotiating the Egyptian-Israeli peace treaty, the United States was able to act as a neutral intermediary, but it was incapable of being neutral when the conflict involved questions more fundamental to Israel's existence. The basic issue arising out of the Carter administration's effort to forge a Palestinian-Israeli peace is whether U.S. policymakers could have acted more independently and forcefully to move Israel toward concessions or whether the conventional frame of reference of Americans, built up over many decades, bound Carter so completely that he would have been unable to move ahead under any circumstances.

The conclusion must be that the old frame of reference had become so automatic as a bracket for U.S. thinking and so widespread—encompassing the entire public, not just Jews or pro-Israeli lobbyists—that Carter could not have altered policy significantly no matter what his own inclinations. His efforts on behalf of the Palestinians certainly loosened the constraints of the conventional wisdom to a great extent, ever afterward making Palestinians a legitimate subject for discussion when matters of peace and negotiations arose. But his political freedom was so constricted that significant change in the frame of reference was not yet possible. A Carter acting in the mid- or late 1980s or in the 1990s—after the changes in the American mind-set about Israel and the Palestinians had taken better hold—might have been able to accomplish more. Had Carter been reelected in 1980, he might with a new mandate have renewed his efforts with some greater hope of success. But in the late 1970s, the idea of Palestinians as partners in a negotiating process and as legitimate claimants to some part of the land of Palestine was still too new to overcome the emotional U.S. identity with Israel.

Carter was part of a process of change that had been going on for several years. After decades of quiescence, the Palestinians had brought themselves and their grievances to world attention in the late 1960s and 1970s—not favorably but in any case as more than refugees. Then Sadat had improved Americans' image of all Arabs—in the words of Andrew Young, "almost single-handedly" balancing "an irrevocable 30-year commitment to Israel" with a new interest in the Arab world.[96] Carter built on this changing image with his efforts to bring the Palestinians into the negotiating process, but he could not completely alter the mind-set himself.

Although a few journalists had shown an interest in the Palestinians as early as 1969 and 1970, the level of attention paid by the serious media to the Palestinians had not significantly increased. Carter was still complaining in the late 1970s that the press criticized him for being anti-Israeli every time he raised the Palestinian issue, and the media were for the most part extremely slow to recognize the Palestinians as a factor in the peace process. News coverage continued almost always to present the Israeli perspective but not the Palestinian. *TV Guide* came to this conclusion after reviewing ten months of television news coverage of the Palestinians and Israel between July 1980 and April 1981. Of twenty-four network news reports about Israeli raids on Palestinian targets in southern Lebanon, the study revealed that only three showed the effects of the raids on the Palestinians and none pictured Palestinian victims. Of the fourteen reports on Palestinian raids against Israel, however, eleven showed Israeli victims. The three reports on the impact on Palestinians of Israeli attacks averaged under twenty-five seconds each, whereas the reports showing Israeli victims averaged over a minute and a half each.[97]

A principal agent for changing, or for conveying changes in, a conventional wisdom or frame of reference, the media clung persistently to their own assumptions about Israelis and Palestinians and, with a few notable exceptions, began to focus attention on the Palestinian question only after Carter himself had given up in frustration. When the press did begin to deal with the Palestinian issue seriously, its treatment was often interesting primarily for revealing media ignorance of the Palestinians and what the media knew to be the public's ignorance. *Time* magazine, for instance, ran a cover story on the Palestinians in April 1980 that was unabashedly wide-eyed at having discovered what Palestinians were actually like. The article, headlined "Key to a Wider Peace: The Palestinian Demand for Self-Determination Is Gaining Acceptance," emphasized what U.S. policymakers had been saying for almost five years about the significance of the Palestinian question, but handled the issue as though *Time* had only just learned anything about the Palestinians beyond the common stereotypes. The article opened on a note of surprise: "Their popular image in the West is that of a throng of terrorists and refugees. Some of them indeed are that, . . . but this community also includes artists and poets, builders and bureaucrats, doctors and teachers. Their industry and zeal for learning . . . have earned them the sobriquet 'the Jews of the Arab world.'" Scattering words like "surprising," "remarkably," and "uncommonly" throughout, the article expressed open wonderment about Palestinians.[98]

Noting that Palestinians were "something of a mystery" to most Americans, the article cited a *Time*-Yankelovich poll taken the week before showing that two-thirds of respondents viewed the Palestinians as either terrorists or refugees.[99] This overwhelmingly skewed perspective would not be overcome by a few cover stories and television features. Three decades in which Israel and Israelis had become a part of the "being" of the United States, in which Americans so automatically viewed events in the Middle East from an Israeli perspective that even a diplomat like Samuel Lewis spoke of trying to help Israel but not the Arabs make peace, could not be overcome in one presidential term. A start had been made; enough of a crack had appeared in the framework that bound thinking on the Middle East to permit a view of the Palestinians. But it remained a small crack at this point and one the Reagan administration would make little effort to expand further.

Even as the Palestinian situation was becoming somewhat better known and understood, Israel was taking concrete steps on the ground in the West Bank and Gaza, through confiscation of Palestinian land and construction of Israeli settlements, to foreclose virtually all Palestinian negotiating options. In the first three years of Begin's tenure, the number of Israeli settlements on the West Bank more than doubled and the number of Israeli settlers reached fourteen thousand. By 1980, Israel had expropriated more than 30 percent of the West Bank's land area for settlements and military bases and had begun to lay the foundation for permanent control of the occupied territories by applying Israeli law to Jewish settlers in these areas. Knowing that in the end the United States could not stop it, the Likud government made no effort to hide its actions or its long-range intentions. As political scientist Mark Tessler has noted, "The Begin government worried little about whether its arguments were judged to be persuasive. From its point of view and that of its supporters, Israel's policies in the West Bank and Gaza derived all the legitimacy they needed from considerations of history, religion, and Jewish nationalism." [100] And most Americans went along.

Despite Carter's most strenuous verbal efforts to halt the process and despite increased attention to Palestinian concerns, at the end of Carter's term the frame of reference had become so accepting of Begin's policies that only a concerted effort by the United States, involving strong pressure on Israel, could have reversed the trend toward the Israelization of the occupied territories. Carter had been unable himself to exert such pressure, and the Reagan administration, which was not bothered by Israeli settlements or land confiscations, would exert no pressure at all.

8 Ronald Reagan
Missed Opportunities

Ronald Reagan's 1980s brought a quantum leap in efforts to promote Israel and delegitimize the Palestinians in the United States. The prominence the Palestinians had gained over the previous decade and particularly the attention paid to them by Jimmy Carter caused considerable alarm both in Israel and among Israeli supporters in the United States. As a consequence, pro-Israeli propaganda, fueled by an efficient Israeli public-relations machine and welcomed by a sympathetic public, press, and Congress, reached a near fever pitch. Equally intense was the concerted campaign by Israel and its supporters to divert attention from the Palestinian issue by denying the legitimacy of the PLO as the Palestinians' designated representative and even denying the Palestinian people's separate existence.

These efforts to recast the frame of reference in its old Palestinian-less mold had a major impact on policymaking. Already a true product of the old framework, Reagan came to office a strong admirer of Israel, had no sympathy for the Palestinians, and was disinclined from the beginning to take an even-handed approach to Middle East policymaking. He then surrounded himself with advisers who were ardent supporters of Israel and who viewed it as a critical element in the Cold War struggle against the Soviet Union. Any policymakers who may not have shared the black-and-white perspective that put Israel and the Arabs into easy, clearly defined categories—anti-Communist ally versus pro-Soviet enemy—tended to be ignored and swept along in the strong tide of pro-Israeli feeling that prevailed throughout the administration.

Thanks to the Palestinians' new prominence, no U.S. negotiating effort could ever ignore their role completely. But the Reagan administration tried hard—at least implicitly supporting Israel's attempts to destroy the PLO, attempting to shut the PLO out of peace negotiations, and in general denying the relevance and the existence of Palestinian nationalism. In their efforts to accommodate the anti-Palestinian position of Israel's Likud-led government and to skirt the Palestinian issue, Reagan administration officials repeatedly missed opportunities to encourage a peace process.

In the end, the administration was forced reluctantly in its last days to authorize an official U.S. dialogue with the PLO—an irony, given its profound distaste for the PLO and its consistent effort over the years to deny legitimacy to the organization. The *intifada,* the West Bank/Gaza uprising launched in December 1987, and the international support and sympathy it brought the Palestinians gave the PLO the confidence to launch a major peace initiative in late 1988, openly and explicitly granting Israel the recognition that Yasir Arafat and PLO moderates had been discussing in private and in circuitous language for over a decade. Because the PLO finally agreed precisely to the formula the United States had always demanded— recognizing Israel's right to exist, accepting UN Resolution 242, and renouncing terrorism—the Reagan administration had no choice but to begin a dialogue with the PLO.

In a real sense, the world was black and white for Reagan. There were few nuances in his register of ideas: there was good and there was evil in the world and little in between; other nations were either democracies or dictatorships and therefore either allies or enemies.[1] Reagan was impatient with details and had little close knowledge of any area of the world, but certain broad concepts governed his view of world affairs. He was strongly anti-Communist and anti-Soviet, once calling the Soviet Union the "evil empire," and he dealt with other nations in large measure according to how closely they were allied to the Soviets. During an interview in the midst of his first presidential campaign, he made a statement that was to define the approach his administration would take to foreign policy, with regard both to the Middle East and to the rest of the world. "Let's not delude ourselves," he said. "The Soviet Union underlies all the unrest that is going on. If they weren't engaged in this game of dominoes, there wouldn't be any hot spots in the world."[2] Israel's role in the competition with the Soviets was central in Reagan's mind. On another occasion during the campaign, he told a group of Jewish leaders that Israel was "the only stable democracy we can rely on in a spot where Armageddon could come. . . . We must prevent the Soviet Union from penetrating the Mideast. . . . If Israel were not there, the U.S. would have to be there."[3]

Israel was a special emotional as well as strategic ally for Reagan. The Holocaust had impressed him deeply, and he told B'nai B'rith during a campaign speech, undoubtedly sincerely, that for him Israel was not only a nation but a symbol. Some analysts have observed that Reagan tended to see foreign affairs as an extension of his personal relationships and that, because he had a great many Jewish friends, largely from his Hollywood days, he was inclined to regard his actions and policies toward Israel as involving the fate of his friends. His "gut instincts" were extremely pro-Israeli, according to one journalist who studied his administration's policies toward Israel closely. A "lifetime of experience," this reporter wrote, "led him to see Jews as part of the 'us' group in his us-against-them mind set." [4] Reagan had no Arab friends and, perhaps for that reason, no empathy for Arab concerns. Arabs were not part of his "us" group.

Reagan's first few years in office were marked by several sharp disagreements with Israel over Israeli actions the United States deemed irresponsible or too militant—for instance, Israel's opposition to the sale of AWACS aircraft to Saudi Arabia in 1981, its June 1981 bombing of an Iraqi nuclear reactor, its annexation of the Golan Heights in December 1981, and some of its heavier bombing raids on Beirut during the 1982 invasion of Lebanon. But the sanctions imposed, if any, were not severe, and Reagan's criticism was seldom harsh. He disliked personal confrontation in any situation, and Ambassador to Israel Samuel Lewis notes that he was at pains to avoid conflict even when he was occasionally, as during the Lebanon invasion, genuinely angry with Israel. He invariably attempted to soften the impact of harsh words with a smiling, apologetic demeanor.[5]

Given Reagan's philosophical outlook on the world, the Middle East was easy for him to define for himself, without additional input from experts. He viewed Arab-Israeli issues, including the Palestinian-Israeli conflict, essentially from within the conventional frame of reference as it had prevailed thirty years earlier, and his perspective did not change significantly while he was in office or afterward. He seemed simply to discard whatever information did not fit into his mind-set. Thus, as late as 1990, when he published his memoirs, he could still seriously propound the old facile tenets of the conventional wisdom—writing, for instance, of regional hatreds with "roots reaching back to the dawn of history" and of the Arabs' supposed "pathological hatred" of Israel, as if unaware of the modern roots of Arab grievances. He still seriously affirmed the old shibboleth that "savagery . . . forever lies beneath the sands of the Middle East." [6]

Because he took his cues primarily from the strong Israeli supporters in his administration, and in many instances from Israeli Prime Minister Menachem Begin, Reagan seems only rarely—the immediate aftermath of the 1982 Lebanon invasion was a notable exception—even to have entertained the notion that there was a legitimate Palestinian perspective. Early in his term, he reportedly told his aides that, with regard to the Palestinian issue, he tended to accept Begin's argument that it was a parochial issue, one of history's "running sores" that was so localized it was easily containable—that it should, in other words, be left to Israel to deal with and not be allowed to interfere with the larger strategic issues of the U.S.-Israeli partnership.[7]

Reagan's strategic thinking and general mind-set reflected the views of a group of neoconservative political thinkers espousing a philosophy that blamed the Soviet Union for most mischief making throughout the world and that tended to assume the United States was losing the Cold War to superior Soviet power. Reagan took most of his specific ideas on international relations from this movement and ultimately surrounded himself with neoconservative writers and thinkers. The neoconservative movement had originated in the 1960s and 1970s among several originally liberal intellectuals concerned about the rise of the radical New Left. These individuals were strong and vocal supporters of Israel and were concerned with what they saw as an anti-Israeli drift on the left of the U.S. political spectrum. For the neoconservatives, Israel represented the kind of hard-hitting anti-Soviet realism in foreign policy that they felt the United States had abandoned in the 1970s. Viewing the Arab-Israeli conflict from a globalist perspective, they heavily promoted the idea that Israel was a vital Cold War ally of the United States and that the Palestinians were tools of the Soviet Union in its campaign of international terrorism. Palestinian nationalism, in this view, had no legitimacy, being only a Soviet invention, and because Israel was so important to U.S. interests, its occupation of the West Bank and Gaza actually served those interests.[8]

The list of prominent new recruits to neoconservative ranks as the movement grew and gained influence in fact reads like a roster of Reagan administration foreign policymakers: Jeane Kirkpatrick, an academic who became U.S. ambassador to the UN; Richard Perle, who became an assistant secretary of defense in Reagan's administration and was a former aide to one of the Senate's greatest Israeli supporters, Senator Henry Jackson; Elliot Abrams, like Perle a former Jackson aide, who became assistant secretary of state first for human rights and later for Latin American affairs; Max Kampelman, a founder of JINSA, which had been formed in the 1970s to bring Israel's security concerns to the attention of Defense Department officials, who became Reagan's arms-control director; Richard Schifter, a cofounder of JINSA who was appointed assistant secretary of state for human rights in late 1985; and Richard Pipes, a Soviet-affairs expert who joined the National Security Council staff. (Pipes's son, Daniel Pipes, is an academic and editor who has written extensively in support of Israel and in opposition to Palestinian nationalism.) Many of these people, including Kirkpatrick and Richard Pipes, were frequent contributors to *Commentary* magazine, edited by neoconservative Norman Podhoretz, which is what brought them to the attention of the Reagan administration.[9]

Although not themselves members of the neoconservative movement, the officials appointed to the foreign-policy portfolios in Reagan's cabinet clearly reflected the philosophy espoused by the neoconservatives on the centrality of East-West issues, the key role of Israel in this Cold War struggle, and the lesser importance of other issues in the Middle East. Secretary of State Alexander Haig came to office believing that the United States had suffered a decline in military strength and a loss of will since the Vietnam war that was causing it to lose its preeminent position in the world and much of its influence to the Soviet Union. In the Middle East, he believed the Reagan administration's principal task should be to rebuild the U.S. position by fighting against Soviet inroads and restoring the faith of friendly Middle East nations in U.S. reliability. Like Reagan, Haig regarded the Carter administration's focus on so-called local issues such as the Palestinian problem, the West Bank autonomy negotiations, and Israeli settlement construction in the occupied territories as a distraction from what should be the primary U.S. goal of creating regional stability.[10]

Believing that both Arabs and Israelis shared the Reagan administration's concern about the Soviet threat, Haig attempted as one of his first orders of business to talk Egypt, Jordan, and Saudi Arabia into joining with Israel in what he called a "strategic consensus," working together to deal with Soviet "interventionism and exploitation" as a first priority before Arab-Israeli peace negotiations were tackled. "Only when local states feel confident of United States reliability and secure against Soviet threats," Haig told the Senate Foreign Relations Committee in March 1981, "will they be willing to take the necessary risks for peace."[11]

Haig's Cold War–oriented frame of reference, formed largely under the guidance of Henry Kissinger during the Nixon administration, naturally favored Israel. His desire to deemphasize the peace process and the centrality of the Palestinian issue was the approach Israel had been pressing for throughout the four years of the Carter administration. Moreover, his attempt to enlist Arab states in a strategic alliance with Israel to combat the

Soviets indicated a failure to understand Arab grievances against Israel. Haig was so centered on U.S.-Soviet issues that he seems not to have recognized that Arabs viewed Israel as a greater threat than the Soviet Union and the unresolved Palestinian issue as a greater source of regional turmoil than Soviet interventionism. Although he was in office for only a short time and his notions of building a "strategic consensus" in the Middle East never took hold, Haig was an activist secretary of state who helped set a tone for Reagan administration foreign policy that would continue through Reagan's eight years in office.

In contrast to Haig and most other top officials in the administration, Secretary of Defense Caspar Weinberger, although a globalist, always opposed the effort to formalize a strategic-cooperation arrangement with Israel and quickly became known among Israeli supporters as an antagonist.[12] Against the enthusiasm for the relationship with Israel elsewhere in the administration, Weinberger's reservations about establishing so close a military tie did not prevail. CIA Director William Casey was a Cold War hawk very much in the mold of the neoconservatives and of his longtime friend Reagan. A highly political animal, he pursued his own foreign-policy agenda, in the words of his deputy Robert Gates, to a degree unparalleled in the history of postwar intelligence directors—who are, in theory and usually in practice, policy implementers but not policymakers. Casey's power was made possible in great measure by Reagan's hands-off management style and inattention to detail. He was almost obsessively fearful of what he saw as Soviet encirclement and was preoccupied with Soviet "surrogates" in the Third World, attributing international terrorism to Soviet inspiration.[13] In his view of the world, the Palestinians stood out as Soviet agents, while Israel was a strong natural ally. Casey increased intelligence cooperation with Israel, agreeing, for instance, under an intelligence-sharing arrangement to provide the Israelis with almost unlimited access to U.S. satellite photography. When Israel used this photography to plan its bombing of an Iraqi nuclear reactor, Casey was said to be pleased, despite the White House's expressed displeasure.[14]

Reagan's first national security adviser, Richard Allen, was another foreign-policy globalist, and he soon became well known as a friend of Israel.[15] Allen had established his general position by writing the introduction to a 1980 book by an extremely pro-Israeli, anti-Palestinian defense analyst, Joseph Churba, who was working as a Reagan campaign aide.[16] Entitled *Retreat from Freedom*, the book affirmed the need to maintain "Israel-American might" against Soviet advances and declared the PLO a Soviet puppet and the Arab states "inherently unstable." Calling Churba's book "indispensable," Allen laid out in the introduction the basic anti-Soviet, neoconservative philosophy by which Reagan administration foreign policy would be governed.[17]

Pro-Israeli lobbyists and committed activists dotted Reagan's administration at key lower levels. Michael Ledeen, who served as a JINSA board member and as executive director for several years in the late 1970s, worked in the Departments of State and Defense and on the National Security Council staff in the Reagan years. Another Reagan appointee heavily involved with JINSA was Stephen Bryen, a close associate of Richard Perle who, after Perle was named assistant secretary of defense in 1981, was appointed to the position of deputy assistant secretary in charge of regulating technology transfer to foreign nations—a particularly sensitive position given Israel's interest in U.S. arms technology. Bryen had briefly succeeded Ledeen as JINSA executive director in 1981 and then turned the directorship over to his wife, Shoshanna Bryen, when he moved to the Defense Department. Stephen Bryen remained on the JINSA advisory board while serving in government, and Shoshanna Bryen was JINSA executive director throughout the Reagan administration and beyond.[18] Howard Teicher was another JINSA member and advocate of Israel's strategic importance who held a key position in the Reagan White House. A Defense Department analyst during the Carter administration, Teicher moved in 1982 to the National Security Council staff, where he served as director of Middle East affairs and later as director of political-military affairs.

The so-called "Arabist" State Department had little influence on Reagan administration policy. Both Reagan and Haig came into office highly suspicious of the Department's Middle East officials and determined to undercut them. Reagan told a group of Jewish leaders during the campaign that he did not have "a great deal of confidence in the present State Department," which he indicated was too much inclined to pursue its own policies and not the president's. Haig felt that the foreign-policy bureaucracy was "overwhelmingly Arabist in its approach to the Middle East and in its sympathies" and clearly set out to ignore its policy advice.[19]

The story of the evolution of Reagan administration policy on the legal status of Israeli settlements gives an illustration of how limited the influence of the State Department was. Reagan's own views on Israeli settlements were apparently influenced by Eugene Rostow, a former Johnson administration official and neoconservative who as a university professor had written frequent legal justifications of Israel's occupation of the West Bank and Gaza and its right to construct Jewish settlements there. Previous U.S. presidents had taken the position that Israeli settlements were illegal and a violation of the Fourth Geneva Convention proscribing settlement of an occupier's own population in an occupied territory. Reagan, however, apparently adopting Rostow's position, began to assert during his 1980 presidential campaign that the settlements were legal, even that Israel had a "right" to construct them. The State Department's director of Israeli affairs from 1978 to 1981 has indicated that after Reagan took office, State officials, trying to devise a formula that would accommodate Reagan's belief in the legality of the settlements while also making it clear to the Israeli government that the United States disapproved, came up with the formula that the settlements were an "obstacle to progress toward peace." When this wording was shown to one of Reagan's senior foreign-policy advisers, however, he responded, "Even if I agreed with this, which I don't, I wouldn't show it to the President." For some time after this, the State Department took no position on the settlements, only later adopting this formulation as its standard position. No one in the administration ever again called the settlements illegal.[20]

Given the heavy emphasis of Reagan administration policymakers on Cold War issues and the strong focus on the U.S. alliance with Israel, any expectation that the Palestinian perspective might have an influence on policymaking was quite forlorn. The administration's frame of reference was almost entirely Israel-centered. The Reagan team did not simply ignore the Palestinians but was actively hostile to the notion of Palestinian nationalism and cooperated with Israel throughout its eight years to undermine the legitimacy of the PLO.

Reagan himself had a particularly negative attitude toward the Palestinians when he came into office. Asked during an interview days after his inauguration whether he had any sympathy for the Palestinians or "any moral feeling toward them and their aspirations," he skirted a direct yes or no answer and condemned the Palestinians for challenging Israel's right to exist. He denounced PLO terrorism and questioned whether the PLO truly represented the Palestinians.[21] Reagan had been fairly vocal on the Palestinian issue during his presidential campaign, repeatedly denouncing the PLO as a terrorist organization, criticizing Carter for not also doing so, and affirming his refusal to deal with the organization even if it accepted UN Resolution 242. He tended to speak in the old stereotypical terms of Palestinians as either terrorists or refugees. Trying to separate "Palestinian refugees" from the PLO, he often took the position that the PLO did not represent the "refugees"; he seldom referred at all to "the Palestinian people" and indicated no understanding of Palestinian national aspirations.[22]

Most others at the policymaking level believed, with Haig, that the Palestinian issue was a distraction from what should be the administration's principal goal in the Middle East of fighting off Soviet advances and building up Israel's military capabilities. UN Ambassador Jeane Kirkpatrick, for instance, was decidedly and actively hostile to the PLO and to the notion of Palestinian nationalism. In an unusual example of outspokenness by a sitting official, Kirkpatrick published an article in the November 1981 issue of the *New Republic* in which she denounced the PLO as "the deadliest enemies of peace in the area."[23] Kirkpatrick's views clearly reflected the attitude of her neoconservative colleagues in government.

In the administration's frame of reference, resolving the Palestinian issue was so unimportant, Israel's priorities and needs took such precedence, and the PLO appeared so monstrous that administration officials found it easy to convince themselves that no one else, not even the Arab states, cared much about the peace process either or viewed the Palestinian problem as central to resolving the Arab-Israeli conflict. As a result, the administration tended to dismiss or ignored altogether the efforts of friendly Arab leaders in Egypt and Saudi Arabia to promote the Palestinian issue. Kirkpatrick, for instance, insisted that Egypt's Anwar Sadat had "scorned" the notion of negotiating with the PLO; her assumption is evidence of how much the administration's thinking was influenced by its own desire not to address the Palestinian issue. In fact, although often highly critical of the Palestinian leadership, Sadat pressed the administration hard on the issue. In August 1981, during his first visit to Washington after Reagan's election, Sadat emphasized in public remarks the urgent need for the United States to open a dialogue with the PLO in order to strengthen moderates among the leadership, and he pointed to the PLO's acceptance the previous month of a cease-fire in Lebanon as a hopeful sign of its willingness to work for mutual and simultaneous recognition with Israel—a sign of moderation that he said "should not escape our notice." In his own public response, Reagan never used the word *Palestinians*.[24]

The fact that virtually no one on the Reagan team appreciated the urgency of Sadat's pleas for progress in the West Bank autonomy negotiations between Egypt and Israel and that most misread his criticism of the PLO leadership as "scorn" for the peace process is an indication of the extent to which the administration was blinded by its own globalist and Israel-centered perspective. According to Hermann Eilts, U.S. ambassador to Egypt throughout most of the 1970s and into the 1980s, Sadat was cha-grined during his August 1981 visit to Washington to observe that although Reagan was well-intentioned, he knew little about the Middle East and was "heavily influenced by Israel." Eilts himself felt that there was scant knowl-edge about Middle East political dynamics anywhere in senior U.S. govern-ment circles.[25]

Little wonder that the administration did not notice or care that Israel was steadily strengthening and consolidating its control over the West Bank and Gaza. Settlement construction proceeded at a rapid pace; the number of Jewish settlers on the West Bank grew by 70 percent during Reagan's first two years in office, and the Israelis laid plans to house three hundred thou-sand Israelis there by the end of the decade. In an effort to undermine the PLO's influence, Israeli occupation authorities also took harsh steps in these years to suppress any sign of Palestinian nationalism—dismissing the pro-PLO mayors of several large Palestinian towns who had been cho-sen in democratic elections several years earlier; disbanding democratically elected councils in Palestinian towns and villages and replacing them with more compliant appointed councils; closing Palestinian universities; cen-soring or closing down Palestinian newspapers; and banning the distribu-tion of books in the West Bank and Gaza. Vigilantism against Palestinians by organized elements of the Israeli settler movement, including random shootings of Palestinian civilians and grenade and car-bomb attacks on Pal-estinian property, also increased markedly. Israeli authorities meted out le-nient punishments to the perpetrators and often encouraged more vigilan-tism by allowing settlers to do their military-reserve duty by patrolling Arab communities.[26]

The Israeli government's concerted effort to suppress all expression of Palestinian nationalism and the fact that virtually none of this effort was reported in the U.S. media guaranteed that the framework in which the PLO and Palestinians had long been viewed in the United States—as ter-rorists rather than as a nation desirous of establishing the institutions of self-government—did not change. Although many in Israel saw through the government's policies, organizing protest demonstrations against its oc-cupation practices, most at senior levels in the Reagan administration did not. Uninterested in anything that distracted attention from the Cold War, the Reagan team remained silent on Israel's harsh policies.

It was little wonder also that senior levels of the administration took virtually no interest in the ongoing negotiations for Palestinian auton-omy, allowing them to languish more or less unattended and eventually downgrading the U.S. representation at the talks. Whereas Robert Strauss and Sol Linowitz, Carter's mediators, were prominent individuals who had served as representatives of the president, in February 1982 Haig appointed Richard Fairbanks, a middle-level State Department official with no Middle East expertise, as his own representative to the talks, not Reagan's.[27]

In August 1981 the administration did authorize an outside mediation effort with the PLO, but contacts ended when Israel invaded Lebanon in June 1982. Arafat initially approached the United States through an intermediary—John Mroz, then director of Middle East studies at a New York-based foundation—suggesting secret talks on developing a way to open an official U.S.-PLO dialogue. Arafat was frustrated that because he was prohibited from dealing directly with the United States, he had always since 1975 heard U.S. views as they were filtered through unofficial and usually non-U.S. intermediaries, and he hoped that as an American Mroz would more accurately convey U.S. thinking. Assistant Secretary of State for Near Eastern and South Asian Affairs Nicholas Veliotes persuaded Haig to follow up on the overture, and Haig obtained Reagan's personal approval for Mroz to begin talks with Arafat. Over a nine-month period, Mroz and Arafat held more than fifty meetings, Mroz reporting back to Veliotes as the designated U.S. contact point. Saudi Arabia was brought in on the effort, but the other Arab states and Israel were not informed. By May 1982, the talks had progressed to the point that Arafat was promising a PLO response the following month to a suggested U.S. plan for facilitating a dialogue, but after Israel invaded Lebanon the response never came.[28]

Both Mroz and Veliotes have indicated that they were uncertain whether the mediation effort would have produced any results had the Israeli invasion not occurred, although Mroz says he believed at the time that an agreement was close. Harold Saunders, who had been involved in the Carter administration's efforts to obtain PLO agreement to the U.S. conditions, regarded this effort as "a more elaborate and more official exchange" than any the Carter administration had engaged in.[29]

Although Haig was initially intrigued by some of the mechanics of the Mroz contact, he and other senior officials were not particularly interested in pursuing a dialogue with the PLO under any circumstances. Reagan had said during his campaign that he probably would not negotiate with the PLO even if it accepted Resolution 242 because he did not believe the organization represented the Palestinians, and neither he nor most of his senior foreign-policy team significantly altered their negative attitude toward the PLO. The possibility many have raised that the United States colluded with Israeli Defense Minister Ariel Sharon in his intention to destroy the PLO's military and political infrastructure, giving him a "green light" to invade

Lebanon in 1982 for the purpose of going after the PLO, is less clear. But it seems likely that some important senior officials in the administration would have been pleased to see the PLO destroyed and that the administration's extreme distaste for the PLO, its identity of interests with Israel, and its concentration on fighting the Soviets and Soviet agents combined to create an atmosphere in which Israeli leaders knew there would be little protest from Washington if they attacked the PLO in Lebanon.

Haig has denied that he gave Israel a green light,[30] and he probably did not, in so many words. But virtually all evidence indicates that the general mind-set throughout high levels of the administration was such that Israel could only have felt it had at least an implicit go-ahead. As former Assistant Secretary of State Veliotes has observed, Haig's point of view was that "we'd all be better off if we didn't have to worry about the Palestinian problem," and this attitude gave Sharon the freedom to act.[31] The likelihood of an invasion was certainly no secret. Sharon had begun dropping hints to U.S. officials in 1981 about his contingency plans to go after the PLO, and he had bluntly informed a shocked special negotiator, Philip Habib, that the time was coming when Israel would have no choice but to "eradicate" the PLO in Lebanon. By the spring of 1982, the likelihood of an Israeli attack was being openly discussed in the U.S. press. There were no public warnings against it from the United States.[32]

Although the administration may have been disconcerted by the scale of the assault, it was generally not displeased about the course the invasion took.[33] In particular, there was no distress over the weakening of the PLO or the possibility of its destruction. A former National Security Council staffer says that as early as May 1981, a high-level Haig aide had suggested at a meeting of experts that U.S. policy in Lebanon should be directed toward bringing about the "neutralization" of the PLO, a word Sharon himself often used.[34] U.S. special envoy Habib later told a Palestinian scholar that he believed at the time that Sharon had some sort of understanding with Haig about Lebanon; whether this was the case or not, Habib said he found it exceedingly hard before Haig was forced to resign in late June, three weeks into the invasion, to induce Washington either to restrain Israel or to support his own negotiating efforts.[35]

The advent of George Shultz, who succeeded Haig as secretary of state in July 1982 at the height of the Lebanon invasion, and Reagan's shock at the plight of Palestinians during the invasion at least temporarily focused the administration's attention on the need to resolve the Palestinian problem. Shultz came to office believing that the United States had been too closely tied to Israel and too disinterested in the peace process and that it needed to offer the Palestinians a realistic way to achieve a solution. He had noted during Reagan's 1980 campaign that the only area on which he faulted Reagan was the imbalance in the candidate's pro-Israeli position. During his own confirmation hearings and in speeches just afterward, Shultz criticized Israel's West Bank policies and spoke of the need to satisfy the Palestinians' "political aspirations."[36] His first order of business after the Lebanon situation appeared to quiet down was to craft a peace initiative, the Reagan Plan, that took account of the Palestinian issue.

Reagan himself had been undergoing a slight change of heart about the Palestinians that Veliotes dates to the summer of 1981. Habib, who had been designated to negotiate an end to a series of Israeli-PLO clashes across Israel's northern border, took the opportunity in his meetings with Reagan to impress on him the importance of resolving the Palestinian problem. Describing Reagan as an intensely personal individual who learned by talking about a topic, Veliotes says the president was deeply impressed by the direct, personal nature of Habib's presentations and took note of Habib's emphasis on the fact that Palestinians were more than just terrorists, as well as his conviction that the United States had to take action to solve the problem. During the Lebanon invasion, Reagan's views were further changed by dramatic television images of Palestinian children injured and killed during Israeli bombing attacks.[37]

The Reagan Plan came out of these changing perceptions. Within days of his confirmation in July, Shultz had convened a group of experts to devise an initiative intended, after the turmoil of Lebanon, to give the peace process new impetus by addressing the Palestinian question. Launched on September 1, 1982, in a nationally broadcast speech by President Reagan, the Shultz-authored peace plan proposed autonomy for West Bank and Gaza Palestinians during a five-year transition period leading to negotiations on a final disposition of these territories. The plan concentrated on the West Bank and Gaza and did not mention Syria at all or the need for a peace settlement on the occupied Golan Heights. Although the plan ignored the PLO altogether, took no note of the interests and claims of exiled Palestinians, and reaffirmed U.S. opposition to the establishment of an independent Palestinian state, the initiative did break new ground in many respects and constituted the most far-reaching U.S. initiative on the Palestinian issue yet proposed.

Noting in his speech that the Lebanon crisis had dramatized Palestinian homelessness and acknowledging that the Palestinians "feel strongly that their cause is more than a question of refugees," Reagan proposed specifics that went beyond the autonomy conceived in the Camp David accords.

Under the Reagan Plan, East Jerusalem Palestinians would have been permitted to vote along with other West Bank and Gaza Palestinians for a self-governing authority, and the autonomy proposed would have included land and resources as well as people, which Israel had been strongly opposed to throughout the post–Camp David autonomy talks. The plan called for an immediate freeze on construction of Israeli settlements. Also in opposition to Israel's Likud government, Reagan affirmed the principle of exchanging territory for peace and noted specifically that the United States believed the withdrawal provision of UN Resolution 242 applied to all fronts, including the West Bank and Gaza. Although not laying out a clear vision of a final peace, Reagan said the United States would not support either independent statehood for the Palestinians or permanent Israeli sovereignty or control over the West Bank and Gaza. The U.S. preference was for Palestinian self-government in association with Jordan.[38]

Despite the promise of the Reagan Plan, and despite Reagan's and Shultz's increased appreciation of the importance of pursuing the peace process and addressing the Palestinian problem as part of it, there was basically no change in the administration's hostility toward the PLO itself or in its ill-concealed desire to see the PLO at least emasculated if not destroyed. Throughout the remainder of Reagan's two terms, he and Shultz proved to be as deeply opposed to the PLO as Haig had ever been and as desirous of circumventing the organization.

Shultz seemed from the beginning almost fearful, perhaps for domestic political reasons, of dealing even indirectly with the PLO. Palestinian intellectual Walid Khalidi tells a story of contacts with Shultz that gives an idea of his mind-set. According to Khalidi, he and another Palestinian who was a long-time friend and business associate of Shultz approached Shultz twice before he became secretary of state with messages for the administration that Shultz willingly passed on. The first involved a message to Reagan from Arafat, passed through Shultz just before Reagan's inauguration in January 1981. The message, informally written on one page of foolscap, contained nine points, including statements to the effect that only a Palestinian state could meet the political and psychological needs of the Palestinians and produce a stable peace, that such a state would live in peaceful coexistence with Israel under international guarantees to both states, and that such a state would not become the base for any outside power. The PLO, the statement read, was eager to start a dialogue with the new administration. Shultz later told the two Palestinians that the administration's reaction had been favorable, but nothing further came of this initiative.

The second contact came at the start of the Israeli invasion of Lebanon in early June 1982. Khalidi and the other Palestinian urged Shultz to use his administration contacts to secure an Israeli standdown. Agreeing with the Palestinians, according to Khalidi, that Israel's invasion went beyond self-defense, Shultz said he would convey his assessment to the administration. A few weeks later, when Shultz became secretary of state, Khalidi and the other Palestinian attempted to reach him again. On the strength of the attitudes the new secretary had previously expressed to them, the two men believed that his appointment opened a new opportunity "to push for an honorable and durable peace in the Middle East." When Shultz's old friend tried to get in touch with him, however, he was told that he should henceforth desist from trying to make any contact, even socially. An aide of Shultz would meet with the two Palestinians if they wished to send a message to the secretary, but there would be no direct contact. A few days later, Khalidi and the other Palestinian, having been told they could not be received in the State Department, met with a Shultz aide at a prearranged spot in the State Department parking lot. The two men, according to Khalidi, "turned up at the rendezvous place at the agreed time. There we were rather furtively approached by a gentleman who gave us a paper on which a name and an address were typed. He explained that if we wanted to send Shultz any message we should do so via the indicated name and address. He thereupon departed." Over the next few weeks, the two Palestinians sent three or four messages to this address, but, receiving no response or any indication that the messages were getting through, they ceased. Khalidi takes this episode as an indication of "how mesmerized American officials are with fear vis-à-vis the pro-Israeli lobby."[39]

Shultz was adamant in his refusal to deal with the PLO. He is reported to have told Sharon in August 1982 that Reagan and he both believed that the PLO "must be scattered and its credibility destroyed. But unless the Palestinian problem is solved, a new PLO will arise."[40] Sharon's aims were no secret; Shultz himself indicated in his memoirs that in early August the Israeli general had mentioned to U.S. diplomats the need to "clean out" the refugee camps in Beirut[41] and, as noted, he had reportedly mentioned "eradication" to Habib. Shultz must have known that his virtually simultaneous statement to Sharon about destroying PLO credibility would only have encouraged the Israeli in his efforts to destroy the organization altogether.

Shultz tended to be a policy manager rather than a policy conceptualizer, and, as a loyal servant of Reagan, he operated out of the president's frame of reference, in many ways taking his starting points and his definitions of the world from Reagan. The story of how Shultz evolved from being a sometime critic of Israel and defender of Palestinian "political aspirations" to what by 1987 AIPAC officials were calling "a friend beyond words" to Israel who had "transformed U.S. policy" and raised the relationship to a new level[42] is the story of a man disinclined to take bold steps, who knew little about Arab political dynamics and was easily angered when the Arabs refused to play the roles he scripted. Confronted when he entered office with a crisis in Lebanon not of his making, Shultz responded with a poorly conceived policy, reacted intemperately when it went wrong, and ultimately took refuge in an administration mind-set so completely focused on Israel and its needs that in the end no other perspective was admissible.

Everything that could possibly have gone wrong in Lebanon did during Shultz's first eighteen months in office, although the period began on an optimistic note. The administration issued the Reagan Plan when the Lebanon crisis appeared to have quieted down and, from Washington's perspective, the atmosphere for peace appeared promising: the fighting had subsided; PLO forces had been evacuated from throughout Lebanon under an agreement negotiated by Habib, and the organization was badly weakened; Syria's military had also been weakened; Israel's siege of Beirut had been lifted and a multinational peacekeeping force of French, Italian, and U.S. troops stationed around the city; a new president of Lebanon had been elected; and the Soviets had lost prestige and credibility because of their quiescence throughout the crisis.

Within days of the Reagan Plan's publication, however, this promising proposal was a dead letter, and the Lebanon situation, which the United States had hoped to put on the back burner again, had collapsed. Although the initial Arab reaction to the Reagan Plan was cautiously favorable, Israel, angered at not having been consulted in advance, objected to virtually every aspect of the proposal and soundly rejected it. The Israelis underscored their objections by immediately approving the construction of ten new settlements on the West Bank.[43]

Like the peace plan itself, the Lebanon situation also began to unravel immediately. Within a month of the plan's issuance, the multinational peacekeeping force had been withdrawn, in the mistaken belief that all was calm; Lebanon's president-elect Bashir Gemayel had been assassinated, apparently by pro-Syrian elements; Israel had moved its troops back into Beirut; Lebanese Christian militiamen loyal to Gemayel and allied with Israel had, with the knowledge of Israeli forces in the vicinity, entered the Palestinian refugee camps of Sabra and Shatila in Beirut and systematically murdered at least eight hundred men, women, and children, possibly many more; and, following the massacre, the multinational force, led by a U.S. Marine contingent, had been returned to Beirut. These developments were the prelude to a further series of disastrous events over the next year and a half, during which, without intending to do so or understanding how to extricate itself, the United States became more and more deeply embroiled in Lebanon's morass, allowed itself to be diverted from pursuing an Arab-Israeli peace settlement, and became not only more closely allied with Israel but deeply estranged from the Arab world.

Concluding after the Sabra and Shatila massacre that the Lebanon situation would have to be tackled before an attempt could be made to begin Arab-Israeli peace talks and deluded by the U.S. success in negotiating the evacuation of PLO forces from Lebanon, Shultz turned his attention to an attempt to secure the departure of Syrian and Israeli forces from the country as well. By explicitly linking progress toward a peace settlement to progress in Lebanon, however, the United States encouraged the Israelis and the Syrians, those most opposed to the Reagan Plan and least eager to work on a peace arrangement for the West Bank, to make as much trouble in Lebanon as possible. The effect was to delay a resolution of the West Bank/Gaza problem while Israel consolidated its control over these territories.[44]

Both because the United States allowed its attention to be diverted to the Lebanon situation and because it was unprepared to confront Israel, which clearly wanted to forestall movement toward peace negotiations, Shultz never pursued the Reagan Plan after Israel's rejection and allowed a promising Arab initiative to die on the vine as well. The administration was clearly disturbed by Israel's continued efforts to expand settlement construction in the West Bank and Gaza, but all the U.S. signals carried a different message to Israel. As had occurred during the Lebanon war, U.S. protests were weak, specifically disavowing sanctions, and for all intents and purposes the administration never again mentioned the Reagan initiative to Israel. Turning to a policy of trying to influence the Israelis by placating them, Shultz and other officials began speaking vaguely of the "leverage given by the possibility of peace" and held out "the objective of peace" as the principal U.S. inducement to Israel, but there was no serious effort to obtain Israeli compliance.[45]

Despite the fact that the Reagan Plan specifically excluded the possibility of independence for the Palestinians or a role in negotiations for the PLO, the PLO and Jordan did not initially reject it. Because the plan seemed to provide a promising basis for discussion, they continued to consider it for several months before finally rejecting it in April 1983, in large measure out of concern that the United States would not be able to bring Israel to the negotiating table. The Arabs had gauged U.S. seriousness about dealing with the Palestinian issue by how it handled the Lebanon problem and concluded that if the Americans were unable to get Israel out of Lebanon, they would have no success getting it out of the West Bank either. Some scholars believe that had there been any reason for the Arabs to expect meaningful U.S. support in the form of pressure on Israel to accept the Reagan Plan, Jordan and the PLO might have been more willing to respond favorably and move beyond ambiguous positions. During the months of meetings between King Hussein and Arafat over whether to accept the Reagan Plan, considerable discussion focused on the likely U.S. response to further Arab concessions. The Arabs, particularly the PLO leaders, were highly skeptical of U.S. sincerity about pursuing peace, but the fact that much of their discussion centered on the possible interplay of Arab concessions and the U.S. response indicates that any reasonable expectation of U.S. movement might have produced greater Arab movement. But in the Reagan years, there was no such expectation.[46]

It is a measure of the extent to which the U.S. attitude on Middle East issues was oriented toward the Israeli perspective that responsibility for the failure of the Reagan Plan has generally been placed on the Arabs and not also on Israel for its outright rejection of the plan or on the United States for its own inertia in pursuing it. Shultz and Reagan themselves blamed the Arabs. Many scholars and perhaps the majority of nonscholarly commentators have also placed the onus on the Arabs. The scholar Steven Spiegel, for instance, in his book *The Other Arab-Israeli Conflict*, concluded a section analyzing the Reagan Plan and reaction to it with the remark that "once again an American Mideast initiative was sacrificed on the altar of intra-Arab rivalry."[47]

The Arabs had actually responded to the Reagan Plan only a week after its issuance with an initiative adopted at an Arab summit held in Fez, Morocco. The United States rejected the Fez Plan, however, despite the fact that it signaled a significant change in Arab attitudes and might have constituted a serious basis for discussion with Washington. With the exception of Libya, all Arab states and the PLO signed on to the Fez Plan. The plan—advocating a UN Security Council guarantee of the right of all states in the region to live in peace and a guarantee of freedom of worship for all religions at holy places—called for Israeli withdrawal from all territories occupied in 1967, including East Jerusalem; the dismantlement of Israeli settlements in the occupied territories; a guarantee of the right of self-determination for the Palestinians; and establishment of an independent Palestinian state with East Jerusalem as its capital. In a preamble, the Fez declaration made reference to a peace plan issued in 1965 by Tunisian President Habib Bourguiba, which had urged acceptance of the 1947 partition plan as the solution to the Palestine problem.[48] Although the Fez Plan did not specifically advocate the right of any state to exist, by urging that all states be allowed to live in peace and accepting the legitimacy of partition, it implicitly recognized Israel and accepted a two-state solution for Palestine.

Given past Arab attitudes, this plan was a highly conciliatory gesture and a significant concession. "Its essence," Palestinian intellectual Walid Khalidi has observed, "was acceptance of the existence of Israel . . . *guaranteed acceptance by the Arabs*"—which had always been Israel's principal demand of the Arabs and a concession that had never before been granted by the Arab side in public and at "such a collective authoritative level." The Arab leaders themselves regarded the plan as a major breakthrough— a "major milestone in the annals of the Arab world," Jordan's King Hussein pronounced; "little short of revolutionary," according to Khalidi.[49]

The United States did not see it that way. Rather than encourage the plan or probe for points of agreement and areas of possible flexibility in the objectionable portions of the Arab position, the Reagan administration essentially disdained the initiative. National Security Council staffer Teicher described it in a later book as not breaking any new ground on the question of recognition of Israel, indicating he had missed the significance of the Arab concessions. Shultz later characterized it as having made the peace process more difficult because of its endorsement of Palestinian statehood. When an Arab League delegation visited Reagan to discuss the plan in October 1982, the United States would not allow a PLO representative to accompany the other Arabs, even though this was the first time the PLO had publicly given its implicit recognition of Israel.[50]

The fact that the United States could ignore a plan that the Arabs regarded as so major a step is an indication of how firm the Reagan administration's mind-set was. Two Israeli journalists, commenting on Israel's equally negative reaction to Arab overtures, captured the limited U.S. frame of reference as well. Speaking of an earlier Saudi Arabian initiative, on which the Fez Plan was based, journalist Amos Elon wrote, "Are we so accustomed to war that we are simply afraid of peace? Are we so taken aback, so angered and unsure of ourselves that we do not even bother to examine whether the Saudi plan . . . is a first step, an opening to a process of negotiation?" Another well known Israeli journalist, Yoel Marcus, noted pointedly that if the PLO were suddenly to offer to negotiate with Israel, "the government would undoubtedly declare a day of national mourning."[51] These two commentaries describe a frame of reference in which the very notion of Arabs and particularly Palestinians offering peace was so foreign as to be frightening. There simply was no room in this mind-set for a PLO that might have been ready to make peace with Israel.

The conclusion to be drawn from the U.S. handling of its own Reagan Plan and the Fez initiative is that, whatever they might have said about the importance of resolving the Palestinian issue, Reagan and Shultz were not interested enough to risk an argument with Israel. Reagan's basic attitude on the Palestinian issue, it will be remembered, was that it was just a "running sore" that could be ignored. Although apparently persuaded by the Lebanon war and by Shultz's early activism that the issue should probably be addressed, he backed down at the first sign of difficulty. Shultz himself had not been prepared for Israel's vehement reaction and was clearly not prepared to press the Israelis hard. He had come to office with a reputation among Israelis and Israeli supporters and in the press for being pro-Arab and was concerned, according to some White House sources, not to confirm Israeli suspicions. Some in the State Department have explained his conversion from occasional critic to strong champion of Israel as a deliberate move intended to escape attacks in the media by pro-Israeli elements.[52] Others have indicated that by the time the United States had extricated itself from the Lebanon morass, Shultz felt so embattled and was so frustrated over his dealings with the Arabs that he simply found it more comfortable to deal with Israel, despite the fact that he was frustrated with Israel as well; he is said to have found "emotional, intellectual, and policy haven with Israel."[53]

By the time Jordan and the PLO finally turned away from the Reagan Plan in April 1983, seven months after it had been issued and Israel had rejected it, the Reagan administration, now deeply involved in attempting to negotiate a peace treaty between Lebanon and Israel, had already put aside its interest in a West Bank solution. In later years it halfheartedly attempted to find a West Bank leader or leaders who would agree to abandon allegiance to the PLO and speak for the Palestinians, and in Reagan's second term Shultz proposed to defuse Palestinian discontent by "improving the quality of life" in the occupied territories through a small aid program and encouragement of private investment.[54] But until the outbreak of the *intifada* in December 1987, very near the end of Reagan's presidency, no serious attempt was made to address the Palestinian political issue or to ease the conditions of Palestinian life under the "iron-fist" policy the Israelis imposed in the mid-1980s.

For the remainder of Reagan's presidency, the administration and particularly Shultz had what must be called a mental block about the PLO. Administration officials constantly spoke—in an oddly disconnected way, as if there were no existing spokesperson for the Palestinians—about how difficult it was to find someone to represent the Palestinians. Assistant Secretary of State Richard Murphy, for instance, speaking at a forum in 1988, said, "Who represents the Palestinians is something the Arabs need to deal with"[55]—not recognizing that the Arabs had already dealt with the question. The failure in general to recognize the reality of Palestinian allegiance to the PLO and often even to say the words *Palestine Liberation Organization* or *PLO*, as if the problem would vanish if it were not mentioned, was typical of the way the administration dealt with the issue throughout two presidential terms.

During a meeting in March 1988, at the height of the *intifada*, with a prominent Palestinian American, Shultz himself spoke about the "dilemma" of finding someone to represent the Palestinians. The Palestinian American recalls the conversation as puzzling and found the way Shultz was able to ignore reality jarring. Acknowledging that Jordan could not represent the Palestinians in peace negotiations, Shultz began talking about the need to find credible and representative Palestinians to speak for the Palestinian people. The Palestinian American remembers:

> So I said, "But everybody knows who represents Palestinians." And he said, "Who?" And I said, "The PLO." . . . He put his hand up, . . . and he said, "I don't want to talk about the PLO." I said, "Why not?" And . . . he said, "It's too complicated." . . . That's literally what he said—it's too complicated, and it's too involved. . . . And I said, "Well, you know, it isn't for the Palestinians." And he said, "Well, let's not talk about it." So I said, "Fine." I mean, what's one to say? He just didn't want to talk about it. It was strange. We were at a dead end right there.[56]

It is clear that Shultz's blind spot had to do specifically with the PLO rather than with the Palestinians and their aspirations. He had always had an understanding at some level of Palestinian needs and had never totally lost the feeling he came into office with that resolving the Palestinian issue was essential to a resolution of the Arab-Israeli conflict. Whatever empathy Shultz may have had for the Palestinians' situation at occasional moments during the Lebanon invasion or later during the *intifada* did not, however, overcome his determination to shun the PLO. His inability to see past what he considered the PLO obstacle interfered directly with U.S. policymaking.

The United States, Israel, and the world were genuinely shocked by the Sabra and Shatila massacre in September 1982, but there was in the reactions an element of denial and unconcern that throws an interesting sidelight on the mind-set through which Palestinians were generally observed.

Shultz was "shaken and appalled" and believed that Israel had been complicit in the massacre.[57] As part of the agreement on the evacuation of the PLO in August 1982, the United States had officially guaranteed the safety of Palestinian civilians left behind, having received formal assurances from both Israel and the leadership of the Lebanese Christian militias that civilians would not be harmed.[58] When the United States precipitately withdrew its peacekeeping contingent, however, leading to the withdrawal of the French and Italian elements of the multinational force as well, there was no one to enforce the guarantee, and the massacre occurred ten days later. U.S. officials felt a moral responsibility for having permitted the circumstances in which a massacre could occur.

Reaction to the massacre nonetheless showed a lack of concern for the Palestinians, having to do, it must be assumed, with their generally unsavory image as terrorists. In the United States, despite the sense of moral responsibility, the massacre was soon forgotten and never had an impact on policy. In Israel, although a special judicial committee of inquiry found Defense Minister Sharon and commanders on the scene responsible and Sharon was dismissed from the cabinet, no judicial punishment was imposed on anyone shown to have been involved.

British journalist Robert Fisk, who was in Beirut at the time and is a careful observer of how the conventional wisdom affects thinking on Palestinian issues, has described an incident that demonstrates the widespread image of Palestinians as terrorists and the mind-set this stereotype can produce in those absolutely convinced of its veracity. Fisk walked through both the Sabra and the Shatila camps after the massacre was discovered. While in Shatila, he was ordered repeatedly by a group of Israeli officers to leave but refused.

> One of the three soldiers put his hand on my arm. "There are terrorists in the camp and you will be killed." That's not true, I said. Everyone there is dead. Can't you *smell* them? The soldier looked at me in disbelief. . . . [Israeli soldiers patrolling the camp] believed—they were possessed of an absolute certainty and conviction—that "terrorists" were in Cha-

tila. . . . I walked alongside these soldiers. . . . After some minutes, they grew used to my presence. So I met Moshe, Raphael, Benny, all carrying their heavy rifles down the road past Chatila, all fearful of terrorists. Terrorists, terrorists, terrorists. The word came up in every sentence, like a punctuation mark. . . . But hadn't the PLO *left* Beirut? Had he not seen the evacuation or read about it in the papers? "They didn't leave," he said. "Lots of them are still here. That is why we are here." But everyone in this area of Chatila was dead. "I don't know about that. But there are terrorists everywhere here." [59]

An element of denial and disbelief was prevalent throughout the media as well. For instance, while *Time* magazine immediately ran the massacre as a cover story, its competitor *Newsweek* chose the death of Princess Grace of Monaco in a road accident, rather than the massacre, as its first post-atrocity cover story. When *Newsweek* did put the massacre on the cover the following week, its story concerned the effect on Israel, not on the Palestinians. The cover headline read "Israel in Torment"; subsidiary articles concerned "The Anguish of American Jews" and "The Troubled Soul of Israel." Whereas the *New York Times* published an editorial forthrightly condemning the massacre, the *Wall Street Journal* minimized it, treating this atrocity as little different from others occurring in Lebanon over the years, excusing Israel's role, and lamenting the attempt by "enemies of the U.S. and Israel" to convert what was a revenge attack by Christian Arabs into a "political victory for the left." [60]

Fisk also recounts a revealing conversation among some U.S. correspondents who could not absorb the fact of the massacre. When he returned from the camps to the Associated Press (AP) office from which he filed his dispatches to London, the AP bureau chief, Steve Hindy, was arguing with AP correspondent Bill Foley about what Foley and another correspondent had seen.

> "Are you sure it was a massacre?" [Hindy asked.]
> Foley was waving pictures in front of him. "Look at them Steve, look at them. You haven't been there yet."
> "But how many dead are there?"
> "What the fuck does it matter? It was a massacre."
> "Yes, but was it? People have been killed in Lebanon like this before."
> I sat in the corner of the room, listening to this. . . . When does a killing become an outrage? When does an atrocity become a massacre? . . . When is a massacre not a massacre? When the figures are too low? Or when the massacre is carried out by Israel's friends rather than Israel's enemies?
> That, I suspected, was what this argument was about. If Syrian troops

had crossed into Israel, surrounded a kibbutz and allowed their Palestinian allies to slaughter the Jewish inhabitants, no Western news agency
would waste its time afterwards arguing about whether or not it should
be called a massacre.[61]

In a frame of reference in which Israel has always been the focal point,
its Palestinian enemies are almost by definition less important; there can be
only one focal point. If the conventional wisdom gives Israel a central emotional and political place, there cannot also be a central place for anyone
else. Thus, it becomes easy to dismiss Palestinians as terrorists and, having
done so, to feel less outrage if they are victimized. The word *terrorist*, Fisk
observes, "had become a murderous word, a word that had helped to bring
about this atrocity"[62]—a word also that made ignoring the political fate
of the Palestinians because they were "terrorists" that much easier for
policymakers already accustomed to viewing Palestinians from an Israeli
perspective.

The United States essentially gave up the policy initiative in the Middle
East after its Lebanon debacle, retreating into inaction and a closer alliance
with Israel that allowed the Israelis to take the policy lead and gave them a
free hand to proceed with settlement construction and a crackdown on Palestinians in the West Bank and Gaza. U.S. policy in Lebanon had been a series of miscalculations, some based on Israel's actions and policy advice, but
by the time the U.S. Marine contingent was withdrawn in 1984, the United
States had concluded that the only way to ensure stability in the area was
to work closely with Israel.[63] Shultz was angry with the Arabs for not having cooperated with his efforts in Lebanon and extremely gun-shy about
again becoming involved in mediation efforts in the Middle East, and so
he turned to Israel. In October 1983, President Reagan signed a National
Security Decision Directive formalizing the administration's decision to
raise the level of cooperation with Israel. Undersecretary of State Lawrence
Eagleburger was sent to Israel a few days after the directive was signed to
discuss closer strategic ties, and a month later the strategic alliance was
sealed with the signing of a memorandum of understanding.[64]

Even Israel was surprised by the move.[65] It was an unusual twist of logic
to forge closer strategic ties with Israel in the immediate aftermath of Israeli actions that had involved the United States in a civil war in which it
had no direct interest. But the rationale behind rewarding Israel gives a picture of how tightly the Israel-centered frame of reference bound the thinking of policymakers and limited their ability to see beyond Israel's interests.

Shultz, for instance, described in his memoirs a catalog of U.S. grievances against Israel with regard to Lebanon but in the end was able to think only of the U.S. need "to lift the albatross of Lebanon from Israel's neck." [66] Similarly, Teicher describes the genesis of the policy of closer ties with Israel as a perceived need to "restore Israeli confidence in American reliability." The United States had made so many mistakes in Lebanon and had so often criticized Israeli policy in Reagan's first two years, Teicher writes, that Israel's "confidence in the U.S. commitment to Israel's security had weakened." [67]

This policy marked the beginning of a period of unprecedented closeness in the U.S.-Israeli relationship. The November 1983 memorandum of understanding established a joint military-political planning group that met regularly and effectively institutionalized the relationship. [68] Thomas Dine, executive director of the principal pro-Israel lobby, AIPAC, quoted Shultz as saying that his goal was to build institutional arrangements in such a way that if in the future a secretary of state was less than wholly supportive of Israel, he would not be able to overcome the bureaucratic ties that existed between Israel and the United States. [69]

AIPAC was a major force behind the intensive drive to forge closer ties with Israel, and in a real sense AIPAC became a partner in U.S. Middle East policymaking in the mid-1980s. But this was a symbiotic relationship; AIPAC channeled U.S. policy, but it could not have been successful had the administration not in the first place been operating from a frame of reference centered on Israel. Led after 1980 by Dine, an energetic former congressional aide who aggressively pushed expanded contacts with Congress and a vastly expanded program of policy analysis, AIPAC made a major effort to increase its membership, its budget, and its influence in Congress and among policymakers after failing in an attempt to block the proposed sale of AWACS surveillance aircraft to Saudi Arabia in late 1981. Although AIPAC lost the AWACS battle in a head-to-head confrontation with President Reagan—who regarded the sale as an important part of the administration's program of building strategic consensus and came to see the battle in Congress as a test of his own prestige—the struggle actually became a victory for the pro-Israel lobby, for it tended to demonstrate graphically just how limited policymaker freedom of action was on sensitive issues involving Israel. On the one hand, the struggle showed that a determined administration can do enough arm-twisting and cajoling to push an issue opposed by Israel through Congress, but, on the other hand, it demonstrated the heavy and exhausting expenditure of political capital that can be involved in such a fight. [70] In fact, no one in the Reagan administration was willing to attempt such a fight again. "We blew three fuses with those guys," one former White House official said, "and we don't want to go to the mat with them again."[71]

AIPAC's grass-roots support grew immensely after the AWACS fight. Both its membership—primarily among U.S. Jews but including as well a small number of evangelical Christians—and its budget quadrupled between 1980 and 1987. Its propaganda effort also increased. Dine believed, according to one source, that policymakers need to be supplied with arguments and that anyone who wrote books and papers that policymakers read would effectively "own" the policymakers. When he took over the directorship of AIPAC, he hired two Middle East experts of a pro-Israeli bent who began publishing a series of position papers focusing on Israel's strategic value to the United States. One of these AIPAC experts was Martin Indyk, an Australian who would later cofound and direct a pro-Israeli think tank, the Washington Institute for Near East Policy, which had a major influence on Bush administration policymaking, and would serve in several key positions inside the Clinton administration.[72]

As Begin had argued unsuccessfully with Carter, the AIPAC experts and others who now advocated closer strategic ties with Israel explicitly discarded the notion that the U.S. commitment to Israel was a moral one, for this implied that Israel was dependent on and possibly even a liability to the United States. The AIPAC papers, directed not at the membership but specifically at policymakers, found a particularly receptive audience inside an administration already convinced of the need to guard against Soviet aggressiveness and already convinced of Israel's strategic value. By 1987, the United States had formally designated Israel as a "major non-NATO ally," which gave it access to military technology not otherwise available.[73]

Congress became so pro-Israeli under AIPAC's tutelage in this period that as two Israeli journalists have observed, it embraced virtually every legislative initiative suggested by the lobby. Lobby officials boasted, probably without exaggeration, that any legislation important to Israel started with a dependable base of two hundred supporters in the House and up to forty-five senators. Members of Congress relied on AIPAC as a source of information on all issues related to Israel and the Middle East, often asked AIPAC to draft speeches, and consulted the lobby group on pending legislation, including annual budget bills.[74] By the mid-1980s, it had become so accepted that Congress was almost automatically pro-Israeli and particularly that Jewish members of Congress would always support Israel that the following statement in a 1985 book by correspondent Wolf Blitzer raised no eyebrows. After describing former Connecticut Senator Abraham Ribicoff's frequent criticism of Israel during the Carter administration and support for Carter's policies, Blitzer wrote that, despite occasional lapses like Ribicoff's, "most Jewish members of Congress accepted their special responsibilities" to Israel.[75]

AIPAC's heightened activism gave it power in policymaking circles throughout the Reagan years. Administration officials took to consulting and sometimes negotiating with AIPAC in advance of presenting legislation in order to help assure passage. The lobby became so powerful and so ambitious that it even attempted openly to exert influence on the staff choices of presidential candidates. As early as a year and a half before the 1988 election, almost all the several Democratic and Republican candidates had already submitted to interviews with AIPAC to answer questions about their policy positions on the Middle East.[76]

The administration's close cooperation with Israel and AIPAC's heavy involvement in policy formulation foreclosed the possibility that the Palestinian point of view might penetrate policymaker considerations. State Department Middle East experts, almost completely cut out of the decision-making process, lamented that where once there was a two-track policy, now only Israel's interests were considered.[77] AIPAC's presence in the policymaking process had a stifling effect on debate. Not only were most officials who would speak for the Arab perspective excluded from policymaking councils, but fewer and fewer officials of any political bent were willing to raise options known to be anathema to AIPAC or likely to encounter strong resistance in Congress. As a result, as one official remarked at the time, "a lot of real analysis is not even getting off people's desks for fear of what the lobby will do."[78]

The Reagan administration's unusually close ties to Israel also tended to have a chilling effect on debate inside Israel, discouraging opposition to the Likud government's annexationist policies and undermining the efforts of the sizable number of Israelis who would have been prepared, if they had received some encouragement, to resist the Likud's uncompromising stance on the Palestinian issue and the peace process. The Israeli electorate was more or less evenly split in the 1980s between those opposed to any movement toward peace negotiations and those ready to make some compromises on West Bank issues in order to move the process forward. Direct and obvious pressure by the United States might have tended, particularly with a leader like Begin, to unite Israelis to resist, but psychological pressure might have had a telling impact. As former State Department official Saunders has noted, just the knowledge among Israelis that Israel's extreme positions might jeopardize U.S. support in the peace process would probably have strengthened the hand of moderate Israelis.[79] Israeli scholars and diplomats have indicated repeatedly that in fact U.S. acquiescence in Israel's uncompromising stance tended to encourage the Likud's resistance to compromise. Some believe, for instance, that there could have been a showdown between the two Israeli camps as early as 1982, in the aftermath of the Lebanon invasion, if a serious plan for resuming the peace process had been placed on the table and vigorously pursued. The Reagan Plan constituted such a plan, but the administration's failure to work for Israeli acceptance stifled an internal contest in Israel. Others believe that the absence of U.S. pressure delivered to Israelis the dangerous message that there was no cost to retaining the occupied territories and undermined any pressures on the leadership from inside Israel to change the status quo.[80]

In late 1982 *New York Times* editorial page editor Max Frankel wrote a series of columns reporting that opposition Labor Party leaders had privately indicated to him that they wanted the United States to exert pressure on Begin's government and hasten its end by reducing the level of economic assistance. Labor officials denied Frankel's allegations, but there seems to be little doubt as to their authenticity. Some saw the Labor overture as nothing more than a cynical election ploy, but the appeal was more likely a plea to the United States for help in moving Israel toward moderation and peace negotiations. Labor's plea found virtually no listeners in the United States. Congress increased aid levels over those requested by the administration in December 1982, and the White House responded to Frankel's columns by assuring Israel that Washington would never use pressure to advance the peace process.[81]

By the mid-1980s, the frame of reference in which Middle East policy was pursued had become constricted to an unprecedented degree. Everything converged during the Reagan years to create this quantum tilt toward Israel. It is common to attribute all pressures in this direction to the power of the pro-Israel lobby and the electoral strength of the U.S. Jewish community, but this explanation is probably too facile. Unquestionably, AIPAC grew exponentially in size and power during the Reagan years, and it was a strong limiting influence on policymaking. But, far from causing the administration's pro-Israeli tilt, AIPAC was able to grow precisely because the administration provided a friendly, fertile atmosphere in which its activists and analyses had a ready audience. AIPAC helped to focus policymaking, providing certain themes, such as Israel's strategic value, that channeled policymaker thinking, and by its vigilance and activism it helped to guarantee that the administration followed a firm and unwavering pro-Israeli course. But with an administration of the Reagan team's mind-set, the lobby did not make or control policy, largely because it did not need to. AIPAC helped to give increased definition to the country's and the Reagan administration's frame of reference in this era, but it did not create that frame of reference, and ultimately it would not have thrived without the administration. The lobby was only as strong as those it leaned on were inclined to bend.

Two trends in U.S. public opinion on Israel and the Palestinian-Israeli conflict emerged in the 1980s. One trend was toward increased criticism of Israel, particularly after its invasion of Lebanon. The second was largely a reaction to the first, a concerted effort by Israel and its U.S. supporters to counter the unfavorable image; this trend was facilitated by the fact that Americans had a large and basically unchanging reservoir of affection for Israel and tended to make excuses for its actions. Ironically, although the level of public criticism of Israel had never been higher than during the early and mid-1980s and the Palestinians received increased media attention and public sympathy during this time, the level of media sympathy for Israel and the degree to which Israel's supporters attempted to guide press treatment of Middle East issues remained extremely high.

The United States began to see a different, less benign side of Israel during the Lebanon invasion, with nightly television pictures of Israeli planes bombing civilian targets in Beirut and news of the Sabra and Shatila massacre occurring while Israel controlled the city. Israel's tight censorship of reporting from Lebanon antagonized reporters. To counter this unfavorable impression, Israeli supporters in the United States went into high gear to bring back the image of old. In 1983, the American Jewish Congress organized a conference in Jerusalem to seek ways to improve the Israeli image. Chaired by a U.S. advertising executive and attended by advertising, communications, and public-relations experts from the United States and journalists from both Israel and the United States. the conference launched a *hasbara*, or propaganda, campaign to sell Israel to the U.S. media. The themes to be emphasized were Israel's strategic value to the United States, as well as its affinity with Western culture and values, its security problem and physical vulnerability, and its fervent desire for peace in contrast to the Arabs' supposed opposition to peace.[82]

Among other activities, the Hasbara Project organized an internship program for Israeli career diplomats to train them in the United States in communications and public relations. The Israeli government also made its own much more direct effort to influence media treatment of Middle East issues. Menachem Shalev, press officer for the Israeli consulate in New York in 1985 and 1986, told a reporter that he and other Israeli press attaches regularly received "favors"—in the form of sympathetic coverage of Israel or help in getting negative stories killed—from U.S. Jewish news bookers and producers who he claimed were more loyal to Israel than to their employers. Shalev said his principal function was to help shape the U.S. media's perceptions of Israel and the Arabs. To this end, he was in constant contact with journalists, called news and talk-show producers daily to determine what stories and guests they intended to have on, and then, in a "kind of joint formulation of ideas," suggested story lines or different or additional guests.[83]

The efforts specifically made to counter Israel's unfavorable image had a powerful impact. Some of the reporters and networks who had been harshly critical of Israel during the Lebanon war were subjected to such strong pressures by pro-Israeli media monitors that they softened the tone of their coverage or explicitly apologized. Shalev observed that after "the hullabaloo over Lebanon [coverage], the press doesn't do anything without calling us for comment." The mere knowledge that supporters of Israel were ready to call newsrooms and write letters to the editor about critical coverage of Israel tended to produce self-censorship among the press.[84] For instance, NBC correspondent John Chancellor broadcast a report from Beirut in the midst of an Israeli bombing campaign against the city in July 1982 and referred to "savage Israel" and "an imperialist state that we never knew existed before." A week later, however, broadcasting from Jerusalem, he said his Beirut report had been a "mistake" and that he now believed Israel had not intended to lay siege to Beirut but had "bumbled into" it.[85]

In fact, the mind-set in most of the media was so pro-Israeli, the residual affection for Israel so strong, that direct pressures often only reinforced an existing tendency among the media to soft-pedal criticism. Whatever Israeli warts may have been revealed by the Lebanon invasion, the press still tended to accept the Israeli spin on stories more or less unquestioningly basically because this was the way most journalists felt, whether they were Jews or non-Jews, and also the way in general that their readers and listeners felt. A retired CBS executive said in the mid-1980s that although every good journalist makes an effort to be fair and unbiased, "over the years, I've detected—and it was certainly true of my own news judgments—that Israel is given the 'benefit of the doubt' whenever possible." An ABC News correspondent attributed the pro-Israeli slant in television newsrooms to the perception of editors that there was a "tremendous interest in and sympathy for Israel" among audiences.[86]

The corollary of this sympathy remained, as had long been the case among journalists, an element of hostility to the Palestinians and most Arabs. What some journalists called a subtle and some a not-so-subtle prejudice against Arabs was so common in newspaper and television newsrooms that few hesitated to talk openly about it. "TV news executives in New York figure that the American population cares less and less about what happens to people the darker their skin is," said one television correspondent.[87] Despite greater interest in the Palestinians since the 1970s, real knowledge and understanding of the Palestinian problem required a more sophisticated, in-depth analysis than was possible in television's forty- or sixty-second news spots. Stereotyping was easy, and there was not the time in television's short-news-item format to counter stereotypes that had been built up over a century or more. The old clichés inevitably influenced what journalists aired in the 1980s.

The concerted effort made by Israel's supporters during the 1980s to feature Israel more prominently in news coverage was accompanied by a major effort to delegitimize Palestinian nationalism. One of the major themes in this campaign was the "Jordan-is-Palestine" position propounded by Israel's right wing and adopted by neoconservative supporters of Israel in the United States. The argument was that because, according to Likud doctrine, Jordan had been part of Palestine until separated by Britain and given a semi-independent status under King Abdullah, a Palestinian state therefore already existed in Jordan.[88] Reagan himself frequently put forth this position during his 1980 election campaign. He observed in one speech that Jordan had 80 percent of the responsibility for handling the Palestinian refugee problem and Israel 20 percent because, as he contended, this was the ratio by which the former Palestine Mandate had been divided. At other times, Reagan urged that the refugees be assimilated into Jordan, arguing, like the Likud, that Jordan was a Palestinian state.[89] In fact, the entire line of argument was a Likud creation designed to undermine the notion of Palestinian separateness. Jordan was not considered part of Palestine by anyone except the Israeli right wing, principally not by the Palestinian people, who traced their origins to the area west of the Jordan River that became Israel, the West Bank, and Gaza. Jordan did not consider itself a Palestinian state.

One of the major instruments in the campaign to undermine Palestinian identity was a lengthy book published in 1984, *From Time Immemorial* by Joan Peters, which purported to demonstrate through voluminous research that most of those who claimed to be Palestinians dispossessed by Israel were not from Palestine at all but had immigrated from elsewhere in the Arab world only a few years before Israel was created.[90] Far from having been dispossessed by Israel, Peters maintained, these Arabs simply re-turned to their original homes during the 1948 war; the number of true refugees from Palestine was relatively small. One Palestinian American scholar described the Peters book as representing "a natural analogue to the concerted, sustained Israeli attack upon Palestinian nationalism"—with the difference that whereas arguments against the existence of the Pales-tinians had previously been confined to specialized journals or local Israeli audiences, now they were being made for a general U.S. audience. The book's principal thesis, the scholar commented caustically, is something like this: "If you thought you were a Palestinian, you were wrong. You really came from someplace else, and therefore *are* someone else. . . . You are not who you say you are because I can prove you were never really you." [91]

The book was initially hailed throughout the country as a startling piece of original research that would dramatically alter the course of debate in the Middle East. Carrying endorsements on the jacket by luminaries such as Barbara Tuchman, Saul Bellow, Angier Biddle Duke, Elie Wiesel, and Arthur Goldberg, and acknowledging research assistance from well-known scholars such as Bernard Lewis, P. J. Vatikiotis, Elie Kedourie, and Martin Gilbert, the book was reviewed favorably and at great length in numerous mainstream periodicals. [92] Saul Bellow called it the first "clear account of the origins of the Palestinians," which would "dissolve the claims made by nationalist agitators." Daniel Pipes, writing in *Commentary* magazine, declared that the book showed that the Palestinian problem "lacks firm grounding" and "reinforces the point that the real problem in the Middle East has little to do with Palestinian-Arab rights."

The book's fame was short-lived. Careful analysis by Israeli, European, and a few U.S. scholars revealed that Peters had fabricated some evidence, misquoted other evidence to suit her argument, omitted evidence that did not support her case, and plagiarized from old Zionist propaganda tracts. [93] The major critical review, an analysis by Israeli historian Yehoshua Porath labeling Peters's thesis a set of "tired and discredited arguments," appeared in the *New York Review of Books* in January 1986—almost two years af-ter the book's publication. [94] Although the book was discredited, none of the journals that had initially published favorable reviews issued retractions, and no scholar who assisted Peters or endorsed the book dissociated him-self. *Commentary* magazine, in fact, ran a second favorable review in mid-1986 that criticized the critiques. [95]

In 1987 and 1988, when Israeli scholars Benny Morris and Avi Shlaim published major revisionist histories of the period surrounding Israel's creation—histories that did change the course of debate on the Palestinian problem—none of the mainstream periodicals, with the exception of the *New York Times*, that had praised Peters's anti-Palestinian book reviewed the revisionist books at all.[96]

The Peters book was accompanied in the summer of 1984 by publication of a novel about Palestinians by Leon Uris, who in the 1950s had introduced a generation of Americans to a heroic image of Israel with the novel *Exodus*. Uris's 1984 novel, *The Haj*, about a Palestinian family during the time of Israel's creation, was a strong anti-Arab diatribe that attempted to delegitimize the Palestinians via fiction. As in *Exodus* a quarter century earlier, *The Haj*'s anti-heroes were cowardly, ignorant, sexually deviant, and unmotivated by any sense of nationalism. Although less popular than *Exodus*, *The Haj* managed to acquaint another generation of Americans with Uris's picture of Palestinians. The book was on the hardback bestseller list for five months in 1984 and on the paperback bestseller list for three months the following year.[97]

The self-perpetuating aspect of the heavy media and publishing attention to Israel perpetuated in turn the minimal and stereotypical coverage of the Palestinians. Jim Lehrer, co-anchor of PBS's *MacNeil-Lehrer News Hour*, was asked in 1982 why his own and other programs always did more items on Israel. "Because," he said, "Israel is more involved in the news. You can argue with the definition of news, but it is a fact that the United States is the major ally of Israel, and that one-fourth of all U.S. aid goes to Israel."[98] This phenomenon becomes a never-ending cycle: Israel is more involved in the news because it receives more U.S. aid, which in turn is because Israel is more involved in the news, is seen more often on programs like Lehrer's, and is more often on the minds of Americans.

Certainly not all reporting was automatically pro-Israeli or Israel-centered. The *Washington Post* ran a hard-hitting series of articles on Israel's occupation practices in the early 1980s, and other papers, particularly the *Christian Science Monitor*, were often critical of Israel and careful to report the Palestinian perspective. The weekly periodical the *Nation* sharply criticized Israel during the Lebanon invasion and recognized the PLO as the voice of the Palestinians, advocating that it be included in the peace process.[99] But throughout the 1980s much of the press nonetheless tended to follow a script on Palestinian-Israeli issues. A journalist assigned to Jerusalem in 1983 and 1984 observed that the self-perpetuating nature of the conventional wisdom on Palestinian-Israeli issues was built into the system. Editors, he maintained, were concerned not to be out of step with other media and therefore expected their correspondents to report what other journalists reported. "Being attentive to what others reported initiated newcomers into what passed for 'facts' in the Middle East," he said. "They obediently learned to file story after story that were but part of a larger story, hatched from a line of logic they had brought in on the plane with them and reified by colleagues who shared the same certainties. . . . Reporters invariably sought out sources who sustained the taken for granted." [100] The conventional wisdom was self-perpetuating for the Reagan administration as well, which tended even more than the press to follow a prepared script unquestioningly on Palestinian-Israeli issues.

During the *intifada*, Leon Wieseltier, literary critic of the *New Republic* and a leading U.S. Jewish commentator, wrote an article aptly describing the conventional wisdom as understood by Jews in the United States— a way of perceiving the situation that in fact applied not only to Jews but to much of U.S. opinion. Wieseltier listed what he called "received Jewish ideas about the Israeli-Palestinian conflict": that Israel had not asked for the occupied territories; that Israel had no alternative but to continue control of the territories; that Israel treated the Palestinians under its control better than the Arab states did; that Israel could not cope with terrorists; that all Israel's difficulties were the media's fault. Observing that these ideas either were not true or were beside the point, Wieseltier said they were "powerful platitudes" that served to provide Jews with a kind of "intellectual insulation" against reality. "They protect Jewish consciousness," he wrote, "against the detonation of something it has come to cherish: the status quo . . . a comfortable state of suspension" in which the need for serious decisions is deferred.[101]

Wieseltier's so-called received ideas about the Palestinian-Israeli conflict were not just Jewish ideas but those that most Reagan administration policymakers came to office harboring. With a frame of reference already set in an Israeli mold, Reagan and his team seemed to take in primarily ideas that reinforced rather than altered that mind-set. Policymakers took many of their ideas from the elite media, represented particularly by such influential periodicals as *Commentary* and the *New Republic*. *Commentary* editor Norman Podhoretz, an unapologetic propagandist for Israel, observed in the mid-1980s that although the circulation of periodicals like his was small, the ideas that, in his words, "*run government* or are a part of public debate" originated precisely in these small journals of opinion.[102] Podhoretz's statement may have been too sweeping as a general matter, but for the Reagan administration it was probably no exaggeration. Podhoretz was one of the founders of the neoconservative movement, *Commentary* was neoconservatism's leading mouthpiece, and President Reagan was its preeminent policy exponent. On Middle East issues, the *New Republic,* published by another champion of Israel, Martin Peretz, also shared the administration's point of view.

Both Podhoretz and Peretz were vociferous and emotional in their support of Israel. Podhoretz was one of the most vocal advocates of the position that no U.S. Jew should ever criticize Israel[103] and that much if not all of the criticism Israel received during and after the Lebanon invasion, from Jews as well as non-Jews, was motivated by anti-Semitism. His 1982 article "J'Accuse" was a blistering attack on critics of Israel and still stands out as a landmark defense of Israel.[104] Peretz is said to be so emotionally involved with Israel that debate is generally impossible at the *New Republic,* which the *Jerusalem Post* once hailed as "the single most favorable American voice on Israel." He not only supports Israel but is also apparently emotional about his hostility to the Palestinians, regarding Palestinian nationalism as illegitimate and Palestinian culture as inherently violent.[105]

Members of the Reagan administration wrote for both *Commentary* and the *New Republic,* on Middle East as well as other topics, and members of the administration undoubtedly read both journals. The interchange of ideas was apparently frequent. Both *Commentary* and the administration, for instance, began in the early 1980s to put heavy emphasis on Israel's democratic nature, stretching their analysis to the point of seeming to indicate that Israel's actions were excusable because it was a democracy and its Arab neighbors were not. Podhoretz's article "J'Accuse," for example, concluded on the following note: "Hostility toward Israel is a sure sign of failing faith in and support for the virtues and values of Western civilization in general and of America in particular. How else are we to interpret a political position that, in a conflict between democracy and its antidemocratic enemies, is so dead set against the democratic side?" Podhoretz ignored the undemocratic nature of Israel's rule over West Bank and Gaza Palestinians. Moreover, implicitly equating "democratic" with "moral" allowed him and others of Israel's vocal supporters to equate "nondemocratic" with "immoral." It also allowed them, by concentrating on the element of democracy, to ignore whatever might have been deemed not moral about Israel's practices in the occupied territories.

The preoccupation with Israel's democracy became a new element of the administration's frame of reference as well, allowing it also to ignore Israeli practices in the occupied territories and in Lebanon. Shultz used a variation on the democracy theme in an essay he wrote, while still in office, for a book on terrorism edited by Benjamin Netanyahu, then Israel's ambassador to the UN. Assuming that the principal goal of terrorism was specifically to undermine democracy, and dismissing any notion that terrorists might have other, legitimate goals, Shultz wrote that wherever it takes place, terrorism "is directed in an important sense against *us,* the democracies, against our most basic values and often our fundamental strategic interests. . . . How tragic it would be if democratic societies so lost confidence in their own moral legitimacy that they lost sight of the obvious: that violence directed against democracy or the hopes for democracy lacks fundamental justification." Violence on behalf of democracy, however, was justifiable, according to Shultz. "Resort to arms in behalf of democracy against repressive regimes or movements is, indeed," he wrote, "a fight for freedom, since there may be no other way that freedom can be achieved." [106] Shultz may or may not have taken his cue from Podhoretz and the neoconservatives, but the similarity between Podhoretz's indictment of the moral failure of any society that does not support Israel and Shultz's lament about society's lost moral legitimacy is striking.

The emphasis on Israel's democratic nature proved to be a powerful shield for Israel against strong criticism throughout much of the 1980s, at least until the start of the *intifada.* Even those—including, occasionally, administration officials—who did criticize Israel's continued occupation of the West Bank and Gaza usually expressed concern for what the occupation was doing to Israel rather than for what its consequences were for the Palestinians. The common theme of these friendly critics was that if Israel annexed the occupied territories, either it would cease to be a democracy if it denied democratic rights to the Palestinians, or it would lose its character as a Jewish state if it incorporated Palestinians into Israel. The critics generally viewed the prospects from an Israeli point of view: it was said that the Zionist dream was becoming a "nightmare"; the higher birthrate among Palestinians was considered a demographic "threat" that would overwhelm Jewish numbers. These arguments, which became part of the lore and the frame of reference of the 1980s, ignored the Palestinian side of the equation.

Increasingly, as Israel's Likud government hardened its position throughout the 1980s, debate tended to be closed off in the United States, both inside and outside the government, and even dissident voices from Israel were muzzled. I. F. Stone, the well-known U.S. Jewish journalist and commentator, had complained in the late 1970s that he knew of several leading U.S. journalists who were fearful of writing anything at all sympathetic to the Palestinians because doing so always brought a deluge of letters charging anti-Semitism, and he wondered how "wise solutions [could] be reached and the opportunity for peace rescued when . . . dissident voices are hardly heard here above a whisper." [107] Debate did not take place among policymakers either. Just as the United States failed to probe the PLO's frequent overtures for signs of flexibility or seriously to debate the merits and the means of including the PLO in the negotiating process, it did not engage the Israelis in meaningful discussion of the peace process either. Saunders noted in the mid-1980s that, despite fundamental U.S.-Israeli disagreement over West Bank policy, high levels of the two governments had not had "a profound discussion on the road we are traveling together" since the late 1970s. [108] At one of the most critical stages of the Palestinian-Israeli conflict, public and policy debate on this most critical of issues had effectively ceased, and the situation was being allowed to drift.

Two trends emerged in the 1980s that tended to point away from the kind of reflexive acquiescence in Israel's position on the peace process that the Reagan administration showed, but in neither case were Reagan policymakers inclined to pay significant attention. The first of these trends involved U.S. public opinion. Although Americans had always been, and continued in the 1980s to be, far more sympathetic in emotional terms toward Israel than toward the Arabs in general or the Palestinians, an in-depth study of public opinion polls taken from the late 1970s through the mid-1980s indicated that a significant segment of the public believed as a practical matter that the Palestinians had the right to establish an independent state in the West Bank and Gaza and that the PLO should be involved in peace negotiations—despite the fact that the PLO and Arafat himself were consistently viewed in a negative light. The study showed that the public's readiness to criticize Israel had risen and that the portion of the public inclined toward automatic, hard-core support for any and all positions of the Israeli government was only 25 percent. [109]

At least one poll demonstrated dramatically that when given additional factual information about the Palestinian-Israeli situation, respondents tended to support the notion of Palestinian independence in greater numbers. In May 1982, Republican pollster Richard Wirthlin's organization conducted a survey that probed respondents' views increasingly deeply by supplying more information and asking follow-up questions. Respondents were initially asked, for instance, "In 1947, the United States supported a UN proposal for both a Palestinian and Israeli state. Do you feel the Palestinians should have the right to establish this state?" A total of 76 percent said yes, while 11 percent said no, and 13 percent had no opinion. The one-quarter of respondents who had said no or who had no opinion were then asked, "If you knew that half of the 4.5 million Palestinians in the world

are stateless refugees and the majority of the remaining half live under Israeli occupation in the West Bank and Gaza, would you feel that the Palestinians should have the right to establish a state of their own?" With this
new information, 69 percent of these previously negative respondents now
said yes. The additional increment of knowledge provided by the second
question brought the overall total of those who favored Palestinian independence to over 90 percent.[110] These results demonstrate how thoroughly the reasons for the Palestinian-Israeli conflict had dropped out of
most Americans' consciousness and the difference gaining some part of this
knowledge makes in the public's attitudes.

There is no evidence that the Reagan administration was even aware
of this poll—although it was conducted, ironically, by a Republic Party
pollster—and certainly none that the findings had any impact on policy
decisions. Palestinian American scholar Fouad Moughrabi, who authored
the public opinion study, concluded that any U.S. president who proposed
a peaceful solution that would involve the PLO in the peace process and
lead to an independent Palestinian state would find ample support among
the public, despite the 25 percent of the electorate that constitutes the committed core of Israel's support.[111] But changing public attitudes had no impact on an administration that, probably more than any other, numbered
itself among the hard-core 25 percent. The administration's structure of beliefs remained so solid that only a clear and definite push from public opinion could make a difference; the passive changes emerging in public attitudes could not penetrate.

The second trend, which had a strong impact on the way many observers came to view the origins of the Palestinian-Israeli conflict and the
legitimacy of the Palestinian claim, came late in Reagan's presidency and
was probably not even noticed by Reagan policymakers. In the mid- to late
1980s, a group of young revisionist scholars in Israel, using recently declassified Israeli archival material, began publicizing the details of Israel's
creation in 1948, revealing a less romanticized aspect of Israel and a less demonized aspect of the Palestinians and other Arabs. The "new historiography," as the revisionist scholarship came to be called, provoked a profound
debate—taking place initially almost exclusively among scholars but soon
spilling over into other areas of Israeli society—between the new historians and older mainstream historians devoted to the old images of Israel as
heroic and peace-loving and of Arabs as predatory and warmongering.[112]

For Israelis, the debate, which continued well into the 1990s, became
a debate on their own national legitimacy, for the new historiography exposed what the scholar Ilan Pappé calls "unpleasant, at times shocking chap-

ters in the Israeli historical narrative" and revealed a "basic contradiction between Zionist national ambitions and their implementation at the expense of the local population of Palestine." Perhaps most strikingly, the new history of 1948 legitimized the Palestinians' historical narrative, not only bringing to Israeli consciousness for the first time an awareness that another version existed but demonstrating the scholarly accuracy of a version Israelis had previously regarded as merely propaganda. The new history, Pappé observes, "is the most profound legitimization given by Israeli scholarship to any chapter in the Palestinian narrative."[113]

Wide publication of a serious critique of the past was not possible in Israel until the mid- to late 1980s—in part because the archival material on which the new version was based was not declassified until the late 1970s and 1980s, in part because the task of challenging the conventional dogma on the past had to await the coming of age of a second, less reverent generation of historians, and in large part because only in the late 1980s was the full impact being felt of a series of great changes in Israel's political climate. Developments in the 1970s, particularly the surprise Arab attack in October 1973, revealing a weakness in the Israeli army, had already shaken the ideological firmament for a great many Israelis. In the 1980s, the shock of the Lebanon invasion and the Israeli government's harsh reaction to the *intifada* eroded faith in Israel's moral superiority. The new young historians thus came of age in what some scholars call a post-Zionist environment, an environment in which images of heroism and moral rectitude were no longer relevant and in which the national consensus built around Zionism was breaking down and society was increasingly polarized between expansionist hawks and more conciliatory doves.[114]

The 1980s also saw a change in the United States in the character of scholarly literature on the Palestinian issue. Little had been published at all on this issue before the 1980s, and as late as 1988 historian Charles Smith could write in the preface to the first edition of his *Palestine and the Arab-Israeli Conflict* that he had been unable to find a text suitable for college students that would introduce the history of Palestine in the period before 1948 and explain the bearing this history and the interactions of Palestinian Arabs and Zionists in this early period had on the Arab-Israeli conflict.[115] Several specialized works on Palestinian history had been published earlier in the decade, but virtually none of the more detailed works predated 1980, and there were no general surveys until Smith wrote his.[116]

Little if any of this new scholarship or the revisionist debate in Israel reached Reagan administration policymakers. The twin currents represented by the Israeli debate and the changes in U.S. public opinion, in fact, tended to eddy around policymakers without having a significant impact on them or their attitudes. Most, even at lower levels of the bureaucracy, were not even aware of the debate over the events of 1948, and those who were aware were undoubtedly inclined to discount it as irrelevant to the current task of crisis policymaking. Public opinion polls showing increased but still passive popular support for Palestinian aspirations also did not hold much water for politicians beset by direct congressional and lobby pressures from those prepared to back up their views with votes. The collective mind-set of the Reagan administration was so firmly cast that little could move it.

U.S. Ambassador to Israel Lewis openly criticized the Reagan administration in 1984, just before the U.S. presidential election, for failing to advance the peace process because of its demonstrated lack of urgency. Lewis cited the administration's failure to pursue the Camp David autonomy talks and the Reagan Plan, Reagan's own failure to become personally involved in the peace process, the administration's overemphasis on the global context of Middle East developments, and its tendency to perform a mediating role "only with carrots." [117] Lewis's criticisms accurately summarized the Reagan team's first-term policies; four years later, the same observations would apply to the administration's second-term policies.

The administration did, without much enthusiasm, pursue an initiative launched in February 1985 by Jordan's King Hussein and the PLO designed to lead to a full Israeli withdrawal from the West Bank and Gaza and establishment of a Jordanian-Palestinian confederation to control the territories; Palestinian self-determination would be exercised within the context of this confederation. The initiative proposed to open a dialogue between the United States and a joint Jordanian-Palestinian delegation, leading to an international peace conference that would in turn ultimately lead to direct negotiations between the Arabs and Israel. Early 1985 was widely viewed as the optimum time in which to try such an initiative, with Reagan having just been reelected and the more moderate Shimon Peres of Israel's Labor Party briefly holding the prime ministership in a coalition government with the Likud. But Peres was as chary of dealing with the PLO as the Likud had been, and the United States, also unable to get past the procedural problems involved in negotiating with Palestinians, was never wholly convinced of the merits of the Jordanian-PLO initiative.

The U.S. and Israeli insistence that no one associated with the PLO be involved stymied efforts in the first instance to form a joint Jordanian-Palestinian delegation. In addition, because Shultz and Reagan were unwilling to have the United States become directly involved in negotiations, they focused attention exclusively on encouraging direct talks between the parties and undermined the notion of convening an international conference, even when Peres himself, during a speech to the UN in the fall of 1985, indicated support for such a conference. For its part, the PLO refused, without a recognition of the Palestinians' right to self-determination, to accommodate the U.S. insistence that it adhere precisely to the formula laid down by Washington: unconditional and unambiguous acceptance of UN Resolution 242, explicit recognition of Israel's right to exist, and renunciation of terrorism.[118] As a result, after a year of futile wrangling and maneuvering over procedural issues, the Jordanian-PLO alliance broke down and the initiative collapsed in February 1986.[119]

Shultz blamed the PLO and only the PLO for the breakdown. Washington, however, had failed to encourage the initiative from the beginning. Shultz says in his memoirs that he pursued the negotiations even though they were "against my own instincts." From the start, Shultz and Reagan viewed the prospect of dealing with the PLO with profound distaste and repeatedly threw obstacles in the way of efforts to form an acceptable joint Jordanian-Palestinian delegation, questioning PLO sincerity and even refusing permission for the PLO's UN observer to come to Washington at the invitation of several members of Congress to discuss the initiative. In the summer of 1985, President Reagan upset a planned meeting with a carefully chosen group of Jordanian and Palestinian delegates when he personally intervened to forbid U.S. dealings with any Palestinian even remotely associated with the PLO.[120]

Some small-scale Palestinian terrorist incidents against Israeli targets in the summer of 1985, followed by Israel's bombing raid on the PLO's Tunis headquarters in October, followed in turn by the hijacking by a PLO splinter group of the cruise ship *Achille Lauro*, during which a wheelchair-bound American was murdered, all put a serious pall on peace efforts. The clear apathy with which the United States approached the process undermined it further and tended to encourage radicals and the so-called rejectionists on both sides. After the failure of this initiative, Peres, having rotated out of the post of prime minister to become foreign minister under Yitzhak Shamir, attempted again to pursue with Jordan the possibility of convening an international conference, but Shultz discouraged this attempt as well.[121]

Peres's clear strategy while serving as prime minister had been to start a formal negotiating process that, once begun, might provoke debate within Israel and a coalition crisis, leading to the formation of a majority Labor government. Some have speculated, once again, that U.S. encouragement not only might have strengthened moderate forces within the PLO, who clearly hoped that the PLO alliance with Jordan would elicit a favorable U.S. response, but might have facilitated Peres's strategy and strengthened him for a showdown with the right wing in Israel. One Israeli commentator believes that the Reagan-Shultz policy instead played into the hands of the Israeli right by convincing voters that with the Likud in power Israel "could have its cake—U.S. aid—and eat it too, by continuing to settle the West Bank." U.S. policy also, this analyst believes, ultimately led to the *intifada,* by producing the political gridlock in Israel that finally caused complete Palestinian frustration.[122]

After the failure of the Jordan-PLO initiative, the United States confined itself to a halfhearted effort to "improve the quality of life" of Palestinians in the West Bank and Gaza—an effort intended primarily to undermine the PLO's reputation in the territories and enhance Jordan's standing among Palestinians. No further attempts to restart the peace process were made. The United States seemed, in the view of political scientist Ann Lesch, to have conceded that Israel would rule the occupied territories indefinitely and that only cosmetic improvements in living conditions could be expected.[123]

The Palestinian *intifada* in the West Bank and Gaza, begun in December 1987, sent a message to Israel, the United States, and the world that the Palestinians demanded something more than cosmetic improvements in their quality of life. As the scholar Mark Tessler has noted, the message was, "We exist and have political rights, and there will be no peace until these rights are recognized." The message got through only partially. In Israel, many, perhaps the majority, began to accept the notion that the West Bank and Gaza were not an asset to Israel's security but a burden and that Israel could not continue to rule over another people. The government, however, did not change its attitude and instead cracked down harshly on Palestinian demonstrators. Reaction was mixed in the United States as well, but in general, as Tessler has observed, "there was more continuity than change in American attitudes and foreign policy."[124] The *intifada* received heavy press treatment in the United States and focused a great deal of attention on the Palestinians—most of it sympathetic and tending, for the first time, to show the Palestinians as a distinct people with national aspirations seeking freedom from an occupying power. At the same time, however, Congress and to a large extent the administration tended to rally to Israel's support, the principal concerns being how to extricate Israel from the problems of the *intifada* and how to exclude the PLO from any negotiating process.

The uprising did awaken the United States from its diplomatic torpor, although not from its total opposition to dealing with the PLO. Secretary of State Shultz devised a plan for a peace settlement to be achieved through direct bilateral negotiations between an Israeli and a joint Jordanian-Palestinian delegation. His blueprint would have established a transitional phase for the West Bank and Gaza, to be followed immediately by negotiations on the final status of the territories. Shultz made four trips to the Middle East in early 1988 in an attempt to win the various parties over to his initiative, but although this was the first serious U.S. involvement with the Middle East in five years, the effort came too late and had too little weight behind it to be effective.[125]

None of the parties involved was ready to cooperate at this point. The Palestinians, angry about the PLO's exclusion and resentful of what they viewed as their second-class treatment by Shultz's initiative even as they were showing their political strength through the *intifada*, were basically uninterested in the initiative. Jordan took itself out of the peace process altogether by relinquishing all responsibility for and claims to the West Bank in July 1988. Israel adamantly refused to consider any aspect of the Shultz initiative. Although Shultz was highly irritated with Prime Minister Shamir's inflexible attitude, Washington itself undermined the peace plan by giving Israel new strategic benefits in the spring of 1988. In April, the United States and Israel signed a revised memorandum of understanding on political, security, and economic cooperation, and the United States speeded up delivery to Israel of seventy-five fighter aircraft. An increasing number of Israeli and U.S. commentators began to show open scorn for Shultz for helping to foster deadlock by seeming to reward Israeli intransigence. Israeli journalists chided the United States for allowing Israel to say no to Washington and still giving it a bonus.[126]

In the months following issuance of the Shultz plan, the United States went along with initiatives generated by others but did not initiate any steps in the peace process itself. One of these efforts was begun by Swedish Foreign Minister Sten Andersson, who arranged a series of meetings between PLO leaders and several prominent U.S. Jews in the hope of formulating an agreed statement of the PLO's commitment to a peace settlement with Israel.[127] A second effort was undertaken in August by a Palestinian American, Mohamed Rabie, who had contacts among the PLO leadership. Enlisting the assistance of Middle East expert William Quandt as a go-between with the State Department, Rabie attempted for several months to work out an agreement that would lead to an official U.S.-PLO dialogue.[128]

Both efforts—one to start an Israeli-PLO negotiation, the other to start a U.S.-PLO dialogue—ultimately prepared the way for a groundbreaking initiative in November 1988 by the PNC, the PLO's legislative arm, advocating the coexistence of Israel and a Palestinian state. The PLO had been coming to the point of accepting Israel's existence for years, but the timing of this initiative was directly related to the *intifada* and had been heavily influenced by West Bank and Gaza Palestinians who hoped to capitalize on the uprising to put forth a formal negotiating stance and a message of conciliation that they believed the United States would be forced to accept. In a document drafted in the summer of 1988 by the prominent Jerusalem Palestinian Faisal Husseini, Palestinians from the occupied territories urged the PLO leadership to call for a two-state solution and declare Palestinian independence on the basis of the original UN partition plan.[129] The PLO political platform issued in November did just that, implicitly recognizing Israel, accepting UN Resolution 242, and declaring the existence of a Palestinian state in the West Bank and Gaza.[130]

The Swedish government remained active in this process even beyond the PNC declaration, for it was the intervention of the Swedish foreign minister that led directly to Arafat's issuance, a month after the PNC declaration, on December 14, of a further statement reciting the exact formula laid down by the United States for the opening of an official dialogue with the PLO.

Not only did Shultz do virtually nothing to encourage these developments, but he placed repeated obstacles in the path of this process before he was finally forced reluctantly to agree to recognize the PLO in response to Arafat's December 14 statement. Shultz had ignored a highly conciliatory statement issued by Arafat aide Bassam Abu Sharif in the summer of 1988.[131] Later, although Shultz did make forthcoming statements in the early fall of 1988 about Palestinian "political rights" in response to the Rabie-Quandt initiative, he essentially paid little attention either to this initiative or to the Swedish mediation effort until they were near fruition, irritated at being, as he put it, "drawn into a series of indirect exchanges with the PLO in this fashion." Finally, when the PNC issued its political platform in November—a platform that Palestinians throughout the world regarded as a major peace initiative and a historic compromise— Shultz dismissed it as a unilateral declaration that was too "blurry and ambiguous."[132]

Described by one diplomat as having a "visceral hatred" for Arafat,[133]

Shultz denied Arafat a U.S. visa to address the UN after the November PNC declaration, despite heavy international pressure to grant the visa and despite the likelihood that Arafat would use this forum to repeat unambiguously the formula prescribed for a dialogue with the United States. Again, Shultz placed one after another obstacle before the PLO. When Arafat wrote a letter to the Swedish foreign minister with the precise wording demanded by the United States, Shultz insisted that he issue the statement publicly. When Arafat did so—on December 13 before a special session of the UN convened in Geneva to accommodate his exclusion from New York—but worded his statement somewhat differently from what Shultz expected, Shultz still demanded more. Only after Arafat had held a press conference the next day and said exactly the words in exactly the order the United States dictated did Shultz relent and agree to open a dialogue with the PLO.[134]

Both the Swedish mediation and the Rabie-Quandt effort are examples of what could be accomplished—and what might have been accomplished years earlier—with a serious attempt to expand on PLO openings and probe the limits of Palestinian flexibility. The PLO had made amply clear as much as a decade earlier its readiness to live in peace alongside Israel, and if its position was too "slippery and vague" for the United States, as Shultz characterized it,[135] the U.S. government did not make a serious attempt to ascertain whether the Palestinians could be pinned down to a more definite and acceptable position and made no attempt to encourage the PLO along a conciliatory path. The important point about Shultz's automatic rejection of each PLO opening and his rigorous efforts to dodge PLO overtures and discourage Palestinian moderation is that his inability to move beyond his reflexive hostility to everything about the organization effectively closed off the principal avenue toward a peace settlement for the entire six and a half years in which he was in office.

The Reagan administration's eight years of Middle East policymaking provide a good illustration of how a mind-set can create a policy. Reagan and his political compatriots had the mind-set of a decade earlier, and when they came to office, they took policy back to the thinking of the 1970s. It was as though Carter's efforts to resolve the Palestinian-Israeli conflict had never occurred, as though the Palestinians had never shed the political anonymity in which they had lived for the first decades of Israel's existence. Reagan's team reverted to the old frame of reference—in effect, they created a reality—in which Palestinians and the Palestinian issue did not exist and Israel was preeminent in U.S. considerations, in which the Cold War struggle with the Soviet Union was the highest U.S. priority and Israel was regarded as a necessary ally, no matter what its West Bank policies or its Lebanon policy or its human-rights record.

The Reagan people, particularly Shultz, did recognize that the Palestinian problem had to be solved if there were to be a peaceful resolution of the Arab-Israeli conflict; this much of the great change in the old frame of reference wrought by Carter's policies and by the Palestinians' own rise to prominence had made an impression on the Reagan administration. But, in the end, resolving the Arab-Israeli conflict was not a high priority for the administration, and certainly not if it necessitated dealing with the PLO or angering Israel's U.S. supporters or antagonizing the Likud.

The administration missed repeated opportunities to advance the peace process throughout its eight years in office. The *intifada*, in fact, was launched because the Palestinians had reached a point of hopelessness over those missed opportunities and the prospect of never seeing relief from Israeli occupation. In addition to being an expression of their total frustration, the uprising was also an assertion of the Palestinians' national identity and a source of pride for all Palestinians that strengthened the hand of moderates in the PLO, allowing them to seize the diplomatic initiative and to say explicitly the things about Israel's existence and their own readiness to coexist that they had been saying only indirectly and implicitly for over a decade. Through the *intifada*, the Palestinians seized what no one in Israel or the United States had been willing to grant them: recognition of their existence as a national community willing to share land with Israel in mutual coexistence. Had the Reagan administration broken out of the old mental fetters that kept it from recognizing the reality of Palestinian nationalism and accepting the genuineness of the Palestinian moderates' desire for peace and coexistence, it might have been able to respond to and encourage Palestinian moderation rather than allow repeated opportunities for pursuing a peace process to slip by.

While Reagan policymakers waited for an opportune moment to pursue peace, Israel built more Jewish settlements in the occupied territories, confiscating more Palestinian land, and the Palestinians grew increasingly frustrated. Without opposing pressure from the United States the number of settlements in the West Bank and Gaza grew exponentially. With yearly increases in the number of settlers in the range of 30 percent and often higher, the Israeli settler population of the territories more than quadrupled during the Reagan administration's first six years. As of mid-1987, a total of almost sixty-eight thousand lived in approximately 140 settlements in the West Bank and Gaza; these figures are for the areas outside the expanded limits of Jerusalem, where another several thousand Israelis lived in urban settlements.[136]

The irony of the Reagan years was that the administration most deeply and emotionally opposed to negotiating with the PLO was the very administration that in the end was forced to authorize a dialogue with the organization. But the tragedy of the Reagan years was that the bloodshed of the West Bank/Gaza *intifada*, which ultimately led to the breakthrough that brought about the U.S.-PLO rapprochement, might have been avoided and the same progress toward peace made years earlier if the administration's framework for thinking had not been so oriented around Israel and if Reagan policymakers had been more willing to look past their narrow focus on Israel's point of view to take account as well of the Palestinian perspective.

9 George Bush
No Illusions

George Bush took office in January 1989, during a period that in many ways was the most hopeful, in other ways the most difficult, in the more than forty-year history of U.S. involvement in the Palestinian-Israeli conflict. Never had the Palestinians, strengthened and given political confidence by the *intifada,* been readier to coexist in peace with Israel in a two-state division of Palestine. But never had Israel under the hard-line government of the Likud's Yitzhak Shamir—its control over the West Bank and Gaza consolidated after almost a dozen years of unrestrained settlement construction and its annexationist policies encouraged by eight years of Reagan administration acquiescence—been less ready for compromise.

Bush and his secretary of state, James Baker, wanted to move forward on the peace process but were deterred from taking forceful action during their first year and a half in office by several factors. Neither had a strategic vision of a Middle East at peace; they had no particular interest in what a peace settlement would look like but wanted a solution for the political achievement of finding a solution. The overriding interest in the process of achieving a peace settlement, rather than in peace itself, tended to dampen the administration's commitment when obstacles arose. The political climate in the United States also restrained vigorous action. Despite greatly increased sympathy for the Palestinians and criticism of Israel since the outbreak of the *intifada,* the general sentiment in the country and in Congress remained opposed to exerting the kind of pressure on Israel that was necessary to move its Likud government.

A further impediment to negotiations was the fact that Bush and Baker surrounded themselves with a group of Middle East advisers strongly of the view that the United States could and should do little to move the peace process along. Neither Bush nor Baker was inclined toward activism on any issue, and, without real convictions on the Middle East's problems, both were inclined at the beginning to follow their advisers' cautious approach. As a result, so little was accomplished in the administration's first eighteen months that the peace process went completely off the track in the summer of 1990, and the Persian Gulf crisis of 1990–1991 diverted all attention from attempts to start peace negotiations on the Palestinian-Israeli issue until mid-1991.

By the time Bush and Baker turned their attention again to the Palestinian-Israeli peace process, conditions in the Middle East, in the international arena, and on the domestic political scene made the situation unusually amenable to U.S. intervention. The Madrid peace conference convened in October 1991 was a landmark in Arab-Israeli and Palestinian-Israeli history, marking the first time a comprehensive peace conference was attended by all parties to the Arab-Israeli conflict and the first time Palestinians participated in peace negotiations at any level.

The mere fact of the Palestinians' attendance at the Madrid conference did much to change the way public opinion in the United States viewed them; it altered the Middle East frame of reference in fundamental ways. Palestinians were now seen to a far greater degree as reasonable people with human concerns and legitimate aspirations. Bush and Baker were able to accomplish this alteration in the frame of reference because, in their unsentimental approach to Palestinian-Israeli issues, they recognized what few other politicians did, that the political climate would support an effort to lean not just on the Palestinians but also on Israel for the concessions necessary to begin peace negotiations. The problem with their approach, however, was that with no substantive goal they lost interest after the procedural hurdles of convening peace talks had been cleared and allowed the negotiations to bog down.

Bush and Baker together were a foreign-policy team of rare pragmatism when it came to Middle East issues and policy toward Israel. Both completely unemotional policymakers, they were less bound to the U.S. relationship with Israel and less fettered by the restraints of this relationship than any president and secretary of state except Carter and Vance.

Bush was probably better versed in foreign diplomacy and policymaking when he took office than any president before or since, having served as ambassador to the UN, ambassador to China, and director of the CIA. He did not have an intricate knowledge of the history or politics of individual nations, except possibly China, and he did not know the Middle East any better than any other new president, but he was attuned to the conduct of foreign policy to a far greater extent than most presidents. He was a warm and gregarious person, according to aides, and he carried this personal warmth into his diplomacy. He had a unique sense of the importance of, and usually had great skill in developing, a personal interchange with foreign leaders in order to accomplish mutual goals.[1] Much of his difficulty with Israel, in fact, came about because he took an instant personal dislike to Prime Minister Shamir and was unable to forge a cooperative relationship with the Israeli leader, who misled Bush about Israel's plans for settlement construction in the occupied territories at their first meeting.

But if Bush was a diplomat, he was not a statesman. Uncomfortable with geopolitical rhetoric and strategizing, and impatient, as he himself advertised, with what he called "the vision thing," Bush never articulated a broad vision of U.S. foreign-policy goals beyond a sense of the importance of the United States as a world leader. Indeed, he is said to have favored close interpersonal relations with other leaders precisely because he was so uncomfortable with ideas and so skeptical of the power of ideas to change people's minds. Perhaps overly cynical, *Time* magazine White House correspondents Michael Duffy and Dan Goodgame concluded in their 1992 book on Bush, *Marching in Place*, that he was a wholly practical man who decided that what he most wanted to do in his first term was win a second term.[2]

Bush's diplomatic jobs, none lasting long in the first place, had never involved making or enunciating policy, and even as a presidential candidate in 1980 he did not spell out his views on foreign policy. Throughout the Reagan administration, in stark contrast to Reagan himself and most of his team, Bush had remained for the most part a closed book. It was clear that with regard to the Middle East he was far less emotionally attached to Israel than most of the rest of the administration, but for the most part his viewpoint was kept well hidden. "For a man of wide experience, he had left few traces" before becoming the president, notes one scholar.[3]

Secretary of State Baker, a longtime close friend and political ally of Bush, was a man remarkably like him in both personality and political style. Both status-quo politicians, reluctant to rock the boat or take bold steps;[4] both intrigued more by the workings and the process of foreign policy than by its substance; both impatient with the world of ideas and broad visions, the two men were so much alike and their instincts so much in tune that it is virtually impossible to determine where, on a given issue, the influence of one left off and that of the other began. They coordinated so closely, meeting privately twice a week and talking on the telephone up to a dozen times a day,[5] that their policymaking was all but seamless. No other members of Bush's top-level foreign-policy team felt particularly deeply about the substance of Arab-Israeli issues or had significant input in Middle East policymaking.

Baker pursued policies not because they advanced an ideological or an emotional agenda but essentially because they would work, because they would advance whatever political agenda he and Bush had set. Baker was universally described, by allies and critics alike, as having uncanny political acumen and a keen sense of how to work Congress and the press and to maneuver on the Washington political scene. He also had a rare instinct for knowing what he could accomplish politically; he generally took on only those issues where success was virtually assured, and he is said to have formed a viewpoint on an issue only after having judged its likely political implications.[6]

Like Bush not a man of vision, Baker was far less interested in policy goals themselves than in the process involved in achieving them. Scholar and former government official William Quandt has observed that the United States acted as a convener in the peace process but not as a mediator, never even hinting during the 1991 Madrid peace conference and its follow-up negotiations at any substantive ideas to put before the parties. *New York Times* correspondent Thomas Friedman, a careful observer of Baker throughout the administration's four years, made a similar observation, noting that the "Baker-Bush peace process was at its root an intense negotiation focused primarily on getting the parties to the table. It never really intended to get the parties to agreements, with compromise proposals of its own."[7]

This interest in process over substance, along with Baker's innate tendency toward caution, meant that he could easily be deterred from pursuing a policy objective in the first place if political difficulties loomed, and he could be diverted from a goal if another, more politically feasible or more tactically challenging goal arose to take his attention. Both of these situations arose at various points during Baker's tenure as secretary of state: in the administration's early years, his highly developed political sense and the possibility of failure kept him from vigorously pursuing the peace process or challenging the Middle East status quo, and after the Madrid peace conference had moved on to bilateral negotiations, Baker, no longer interested in the talks as they turned to substantive matters and diverted by the need to campaign for Bush's reelection, ignored the peace process and allowed it to languish.

As a self-described man of action rather than of reflection, and no historian by his own testimony,[8] Baker had little sense of the historical forces behind any of the issues with which he dealt and, specifically with regard to the Middle East, little appreciation for the history that animated either Israelis or Palestinians. Clearly not influenced by the Reagan administration's previous intimacy with Israel and just as obviously not a product of the frame of reference that had always dictated close emotional ties with Israel, Baker was as uninterested in Israel's Holocaust-induced fears and its security concerns as he was in the Palestinians' grievances over the 1948 dispossession. He came to office with a skeptical attitude toward the Likud government's hard-line policy on the occupied territories, and, like Bush, he quickly developed an intense dislike for Shamir's prickly personality.

Lack of empathy for the Israelis did not, however, make Baker pro-Palestinian or give him an understanding of Palestinian concerns. At the start of his term in office, he does not seem to have had a clear understanding of the Palestinian position. He remarks in his memoirs that when the new administration took office in January 1989 there was "no real evidence to believe the climate was ripe for generating any momentum" because "neither side" was ready to make the concessions necessary to start a peace process. Neither the PLO nor the front-line Arab states, he remarked, "appeared interested in searching for common ground" with Israel, and the PLO "remained committed to the destruction of Israel."[9] Referring to a period only weeks after the PLO had formally made major concessions in its diplomatic stance, indicating that it recognized and was ready to coexist with Israel and was eager to begin peace negotiations, Baker's belief that no Arab was ready for peace with Israel indicates that, however free he may have been of the constraints of the frame of reference in some respects, he was very much bound by the rote assumption that Palestinians were incapable of compromise.

What was unique about Bush and Baker in the way they made Middle East policy was their utter lack of sentimentality; they had "no illusions about the Arabs, no illusions about the Israelis."[10] They pursued a policy solely because they judged it to be in their own political interest or that of the United States, not because they had an opinion on the morality or the justice of either the Israelis' or the Arabs' positions. If an issue appeared to be impeding progress, Baker worked to overcome the obstacle purely for the sake of advancing the peace process, not from a judgment that the rights of one side or the other were being infringed. When Baker calculated that Israel's settlement construction had begun to foreclose too many negotiating options for the Palestinians, he exerted heavy pressure on Israel, not because he sympathized with the Palestinians but simply because he perceived that this was the only way to get negotiations started. By the same token, when he concluded that the only way to secure Israel's attendance at the Madrid peace conference in 1991 was to obtain Palestinian concessions on such procedural issues as whether Palestinians from inside Jerusalem or with known ties to the PLO could attend, he forced those concessions not because he cared about the symbolism of who attended and who was barred but because his sole interest was in starting the conference.

Despite his lack of sentimentality, Baker did show occasional flashes of compassion,[11] and the Palestinians with whom he dealt during the months of preparation before the Madrid conference were able to bring him to some understanding of the human dimension of their situation in the occupied territories. He gained a better insight into the vantage point from which the Palestinians were negotiating. This understanding and his recognition that continuation of the status quo was impeding progress in the peace process would not have been possible except for the fact that he was the first high-level U.S. official in a half century of Middle East policy-making ever to meet formally with Palestinian representatives and therefore to encounter Palestinian concerns and grievances firsthand. His experience stands as a prime example of how dealing directly and forthrightly with both sides to a conflict can affect policy by influencing the perspective from which that policy is made.

Bush administration Middle East policy in the first year was influenced heavily by a lengthy report prepared in advance of the 1988 presidential election under the auspices of the pro-Israeli think tank the Washington Institute for Near East Policy.[12] The report had been prepared in the hope that, whichever candidate won election, the new administration would use it as an initial guidepost for Arab-Israeli policy, much as the Carter administration had used the Brookings Institution report in 1976. Campaign advisers and major figures from both political parties were members of the study group that drafted the report, as were several former government officials, journalists, and Middle East experts. Most of these individuals could be described as having a pro-Israeli bent.

As had occurred in the Carter administration when several of the Brookings report's drafters were appointed to important positions in the administration, the Washington Institute report proved to be a stepping stone for several of its authors to key positions in the Bush administration. Lawrence Eagleburger, who had cochaired the study group with Walter Mondale and had been a close associate of Henry Kissinger in the White House and the State Department during the Nixon and Ford administrations, became deputy secretary of state; Dennis Ross, a Middle East and Soviet expert who had been Bush's foreign-policy adviser during the campaign and was the principal drafter of the report, was appointed director of the State Department's Policy Planning Staff, where he became Baker's principal policy adviser; and Richard Haass, another Middle East expert and former Robert Dole campaign adviser, was named director of Middle East affairs on the National Security Council staff.

The Washington Institute report was essentially a blueprint for inaction. Concluding that the *intifada* had made peacemaking more difficult than it had been before and that the conflict between the Arab states and Israel had become more dangerous and volatile, the report asserted that the impediments to the peace process were too great to be overcome "by a direct diplomatic assault" and recommended that the administration shun efforts to achieve a rapid "breakthrough." The administration should instead engage in a more drawn-out "ripening process," attempting through the promotion of "confidence-building measures" to create an atmosphere conducive to negotiations and gradually to alter the two sides' perceptions of each other. Although it observed that continuation of the status quo was dangerous for everyone, including Israel, the report amounted effectively to an endorsement of the status quo since it specifically eschewed any active U.S. intervention against the Likud government's hard-line position.

Largely because it was written from an Israeli perspective by a group with little or no understanding of the Palestinian point of view, the report misunderstood the purpose of the *intifada*, concluding unreasonably that its principal effect had been to increase hatred and suspicion and to radicalize Palestinians in the occupied territories. The report's argument for the radicalizing effect of the *intifada* was based on the conclusion that Palestinian youth and refugee-camp inhabitants were dictating the pace and intensity of events and that "the pragmatic element—the traditional, middle class elites in the West Bank who accommodated themselves to the Israeli occupation—[had] been undermined and intimidated." The Israel-centered thinking behind this conclusion is clear: Palestinians who did not "accommodate themselves to the Israeli occupation" were radicals, and any attempt at rebellion against the occupation was automatically to be condemned.

The report's focus on the Israeli perspective was also evident in the fact that it placed the entire burden of peacemaking on the Palestinians. Asserting, again unreasonably, that the *intifada* had undermined the influence of Israeli advocates of conciliation, the report's authors called on the Palestinians but not the Israelis to make conciliatory moves. Palestinians must, the report said, "go beyond imposing costs on Israel"; unless a Palestinian initiative was "an unambiguous effort to accommodate and reassure Israel," it would surely fail. There was no call for an Israeli initiative or for an Israeli attempt to "accommodate and reassure" the Palestinians.

The report bore quite heavily the imprint of the kind of thinking and the misconceptions about the Palestinian-Israeli conflict that had taken hold during the Reagan administration among large segments of the community of political elites in Washington and throughout the United States. Most of these misconceptions were not new, but the rising prominence of such study institutes and think tanks as the Washington Institute, which had easy access to policymakers, gave this body of perceptions a new currency and a greater level of coherence. This was the set of assumptions that informed the thinking of the report's authors, that found its way into the basic premises of the report, and that formed the initial basis of Bush administration policy. It was also the basic set of assumptions, only slightly altered over the years, that this group of policy advisers eventually took to the Clinton administration.

These stock assumptions had several more or less interrelated elements: that the PLO was incapable of compromise and that, if the Palestinian issue were to be resolved, the PLO had to be bypassed; that Palestinians in the West Bank and Gaza were inherently more moderate than the PLO and could constitute the hoped-for "alternative Palestinian leadership"; that the burden of compromise and movement in the peace process lay with the Arabs; that most Arabs, however, believed that they did not need to make a move, that they could wait the Israelis out in the hope that the United States would exert pressure on Israel; that the Palestinians were not a community or a distinct people and had only lately inserted themselves into what was essentially an interstate conflict between Israel and the Arab states; that Israelis had vital security needs that must be accommodated as part of any solution but that Palestinians, as simply the "intercommunal" element of a more significant interstate conflict, had no similar concerns.

One of the most cogent spokesmen for this mind-set was Martin Indyk, a highly influential Australian who came to prominence in Washington as a strategic analyst for AIPAC during the Reagan years, was a cofounder of the Washington Institute in the late 1980s and became its executive director, served as convener of the study group that produced the Institute's 1988 report, and later served in the Clinton administration in high-level White House and State Department positions.[13] Indyk did not play a direct role in Bush administration policymaking, but he had a major role in formulating the Washington Institute report, and he was a close associate of such individuals as Ross and Haass and shared their mind-set. At a November 1988 symposium at the Institute he gave a presentation on the report that expands on the background thinking and is instructive for what it reveals of this group's approach to policy on the Palestinian-Israeli situation.[14]

Essentially ignoring the fact that just two weeks before his presentation the PNC had issued a political platform implicitly accepting coexistence with Israel,[15] Indyk minimized the importance of the Palestinian element in the Arab-Israeli conflict and overstated the nature of the "complication" introduced by the *intifada*. He said he believed the Bush administration, just elected, would face a much more complex situation than previous administrations because the Arab-Israeli conflict was suddenly no longer only an interstate conflict but "now possesses an additional intercommunal component." Indyk's reference to a new "additional" element betrayed a failure to understand that the Palestinian-Israeli conflict began, and the Palestinian element in the situation emerged, not when the *intifada* erupted in 1987 but a century earlier. Indyk's chagrin at discovering that the Palestinian issue was part of the broader conflict was evident throughout his remarks, as was his apparent reluctance to acknowledge that because of the *intifada* and the PNC's recent concessions, the Palestinian issue was no longer an avoidable problem. He nonetheless still sought ways around the problem, for instance by minimizing the conciliatory aspects of the PNC's political platform and portraying the Palestinians as still intransigent— which allowed him to conclude that he found it "difficult to recall a time when the positions of the parties to the conflict were so far apart and basically unbridgeable."

Israel's Meron Benvenisti, in describing the Israeli reaction to the *intifada*, has made a point about the nature of the Israeli mind-set on the Palestinians that applies equally to Indyk and other like thinkers in the United States. The Israelis, Benvenisti said, refused to see the Palestinians as a community and so could not believe that they would respond as a community to the occupation and its harsh practices. Benvenisti saw the roots of this Israeli misjudgment as lying in what he called the ethnocentric Jewish world-view, the "inability to recognize the existence of another legitimate collective between the Jordan and the sea." As a result of this mind-set, the Israelis internalized only the violent aspect of the *intifada* and were blind to its community, and one might say its national, aspects—among them the Palestinians' mobilization of the entire community and particularly the masses and their attempts to create an independent economic and social infrastructure.[16] The old frame of reference that Indyk represented could fairly be characterized as quite similar to this Israeli mind-set in its inability to see the Palestinians as a people and a community in their own right and as other than perpetrators of violence and opponents of Israel.

The Washington Institute report reinforced Bush's and Baker's own instincts for caution and lack of innovation and gave Baker the excuse he wanted for staying at arm's length from a problem he knew had no guarantees of success.[17] These factors and his own lack of knowledge about the situation gave those individuals involved in the report who moved into key administration positions considerable influence in this early period, particularly Ross, who became Baker's closest adviser on both Middle East and Soviet affairs. Ross was known to share the pro-Israeli community's suspicions of the State Department's so-called Arabists and of other elements of the government bureaucracy.[18] Baker himself liked to work with a small circle of trusted aides, and by concentrating policy formulation on Middle East issues in the hands of Ross as director of the Policy Planning Staff and two other State Department experts, Baker and Ross almost totally shut out the line officers in the Near East Bureau. The other two members of the Ross trio at the State Department were Daniel Kurtzer, a Foreign Service officer fluent in both Hebrew and Arabic who had served in Egypt and Israel, and Aaron David Miller, a Policy Planning Staff analyst who had written two books on the Palestinians and the Palestine question in the 1980s.[19]

All three men worked closely with Baker. They and National Security Council staffer Haass traveled with him on his shuttle missions to the Middle East, particularly the eight trips he made in 1991 in organizing the Madrid peace conference. Most often, Ross was the only adviser Baker took with him when meeting with Israeli and Palestinian leaders. All these advisers, all Jewish and all widely described in the United States and in Israel as having "impeccably pro-Israeli credentials" but with an Israeli Labor Party approach to the issues, came to be known as the bureaucracy's "Israelists," succeeding the generations of Arabists who had once populated the State Department.[20] Hanan Ashrawi, one of the Palestinians who met regularly with this team throughout 1991 and during bilateral peace talks in Washington in 1992 and 1993, has observed that the Palestinians found it ironic that this U.S. team reflected the Israeli domestic political scene, not the U.S. political scene. In Washington in those days, she noted, "there was no question of pro-Israeli versus pro-Arab (or pro-Palestinian) trends and currents, but one had to figure out if the players were sympathetic to Peace Now, Labor, or Likud. . . . It was evident . . . that positions were defined on the basis of what was good for Israel from the different perspectives of the Israeli political spectrum."[21]

Ross had long been espousing the Israel-centered ideas embodied in the Washington Institute report. A scholar who had worked in the Defense Department at various times during both the Carter and the Reagan administrations, briefly in the State Department under Reagan, and in various think tanks before becoming a campaign adviser to Bush in 1988, he had long been a believer in Israel's strategic value to the United States and had a track record as an advocate of the kind of nonactivist approach to the peace process that the Washington Institute had proposed for the United States and that the Bush administration followed in its first year and a half in office. In a policy paper written for the Washington Institute in 1985, aptly titled *Acting with Caution: Middle East Policy Planning for the Second Reagan Administration,* Ross had concluded that because warfare in the Middle East was then unlikely and the Arabs were inflexible and unready to take the steps necessary for progress toward a peace settlement, there was no urgent reason for U.S. action and the United States should therefore pursue "a strategy of motion while patiently awaiting real movement from the local parties." [22]

As demonstrated in this paper, Ross was strikingly focused on Israel and what was good for Israel and had little understanding of the Arab or particularly the Palestinian perspective. For instance, assuming that "the ball is in the Arabs' court" with regard to movement toward peace, Ross advocated appointing a "non-Arabist" special Middle East envoy who would deliver several messages to the Arabs: that the United States was prepared to act, but its actions could not substitute for Arab action toward peace; that the Arabs could not count on the United States to deliver Israeli concessions; and that Israeli concessions would come only when the Arabs agreed to negotiate directly with Israel and gave concrete (this word was emphasized but not elaborated on) demonstrations of their flexibility. Yet Ross would issue no similar messages to Israel: the Israelis would not be told that U.S. action was no substitute for Israeli movement toward peace; no flexibility was demanded of Israel; no concrete actions or demonstrations of Israeli conciliation were required in order to move toward peace.

Ross's colleagues at the State Department, Miller and Kurtzer, although linked by religious and family ties to Israel, appear to have been somewhat more cognizant of the need to involve the Palestinians in the peace process than Ross was in the administration's early months, and they are said to have had considerable understanding of Arab sensitivities. Miller has been described as a brainy historian who tends to look at the broader implications of policy and who has a tendency to lean toward the Arab position. [23] His writings—unlike those of Ross, Haass, or Indyk—show him to be a serious and generally unbiased analyst, better able than the others to distance himself from the Israeli perspective and better able to view the Arab side clearly and dispassionately.[24] Kurtzer wrote a doctoral dissertation in 1976 on the development of the Palestinian resistance movement and Israel's reaction to guerrilla activity that indicates an understanding of the national basis of the Palestinian struggle.[25]

Haass was another principal drafter of the Washington Institute report who, like Ross, took an Israel-focused approach to the problems of the Middle East. A Harvard lecturer who had briefly served in the Defense and State Departments, Haass had participated with Ross and several others in 1981 in drafting a policy paper to set out the formal terms of strategic cooperation with Israel.[26] His own views were clearly laid out in a 1986 article in *Commentary* magazine and, after he had been appointed to the National Security Council staff, in a book, *Conflicts Unending*, published in 1990.[27] It does not appear that Haass's fundamental viewpoint changed significantly over the four years between publication of these two documents, and much in these documents points to his heavy hand in drafting the Washington Institute report.

The principal theme of his own writings, like that of the Washington Institute report, was that the Middle East situation was not "ripe" for movement toward peace and therefore also not for U.S. intervention. Throughout his own pieces, Haass placed the entire burden for making concessions on the Arab side; failed, even in 1990, after the PLO had conceded Israel's right to exist, to give credence to any of the concessions the Arabs had already made; did not appear to expect that any similar concessions should be demanded from Israel; and specifically eschewed any U.S. effort to press Israel for movement. Haass patronized the Arabs and the Palestinians by repeating the old shibboleth, popular for years among supporters of Israel, that "visible efforts by the United States for a comprehensive peace in the Middle East help perpetuate the illusion in the Arab world that the secret to peace in the region lies not in their own willingness to compromise but in an American willingness to pressure Israel."[28] This point failed to give either the Palestinians or other Arabs credit for past compromises or for any seriousness of purpose in pursuing a peace settlement.

Haass gave no evidence of recognizing the centrality of the Palestinian issue to resolution of the Arab-Israeli conflict or of understanding that the roots of the conflict lay in the Palestinians' dispersal in 1948 rather than in Israel's capture of territory in 1967. He also indicated, even as late as his 1990 book, no appreciation of the impediment to progress, from the Palestinian standpoint, posed by such Israeli actions as settlement construction and land confiscation. For instance, although he spoke of the need to accommodate Israeli security concerns in a final resolution, he did not, in a lengthy discussion of the positions of the various parties and of several possible approaches to a final resolution, refer to the impact on the Palestinians of the settlements or any other aspect of living under Israeli occupation. Perhaps the most telling clue to Haass's thinking lay in the fact that he listed as one of four recommended books on the Arab-Israeli conflict Joan Peters's 1984 *From Time Immemorial*—a book of dubious scholarship, discredited in Israeli scholarly circles, that seriously distorted the Palestinians' claim to patrimony in Palestine.

Perhaps the most significant aspect of the frame of reference of Ross, Haass, and others who formulated Palestinian-Israeli policy in this period was the fact that their Israeli perspective obscured for them the impact that U.S. aid had had, particularly during the Reagan years, on stiffening Israel's resistance to demands for concessions. In concluding that the situation was not "ripe" for a serious U.S. initiative, all these individuals argued that neither Arabs nor Israelis were ready to make the compromises necessary for a successful negotiating process; in the case of the Israelis, they contended that the Israeli body politic was polarized and unable to reach a consensus on how to alter the status quo. This observation begged the question, however, of what had encouraged the Likud government in the belief that it need not make hard decisions and whether a massive amount of no-strings-attached U.S. aid was a factor in Israeli complacency. None of the key individuals who wrote so extensively on the need for caution and the inadvisability of exerting pressure on Israel had examined, or apparently given thought to, what if any role U.S. policies played in bringing or failing to bring Israel to the critical point of ripeness.

The realities of dealing at first hand with Arabs and Israelis on the peace process and of working for a consummate pragmatist like Baker did bring about some change in the outlook of these individuals. Ross, for instance, gained a better sense of the Palestinian viewpoint and of what was and was not possible from the Arab standpoint after working on the Palestinian-Israeli problem for a while. He began to understand Palestinian distinctness, telling a symposium in September 1989 that the Palestinians were "not derivative" and "not a function of an Egyptian delegation or a Jordanian delegation." In addition, although he had earlier been a strong advocate of the so-called Jordanian option—that is, negotiating the fate of the West Bank with Jordan rather than with the Palestinians[29]—he observed at the 1989 symposium that the Jordanian option might never have been more than a fiction in the first place and had finally been put to rest by the *intifada.*[30]

The most significant factor in bringing about a change in the approach pursued by these advisers, however, seems to have been the change in Bush and Baker themselves. They had never shared the mind-set that the advisers brought to office, and, from the beginning, although not enthusiastic about the U.S.-PLO dialogue and deeply cautious about how it should be pursued because of the political opposition to it in the United States, they made it clear that they hoped the dialogue would succeed. As a result, even powerful advisers like Ross and Haass, who did not believe in the dialogue, ultimately came to see some utility in it and were forced to defend it. Baker, ever the cautious politician, was happy enough at the start to follow the Ross/Haass/Washington Institute approach, but when later, in 1991, he moved into a more activist mode and it became clear that Bush and he were prepared to exert significant pressure on Israel's Likud government for movement in the peace process, the advisers loyally supported the policy.

The particularly noteworthy aspect of the body of assumptions these advisers brought to government is that these individuals not only played a major role in formulating Bush administration policy but to an even greater extent shaped policy in the Clinton administration, where most of them stayed on as major players in the Middle East peace process. In an administration like Clinton's, whose leadership had few concrete foreign-policy ideas of its own but did, unlike the Bush administration, feel a great sentimental attachment to Israel, the impact of these Israel-focused advisers was considerable.

The real change in Bush and Baker themselves, from timidity to boldness and, in the context of past decades of policymaking, near recklessness in the way they exerted pressure on Israel and advocated for Palestinian participation in peace talks, was long in coming. Baker began in early 1989 by leaning on the parties verbally and attempting halfheartedly to keep the U.S.-PLO dialogue alive and to persuade the parties to move forward with a minimum of U.S. involvement. But this was policy avoidance rather than policymaking, and in the end nothing was accomplished in the year and a half before the peace process collapsed and Iraq's Saddam Hussein diverted all attention by invading Kuwait, leading to the Gulf crisis of 1990–1991.

Quandt has written that the paradox about Bush was that his initial agenda was "probably more consonant with Israeli views than that of any previous president," yet this same administration soon became known as the most hostile ever to Israel.[31] Indeed, it was a paradox that the president and secretary of state who were least sentimentally attached to Israel and least shaped by the old frame of reference should in the first place have chosen advisers whose agenda was so consonant with Israel's views. But it was a greater irony that a group of advisers, all Jewish and all very much in tune with a moderate Israeli viewpoint, would so quickly be castigated by Israel's right wing and the Likud's U.S. supporters as self-hating Jews, labeled in vulgar terms as "Baker's Jew boys."[32]

The paradoxes had much to do with pre–Bush administration policies, with the Reagan era's extremely pro-Israeli approach and the expectations this approach raised. Israel and its supporters, having received affection and acquiescence from the Reagan foreign-policy team, expected the same from the Bush-Baker team. But now the tone was distinctly different. In May 1989, for instance, when Baker addressed the annual AIPAC conference and called on Israel to "lay aside, once and for all, the unrealistic vision of a greater Israel," cease construction of settlements in the occupied territories, forswear annexation of territory, and reach out to the Palestinians "as neighbors who deserve political rights," the reaction from Israel and its friends was outrage. The speech was written by Ross, Kurtzer, and Miller, and the policy was not different from that laid out in the Reagan Plan of 1982. But because the Reagan administration had never mentioned its opposition to the Likud's visions of a "Greater Israel" after 1982, Israel apparently did not expect to hear such admonitions. Nor was it enough for Israel that Baker was equally demanding of the Palestinians, stating U.S. opposition to Palestinian statehood and urging them to end the *intifada*, amend the PLO Charter, and reach out to the Israelis. The Israelis' problem was apparently as much the tone of Baker's remarks as their content. The *Jerusalem Post* commented that in "the vital realm of atmospherics" Baker was nothing like his predecessor George Shultz.[33] The reaction is an interesting commentary on the role of perceptions in policymaking and on the difficulties posed by formulating policy from a constricted framework.

In fact, it is a measure of how laden with emotion Middle East policymaking had always been that Bush's and Baker's lack of sentimentality was widely taken as hostility to Israel. The Reagan administration had been so accommodating to Israel that, in a real sense, no one who followed could have done other than coddle Israel without arousing suspicion and heavy criticism. Bush and Baker, it was clear from the beginning, were determined to deal with Israel as "just another pragmatic foreign policy problem,"[34] but Israel did not know how to cope with this attitude. Israeli officials, U.S.

Jewish officials, and the media devoted great amounts of time and editorial space to taking the temperature of the U.S.-Israeli relationship. Always comparing Baker to Shultz, Israelis talked about their discomfiture with the cool, businesslike attitude now displayed toward them during official meetings. The media counted the number of meetings between Baker and U.S. Jewish leaders, which never matched the regularity of Shultz's meetings, and criticized Bush and Baker for not establishing "an emotional bond of trust" with Israel. *New York Times* correspondent Thomas Friedman actually referred to the fact that Baker never communicated his plans to the U.S. Jewish community as one of his "great failings."[35] That Bush's and Baker's treatment of Israel as "just another pragmatic foreign policy problem" became a subject of such consternation and a major topic of media discussion is an indication of how thoroughly U.S. interests were identified with Israel's in the public mind. Israel had come to expect love, in a literal sense, and indulgence as its due, but Bush and Baker merely wanted a practical way to mediate a peace.

The Palestinians did not receive any indulgence either. One of the principal objectives of the authors of the Washington Institute report had been to sideline the PLO and attempt instead to work through a local Palestinian leadership from the West Bank and Gaza. Despite the PLO's major concessions in late 1988, Bush administration policy remained focused at the beginning on an effort to bypass the organization. The U.S.-PLO dialogue, according to procedures established at the end of the Reagan administration, took place in Tunis, where PLO headquarters was located, between several members of the PLO Executive Committee and U.S. Ambassador to Tunisia Robert Pelletreau. The talks, which proceeded haltingly for eighteen months, were an essentially meaningless diplomatic exercise. The Palestinians were disappointed that the United States would not allow contacts at a higher level and quickly came to feel that the United States was promoting the Israeli position. The meetings were infrequent, averaging only about one every two months in the first year of the dialogue, and amounted to little more than a pro forma exchange of positions by individuals on both sides who were too far removed from the centers of power and decision making to have a real input.[36]

More meaningful negotiations, specifically designed to circumvent the PLO, were going on at a higher level throughout this period among the United States, Israel, and Egypt over a proposal for West Bank/Gaza elections that the United States had urged Israeli Prime Minister Shamir to put forth. Rather than take the domestic political risks of dealing directly with the PLO in these negotiations, the United States used Egypt as an intermediary.[37] Operating initially on the belief that a supposedly more moderate Palestinian leadership from the occupied territories could be split off from the PLO, as well as on the equally erroneous belief that Israel's Likud-led government was interested in negotiating a compromise peace agreement, the new Bush administration had urged the Israelis to come up with a proposal that would form the basis for a new round of diplomacy. Seeing this request as an opportunity—indeed, as an invitation from the United States—to set the agenda for the next round, the Israeli cabinet put forth a plan for holding local elections in the West Bank and Gaza to choose a delegation of non-PLO Palestinians with whom Israel could then negotiate an interim agreement on self-government, in accordance with the Camp David formula.[38] The Israeli proposal addressed no substantive issues and dealt only procedurally with elections of local Palestinians who might or might not then be able to negotiate substantive matters.

The Bush-Baker team of advisers generally operated at the beginning in the belief that the Palestinian issue could somehow be taken care of by dealing with the West Bank and Gaza in this way, promoting the establishment of a local leadership and ignoring that part of the Palestinian community, making up at least half the total worldwide Palestinian population, that lived outside the occupied territories. In his 1985 paper, Ross had advocated that Israel unilaterally impose autonomy on the West Bank and Gaza as a means of promoting an alternative local leadership.[39] According to one former government official, Baker, Ross, and Ross's subordinates did finally, because "it was explained ad nauseam" to them, come to see the importance to all Palestinians of being represented by the PLO because it spoke both for Palestinians in exile and for those inside the occupied territories. But during the 1989–1990 effort to organize a Palestinian negotiating delegation, they still went to considerable lengths to accommodate Israel's refusal to deal with the PLO. Indeed, Haass, virtually alone among the policymakers working on the issue, persisted even beyond 1990 in failing to recognize the PLO's importance to the Palestinians, insisting that "the whole idea is to play on the split, not to help preserve [Palestinian] unity."[40]

Shamir brought the Israeli plan for local elections with him in April 1989 on his first visit to Washington after Bush's election, and it quickly became labeled "the only game in town," meaning it was regarded by the United States as the only starting point for the peace process. The Palestinians had missed an opportunity to take the initiative themselves by failing to put forth substantive proposals of their own. The PLO team engaged in dialogue with the U.S. ambassador in Tunis did not press the United States to discuss substantive issues, and although Arafat apparently composed a letter to Bush in February explaining the PNC resolutions passed three months earlier and emphasizing the Palestinian desire for peace, he delayed sending it in order to consult other Arab leaders on its content; he did not dispatch it until summer, well after Shamir had proposed his elections plan.[41] Although the PLO might have regained some of the initiative by putting forth counterproposals to the Shamir plan, it chose instead to work quietly and indirectly through Egypt's auspices.

Baker and his advisers spent the following year working on Shamir's plan, proposing variations and seeking counterproposals from Egypt. The Egyptians, serving as intermediaries with the PLO and hoping to secure Israel's agreement to broaden its definition of "acceptable" Palestinians to stand for election, offered a proposal in response to Israel's plan, and in late 1989 Baker, trying to bridge the gap, put forth a U.S. proposal. But because Israel's Likud-led government was uninterested in real movement toward peace, because the PLO failed to put itself forward actively, and because the United States was determined not to become engaged in questions of substance, the Israeli-Egyptian-U.S. diplomatic exchanges had no real goal and eventually became entangled in absurd procedural controversies over which Palestinians with which residency status and which address would be allowed to run for election. In the spring of 1990, Shamir, opposed to moving beyond this procedural wrangling and under pressure from right-wingers in his cabinet, finally scuttled his own plan.

The United States had misjudged Shamir's flexibility and essentially wasted a year in the belief that he would ultimately compromise and could be cajoled into real movement toward peace. Apparently believing that Shamir was flexible underneath a tough exterior and interpreting the Israeli's hard-line policy on the occupied territories as a tactical stance that could be changed if he were handled adroitly and cautiously, Ross thought the Likud-led government would eventually take serious steps. Bush and Baker, themselves nonideological pragmatists who could see the possibility for resolution in every problem, had little understanding of anyone like Shamir who was prepared to stand absolutely firm on the basis of ideology. It was a year before U.S. officials began to realize that Shamir had no intention of ever relinquishing control over the West Bank and Gaza.

The belief that the Likud was somehow flexible beneath the surface had been a major misconception in the United States for some time. Indeed, the belief that Israel would eventually "come around" and the inability to recognize that the Likud would not had long been fundamental elements of the basic frame of reference from which U.S. policy was made and had led the United States astray during both the Carter and the Reagan administrations. Baker's public threats to withdraw from the peace process, made in anger after Israel had scuttled the elections plan in mid-1990, and his dramatic statement before Congress giving the White House phone number and telling Israel to call when it was serious about peace were an indication that, even after more than a year of dealing with Israel, Baker did not fully recognize that U.S. disengagement was exactly what Shamir wanted.[42]

Many who knew Israel better felt at the time that while Shamir and his right-wing government could not be moved, Israeli society was ready for change and would have responded to a clear U.S. stance opposing Israel's West Bank policies by changing the political equation. Contrary to the conventional U.S. notion that aid should never be used to exert pressure on Israel, these observers believed that pressure on Shamir would have had a salutary effect and that U.S. encouragement of Shamir had discouraged more moderate Israelis from challenging him. Former Israeli Foreign Minister Abba Eban wrote in early 1990 that opinion polls indicated that the Israeli public was ready for territorial compromise and for dialogue with anyone who truly represented the Palestinians, even the PLO. The United States was hurting its own and Israel's interests, he thought, by so narrowly focusing on Shamir's nonsubstantive elections plan. Noting pointedly that "our region has never been as 'ripe' as it is today for large visions and hard facts," Eban said that Israeli think tanks, political parties, and media were examining a range of substantive formulas for peace but were being frustrated and "sidetracked" by U.S. encouragement of Shamir's delaying tactics.[43]

An Israeli journalist living in the United States, citing a 1990 Israeli public opinion poll showing clear majorities in favor of a halt to Israeli settlement construction and of trading territory for peace with security guarantees, noted that the poll suggested that a strong U.S. message and a clear position could influence Israeli political choices and could "help shatter the status quo." By not sending such a message, through some curtailment in aid to Israel linked to its settlement policies, the journalist asserted, "American policymakers are channeling U.S. tax dollars to increase the power of those forces in Israel whose interests run counter to American values and goals."[44]

The Bush administration did eventually come to accept the utility of using U.S. aid as a lever with Shamir in an attempt to halt settlement construction, and the pressure did result in Shamir's defeat at the polls, the election of a Labor government more willing to move forward on substantive issues, and some curtailment of settlement construction. But this curtailment of aid would not occur until 1991, after a Middle East war had been fought and much time had been lost in the peace process. In the administration's first year and a half, although the acrimony between Israel and the United States reached unprecedented levels, nothing tangible changed. Aid continued to flow uninterrupted, increasing in the aftermath of the 1991 Gulf war by two-thirds, from the standard $3 billion dollars annually to $5 billion,[45] and Israeli settlements continued to be constructed, not only uninterrupted but at an increased pace because of the massive influx of Soviet Jewish immigrants beginning in late 1989. In each of the years 1990 and 1991, the Jewish population of the occupied territories increased by approximately one-quarter.[46]

Although the Bush administration did not take tangible steps early on to impede Israel's West Bank policies, the settlements issue was a major source of contention between the administration and Israel from the beginning. President Bush became preoccupied with the issue at the time of Shamir's April 1989 visit. Firmly believing that settlements posed an obstacle to peace, he spoke to Shamir in strong terms during a private meeting and came away from the meeting under the impression that the Israeli leader had agreed to slow or halt the settlement process. A few days later, however, in an episode reminiscent of Jimmy Carter and Menachem Begin, Bush learned from the newspapers that the Israeli government was planning to establish several new settlements. He is said to have been outraged, concluding that Shamir was playing him for a fool, and thereafter he viewed the settlements issue as the litmus test of whether the Israelis were taking him seriously.[47]

Matters came to a head again less than a year later, when Shamir said publicly that a "big Israel"—meaning an Israel including the occupied territories—was needed to absorb tens of thousands of Soviet Jewish immigrants to Israel and in a private conversation misled Bush about how many of the immigrants were being housed in the occupied territories. Bush reportedly "went ballistic" when he learned that, contrary to Shamir's assurances that only 1 percent of the Soviet Jews were living in the territories, in actuality 10 percent were moving into East Jerusalem.[48] Although rarely made a public issue, the United States had not since 1948 recognized Israel's control over any part of Jerusalem, which under the UN partition plan was designated as an international zone under neither Arab nor Israeli sovereignty. Neither had the United States recognized Israel's annexation of East Jerusalem following the 1967 war or its incorporation of substantial expanses of West Bank land into the city's borders. By strict U.S. definition therefore—and a definition Bush intended to press—East Jerusalem was part of the occupied territories.

At this point Baker first raised the possibility, in an off-the-cuff remark before a congressional committee, of refusing an Israeli request for a $400-million loan guarantee for housing construction unless Israel agreed to halt the construction of new settlements. Although Baker backed off a bit from the statement, Bush pursued the issue and, having been shown maps detailing extensive settlement construction in East Jerusalem, announced at a news conference in March 1990 that the United States did not believe Israel should build new settlements in either the West Bank or East Jerusalem.[49]

Despite the verbal fireworks between the United States and Israel, Palestinian frustration over the halt to the peace process and Israel's expanding control over the occupied territories began to mount rapidly in the spring of 1990. Mainstream Palestinian moderates and PLO loyalists in the occupied territories came under increasing attack from "rejectionist" factions and Islamic fundamentalists who were able to point to the fact that a moderate diplomatic approach had failed to produce results and began to urge a return to more militant armed tactics.[50] At the same time, developments on the ground in the occupied territories appeared rapidly to be eliminating the possibility of a meaningful solution. The influx of Soviet Jews was forecast to number as many as five hundred thousand in 1990 alone, and Shamir was openly boasting that Jewish immigration would soon dramatically alter the demographic character of the West Bank and Gaza. In the event, actual Jewish immigration reached only about a quarter of the total predicted,[51] but the demographic changes nonetheless had a dramatic impact on the occupied territories. Housing construction for Jewish settlers soared, reaching a total of thirteen thousand units under construction in 1991 alone, compared to twenty thousand units in all the previous quarter century. By the end of 1991, over a quarter million Israeli settlers lived in the West Bank, Gaza, and East Jerusalem. Israel had confiscated 68 percent of the land area of the West Bank.[52] With no expectation that movement in the peace process would halt this inexorable absorption of the occupied territories, with the United States not only doing virtually nothing to move the peace process along but threatening to back off entirely, and with the *intifada* sputtering to a halt, Palestinians began to feel frustrated that their situation would never improve.

The situation was further aggravated when in May 1990 a mentally unbalanced former Israeli soldier murdered seven West Bank Palestinians working in Tel Aviv. The incident became a symbol for the Palestinians of their vulnerability under Israeli control and their inability to affect their own fate. In the wake of the killings, the UN Security Council held a special session in Geneva to discuss a resolution authorizing a Security Council investigation of the safety of Palestinians living under Israeli occupation.[53] U.S. action on a Security Council resolution that would have stood as a kind of guarantee of international protection for the Palestinians became a test for them of U.S. resolve in the peace process and of U.S. willingness to stand up for the protection of Palestinians against Israel. The issue was so important to the Palestinians that local Palestinian leader Faisal Husseini and forty others staged a two-week hunger strike following the massacre of the West Bank workers to underscore the Palestinians' sense of vulnerability and draw international attention to their situation.

The Bush administration was uncomfortable with the resolution. Under intense pressure from Israel and U.S. supporters of Israel to veto it, U.S. negotiators attempted to weaken the powers of the proposed UN investigatory commission, and the United States was already near a decision to veto when, the night before the Security Council vote, an abortive terrorist attack by a Palestinian splinter group on a Tel Aviv beach ended any uncertainty and induced the United States to cast a veto. The vote—fourteen votes for the resolution, no abstentions, and the one U.S. veto—was characterized by Husseini and the other hunger strikers as a "rude slap in the face" by the United States. Speaking for all Palestinians in the occupied territories, Husseini said at a press conference marking the end of the hunger strike that "instead of encouraging us we are being punished for seeking protection."[54]

Seeming to ignore the Palestinians' growing sense of hopelessness and under intense pressure from Congress and the pro-Israel lobby to end the U.S.-PLO dialogue, President Bush demanded that Arafat condemn the abortive terrorist act and discipline its author, Muhammad Abbas (Abu al-Abbas), a maverick member of the PLO Executive Committee, leader of the small Palestine Liberation Front (which conducted the attempted Tel Aviv beach attack), and mastermind of the *Achille Lauro* hijacking in 1985. Although the beach raid had not been planned or authorized by the PLO and Arafat dissociated the PLO from the attack, he would not explicitly condemn it. Angered by the U.S. veto and the apparent U.S. withdrawal from active involvement in the peace process, Arafat had turned to Iraq's Saddam Hussein, whose strident threats against Israel earlier in the year made him appear a champion to many desperate Palestinians, as well as a pressure point on the United States and a possible means of moving Washington out of its inertia. Arafat began to spend more time in Baghdad and, according to his principal deputy Salah Khalaf, was increasingly coming under

Saddam's influence. It was generally believed, in fact, that the attempted Tel Aviv beach raid was engineered by the Iraqi leader as a means of scuttling the peace process and drawing the PLO more closely into his orbit.[55] With the United States and Arafat at loggerheads—the one adamant in its demands of the PLO, the other equally adamant in his refusal—Bush took the decision in late June to suspend the U.S.-PLO dialogue. The stage was thus set for Iraq's invasion of Kuwait and the beginning of the Gulf crisis only six weeks later.

There was clearly no love lost between Israel under Shamir and the United States under Bush, but in the early years of the Bush administration and particularly as the summer of 1990 wound on, it was equally clear that neither Bush nor Baker sensed the seriousness of the situation or the urgent need for movement in the peace process. Quandt observed after the Gulf war that the collapse of the peace process had played into Saddam's hands; it was, Quandt said, "difficult to imagine his making such an audacious move as the invasion of Kuwait if Israelis and Palestinians had been engaged in peace talks." [56] It is also difficult to imagine Arafat casting his lot with Saddam if peace talks had been in progress.

The events leading to suspension of the U.S.-PLO dialogue closed a book that would not be reopened until after the Gulf war. The war itself might have been avoided if the Bush administration had better read the signs. Had there been recognition within the administration that Shamir could not be moved without arm-twisting; that much of Israel outside Shamir's circle was ready for compromise if it appeared the United States was serious; that Congress would probably have allowed the administration as much or nearly as much leeway to exert pressure on Israel in 1989 or 1990 as it later would permit in 1991; that desperation was growing among Palestinians; and that U.S. inaction and the lack of a vision or a plan almost always had grave consequences in the Middle East—the peace process might have moved along somewhat more rapidly.

A unique constellation of forces made real movement in the peace process possible in the aftermath of the Gulf war. The Palestinians had been badly weakened both diplomatically and financially by their alliance with Saddam during the Gulf crisis and were malleable; Israel was more obviously obligated to the United States, which had effectively destroyed the military capability of its most powerful enemy, Iraq, and the Likud government was more susceptible to U.S. pressure; the Soviet Union was on the verge of collapse and was, as it had demonstrated during the Gulf war, much more willing to cooperate with the United States; the U.S. public, increasingly impatient with foreign involvements and massive allocations of foreign aid, was willing to go along with economic pressures on Israel; and, most important, Bush and Baker themselves, emboldened by these developments and by Bush's unprecedented popularity in the wake of the war, were more than usually willing to take the political risks and use the political muscle necessary to get the peace process moving.

On the face of it, many of these factors might have indicated that there was diminished urgency and no vital U.S. interest in becoming involved in peacemaking. But dangers in the status quo dictated a U.S. interest in attempting to produce movement toward peace. Regional stability continued to be threatened by a perpetuation of the Palestinian-Israeli conflict. Continued lack of movement promised to increase the radicalization of both sides, as had been occurring before the Gulf war. There was also some danger that the Egyptian-Israeli relationship, which had been cool from its beginnings over a decade earlier because of the stalemate in the Palestinian situation, would sour further in the absence of some progress for the Palestinians. Perhaps most seriously, without a peace settlement the danger of warfare between Israel and one or more Arab countries was always a possibility, and the existence of unconventional weapons and long-range delivery systems intensified the risks of a major confrontation.[57]

Domestic U.S. political factors, however, probably most directly led Bush and Baker to decide to reopen the peace process and intervene forcefully. In the spring of 1991, Bush had extremely high popularity ratings, and, with an election approaching the following year, he and Baker calculated that a successful Middle East peace, coming on top of a successful Middle East war, would help ensure electoral victory. Presidents normally shied away from tackling the Arab-Israeli issue at this point in their terms, but in this instance Bush seems to have judged that the usually powerful Jewish vote would not be a major factor. He had received less than 30 percent of this vote in 1988, which had all along given him an unusual degree of freedom from political pressure, and with his popularity ratings so high, he felt no need to accommodate this bloc for the 1992 election. Administration political strategists reasoned that with a peace process successfully started, criticism from the Jewish community would be muted in any case.[58] Bush and Baker believed they could challenge Israel and face down Israel's friends in Congress with relative impunity, accomplishing something, as Bush wrote in his diary, that "no president has done since Ike."[59]

Developments in the Middle East over the previous several years, particularly the *intifada* and the Gulf war, had also produced a sea change in U.S. public perceptions of Israel and the Arabs and thus a major change in the frame of reference from which both the Arabs and Israel were viewed. The changed perceptions produced a shift in the balance of public sympathy, to some degree reducing automatic support for Israel and increasing support for the Palestinians and other Arabs. Public opinion polls began to show that Americans, although still highly supportive of Israel, were more sympathetic to the Palestinians than ever before, more inclined to fault Israel equally with the Arabs for holding up progress toward peace, and eager for the United States to move the peace process along. Consistently, a majority or plurality of respondents in various polls said they favored establishment of an independent Palestinian state in the West Bank and Gaza.[60]

Changed sympathies also tended to raise the level of tolerance for steps that in furtherance of the peace process might exert pressure on Israel and accommodate Palestinian demands. Americans were becoming impatient with foreign entanglements and high levels of foreign aid and, although by no means turning away from Israel, were increasingly impatient with Israel's hard line. To a much greater extent, the relationship came to be seen as a burden, the peace process as a way out. The *intifada* and Israel's harsh response had cast something of a pall on Israel's image. In addition, the demanding attitude of Israel's right-wing leaders—who repeatedly defied U.S. attempts to advance the peace process by building new West Bank settlements, even as they were asking the United States for $10 billion in loan guarantees for immigrant housing construction—had begun to irritate many Americans. Editorial cartoonists and commentators openly criticized Shamir for ignoring U.S. requests for concessions while demanding additional aid.[61]

Israel's attitude and increasing U.S. impatience made it more possible for the Bush administration to disengage from Israel somewhat and in effect to force the Palestinians down Israel's throat. Whereas aid to Israel had for years been sacrosanct, its demands were now widely seen as excessive, and the new atmosphere made it possible in September 1991 for Bush to request a four-month delay in congressional action on Israel's loan-guarantee request without provoking a significant outcry from Israeli supporters.[62] It also became possible at no political cost to talk to Palestinians and to force Israel to talk to Palestinians. The frame of reference had perceptibly changed. "The *Exodus* syndrome is in trouble," one pro-Israeli activist lamented. It had formerly been the case, he said, that when Americans were asked what they thought of when they heard the word "Israeli," they would think of Paul Newman in the movie *Exodus*. "President Bush changed that," he observed. "People now weigh the liabilities and pluses of Israel differently."[63]

Israelis also began to weigh the liabilities and pluses of the Likud government differently because of President Bush. As many Israeli observers like Eban had said it would, the Israeli electorate, needing to be challenged to move the peace process forward and encouraged in the knowledge that the United States now actively intended to foster movement, voted Shamir out of office in June 1992 and replaced his government with a Labor government more willing to pursue peace negotiations.

Hanan Ashrawi, a leading Palestinian negotiator who became well known in the United States as a spokesperson for the Palestinians during the run-up to the October 1991 Madrid peace conference and afterward, has written that the most notable aspect of Palestinian political discourse was the human dimension and that the rigidly pragmatic approach taken by the Bush administration—working incrementally for what was possible and achievable without setting long-range goals, leaving the difficult issues undefined until a later phase, and ignoring history and the human element—overlooked what she and most Palestinians regarded as the essential elements in a peace settlement. Palestinians had a keen sense of the importance of getting their story across, "to gain it the legitimacy of human identification and recognition." Yet the Americans approached the problem reductively, Ashrawi believed, leaving out the "complexity of the conflict with its historical, cultural, and existential dimensions."[64]

Bringing a consummate pragmatist like the unsentimental Baker—who did not care what the peace process achieved as long as there was an achievement, who was impatient with history and unsympathetic to questions of justice or morality—to an appreciation of the "historical, cultural, and existential dimensions" of the Palestinian question was no easy task. But Ashrawi herself achieved a measure of success in breaching Baker's reserve and accomplished much in bringing the U.S. public to a better understanding of the Palestinian perspective. More significant, although Baker may not, from the Palestinian standpoint, have been receptive enough to Palestinian concerns, that he listened to these concerns at all, that he negotiated directly with any Palestinians and particularly with those known to be affiliated with the PLO, and that he effectively forced the Palestinians on Israel, all constituted a major change in the U.S. approach to the peace process. Baker himself has explained his change of heart, from reluctant peacemaker to activist peacemaker after the war, as emanating both from a practical sense that the United States, having promised to address the Arab-Israeli conflict after the Iraqi crisis had been taken care of, would be criticized if it did not do so, and from a moral obligation because he had given his word. He received some opposition, he says, from administration officials who thought it would be impossible to bring Israel into dialogue with the Palestinians, but Bush, genuinely concerned to resolve the Palestinian problem, was wholly behind the effort.[65]

Baker's lack of sentimentality and his single-minded and wholly pragmatic pursuit of a formula to convene the Madrid conference brought the wrath of both Palestinians and Israelis down on him. *New York Times* correspondent Friedman, who followed Baker closely throughout the negotiating process, noted after the Madrid conference had convened that the only way Baker had been able to obtain agreement among Israelis and Arabs on even the shape of the table was by simply deciding what he thought was fair and imposing it.[66] To the Palestinians, this approach appeared to favor Israel. Ashrawi, a key player in a series of eighteen meetings with Baker during his eight shuttle missions before the conference, complained that Baker and his team constantly told the Palestinians that Israel would never agree to this or that Palestinian demand; she thought the principal U.S. motivation was to do what was good for Israel and that the Americans believed peace was good for Israel in spite of itself.[67] Baker clearly did lean on the Palestinians hard. When one Palestinian negotiator protested that "we are a people with dignity and pride. We are not defeated," Baker bluntly responded, "It's not my fault you backed the losing side" in the Gulf war and reminded the Palestinians that there was a big price to be paid for their "absolutely stupid" behavior. Baker constantly egged the Palestinians on with admonitions like "Don't let the cat die on your doorstep" or by observing that the train was leaving the station and would go whether they were on board or not. He frankly reminded the Palestinians that their only alternatives were to accept the conditions he was imposing and agree to negotiate or to wait until Israel had confiscated virtually all the land in the occupied territories. The issue, he always insisted, was not what was fair or right but what was realistic.[68]

Baker was hard on Israel as well. At one point when Shamir demanded that Palestinians who attended the peace conference issue a letter explicitly disavowing the PLO, Baker flatly told Shamir that such a condition would make it impossible to move forward and he could not insist that the Palestinians "commit suicide."[69] Simply forcing the Israelis to deal with the Palestinian issue was a rare accomplishment.

Another rare development was the fact that after numerous meetings, during which the Palestinians made their objections to Israeli settlement construction a major theme, Baker understood something of their perspective, particularly why the settlements were so significant to them. By dealing directly with Palestinians rather than through intermediaries, Baker began to see the West Bank/Gaza situation and the general Palestinian situation more nearly as Palestinians themselves did, more nearly in the human terms of which Ashrawi spoke. He began referring in congressional testimony to the Palestinians' situation as "really quite desperate"[70] and made note of the "human dimension" during his speech at the opening session of the Madrid conference. He is said to have purchased several hundred copies, for distribution to friends, of a 1990 book on the Palestinian issue, *We Belong to the Land,* by Israeli-Palestinian priest Father Elias Chacour.[71]

The Madrid peace conference put a new, human Palestinian face before the U.S. public as well—the face of Dr. Haidar Abdul-Shafi, who headed the Palestinian delegation, and of Hanan Ashrawi. Abdul-Shafi and Ashrawi had first become known to many Americans in April 1988, when both appeared on ABC television's *Nightline* show; host Ted Koppel staged a "town meeting" between Palestinians and Israelis in Jerusalem. Running for several nights, the program brought the two Palestinians—one a senior political figure from Gaza, the other a relatively unknown university professor—to some prominence. But the face they presented at Madrid was new to vast numbers of the U.S. public and the media. The press seemed to discover the Palestinians for the first time at Madrid. *Time* magazine, which had expressed such surprise in a 1980 cover story that Palestinians were teachers and doctors as well as terrorists and refugees, seemed surprised again that at Madrid they had "presented an image of intelligence, professionalism and sensitivity" that contrasted with the "unshaven face of Yasser Arafat."[72] CNN spoke of the Palestinians' "unexpected dignity" and of the previously "hidden" face of Palestinian moderation.[73]

Whatever the magnitude of the changes in the conventional wisdom wrought by the mere presence of Palestinians at a comprehensive peace conference, much remained unchanged, and many of Israel's most ardent supporters actively sought to maintain the basic structure of the old frame of reference. New themes emerged to compensate for the greater acceptance of Palestinians as legitimate participants in the peace process, making it clear that although the conventional wisdom had been fundamentally changed, the guardians of the old Israel-centered framework would make continued efforts to undermine the Palestinian claim to a hearing.[74]

The Bush administration not only started the peace process but forever altered the framework that shaped both public discourse and policy on Palestinian-Israeli issues. The decision finally to deal directly with Palestinians and listen to the Palestinian point of view loosened constraints on thinking and on policy that had impeded progress for decades. But the essential qualities of Bush and Baker as policymakers, the very qualities that had made them so dogged in pursuit of the peace conference, quickly emerged to thwart further progress. Their overriding interest had been in the challenge of convening the conference, and, having achieved that goal, they quickly lost interest. Never particularly interested in the substance of the negotiations, they did not care what direction or pace the talks took. Other challenges, especially Bush's troubled reelection campaign, diverted their attention, and the peace process was left to the care of the Ross-Haass team, whose frame of reference had not changed substantially from the days when they approached the Palestinian-Israeli conflict from an Israeli perspective, knew little of the Palestinian viewpoint, and advocated a hands-off approach to negotiations.

It is difficult to judge Bush administration policymaking in its totality. Its achievement in bringing all parties to the conflict together in a comprehensive peace conference for the first time since Israel's creation was a major and unprecedented breakthrough. Specifically on the Palestinian-Israeli conflict, the administration's acceptance of Palestinian political existence and legitimacy changed the U.S. mind-set about the Palestinians, broadening the framework within which all Americans viewed both Palestinians and Israelis. Although many of the old images and perceptions of Palestinians would remain and both the popular and the policymaking frame of reference would continue for the most part to be Israel-centered, the Palestinians would never in the future be politically invisible and would never be completely excluded from policy calculations. It is probably safe to say that, without Bush's and Baker's readiness to work with the Palestinians as a principal party to the negotiations and without the functioning structure of a peace process in place, Israel would not have been encouraged to negotiate with and ultimately recognize the PLO.

At the same time, however, the administration's accomplishments were diminished by its failure of vision, its failure to follow through, and its imperfect understanding of both Arabs and Israelis. The fact that policymakers were so unwilling to challenge the Middle East status quo during the administration's first year and a half contributed to the growth of radicalism among both Arabs and Israelis and allowed Israel's Likud government a free hand in that period to expand settlement construction in the West Bank and Gaza and thereby foreclose many options for peace. Furthermore, having finally begun the peace process so auspiciously in 1991 and so dramatically faced down Shamir over the settlements question the following year, bringing about a change of government in Israel, the Bush team failed to follow through on either issue.

Immediately after the multilateral Madrid conference broke up into separate bilateral groups, Baker and the administration in general lost interest in the peace talks and again pursued the low-key, no-U.S.-intervention policy that had characterized the early period. When Prime Minister Yitzhak Rabin came to the United States in August 1992, two months after his election, Bush and Baker appeared to lose their resolve about imposing a meaningful halt to settlement construction. In return for Israel's loose agreement to halt construction of new settlements, the United States granted the requested $10 billion in housing loan guarantees, which had been delayed from the previous year. The guarantees were to be spread out over a five-year period. The two sides agreed to terms that allowed Israel considerable leeway to continue construction already in progress and at the same time enabled the United States to deduct from each year's loan guarantees those construction costs that went beyond permissible limits. Israel agreed to cancel construction of six thousand planned housing units in the West Bank, but because construction necessary to accommodate "natural growth" in existing settlements was permitted under the agreement without penalty, some eleven thousand units already under construction were allowed to be finished. Construction was also permitted without restriction in areas that Israel deemed "security areas"—which included nearly half the West Bank and all of East Jerusalem, an area of such concern to Bush in 1990.[75]

The generous terms of this agreement, which was approved by Congress in October 1992, undercut much of what Bush and Baker had attempted to accomplish in halting the expansion of settlements and gave Israel almost everything Shamir had asked for. During the four years of Labor Party rule from 1992 to 1996, even with the restrictions on settlement construction, the number of Israeli settlers in the occupied territories would grow by 49 percent, from 101,000 to 150,000.[76]

In the midst of intensive negotiations with the Palestinians, Baker momentarily understood aspects of the Palestinian perspective, but in his concern to avoid becoming involved in substance he also often misunderstood the Palestinians, occasionally mistaking highly substantive demands for mere points of process. During the negotiations over whether Palestinians from outside the occupied territories and those residing in Jerusalem would be allowed to sit on the Palestinian delegation, for instance, Baker interpreted the Palestinians' demands as nonsubstantive and accused them of being "hung up on symbols."[77] This characterization defines the gap between the U.S. and the Palestinian approaches. To Palestinians—and indeed to Israelis—permitting the Palestinians to be represented by the PLO, to display the Palestinian flag, to have representatives of the exile community and Jerusalem residents accepted as legitimate members of the Palestinian collective were all issues of identity that went to the essence of Palestinian national existence. Israelis understood the identity issue well, even if the United States did not, which is why Shamir and the Likud—deeply concerned *not* to permit Palestinians to be seen as a national entity—were also hung up on these very symbols. In Baker's process-oriented frame of reference, symbols simply stood as obstacles to progress.

Palestinian novelist Anton Shammas wrote in April 1991, shortly after the first of Baker's eight trips to the Middle East to organize the Madrid conference, that upon his arrival in Israel Baker had gone straight from the airport to the Yad Vashem Holocaust memorial in Jerusalem to lay a wreath. "Inadvertently," Shammas observed, "he was signaling to the Palestinians, up front, that their voice was going to remain inaudible, not only because their dialect lacks what a language has (an army, a navy, an air force), but because their pain is deemed to be forever filtered through the dark, larger-than-life muffler of the Holocaust, forever insignificant in juxtaposition."[78]

Even with a U.S. administration intent on involving the Palestinians in negotiations and on not totally accommodating Israel, the Palestinian voice was and would remain far less audible than Israel's, its symbols less important than Israel's, as had always been the case. Discussing the vital role of language in political discourse, Shammas noted that Zionists viewed the creation of a Jewish state as the "re-territorialization of the Hebrew language," and when Palestinians were displaced, their scattering was done in Hebrew. Until the *intifada*, Palestinians had remained completely inaudible, the hidden component of what came to be known as the Arab-Israeli

rather than the Palestinian-Israeli conflict. The *intifada* gave the Palestinians "a voice within the language of the conflict," Shammas said, but in
their present state they would remain people "without a territorialized language, people of dialect."[79] Although it did much to change the framework
of thinking on the conflict and to help the Palestinian voice be heard, the
Bush administration did not change the reality that the Palestinians still
had no real language.

10   The Pictures in Our Heads

Political philosopher Walter Lippmann often commented that we are all captives of the pictures in our heads. People make mistakes, he once wrote, "because an important part of human behavior is reaction to the pictures in their heads." Human behavior takes place in "a pseudo-environment," a representation of what we suppose to be, but not what actually is, the reality. "This man-made, this cultural environment, which has its being in the minds of men, is interposed between man . . . and the external reality. . . . Men react to their ideas and images, to their pictures and notions of the world, treating these pictures as if they were the reality."[1]

We all function on the basis of what one scholar calls "perceptual predispositions," fitting the realities that confront us into our own set of images. Policymakers are no different. Confronted with the need to draw conclusions and make policy on the basis of ambiguous evidence, they tend to fit data into a preexisting framework of beliefs, establishing a paradigm that "sets limits on what explanations 'make sense,' . . . helps determine what phenomena are important, . . . [and] marks out areas to be ignored." The paradigm will lead scientists and policymakers alike to "reject flatly evidence that is fundamentally out of line with the expectations that it generates. An experiment that produces such evidence will be ignored by the scientist who carries it out. If he submits it to a journal the editors will reject it. Even if it is printed, most of his colleagues will pay no heed even if they cannot find any flaws in it."[2]

Perceptual predispositions have governed policymaking on Palestinian-Israeli issues from the beginning, from the earliest days of the Palestine problem, when British and U.S. policymakers, perceptually predisposed to view Arabs as backward and unready for self-governance and to see Palestine as a biblical land peopled with Jews and Christians, were able to block out and totally override the interests of an overwhelmingly majority Arab population in order to further the Zionist enterprise. Perceptual predispositions function today as well, for despite the fact that Palestinians are now widely recognized to have a national existence and national aspirations, U.S. policymakers are still, in their focus on Israel's interests and perspective, able to a great extent to block out the Palestinian viewpoint. For instance, although the United States still considers itself a neutral "honest broker" between the two sides, Israel's security still takes precedence in U.S. calculations of what constitute fair and reasonable peace terms, and Israel's readiness to negotiate still determines U.S. readiness to mediate. The question of Palestinian security has rarely entered U.S. calculations, and Palestinian readiness to negotiate has rarely pushed the United States to press forward with a mediation effort.

Washington Post editor and columnist Stephen Rosenfeld observed in 1997 that "Palestine is always going to be, at best, a struggling little country perceived first, by most Americans, through an Israeli lens."[3] This succinct description of the situation undoubtedly also accurately predicts the future state of public perceptions and of policymaking. But it does not accurately state the magnitude of the problem, for it is reasonable to suggest that an approach to the conflict that did not always look through an Israeli lens—that was less focused on one side, more cognizant of the concerns and, at the beginning, of the very existence of the other side, and less dismissive of the true origins of the conflict—might have, and indeed probably would have, led to a resolution years and perhaps decades earlier. Many wars and much bloodshed resulted because Israel denied and few United States policymakers ever understood the real reasons the conflict arose in the first place.

Clinton administration policy on the Palestinian-Israeli situation gives clear evidence of the truth of the old adage *"plus ça change, plus c'est la même chose,"* for it demonstrates both how dramatically the policymaking frame of reference has changed and how much it has stayed the same. In the wake of the 1991 Madrid conference and the Oslo Declaration of Principles, signed by Israel and the PLO in September 1993, Palestinians became more "respectable" in many senses in the United States. PLO leader Yasir Arafat is now received at the White House, he shakes hands with presidents and secretaries of state, and he is referred to as "President Arafat" in many circles, although not by U.S. officials. The Palestinian perspective is sought in most news programs, talk shows, and other media presentations on the

Middle East. Palestinians are considered full participants in the peace process and to a great extent are treated diplomatically like a sovereign nation.

Criticism of Israeli policies is also much more widely acceptable; many former policymakers and numerous media commentators have been openly critical of the policies of Prime Minister Benjamin Netanyahu on the basis that they have foreclosed negotiating options for the Palestinians and left them with no stake in the peace process. In December 1996, eight former high-ranking U.S. officials addressed a letter to Netanyahu stating their belief that a lasting solution to the Arab-Israeli conflict must ensure "equity for all sides" and criticizing Israel for taking "unilateral actions, such as the expansion of settlements, [that are] counterproductive to the goal of a negotiated solution and, if carried forward, could halt progress made by the peace process over the last two decades. Such a tragic result would threaten the security of Israel, the Palestinians, friendly Arab states, and undermine U.S. interests in the Middle East." The letter was signed by former secretaries of state James Baker, Lawrence Eagleburger, and Cyrus Vance; former national security advisers Zbigniew Brzezinski, Frank Carlucci, and Brent Scowcroft; and former Middle East negotiators Richard Fairbanks and Robert Strauss. Former secretaries of state Henry Kissinger, Alexander Haig, and George Shultz did not sign the letter.[4]

Nonetheless, despite statements such as this, the Palestinians are still not fully accepted as legitimate contenders for public and policymaker attention, and in many subtle ways the national mind-set remains closed to the Palestinian viewpoint. The Clinton administration—from President Bill Clinton, who as a Southern Baptist feels the biblical affinity for Israel that large numbers of his predecessors felt; to Vice President Al Gore, whose earlier record in the U.S. Senate placed him in the ranks of Israel's staunchest congressional supporters;[5] to special Middle East negotiator Dennis Ross, who brought his Israeli perspective from the Bush administration; to Martin Indyk, who moved from directing the Israeli-oriented Washington Institute for Near East Policy to holding several key posts under Clinton, first becoming director of Middle East affairs on the National Security Council staff, then ambassador to Israel, then assistant secretary of state for Near East affairs—has in most ways operated according to the old Israel-centered frame of reference. Like the team recruited into the Bush administration from the Washington Institute, the Clinton administration Middle East team generally has an Israeli Labor Party orientation.[6] Administration officials were openly chagrined when Labor Prime Minister Shimon Peres was defeated at the polls in May 1996 by the Likud's

Benjamin Netanyahu, but the restoration of Likud rule in the end has had little impact on U.S. policymaking.

The peace process had moved forward slowly under the Labor governments of Yitzhak Rabin and, after his assassination in November 1995, of Shimon Peres, but under Netanyahu it caromed from crisis to crisis, stuttering to a nearly total collapse. These crises included most notably: Israel's opening in September 1996 of an archeological tunnel running along the al-Aqsa mosque compound in East Jerusalem, which led to Palestinian demonstrations and clashes between Israeli troops and Palestinian police; the failure until January 1997 to reach agreement on the redeployment of Israeli troops in the West Bank town of Hebron; Israel's expansion of settlement construction in East Jerusalem and the West Bank, including particularly construction of settlements and takeover of homes in Arab neighborhoods of East Jerusalem in mid-1997; several 1997 bombings in Jerusalem by Palestinian Islamic fundamentalist terrorists; and Israel's delay in implementing further withdrawals from the West Bank, as called for initially by the Oslo agreement and spelled out further in the Wye agreement of October 1998.

Each of these crises necessitated some U.S. intervention, and the Wye agreement involved intensive negotiation by Clinton himself over a nineday period. But in the final analysis the United States took few concrete steps to move the peace process along, demonstrating a clear reluctance to exert pressure on or to force an open confrontation with Netanyahu and ultimately always taking refuge in the old notion that it was powerless to move until the parties themselves were ready. With a Likud government in power in Israel, this requirement automatically meant virtual deadlock. Long experience with Likud governments had previously demonstrated that Israel's right wing did not want progress in the form of territorial concessions and indeed was fundamentally opposed to the peace process. Throughout the process, for a variety of reasons ranging from the Ross team's longstanding advocacy of a hands-off approach to peacemaking, to Clinton's entanglement in scandal, to his aversion to confrontation of any kind and particularly with Israel and its congressional supporters, Clinton and his team allowed Netanyahu to play a dominating role. As *New York Times* diplomatic correspondent Steven Erlanger observed, in mid-1998, in order to avoid a politically damaging showdown with Netanyahu and in hope of ultimately forging some sort of acceptable withdrawal arrangement, Clinton seemed "to be willing to take a degree of humiliation—quite an extraordinary degree, in my view"—from Netanyahu.[7]

Throughout its first term, which more or less coincided with Labor Party rule in Israel, as well as during its second term, when the Likud governed in Israel, the Clinton administration set policies that in small ways and large automatically gave Israel an advantage in peace negotiations. The basic policy of doing virtually nothing until Israel was ready favored the Israeli position in the first instance. Almost from the beginning, moreover, the United States changed the ground rules in subtle ways that favored Israel. In June 1993, for instance, only a few months into Clinton's first term, Ross authored a statement of principles, released under Secretary of State Warren Christopher's name,[8] that in a key way reframed the objectives of the peace process. The statement subtly but fundamentally altered the U.S. position on the ultimate disposition of the occupied West Bank and Gaza, undermining the concept of territory for peace, which had always been a bedrock of U.S. policy. Heretofore, the essence of the territory-for-peace concept embodied in UN Resolution 242 had been that the territories were ultimately Arab and that all should be returned to Arab control, allowing for "minor border adjustments," in return for Arab agreement to recognize and live in peace with Israel. In the 1993 statement of principles, however, the idea of exchanging territory for peace was not mentioned, and the entire question of the extent of territory to be relinquished by Israel— even the ultimate sovereignty over those territories included during the interim stage in the Palestinian self-governing area—was left to future permanent-status talks.[9] Thus, even in the interim self-governing areas, Palestinian jurisdiction was not assured and was considered to be temporary and functional rather than territorial.

The United States thereby came to consider the territories to be "disputed"—not, as previously, "occupied." Whereas longstanding U.S. policy had always been that Israel's control of these territories was temporary, it now adopted the Israeli position that Israel had the right to negotiate the retention of some or all of the territory. Under these new terms of reference, what had always previously been understood to mean "full territory for full peace" had become instead, as far as the United States was concerned, "some territory for full peace." Ironically, this U.S. statement of principles went further toward accommodating Israel than Israel's Labor government itself was demanding in the secret Oslo negotiations then going on with the PLO, and the Oslo Declaration of Principles signed three months after the United States put forth its guidelines did not carry the connotation that those areas turned over to Palestinian jurisdiction in the interim stage might be taken back as a result of final-status negotiations.

Ross had formulated his own basis for the notion that the occupied territories were open to negotiation almost a decade before, in the Washington Institute for Near East Policy paper that he authored in 1985 recommending Middle East policy for Ronald Reagan's second term. Speaking of the demands the United States should make of the Soviet Union, he observed that the Soviets should show their good faith by, among other things, recognizing Israeli security requirements by "going beyond UN Resolution 242 and accepting the need for 'defensible borders,' meaning the acceptance [by the Soviets and the Arabs] of the principle of territorial compromise, rather than total withdrawal."[10] The concept of "territorial compromise" had heretofore implied compromise by Israel in return for full peace from the Arabs—not, as Ross indicated here, territorial compromise by the Arabs in order to guarantee Israeli security.

The Clinton administration also changed the language of negotiations and altered the ground rules in other areas. Israeli settlements, for instance, which the Carter administration had called "illegal" and the Reagan administration had termed "obstacles to peace," were labeled mere "complicating factors" by the Clinton administration. The administration seemed to take the existence of the Oslo accords and the fact that Israel and the PLO had signed an agreement leaving such issues as Israeli settlements and the status of Jerusalem until final-status negotiations as a reason to refrain completely from stating its own view on any of these key issues. Thus, the United States refused during the UN session following the signing of the Oslo accords to condemn or debate Israel's settlement activity because it was "unproductive to debate the legalities of the issue." Also in 1993, it failed for the first time in over forty years to support the UN General Assembly's annual reaffirmation of Resolution 194, adopted originally in 1949, which expressed support for the right of Palestinians who fled Palestine in 1948 to return to their homes as long as they were willing to live in peace with Israel. The United States had voted for the original resolution and forty subsequent reiterations of it, but refused to do so in 1993. In 1994, U.S. Ambassador to the UN Madeleine Albright suggested in a letter to General Assembly members that, in light of the recent peace agreements, the General Assembly "consolidate," "improve," or "eliminate" certain resolutions judged by the United States to be contentious.[11]

The body of UN resolutions, including particularly the 1970 General Assembly resolution extending the universal right of self-determination to Palestinians, constituted the basis of what international support the Palestinians enjoyed, symbolic and ineffectual though it was. Eliminating these resolutions, as the United States advocated, would have undermined those few aspects of the ground rules that helped the Palestinians, amounting to what a Jordanian journalist called "an attempted assault on the past and theft of the collective memory." [12] By stepping back itself from voicing an opinion on such things as Israel's occupation practices and urging the international community to do the same, the United States was in fact placing its support behind Israel. It was attempting to create a supposedly level playing field by removing the Palestinians' international support in a situation in which Israel enjoyed the tangible advantages—a state, actual physical control of the land, and clear military superiority—and the United States itself underwrote that advantage.

Indeed, it is an irony that the mere fact of a peace agreement between Israel and the PLO, an agreement that had altered the political and diplomatic frame of reference in the United States overnight by making the Palestinians acceptable, had also made it possible to continue ignoring the Palestinian perspective on the conflict. It became so widely assumed, particularly while the Labor government was in power, that the peace process was on track—that the Palestinians had the recognition they wanted and Israel had given all that was necessary—that few noticed or cared about events occurring on the ground that might undermine further progress. The peace process provided a kind of shield that in some ways made it increasingly difficult for the Palestinians to put their views forward.

Israeli writer Meron Benvenisti observed this phenomenon early on. Even as the bilateral Israeli-Palestinian talks were proceeding in Washington, before Oslo, Benvenisti noted that Prime Minister Rabin was cracking down on Palestinians in the occupied territories. Life became harsher in the West Bank and Gaza, he wrote, "in a way unseen by eyes blinded by the bilateral talks." Violence had been raised to a new level, Benvenisti observed, by Israel's mass deportations of Palestinians, by its closure of egress from the occupied territories so that Palestinians could not enter Israel to work, by its increased demolition of Palestinian houses. Construction of Israeli settlements increased. "Yet this quantum leap did not," he said, "disturb the sleep of the Israeli consensus [or of the U.S. consensus]. When the Palestinians came to U.S. Secretary of State Christopher and presented their protests about the situation in the territories, he responded: 'How long will you go on complaining? The time has come to start talking business!' In other words, talk to me in the jargon I know and don't bother me with the street talk of reality." [13]

The jargon the United States knows is to a great extent that of the old frame of reference, and the partial peace that now exists has made it far more difficult to change that jargon. The general attitude in the United States about the ultimate fate of Jerusalem is a case in point. Many U.S. supporters of Israel, particularly in Congress, have long urged the United States to declare officially its recognition of Jerusalem as Israel's capital by moving the embassy from Tel Aviv to Jerusalem. But until the Oslo process began, more moderate heads, recognizing that moving the embassy would constitute a major change in policy and aware of the serious political repercussions such a move would have in the Arab world, had always prevailed. In October 1995, however, by an overwhelming majority (95–5 in the Senate and 374–37 in the House), Congress passed a bill mandating the move to Jerusalem by May 1999. The bill, which automatically became law when Clinton neither vetoed nor signed it, gives the president the power to delay the move for periods of six months if a delay is deemed necessary to protect U.S. national security interests.

Had the peace process not been moving forward at the time, this proposal might not have come up at all or been voted on so overwhelmingly by Congress. But because peace appeared to so many people to be so nearly accomplished, it seemed no longer necessary to withhold approval for the embassy move. Vast numbers of the U.S. public believed in any case that Jerusalem belonged and should always belong to Israel. *New York Times* columnist William Safire spoke for a far broader sampling of public opinion than his politically conservative views normally represented when he wrote in mid-1996 that "plain justice and the new realism" demanded that the United States recognize Jerusalem as Israel's capital. Assuming that Jerusalem was Israel's capital because Israel had declared it to be—and assuming that "every realist" knew this would always be the case—Safire expressed annoyance that anyone could think otherwise.[14]

The Clinton administration did virtually nothing to counter the widely held viewpoint expressed by Safire. It remained official policy that the final status of Jerusalem was open to negotiation, and administration spokespeople criticized the Netanyahu government for its repeated efforts to prejudge the negotiations by building in Palestinian neighborhoods. But the administration essentially acquiesced in Netanyahu's aggressive assertion of Israeli control. Its criticism, if voiced at all, lacked force; it took no action to curtail aid to Israel and in fact increased aid by offsetting almost all the penalty that would have been deducted from the $10 billion in housing loan guarantees;[15] and when it had an opportunity to send a clear and meaningful signal of disagreement with Israel's policies—as with the Jerusalem embassy bill and several UN resolutions in 1997 criticizing Israel's increased settlement construction in East Jerusalem, all of which the United States vetoed[16]—it instead sent clear signals of U.S. acquiescence and even approval. The United States also did not speak out against, and thus seemed to condone, Israel's well-publicized practice since 1996 of revoking the residency permits of many Palestinians living in East Jerusalem.[17]

The rote assumption embodied in Safire's column, in the opinions of most conservative commentators, and in Congress's embassy vote that all Jerusalem is and should be Israeli because Israel said so; the refusal to debate the legalities of the issue or accept the basis for past U.S. policy; the refusal to take account of the Palestinian viewpoint or of Palestinian history in the city; the assertion of the Jewish right to control all Jerusalem and to live in any part of Palestine without recognizing a comparable Palestinian right—these have all become a widely accepted part of the national mind-set.

Many liberal commentators speak out against this body of assumptions, but their voice has been muffled. The resurgence of the conservative wing of the Republican Party in the United States in the mid-1990s brought with it a new trend in the community of U.S. supporters of Israel—a trend that increased pressures on the Clinton administration to go along with the hard-line policies of Israel's Likud government. Decisive Republican victories in congressional elections in 1994 and 1996 brought back to the fore many of the neoconservative opinion molders and intellectuals of the Reagan era, most of whom aligned themselves with Israel's Likud Party and its policies and opposed the peace process. The conservative resurgence gave a strong boost to the think tanks and editorial offices where the neoconservatives hold sway and again gave them a key voice in setting the parameters of public and congressional discourse on Palestinian-Israeli issues. Think tanks such as the American Enterprise Institute and the Heritage Foundation became major forums for opponents of the peace process in the mid- and late 1990s, and conservative commentators who supported Israel's right wing—particularly A. M. Rosenthal and William Safire of the *New York Times* and the *Washington Post's* George Will and Charles Krauthammer—maintained a steady drumbeat of opposition to efforts to further the peace process. Even before Netanyahu's electoral victory in 1996, a pro-Likud, anti-Labor, and anti-peace lobby had begun to emerge in Washington. While still in the opposition, Netanyahu and other conservative Israelis frequently lobbied Congress against Labor's peace policies and against such measures as giving financial aid to the Palestinian Authority, and many of the most politically conservative U.S. Jewish groups joined in a coalition to promote the Likud line. The lobbying coalition had already gained a foothold with Congress when Netanyahu's election gave it further impetus.[18]

Calling this union of right-wing Israelis and conservative U.S. lobbyists "peacebreakers" rather than peacemakers, one scholar, political scientist Ian Lustick, has noted that their tactic has been to look for the worst about the Oslo peace process—not to look for the possibilities or seize opportunities for peace and cooperation but to seek out legalistic evidence of violations. On the issue of the revision of the Palestinian Charter, for instance, although the PNC voted in April 1996, in accordance with the Oslo accords, to rescind those articles in the charter that called for Israel's destruction, Netanyahu and his conservative U.S. allies pressed for, and secured as part of the 1998 Wye agreement, a requirement that the PNC formally reaffirm the decision to rescind. (This was accomplished in December 1998 at a special PNC session attended by Clinton.) The "peacebreakers," says Lustick, chose to treat the Oslo accords "not as a basis for an evolving partnership, but as an array of legalistic and public relations weapons that can free Israel of its commitments, prevent further transfers of territory to Palestinian control, and delegitimize Arafat and the idea of a Palestinian state." [19]

The upsurge in anti-Palestinian, pro-Likud sentiment among conservative opinion molders in the United States reaches and helps shape the thinking of a wide audience. The major think tanks essentially set the tone and much of the content of Republican political thought. Conservative, pro-Likud columnists such as Will and Krauthammer are widely syndicated and reach an audience throughout the country. Other media vehicles that espouse the same rightist line, such as the *Wall Street Journal's* editorial page, have huge national circulations.

Radio talk-show hosts like Rush Limbaugh, who claims to have an audience of regular listeners numbering in the millions, also frequently treat their audiences to anti-Palestinian, pro-Israeli diatribes. In April 1997, at the height of the crisis sparked by Israel's construction of the 6,500-unit Har Homa settlement in the Jabal Abu Ghunaym section of East Jerusalem, Limbaugh delivered a lengthy monologue on his understanding of the Middle East situation. He had visited Israel four years earlier and met with several Israeli leaders—including Ariel Sharon, who gave him a three-hour tour of the West Bank—and only two months previously had been invited by Netanyahu to meet with him in New York during a U.S. trip. As a result of these meetings, Limbaugh, who sympathized with Netanyahu as a fellow conservative, considered himself qualified to educate his audience about the true situation in Israel. Asserting during his radio monologue that Arafat's "ultimate objective . . . has never changed. It's the elimination of Israel. There are no two ways about it," Limbaugh summed up his view of the peace process as follows: "How in the world you think you can have peace with people who swear to exterminate you is beyond me. And so a peace that seeks to accommodate those enemies is an illusion." Netanyahu, he said, understood this, although the United States did not.[20]

In a similar vein, right-wing pro-Israeli organizations such as the Zionist Organization of America, the U.S. extension of the Israeli parties Herut and Likud, have waged concerted campaigns in Congress and in the media to portray the Palestinians as untrustworthy for failing to live up to the precise legal terms of the Oslo agreement.[21] Other right-wing organizations like FLAME (Facts and Logic about the Middle East), which enjoys tax-exempt status in the United States as an educational institution, place political ads in major mainstream magazines such as the *New Yorker* denouncing the peace process under the guise of giving readers the true facts. Referring to "the so-called 'peace process,'" FLAME ads assert, "Only Israel should determine whether its national rights and its security requirements are being honored and fulfilled. Only then, and not before, should it be prepared to continue its negotiations with the Palestinian Arabs."[22] The assumption is that only Israel has national rights and security requirements.

The significance of this trend is not only that this sentiment constitutes a major political voice but that it has a major and direct impact on policy-making. With a president basically uninterested in foreign affairs in the first instance, enmeshed in scandal, and disinclined toward confrontation with his domestic political foes, the Clinton administration has probably been even less inclined than most of its predecessors to confront Israel's most vocal supporters by pressuring Israel for greater movement in the peace process. In fact, the administration frequently undermined the strength of its own bargaining position by seeming to reward Netanyahu when he was at his most uncompromising—as when, for instance, in January 1998, the U.S. delivered to Israel the first F-15 combat aircraft only hours before what was being advertised as a hard-hitting meeting between Clinton and Netanyahu over the extent of proposed Israeli West Bank withdrawals.[23] As occurred during the early years of the Bush administration, when the United States was failing to push Shamir's Likud government, opponents of the Likud in Israel again began to plead with the United States to exert meaningful pressure on Netanyahu.[24]

The intensive burst of energy expended to bring about the 1998 Wye agreement stands as an exception to Clinton's general reluctance to exert pressure on Israel, and it is a real irony that, despite his usual reticence, his pressure at Wye probably ultimately led to the breakdown of Netanyahu's governing coalition by forcing a right-wing Israeli government to undermine its own ideological underpinnings by implementing territorial withdrawals. In the particular case of the Wye agreement, Clinton, facing a congressional election in November 1998 and the danger of impeachment, needed a diplomatic success for his own political position more than he feared antagonizing Israel's supporters. In the end, Clinton achieved the Wye agreement—which simply provided for the implementation of steps originally scheduled to be carried out a year earlier under the Oslo timetable—more for Clinton himself than for the sake of the peace process.

Whereas in the Bush administration both the president and Baker counterbalanced their advisers' Israeli orientation, in the Clinton administration everyone in key positions viewed the Palestinian-Israeli conflict primarily from an Israeli perspective and was emotionally connected to Israel in some way. As a result and because Clinton and most others at high levels of the administration, including Christopher and Albright, Christopher's successor as secretary of state, rarely took an interest in the details of Palestinian-Israeli policy, as Bush and Baker both did, Ross and his team generally had a free hand to formulate policy. Although Clinton himself and his policymakers came to despise Netanyahu and his government, and the verbal fireworks were occasionally intense, the fundamental emotional attachment to Israel and its security needs and the tendency to view the conflict through an Israeli lens always principally determined Clinton administration policy.

From the beginning of the Palestinian-Israeli conflict almost a century ago, Palestinians have been particularly ineffective in advancing their own case and attempting to insert themselves and their cause into the framework that forms public thought and policy in the United States, although it is doubtful that greater organizational and public-relations skills would have altered the course of events significantly.

Palestinian political disorganization, the lack of a national political structure, and the lack of any public-relations effort in the years leading up to Israel's creation, as well as during the two decades in which Palestinians languished in shock and political quiescence following their dispossession and dispersal, have been noted. When Palestinians finally began to bring themselves to international attention in the late 1960s with a series of international terrorist incidents, the Palestinian leadership failed to put forward to the world a political face that anyone could relate to, a face that adequately explained the reasons for the terrorism, the underlying grievances that Palestinians were attempting to enunciate, and the aspirations Palestinians were pursuing. For the next two decades, Arafat dodged and weaved, promising moderation and then withdrawing it, offering secret initiatives but failing to pursue them forcefully, tantalizing U.S. policymakers with overtures but so seldom offering anything definite and tangible that it was relatively easy for them to dismiss him.

When the Palestinian people forced the issue and brought their desperate situation under Israeli occupation to the attention of the world and of their own leadership with the *intifada* in the late 1980s, the PLO leadership again failed to press the Palestinian case adequately. Although in the wake of the uprising, the PLO did issue a message of political conciliation and coexistence with Israel, with its initiative of November 1988, Palestinian spokespeople did virtually nothing to follow up on this conciliatory move. The PLO took no steps to capitalize on the considerable public sympathy for the Palestinians aroused by the *intifada,* to emphasize the historical significance of PLO concessions, to reiterate its readiness for coexistence with Israel, to combat Israel's portrayal of Palestinian concessions as a sham, or to fight continued skepticism in the United States.[25] The PLO then severely tarnished its own and its people's image by supporting Iraq's Saddam Hussein during the Persian Gulf crisis of 1990–1991, without being able to explain adequately the sense of hopelessness about the peace process that had led the Palestinians to throw in their lot with Iraq.

Edward Said has complained about the Palestinians' "historical inability as a people to focus on a set of national goals, and singlemindedly to pursue them with methods and principles that are adequate to these goals." Whereas the Zionists and later the Israelis have always had an unchanging guiding principle and have always been able to formulate concrete steps to accomplish their goals, Said writes, "the Arab technique has always been to make very large general assertions, and then hope that the concrete details will somehow work out later." Israel has always had the plans, he says; "*we* have the wish."[26] Similarly with the pro-Israel and the Arab American lobbies in the United States, one has had the plans and the other—no match for the pro-Israel lobby in size, unity, skill, dedication, or persistence—has had only the wish, with little clear and cohesive sense of its goals.

These problems and shortcomings have unquestionably had an impact on how well the Palestinian message and perspective have penetrated the consciousness of Americans. A more competent Palestinian leadership could certainly have done things differently. A more skilled propaganda arm might have competed on a more nearly even level with the pro-Zionist and later the pro-Israel lobby. Ultimately, however, it is doubtful that Palestinians would have received a much better hearing in the United States, that their message would have penetrated significantly better, even had these problems not existed. Even if their political leadership had been better able over the decades to articulate its case credibly or organize the Palestinian people or lay out a coherent strategy—even with a charismatic leader who captured the imagination of Americans as, for instance, Anwar Sadat did—it is unlikely that perceptions would have been changed appreciably. For, ultimately, Americans had no place in their mind-set for Palestinians and what they had to say about their grievances and aspirations. The U.S. frame of reference on the Palestine situation had been essentially anti-Arab and "Palestinian-less" before it was ever Zionist- or Israel-centered; the advent of Zionism as a factor and the great affection for Israel in the United States in effect set the Palestinians' already predetermined fate in concrete. U.S. presidents from Wilson on believed the Zionists had a right to Palestine; that the United States was solemnly committed to assist in, or at least not to impede, this endeavor; and that Palestinians were a primitive people with no rights, who constituted nothing so much as an obstacle to the Zionist enterprise. Charisma and a more engaging leader than the Mufti of Jerusalem in the early days would not have been enough to overcome this mind-set.

Each U.S. president since Israel's creation has put his own imprint on policy toward the Palestinians, but one principal factor has influenced the policy of each of them: the affinity each president has or has not felt for Israel has had a direct and significant impact on how the Palestinians have been dealt with. Each has been influenced to one degree or another by a national mind-set that is focused principally on Israel. Those presidents with the greatest emotional bond to Israel, particularly Johnson and Reagan, have been the most inclined to ignore or to try to ignore the Palestinians. But every president has brought to Middle East policymaking a perspective centered to a greater or lesser degree on Israel. Eisenhower, who dealt harshly with Israel, nonetheless never took the Palestinian viewpoint into consideration. Bush clearly had no emotional feeling for Israel, and he saw the need to involve the Palestinians in the peace process if a resolution were to be achieved, but neither he nor most of the foreign-policy team under him understood what the Palestinian point of view was. Even Carter never thought to challenge the assumption that had prevailed for thirty years when he took office that establishment of a Palestinian state was out of the question.

The strictures that bound the thinking even of someone as open to the Palestinian viewpoint as Carter, as well as the serious domestic political problems he confronted when attempting to bring Palestinian concerns into the negotiating process, give a clear indication of how difficult it was and probably will always be to alter the fundamental aspects of the frame of reference. What Bush was able to accomplish in pressing Israel to accept Palestinian participation in negotiations demonstrates on the one hand what is possible if policymakers step outside the usual framework. On the other hand, Clinton's quick return to the old ways and the old mind-set— and particularly the fact that, faced like Bush with a hard-line Likud government in Israel, he did not confront the Israelis as Bush did but acquiesced in policies that undermined the peace process, much as Reagan did—indicates that in the end little has changed. Each president and each administration's policymakers have ultimately been influenced by the prevailing mind-set on the issue throughout the United States, and Americans remain bonded to Israel. The pictures in the nation's heads are basically Israeli, the jargon the country knows is basically Israeli, Israel remains part of the "being" of the United States. However individual each president's style may have been, the frame of reference has more or less been a constant.

Setting the parameters of public and policymaker discourse on Palestinian-Israeli issues has always been far more than a matter of manipulation by a powerful pro-Israel lobby, more than a matter of the dictates of a controlling press, more than a matter of government or congressional manipulation. These pressures have helped to intensify and perpetuate the differences in the perceptions of Palestinians and Israelis, but it is far too simplistic to conclude that the U.S. frame of reference has been molded through a kind of conspiracy of interest groups. The public wisdom on the Palestine situation that has evolved over the decades, however inaccurate, however distorted or one-sided, has become rote, a set of blinders that permit only brief side glances into the Palestinian viewpoint. New information and new perceptions barely penetrate this set of assumptions. The lore thus constructed takes on a life of its own. It is rarely challenged, and challenges are rarely believed. In this situation, only minimal lobby pressure and media manipulation are necessary to sustain it.

More Americans know more about Israel—its history, its politics, its foreign relations, its society—than about any country in the world. In the mind of Americans, Israel is something apart. Scholar Bernard Reich has explained this special identity as emanating from a sense that Israel is "a like-image state whose survival is crucial to the ideological prospering of the United States. This perspective goes beyond the more general concern for all similar states, to one associated particularly with Israel."[27] Reich's view may be somewhat overdrawn, but it is not distorted by much, and, however imprecise, it describes a mind-set that Palestinians will obviously never penetrate. Palestinian scholar Camille Mansour has made a similar observation.

> The [U.S.] pro-Israeli predisposition [is] . . . a stubborn and enduring given that "precedes" any consideration of interest, any concern with cost or damage. . . . Cultural identification causes people to perceive that those with whom they identify are also contributing to their own strategy. By taking part in the "being" of American society, Israel also participates in its integrity and its defense. Does one think spontaneously of costs when the problem is to defend one's being, one's space, one's border? . . . Since [U.S. political leaders] cannot decide rationally whether supporting Israel against its neighbors promotes or undermines American interests, they follow their spontaneous pro-Israeli sentiments and the persuasive force of the lobby.[28]

The cultural identification of the United States with Israel simply by its nature excludes the Palestinians. Palestinians will never be part of the being of the United States and will never be perceived as contributing to U.S. strategy and defense. However perceptions of the Palestinians may change, their viewpoint will never become an integral part of the frame of reference.

In the final analysis, the key question arising from these realities is why the existence of a mind-set or frame of reference that is more or less locked into the Israeli perspective matters in the overall scheme of U.S. foreign relations. The short answer is that by its attempt since the late 1940s to avoid intervening in the conflict (an avoidance that Israelis but not Arabs have desired), by its failure to recall the root of the conflict, by its general failure to take account of Palestinian concerns, the United States has prolonged the Arab-Israeli and specifically the Palestinian-Israeli conflict. Sociologist Gershon Shafir has written that ideological convictions in Israel prolonged the conflict by leaving Palestinian interests unfulfilled and invisible and rendering even the expression of these interests illegitimate. Until Israel's young revisionist historians and the "critical sociologists" such as Shafir himself and Baruch Kimmerling came along in the late 1980s, most Israelis lived with the sense of security that came from "ideological and mythical certainties," that arose from the apparently certain knowledge that Israel's cause was and had always been entirely just and its behavior above reproach. These myths and ideological convictions required blinders that actually produced views of a far more sinister nature, Shafir maintains; in the end, they "championed behavior that brought on repeated conflict and, by justifying the mistrust of peace, offered no way out." [29]

Shafir's analysis of Israeli thinking and behavior applies as well to U.S. thinking, for the United States, following Israel's lead, has essentially taken refuge over the decades in the comfort of the status quo. By blinding policymakers to the Palestinian side of the conflict and the Arab side in general, the convictions and assumptions of the status quo prevented them not only from taking serious steps to resolve the conflict but even from recognizing when the conflict was ready to boil over.

Those policymakers and analysts who advocate that the United States maintain a hands-off or a low-key posture with regard to Palestinian- and Arab-Israeli issues, who maintain that only the parties themselves can achieve peace, point to the fact that the Oslo Declaration of Principles was negotiated without the assistance of the United States but came about when Israel and the Palestinians themselves decided to move ahead, negotiating directly and using the Norwegians not as mediators but as facilitators to arrange a venue for the secret talks, to carry messages, and in some of the final stages to clarify points and assist in devising wording. But Israelis and Palestinians came together for these direct, unmediated talks in 1992 and 1993 for a combination of reasons that had not existed previously and probably will not again—reasons that in the end bring no credit to U.S. policymaking.

First, Israel under a Labor government was ready to talk and make concessions and was pushed by a young government minister, Yossi Beilin, and two unknown Israeli academics interested in taking new risks and exploring new avenues. This circumstance is not likely to be repeated under a Likud government avowedly opposed to any peace arrangement involving Israeli territorial concessions. Second, Arafat was eager to probe the Oslo channel precisely because he and the PLO had been excluded from the main peace talks by U.S. design and he was fearful of being sidelined by the West Bankers engaged in the Washington bilateral talks. Had U.S. policymakers not been so determined to bypass the PLO and seek an alternative leadership for the Palestinians among the West Bank negotiators, similar progress would undoubtedly have been possible in the principal negotiating venue in Washington. Finally, the United States itself undermined the official negotiations during the last year of the Bush administration and the first few months of Clinton's presidency by playing the role of spectator, failing to intervene with positive proposals of its own when Israelis and Palestinians were unable to bridge the gap between them and seeming to take Israel's part on the essentials.

U.S. policymakers did know about the Oslo channel, but, apparently unable to believe that anything could be accomplished without U.S. participation and perhaps believing, because of their own anti-PLO views, that Israel would never negotiate with the PLO, they missed the significance of the secret talks. In late 1992, the Norwegians and Beilin each asked U.S. officials for their views on the possibility of negotiating with the PLO and in both instances were given dismissive answers: it was premature, or Arafat was an unreliable negotiating partner. Again in January 1993, the Norwegians gave the new Clinton administration a general report on the secret talks, without elaborating on details, and conveyed a request from the PLO negotiators that the Americans engage in secret direct talks with the PLO, and again the United States showed no interest. Several times throughout 1993, including in July and August, only weeks before the Declaration of Principles was signed, the Norwegians informed the United States, including Secretary of State Christopher, in general terms about the secret channel, but the United States never followed up on offers to use the channel as a means of overcoming impasses in the Washington talks and did not appear to consider the Oslo talks a serious venture. One U.S. official flatly turned down an offer to join the secret talks, apparently considering them too vague and exploratory, even after becoming aware that Foreign Minister Peres had become involved.[30]

The Oslo talks ultimately succeeded in large measure because the Israelis, particularly Beilin and his mentor Peres, began to take the PLO seriously, finally coming to realize that only the PLO could deliver. The Washington talks were stagnating, they realized, because the PLO had been shut out and Palestinian negotiators would not make decisions independent of their leadership.[31]

Harold Saunders has recounted a conversation he had with an Egyptian official in early 1974 during one of Secretary of State Henry Kissinger's shuttle missions following the October 1973 war. The Egyptian lamented that the United States had not been decisively involved in the search for peace between the 1967 and the 1973 wars. When Saunders observed that the United States was certainly involved now, the Egyptian replied, "Yes, but it took a war to get you here."[32] Unfortunately, this has been the case more than once throughout the history of the Arab-Israeli conflict, and it is not unreasonable to argue that many wars, perhaps all wars, could have been avoided over the last half century if the United States had better understood and paid better heed to the concerns of both sides in the conflict. The possibility that Iraq's invasion of Kuwait and the Persian Gulf war that followed could have been avoided if an active peace process that addressed Palestinian concerns had been in train has been noted. Similarly, the *intifada* and its accompanying bloodshed might have been avoided if Palestinians had felt any reason to hope that the United States would press for serious negotiations and would not continue to underwrite Israel's occupation.

It is possible to continue going back in time with this line of thought. What might have been the possibility of avoiding Israel's 1982 invasion of Lebanon if the United States had not encouraged Israel to believe it had Washington's support for its harsh anti-Palestinian policies in the occupied territories and indeed for its ill-concealed intention of permanently absorbing the territories into Israel? Going back to 1967 and before, what might have been the likelihood of avoiding this conflict if the United States had recognized that the Palestinian problem was the core of the conflict and had treated this issue from the beginning in its national and political dimension rather than only as a humanitarian issue of refugees? By dealing only with the broader Arab-Israeli issues arising from the events of 1948—that is, by adopting Israel's self-interested denial of the Palestinian issue's relevance and by allowing the Arab states' self-interested focus on their own territorial issues to divert it from the Palestinian question—the United States missed the point and tried to treat the symptoms while never attempting to cure the disease.

What might have been accomplished in a positive sense toward reaching a real peace, one wonders, if the United States had ever thought to examine the Palestinian perspective on the conflict? In retrospect, it is remarkable to recall that the United States did not talk to a Palestinian about political issues for forty years after 1948 and, for over a decade after 1975, actually forbade itself from talking to the Palestinians' political representative. One has to ask how slippery and hard to pin down Arafat might have been had any U.S. official ever addressed him, how many opportunities he would have missed if the United States had presented him with any, how much more forthcoming he and the PLO might have been had they received encouragement from the United States. There are no definitive answers to these questions, but the possibilities are intriguing.

During the secret Oslo negotiations, it quickly became clear to both the Palestinians and the Israelis that the personal relationships formed by the mere fact that individuals from the two sides were talking seriously to each other gave this negotiating track its momentum. Attitudes on both sides changed dramatically because each side realized that the other was legitimizing it simply by talking. One of the Israeli negotiators, Uri Savir, has indicated that he realized early in the negotiations that simply by talking to the PLO, Israel was legitimizing Arafat and that doing so would produce a change in the Palestinians' own refusal to legitimize Israel. The confidence and security each side gained in the knowledge that it was being accepted and taken seriously enabled both to make concessions. For instance, a British journalist who studied the negotiations has observed that after one crisis when the talks seemed to be in danger "the bonds already created had been strengthened; there were new understandings and some honest talking" and the crisis was overcome because there was "a shared will to succeed even when the outlook was at its most bleak." [33] It is tantalizing to imagine the results if this process had been initiated years earlier.

In the end, the singular U.S. focus on Israel's perspective in the conflict renders the United States unable to perform the role it has always set for itself as ultimate mediator and peacemaker. If the United States wants to side with Israel, policymakers, Congress, and the people may justly decide to do so; neutrality has never been necessary for successful foreign policy. But the United States cannot act as an impartial mediator or honest broker if it approaches the mediation with one eye closed. From the beginning of the Palestinian-Israeli conflict, the positions of both sides have been reasonable from their individual perspectives: Israel's denial of the Palestinians' existence as a nation was a reasonable position for Israelis fighting to maintain their national integrity; the Palestinians' denial of Israel's right to exist was a reasonable position for a dispossessed people struggling to restore their national integrity. The failure of the United States, if it expected to put itself forward as a truly neutral and effective mediator, has always lain in so thoroughly adopting the Israeli perspective that it does not recognize the Palestinian point of view. The issue is not fairness, by anyone's definition, or justice or morality. In purely practical terms, the United States cannot be a peacemaker if it continues to underwrite measures, such as Israeli settlements and Israeli land expropriations, that prevent peace from evolving. It cannot honestly maintain that its own intervention is impossible because the parties are not ready to make peace when U.S. support has a direct bearing on Israel's readiness to make concessions. It cannot expect peace in the Middle East if it supports only one side in a conflict that cries out for reconciliation.

Notes

INTRODUCTION

1. Malcolm H. Kerr, *America's Middle East Policy: Kissinger, Carter and the Future*, IPS Papers 14(E) (Washington, D.C.: Institute for Palestine Studies, 1980), pp. 8–9.

2. Ibid., p. 8.

3. Ibid., p. 9.

4. Avi Shlaim, "The Debate about 1948," *International Journal of Middle East Studies* 27, no. 3 (August 1995): 287–304.

5. Peter Theroux, *Sandstorms: Days and Nights in Arabia* (New York: Norton, 1990), p. 23.

6. William B. Quandt, *Decade of Decisions: American Policy toward the Arab-Israeli Conflict, 1967–1976* (Berkeley: University of California Press, 1977), p. 16.

7. Peter Grose, *Israel in the Mind of America* (New York: Knopf, 1983), p. 316.

8. Camille Mansour, *Beyond Alliance: Israel in U.S. Foreign Policy*, trans. James A. Cohen (New York: Columbia University Press, 1994), p. 277.

9. Edward W. Said, *Orientalism* (New York: Vintage Books, 1979), pp. 62, 93–94. Emphasis in original.

10. Henry Kissinger, "Stone's Nixon," *Washington Post*, 24 January 1996.

11. Dan Kurzman, *Genesis 1948: The First Arab-Israeli War* (New York: New American Library, 1970), pp. 190–191.

12. Outside the United States, Irish journalist Erskine Childers had investigated the broadcasts myth much earlier and found no evidence of any broadcasts or blanket orders from military commanders. His detailed analysis of the myth appeared in *The Spectator*, 12 May 1961, reprinted in Walid Khalidi, ed., *From Haven to Conquest: Readings in Zionism and the Palestine Problem until 1948* (Washington, D.C.: Institute for Palestine Studies, 1987), pp. 795–803.

13. Benny Morris, *The Birth of the Palestinian Refugee Problem, 1947–1949* (New York: Cambridge University Press, 1987), pp. 290, 287.

14. Meron Benvenisti, *Intimate Enemies: Jews and Arabs in a Shared Land* (Berkeley: University of California Press, 1995), p. 200.

15. *Ha'aretz*, English Edition, 12 May 1998; *Jerusalem Post*, 12 May 1998; *New York Times*, 15 May 1998.

16. Bernard Reich, ed., *An Historical Encyclopedia of the Arab-Israeli Conflict* (Westport, Conn.: Greenwood Press, 1996). Philip Mattar pointed out the Israel-centered terminology and interpretation in a review of the encyclopedia in the *International Journal of Middle East Studies* 29, no. 3 (August 1997): 474–476.

17. Mattar review in the *International Journal of Middle East Studies*.

18. Baruch Kimmerling, "Academic History Caught in the Cross-Fire: The Case of Israeli-Jewish Historiography," *History & Memory: Studies in Representation of the Past*, spring/summer 1995, 48.

19. Robert Fisk, *Pity the Nation: The Abduction of Lebanon* (New York: Simon & Schuster Touchstone, 1990), pp. 452–453.

20. Rashid Khalidi, *Palestinian Identity: The Construction of Modern National Consciousness* (New York: Columbia University Press, 1997), pp. 14–15. Khalidi notes that Israel frequently imposes Hebrew or Arabicized Hebrew names on Arab locations. For instance, Jerusalem is called Yerushalaim in Hebrew and al-Quds al-Sharif in Arabic, but official Israeli documents in Arabic, as well as Israel's radio and television broadcasts in Arabic, use the word Urshalim, the Arabic translation of the Hebrew name

21. Kimmerling, "Academic History," pp. 48, 53–54.

22. Robert I. Friedman, "Selling Israel to America: The Hasbara Project Targets the U.S. Media," *Mother Jones*, February/March 1987, 25.

23. The statement was by Bassam Abu Sharif, a close adviser to Arafat. Martin A. Lee and Norman Solomon, *Unreliable Sources: A Guide to Bias in News Media* (New York: Carol, 1990), pp. 323–324. For a text of Abu Sharif's statement, see *Journal of Palestine Studies* 69 (autumn 1988): 272–275.

24. Article in the Israeli paper *Davar*, 5 August 1983, quoted in Noam Chomsky, *Pirates and Emperors: International Terrorism in the Real World* (Brattleboro, Vt.: Amana Books, 1990), pp. 27–28.

25. Edward W. Said, *The Politics of Dispossession: The Struggle for Palestinian Self-Determination, 1969–1994* (New York: Pantheon Books, 1994), pp. 372–373.

26. Robert Jervis, *Perception and Misperception in International Politics* (Princeton, N.J.: Princeton University Press, 1976), pp. 410–411, 417.

27. Interview with a former government official who asked to remain anonymous.

28. Harold H. Saunders, *The Other Walls: The Politics of the Arab-Israeli Peace Process* (Washington, D.C.: American Enterprise Institute for Public Policy Research, 1985), p. 10; interview with Saunders, 13 October 1997; and letter from Saunders, 9 July 1998.

29. Jervis, *Perception and Misperception*, pp. 143, 146.

30. Yossi Melman and Dan Raviv, *The Imperfect Spies: The History of Israeli Intelligence* (London: Sidgwick & Jackson, 1989), p. 215.

31. Interview with former government official.

32. Jervis, *Perception and Misperception*, p. 253.

33. Ibid., p. 237.

34. Richard B. Parker, *The Politics of Miscalculation in the Middle East* (Bloomington: Indiana University Press, 1993), pp. 213–214.

35. Jervis, *Perception and Misperception*, p. 417.

36. Kissinger, "Stone's Nixon."

CHAPTER 1. PALESTINIANS IN
THE NINETEENTH-CENTURY MIND

1. Mark Twain, *The Innocents Abroad, or The New Pilgrim's Progress, Being Some Account of the Steamship* Quaker City's *Pleasure Excursion to Europe and the Holy Land* (reprint, Pleasantville, N.Y.: Reader's Digest Association, 1990), pp. 322–323, 394.

2. British journalist Robert Fisk in *Pity the Nation*, pp. 21–22, describes a meeting with an Israeli spokesman in 1980 in which he was given an undated book entitled *Land Ownership in Palestine 1880–1948* filled with quotes, including Twain's, describing early Palestine as "a land of brigandage, destitution and desert."

3. Said, *Orientalism*, p. 192.

4. Khalidi, *Palestinian Identity*, p. 47.

5. Victor Wolfgang von Hagen, "Introduction," in John Lloyd Stephens, *Incidents of Travel in Egypt, Arabia Petraea, and the Holy Land* (reprint, Norman: University of Oklahoma Press, 1970), p. xl.

6. Joseph L. Grabill, *Protestant Diplomacy and the Near East: Missionary Influence on American Policy, 1810–1927* (Minneapolis: University of Minnesota Press, 1971), pp. 38–39. Thomson's book, first published in 1859, has been reprinted several times. One of these reprints is William Thomson, *The Land and the Book: Biblical Illustrations Drawn from the Manners and Customs, the Scenes and Scenery of the Holy Land* (Grand Rapids, Mich.: Baker, 1954).

7. Fuad Sha'ban, *Islam and Arabs in Early American Thought: The Roots of Orientalism in America* (Durham, N.C.: Acorn Press, 1991), p. 117.

8. Von Hagen, "Introduction," p. xxxviii.

9. Quoted in Sha'ban, *Islam and Arabs*, pp. 118–119, 178–179.

10. Said, *Orientalism*, pp. 3, 19. Emphasis in original.

11. Thierry Hentsch, *Imagining the Middle East*, trans. Fred A. Reed (Montreal: Black Rose Books, 1992), p. xii.

12. Said, *Orientalism*, pp. 45–46, 86, 205.

13. Sha'ban, *Islam and Arabs*, pp. 20, 25, 195–199.

14. Hentsch outlines the progression of this enmity in *Imagining the Middle East.*

15. Ibid., pp. 130–131, and Ammiel Alcalay, *After Jews and Arabs: Remaking Levantine Culture* (Minneapolis: University of Minnesota Press, 1993), p. 145.

16. Michael W. Suleiman, "Palestine and the Palestinians in the Mind of America," in *U.S. Policy on Palestine from Wilson to Clinton,* ed. Michael W. Suleiman (Normal, Ill.: Association of Arab-American University Graduates, 1995), pp. 10–11.

17. Sha'ban, *Islam and Arabs,* pp. 32–34, 46.

18. Suleiman, "Palestine and the Palestinians," p. 13.

19. Sha'ban, *Islam and Arabs,* p. 91.

20. Beshara Doumani, "Rediscovering Ottoman Palestine: Writing Palestinians into History," *Journal of Palestine Studies* 82 (winter 1992): 8.

21. Barbara McKean Parmenter, *Giving Voice to Stones: Place and Identity in Palestinian Literature* (Austin: University of Texas Press, 1994), p. 12.

22. Sha'ban, *Islam and Arabs,* pp. 132, 134–135.

23. Twain, *The Innocents Abroad,* pp. 355–357.

24. Sarah Graham-Brown, *Palestinians and Their Society, 1880–1946* (London: Quartet Books, 1980), p. 10.

25. Stephens, *Incidents of Travel,* p. 330.

26. Sha'ban, *Islam and Arabs,* pp. 97–98.

27. Grabill, *Protestant Diplomacy,* p. 157, and Suleiman, "Palestine and the Palestinians," p. 13.

28. Cited in Alcalay, *After Jews and Arabs,* p. 67.

29. The original quote—"a country without a nation for a nation without a country"—came from Lord Shaftesbury in 1839. Suleiman, "Palestine and the Palestinians," p. 11.

30. Doumani, "Rediscovering Ottoman Palestine," p. 9.

31. See Khalidi, *Palestinian Identity,* particularly chs. 5 and 6, for a discussion of the development of Palestinian identity in the early years of the twentieth century.

32. Mark Tessler, *A History of the Israeli-Palestinian Conflict* (Bloomington: Indiana University Press, 1994), p. 53.

33. Parmenter, *Giving Voice to Stones,* p. 26.

34. Grabill, *Protestant Diplomacy,* pp. 27, 55–56.

35. Ibid., p. 27.

36. I. L. Kenen, *Israel's Defense Line: Her Friends and Foes in Washington* (Buffalo, N.Y.: Prometheus, 1981), p. 8.

37. The Division of Near Eastern Affairs, so named from the 1920s through the 1940s, was the State Department's line office dealing with the Middle East. During this period, the division answered to the Office of Near Eastern and African Affairs. In the 1950s, these organizations were renamed and, in the case of the higher level entity, given new geographical responsibilities. The Division

of Near Eastern Affaris was redesignated an "office," and the Office of Near Eastern and African Affairs became the Bureau of Near Eastern and South Asian Affairs.

38. Grose, *Israel in the Mind of America*, pp. 42–43.

39. Quoted in Jack G. Shaheen, "Remembering Both Qana and Oklahoma City Massacres," *Washington Report on Middle East Affairs*, July 1996, 20.

CHAPTER 2. WOODROW WILSON:
"RISING ABOVE" SELF-DETERMINATION

1. August Heckscher, *Woodrow Wilson* (New York: Scribner, 1991), p. 23.

2. Ibid., pp. 138, 396.

3. David Jacobs, *An American Conscience: Woodrow Wilson's Search for World Peace* (New York: Harper & Row, 1973), p. 50, cites an incident illustrative of Wilson's attitude toward blacks and possibly toward colonial peoples. Questioned during his presidency by a cabinet member who asked him whether he was aware of a policy in federal government agencies that forced black and white workers to sit in separate rows of desks and use separate lavatories and other facilities, Wilson replied in a memorandum that he knew of the policy and approved of it. This was a "natural" way for blacks and whites to share office space, he observed, and was the way each race wanted things.

4. For a recapitulation of Wilson's views on the Palestine question, see Hisham H. Ahmed, "Roots of Denial: American Stand on Palestinian Self-Determination from the Balfour Declaration to World War Two," in *U.S. Policy on Palestine from Wilson to Clinton*, ed. Michael W. Suleiman (Normal, Ill.: Association of Arab-American University Graduates, 1995), pp. 27–58.

5. Edward Tivnan, *The Lobby: Jewish Political Power and American Foreign Policy* (New York: Simon & Schuster Touchstone, 1988), p. 17.

6. Ahmed, "Roots of Denial," pp. 35–36.

7. Grabill, *Protestant Diplomacy*, pp. 80–83, 88–89.

8. Ibid., pp. 89–91, 102, 155–162.

9. Ibid., p. 178.

10. Seth P. Tillman, *The United States in the Middle East: Interests and Obstacles* (Bloomington: Indiana University Press, 1982), p. 59.

11. Ahmed, "Roots of Denial," p. 35.

12. "An Interview in Mr. Balfour's Apartment, 23 Rue Nitot, Paris, on June 24th, 1919, at 4:45 P.M.," in Khalidi, *From Haven to Conquest*, p. 198.

13. Ibid., p. 197.

14. "Memorandum by Mr. Balfour (Paris) Respecting Syria, Palestine and Mesopotamia, 1919," in Khalidi, *From Haven to Conquest*, p. 208.

15. See George Lenczowski, *The Middle East in World Affairs* (Ithaca, N.Y.: Cornell University Press, 1980), pp. 80–81, and David Fromkin, *A Peace to End*

All Peace: The Fall of the Ottoman Empire and the Creation of the Modern Middle East (New York: Avon, 1989), pp. 182–183.

16. Quoted in Ahmed, "Roots of Denial," p. 29.

17. Grose, *Israel in the Mind of America*, p. 91.

18. Ahmed, "Roots of Denial," p. 36, and Grabill, *Protestant Diplomacy*, pp. 199–200. The text of those sections of the King-Crane Commission report on Palestine is contained in Khalidi, *From Haven to Conquest*, pp. 213–218.

19. Ibid.

20. Ahmed, "Roots of Denial," p. 44.

21. Grabill, *Protestant Diplomacy*, p. 206.

22. Ahmed, "Roots of Denial," pp. 41, 43.

23. Grabill, *Protestant Diplomacy*, p. 178.

24. Ahmed, "Roots of Denial," p. 36.

25. "An Interview in Mr. Balfour's Apartment," pp. 196–197.

26. Charles D. Smith, *Palestine and the Arab-Israeli Conflict*, 3d ed. (New York: St. Martin's Press, 1996), p. 73.

27. Ahmed, "Roots of Denial," p. 45.

28. Ibid., p. 49.

29. Lawrence Davidson, "Competing Responses to the 1929 Arab Uprising in Palestine: The Zionist Press versus the State Department," *Middle East Policy* 5, no. 2 (May 1997): 100–102, 106, and Lawrence Davidson, "Press, State Department and Popular Perceptions of Palestine in the 1920s" (paper presented at the annual meeting of the Middle East Studies Association, November 1994), p. 34.

30. Grose, *Israel in the Mind of America*, p. 69.

31. Examples are cited in Ahmed, "Roots of Denial," p. 36; Davidson, "Competing Responses," pp. 101–103; and Frank E. Manuel, *The Realities of American-Palestine Relations* (Washington, D.C.: Public Affairs Press, 1949), pp. 182–201.

32. Quoted in Davidson, "Press, State Department and Popular Perceptions," p. 15.

33. Quoted in Grose, *Israel in the Mind of America*, p. 90.

34. Manuel, *The Realities of American-Palestine Relations*, p. 218.

35. Quoted in Davidson, "Press, State Department and Popular Perceptions," p. 7.

36. Ibid., p. 17, and Ahmed, "Roots of Denial," p. 32.

37. Davidson, "Press, State Department and Popular Perceptions," p. 16.

38. Quoted in Mohammed K. Shadid, *The United States and the Palestinians* (New York: St. Martin's Press, 1981), p. 26.

39. Quoted in Lawrence Davidson, "Zionism, Socialism and United States Support for the Jewish Colonization of Palestine in the 1920s," *Arab Studies Quarterly*, summer 1996, 5.

40. See Lawrence Davidson, "Historical Ignorance and Popular Perception:

The Case of U.S. Perceptions of Palestine, 1917," *Middle East Policy* 3, no. 2 (1994): 125–147.

41. Grabill, *Protestant Diplomacy*, pp. 71–72, 101.

42. Davidson, "Press, State Department and Popular Perceptions," pp. 2, 5, 9, 19, 24, 27, and Davidson, "Competing Responses," p. 96.

43. Davidson, "Press, State Department and Popular Perceptions," pp. 14, 17–20, and Davidson, "Competing Responses," pp. 95–96, 99–100.

44. Davidson, "Competing Responses," p. 96.

45. Ibid., pp. 95–97, 99–100, and Davidson, "Press, State Department and Popular Perceptions," pp. 14, 17–20.

46. Davidson, "Press, State Department and Popular Perceptions," pp. 2–4, 17, and 35, note 29.

47. Ibid., p. 34, note 2.

48. Davidson, "Competing Responses," p. 95.

49. Laurence Michalek, "The Arab in American Cinema: A Century of Otherness," *Arab Image in American Film and Television*, supplement to *Cineaste* 17, no. 1 (n.d.), copublished with the American-Arab Anti-Discimination Committee, pp. 3–9.

50. Ibid., p. 3.

51. Grose, *Israel in the Mind of America*, p. 51, and Donald Neff, *Fallen Pillars: U.S. Policy towards Palestine and Israel since 1945* (Washington, D.C.: Institute for Palestine Studies, 1995), p. 18.

52. Kenen, *Israel's Defense Line*, p. 9.

53. Lawrence Davidson, "The Press-Zionist Connection vs. the State Department: Competing American Responses to the 1929 Arab Uprising in Palestine" (paper presented at the annual meeting of the Middle East Studies Association, November 1996), pp. 23 and 35, notes 79 and 80.

54. Lawrence Davidson, "Debating Palestine: Arab-American Challenges to Zionism, 1917–1929" (unpublished manuscript, 1997), pp. 5–21.

55. J. C. Hurewitz, *The Struggle for Palestine* (New York: Norton, 1950), p. 18.

56. Grose, *Israel in the Mind of America*, p. 67, suggests that the American Federation of Labor's 1916 endorsement of Zionism was motivated by leader Samuel Gompers's fear of a glut of Jewish immigrant workers.

57. Tessler, *A History of the Israeli-Palestinian Conflict*, pp. 121–122.

58. Tessler believes that the refusal of most mainstream Zionist leaders to accept the legitimacy of Palestinian Arab desires for self-determination intensified the Arab view of Zionism as a mortal threat. Ibid., p. 168.

CHAPTER 3. FRANKLIN ROOSEVELT: LOCKED IN

1. Doris Kearns Goodwin, *No Ordinary Time: Franklin and Eleanor Roosevelt: The Home Front in World War II* (New York: Simon & Schuster, 1994),

p. 393, and Ted Morgan, *FDR: A Biography* (New York: Simon & Schuster, 1985), p. 69.

2. Grose, *Israel in the Mind of America*, p. 115.

3. See Abba Eban, *Personal Witness: Israel through My Eyes* (New York: Putnam, 1992), p. 80; Grose, *Israel in the Mind of America*, pp. 130–131; Morgan, *FDR*, pp. 583–588; and Goodwin, *No Ordinary Time*, pp. 101–102, 453–454.

4. Grose, *Israel in the Mind of America*, pp. 130–131.

5. Geoffrey C. Ward, *A First-Class Temperament: The Emergence of Franklin Roosevelt* (New York: Harper & Row, 1989), pp. 59, 250–255, and Morgan, *FDR*, p. 23.

6. Tivnan, *The Lobby*, pp. 19, 22, and Evan M. Wilson, *Decision on Palestine: How the U.S. Came to Recognize Israel* (Stanford, Calif.: Hoover Institution Press, 1979), p. 55.

7. Dan Tschirgi, *The Politics of Indecision: Origins and Implications of American Involvement with the Palestine Problem* (New York: Praeger, 1983), pp. 72–74.

8. Goodwin, *No Ordinary Time*, pp. 100–102, 173–174, 397.

9. Tschirgi, *The Politics of Indecision*, p. 36. Roosevelt had earlier referred to Britain's having "promised Palestine to the Jews." See Grose, *Israel in the Mind of America*, p. 134.

10. Tessler, *A History of the Israeli-Palestinian Conflict*, p. 173.

11. Tschirgi, *The Politics of Indecision*, p. 36.

12. See Table l, "Number of Immigrants Annually by Race. Total Number of Persons Registered as Immigrants," in *A Survey of Palestine: Prepared in December 1945 and January 1946 for the Information of the Anglo-American Committee of Inquiry*, vol. 1 (Washington, D.C.: Institute for Palestine Studies, 1991), p. 185. Figures given in Tessler, *A History of the Israeli-Palestinian Conflict*, p. 170, bring the total of Jewish immigrants for the same period to 331,518.

13. Tessler, *A History of the Israeli-Palestinian Conflict*, p. 170.

14. See Appendix I, "Population, Immigration, and Land Statistics, 1919–1946," in Khalidi, *From Haven to Conquest*, pp. 841–843.

15. Grose, *Israel in the Mind of America*, pp. 138–139.

16. Tschirgi, *The Politics of Indecision*, pp. 90–91.

17. Quoted in ibid., p. 113.

18. Quoted in Wilson, *Decision on Palestine*, p. 54.

19. Tschirgi, *The Politics of Indecision*, p. 31.

20. Wilson, *Decision on Palestine*, p. 2.

21. Tschirgi, *The Politics of Indecision*, p. 31.

22. Ibid., p. 47.

23. Kenen, *Israel's Defense Line*, p. 9.

24. Tschirgi, *The Politics of Indecision*, pp. 48–49.

25. Tivnan, *The Lobby*, pp. 22–23.

26. Ibid., p. 24, and Grose, *Israel in the Mind of America,* pp. 172–174.

27. Kenen, *Israel's Defense Line,* p. 18; Wilson, *Decision on Palestine,* pp. 27, 45; and Manuel, *The Realities of American-Palestine Relations,* p. 312.

28. Quoted in Tschirgi, *The Politics of Indecision,* p. 27.

29. Ibid., pp. 25, 27.

30. Ibid., p. 18.

31. Bruce J. Evensen, *Truman, Palestine, and the Press: Shaping Conventional Wisdom at the Beginning of the Cold War* (Westport, Conn.: Greenwood Press, 1992), p. 179.

32. Robert Lacey, *The Kingdom* (New York: Harcourt Brace Jovanovich, 1981), pp. 267–272.

33. Neff, *Fallen Pillars,* pp. 25–26.

34. Ibid.

35. Ibid., p. 25.

36. Wilson, *Decision on Palestine,* p. 33.

37. For a biography of the Mufti, showing his gradual radicalization through the years, his efforts to thwart the Zionists, and his flirtation with the Nazis, see Philip Mattar, *The Mufti of Jerusalem: Al-Hajj Amin al-Husayni and the Palestinian National Movement* (New York: Columbia University Press, 1988).

38. Neff, *Fallen Pillars,* p. 109.

39. Mattar, *The Mufti of Jerusalem,* p. 99.

40. Ibid., p. 122.

41. See Ann Mosely Lesch, *Arab Politics in Palestine, 1917–1939: The Frustration of a Nationalist Movement* (Ithaca, N.Y.: Cornell University Press, 1979), for a study of Arab political organization and the development of local Palestinian nationalism in the British Mandate period. Lesch demonstrates the impact Britain's iron hand and the Zionists' political strength had on the Arabs' ability to establish effective political organizations.

42. See Muhammad Y. Muslih, *The Origins of Palestinian Nationalism* (New York: Columbia University Press, 1988), for an examination of early Palestinian nationalism. Muslih maintains that Palestinian nationalism evolved not only because of and in opposition to Zionism but alongside it and that it would have emerged as separate from broader pan-Arab nationalism even had Zionism not existed.

43. Lesch, *Arab Politics in Palestine,* p. 234.

44. See Avi Shlaim, *Collusion across the Jordan: King Abdullah, the Zionist Movement, and the Partition of Palestine* (New York: Columbia University Press, 1988), for a history of secret British-Zionist-Transjordanian cooperation in the decades before Israel's creation in 1948 and Transjordan's absorption of the areas of Palestine that were to have formed an Arab state according to the United Nations partition resolution.

45. Eleanor Roosevelt, *The Autobiography of Eleanor Roosevelt* (reprint, New York: Da Capo Press, 1992), p. 325.

CHAPTER 4. HARRY TRUMAN:
HISTORY BELONGS TO THE VICTORS

1. Shlaim, "The Debate about 1948."
2. Benny Morris, "A Second Look at the 'Missed Peace,' or Smoothing Out History: A Review Essay," *Journal of Palestine Studies* 93 (autumn 1994): 78–79.
3. Quoted in David McCullough, *Truman* (New York: Simon & Schuster, 1992), p. 620.
4. Quoted in Clark Clifford, with Richard Holbrooke, *Counsel to the President: A Memoir* (New York: Random House, 1991), p. 25.
5. Wilson, *Decision on Palestine*, p. 149.
6. Clifford, *Counsel to the President*, pp. 14, 24.
7. Grose, *Israel in the Mind of America*, p. 294.
8. Michael J. Cohen, *Truman and Israel* (Berkeley: University of California Press, 1990), p. 27.
9. Merle Miller, *Plain Speaking: An Oral Biography of Harry S. Truman* (New York: Berkley, 1974), pp. 230–232.
10. Harry S. Truman, *Memoirs*, vol. 2, *Years of Trial and Hope* (Garden City, N.Y.: Doubleday, 1956), p. 137, and Grose, *Israel in the Mind of America*, p. 200.
11. Truman, *Memoirs*, vol. 2, pp. 137, 140.
12. Cohen, *Truman and Israel*, pp. 50–55, and Grose, *Israel in the Mind of America*, p. 194.
13. Cohen, *Truman and Israel*, pp. 51–53.
14. Dean Acheson, *Present at the Creation: My Years in the State Department* (New York: Norton, 1969), p. 177.
15. See Table 5, "Estimate of Population of Palestine by Race," in *A Survey of Palestine, Prepared in December 1945 and January 1946 for the Information of the Anglo-American Committee of Inquiry*, vol. 1, p. 143.
16. Quoted in Truman, *Memoirs*, vol. 2, pp. 134–135.
17. Ibid., p. 159.
18. Acheson, *Present at the Creation*, p. 177.
19. Truman, *Memoirs*, vol. 2, p. 133.
20. George Lenczowski, *American Presidents and the Middle East* (Durham, N.C.: Duke University Press, 1990), p. 24.
21. See, for instance, Cohen, *Truman and Israel*, p. 27, and Eban, *Personal Witness*, p.140.
22. McCullough, *Truman*, p. 611, and Harry S. Truman, *Memoirs*, vol. 1, *Year of Decisions* (Garden City, N.Y.: Doubleday, 1955), p. 69.
23. Miller, *Plain Speaking*, pp. 232–233. Emphasis in original.
24. Robert J. Donovan, *Conflict and Crisis: The Presidency of Harry S Truman, 1945–1948* (New York: Norton, 1977), pp. 320–321; Tschirgi, *The Politics of Indecision*, p. 236; McCullough, *Truman*, p. 599; and Truman, *Memoirs*, vol. 2, p. 160.

25. Grose, *Israel in the Mind of America*, p. 229, and Miller, *Plain Speaking*, p. 234.

26. Quoted in McCullough, *Truman*, pp. 599, 608.

27. Cohen, *Truman and Israel*, p. 59.

28. Ibid., p. 82.

29. U.S. Department of State, *Foreign Relations of the United States 1948*, vol. 5, *The Near East, South Asia, and Africa* (Washington, D.C.: U.S. Government Printing Office, 1976), p. 695; hereafter *FRUS 1948*.

30. Quoted in Tschirgi, *The Politics of Indecision*, p. 184.

31. See Donovan, *Conflict and Crisis*, p. 316, for another example.

32. Quoted in Cohen, *Truman and Israel*, p. 77.

33. McCullough, *Truman*, p. 604, and Donovan, *Conflict and Crisis*, p. 325.

34. Donovan, *Conflict and Crisis*, p. 321.

35. Cohen, *Truman and Israel*, pp. 83–84, and Grose, *Israel in the Mind of America*, pp. 270–271.

36. Grose, *Israel in the Mind of America*, pp. 264–266, and Cohen, *Truman and Israel*, p. 83.

37. Cohen, *Truman and Israel*, pp. 78, 80–81.

38. Clifford, *Counsel to the President*, p. 5, and Donovan, *Conflict and Crisis*, p. 329.

39. Clifford, *Counsel to the President*, pp. 3–25.

40. Cohen, *Truman and Israel*, p. 59.

41. Grose, *Israel in the Mind of America*, p. 191.

42. Wilson, *Decision on Palestine*, p. 17.

43. Grose, *Israel in the Mind of America*, pp. 190, 207, and Tschirgi, *The Politics of Indecision*, p. 156.

44. Evensen, *Truman, Palestine, and the Press*, pp. 51, 56, 58, and Wilson, *Decision on Palestine*, p. 115.

45. Alixa Naff, *Becoming American: The Early Arab Immigrant Experience* (Carbondale: Southern Illinois University Press, 1985), presents a comprehensive portrait of the early Arab American community.

46. Yossi Melman and Dan Raviv, *Friends in Deed: Inside the U.S.-Israel Alliance* (New York: Hyperion, 1994), p. 364, citing a *New York Times* review of the scholar's book.

47. Eban, *Personal Witness*, pp. 79, 91.

48. Kenen, *Israel's Defense Line*, p. 38.

49. Ilan Pappé, *The Making of the Arab-Israeli Conflict, 1947–1951* (London: I. B. Tauris, 1994), pp. 24–26.

50. Quoted in Tschirgi, *The Politics of Indecision*, p. 299, note 42.

51. Quoted in Neff, *Fallen Pillars*, p. 36.

52. A former British Foreign Office official, Christopher Mayhew, recalls that as a newly appointed junior minister at the Foreign Office in 1946 he was immediately approached by a Zionist group and that Zionist lobbying was constant thereafter, whereas the Arabs exercised no such pressure. He cannot, he says, "remember ever being lobbied by an Arab, let alone a Palestinian."

Christopher Mayhew, "Palestinian Independence Is in Sight," *Middle East International*, 16 February 1996, 21.

53. Wilson, *Decision on Palestine*, pp. 76, 79.

54. Kenen, *Israel's Defense Line*, p. 41.

55. For a review of the UNSCOP mission, as well as of the thinking of UNSCOP delegates before and during the mission, see Pappé, *The Making of the Arab-Israeli Conflict*, pp. 16–33.

56. Evensen, *Truman, Palestine, and the Press*, p. 130.

57. Ibid., pp. 126–129.

58. Ibid., pp. 155, 159–160.

59. See ibid., especially pp. 9, 13, 118, 152–155.

60. Quoted in ibid., pp. 88–89. Emphasis added.

61. Quoted in Abdelkarim A. Abuelkeshk, "A Portrayal of the Arab-Israeli Conflict in Three U.S. Journals of Opinion: 1948–1982" (Ph.D. diss., University of Wisconsin, 1985), p. 132.

62. Evensen, *Truman, Palestine, and the Press*, pp. 155, 181–182.

63. Ibid., p. 162.

64. Abuelkeshk, "A Portrayal," pp. 127–130.

65. Evensen, *Truman, Palestine, and the Press*, pp. 161–163.

66. U.S. Department of State, *FRUS 1948*, pp. 607–609.

67. Morris, *The Birth of the Palestinian Refugee Problem*, pp. 61ff., describes the successful effort by the Jewish military force, Haganah, in early April 1948 to secure key road axes in order to neutralize Arab villages in areas populated by Jews and to relieve the isolation of rural Jewish settlements.

68. For assessments of the comparative strengths of the Jewish/Israeli and Arab forces, see ibid., p. 22; Benny Morris, *1948 and After: Israel and the Palestinians* (Oxford: Clarendon Press, 1994), pp. 14–16; and Nadav Safran, *From War to War: The Arab-Israeli Confrontation, 1948–1967* (New York: Pegasus, 1969), p. 30.

69. Michael W. Suleiman, "American Public Support of Middle Eastern Countries: 1939–1979," in *The American Media and the Arabs*, ed. Michael C. Hudson and Ronald G. Wolfe (Washington, D.C.: Center for Contemporary Arab Studies, Georgetown University, 1980), pp. 24–25.

70. Anne O'Hare McCormick, "'There Is No Present Tense in Israel,'" *New York Times Magazine*, 13 February 1949, 7. This *Times Magazine* article followed a ten-part series by McCormick in the *Times* newspaper that had appeared in January.

71. Gertrude Samuels, "The Three Great Challenges to Israel," *New York Times Magazine*, 16 October 1949, 13.

72. Gertrude Samuels, "Israel of the Future—A Dream and a Plan," *New York Times Magazine*, 20 November 1949, 9.

73. Gertrude Samuels, "Israel: Contrasts and Conflict," *New York Times Magazine*, 30 October 1949.

74. See Morris, *The Birth of the Palestinian Refugee Problem*, pp. 49–52.

75. The examples are from the *Nation*, quoted in Abuelkeshk, "A Por-

trayal," p. 136; Gene Currivan, "Steady Flow of Immigrants Invigorates Life in Israel," *New York Times,* 13 March 1949; Gertrude Samuels, "Report from Dafne in Galilee," *New York Times Magazine,* 18 December 1949, 11; and C. L. Sulzberger, "Growing Israel Is Plagued by Shortage of Technicians," *New York Times,* 22 March 1950.

76. James G. McDonald, *My Mission in Israel 1948–1951* (New York: Simon & Schuster, 1951), p. xi.

77. Manuel, *The Realities of American-Palestine Relations.*

78. Anne O'Hare McCormick, "Israel Alters Levant Balance in Molding of a New Nation," *New York Times,* 10 January 1949.

79. Anne O'Hare McCormick, "Recognizing the Realities in the New Palestine," *New York Times,* 15 May 1948.

80. Cited in Neff, *Fallen Pillars,* p. 73.

81. Ibid.

82. Quoted in Abuelkeshk, "A Portrayal," pp. 141–142.

83. Morris, *The Birth of the Palestinian Refugee Problem,* pp. 293–294; see also the entire chapter "Conclusions," pp. 286–296.

84. McDonald, *My Mission in Israel,* p. 175.

85. Roosevelt, *The Autobiography of Eleanor Roosevelt,* pp. 326–327.

86. Saunders, *The Other Walls,* p. 6.

87. Eban, *Personal Witness,* p. 125.

88. U.S. Department of State, *FRUS 1948,* 22 June 1948, pp. 1133–1134, and 23 June 1948, pp. 1134–1137.

89. Ibid., 15 November 1948, pp. 1595–1596.

90. See Shlaim, *Collusion across the Jordan,* for a lengthy study of the years of discussion and cooperation between the Zionists and King Abdullah that led up to Transjordan's capture of the Arab parts of Palestine in 1948.

91. See Neff, *Fallen Pillars,* p. 111.

92. See, for instance, a Henderson memo to George Marshall dated 22 September 1947, cited in ibid., pp. 46–47.

93. U.S. Department of State, *FRUS 1948,* 1 July 1948, pp. 1173, 1184.

94. Neff, *Fallen Pillars,* p. 69.

95. See Morris, *1948 and After,* Chapter 9: "The Initial Absorption of the Palestinian Refugees in the Arab Host Countries, 1948–1949," pp. 289–321, for a review of Arab problems with the absorption of the refugees and of U.S. and other relief efforts.

96. Morris, *The Birth of the Palestinian Refugee Problem,* Chapter 9: "Solving the Refugee Problem, December 1948–September 1949," pp. 254–285, gives a detailed description of the ultimately fruitless political negotiations about the refugee problem.

97. Pappé, *The Making of the Arab-Israeli Conflict,* p. 230, gives the figure of twenty-five thousand, of whom aproximately ten thousand were allowed back as part of a project of family reunification. Deborah J. Gerner, "Missed Opportunities and Roads Not Taken: The Eisenhower Administration and the Palestinians," in *U.S. Policy on Palestine from Wilson to Clinton,* ed. Michael W.

Suleiman (Normal, Ill.: Association of Arab-American University Graduates, 1995), p. 95, says that about eight thousand Palestinians were allowed to return as part of a family reunion plan that ended in March 1953.

98. Shadid, *The United States and the Palestinians*, pp. 55–68, provides a summary of U.S. resettlement proposals in the Truman and Eisenhower administrations.

99. Abbas Shiblak, "Residency Status and Civil Rights of Palestinian Refugees in Arab Countries," *Journal of Palestine Studies* 99 (spring 1996): 36–45, details the restrictions on residency and civil rights imposed on Palestinians living throughout the Arab world.

100. U.S. Department of State, *FRUS 1948*, 13 December 1948, pp. 1660–1661. Emphasis added.

101. Shlaim, *Collusion across the Jordan*, p. 388.

102. Eban, *Personal Witness*, pp. 49–50.

103. Quoted in Shlaim, *Collusion across the Jordan*, p. 475.

CHAPTER 5. EISENHOWER, KENNEDY, JOHNSON:
POSSESSION IS NINE-TENTHS OF THE LAW

1. Suleiman, "American Public Support," p. 26.

2. Eban, *Personal Witness*, p. 225.

3. See Robert H. Ferrell, ed., *The Eisenhower Diaries* (New York: Norton, 1981), p. 318.

4. Emmet John Hughes, *The Ordeal of Power: A Political Memoir of the Eisenhower Years* (New York: Atheneum, 1963), pp. 17–18, 25.

5. Eban, *Personal Witness*, p. 178.

6. Hughes, *The Ordeal of Power*, p. 26, and Gerner, "Missed Opportunities," pp. 105–106, note 5.

7. Steven L. Spiegel, *The Other Arab-Israeli Conflict: Making America's Middle East Policy, from Truman to Reagan* (Chicago: University of Chicago Press, 1985), p. 60.

8. Ferrell, *The Eisenhower Diaries*, p. 318, and Spiegel, *The Other Arab-Israeli Conflict*, p. 64.

9. Gerner, "Missed Opportunities," p. 91.

10. For a summary of Eisenhower administration Middle East policy, see Lenczowski, *American Presidents and the Middle East*, pp. 31–66.

11. Quoted in Gerner, "Missed Opportunities," p. 87.

12. Spiegel, *The Other Arab-Israeli Conflict*, p. 92.

13. Quoted in Gerner, "Missed Opportunities," p. 88. Emphasis added.

14. Ibid., pp. 95–97.

15. Eban, *Personal Witness*, pp. 218–221.

16. Ibid., pp. 218, 294.

17. Ibid., p. 223, and Kenen, *Israel's Defense Line*, pp. 66, 69.

18. Melman and Raviv, *Friends in Deed*, pp. 84, 88.

19. Quoted in Grose, *Israel in the Mind of America*, pp. 314–315.

20. Quoted in Abuelkeshk, "A Portrayal," pp. 150–152, 165–167.

21. Melman and Raviv, *Friends in Deed*, pp. 107–108.

22. Michalek, "The Arab in American Cinema," p. 5.

23. Art Stevens, *The Persuasion Explosion: Your Guide to the Power and Influence of Contemporary Public Relations* (Washington, D.C.: Acropolis Books, 1985), pp. 104–105.

24. Melman and Raviv, *Friends in Deed*, p. 109, and Tivnan, *The Lobby*, p. 51.

25. William Stivers, *America's Confrontation with Revolutionary Change in the Middle East, 1948–83* (New York: St. Martin's Press, 1986), pp. 38–42.

26. Zaha Bustami, "The Kennedy-Johnson Administrations and the Palestinian People," in *U.S. Policy on Palestine from Wilson to Clinton*, ed. Michael W. Suleiman (Normal, Ill.: Association of Arab-American University Graduates, 1995), p. 115.

27. Ibid., pp. 114–116, and Shadid, *The United States and the Palestinians*, pp. 68–69.

28. Bustami, "The Kennedy-Johnson Administrations," pp. 113–114.

29. Tivnan, *The Lobby*, pp. 53–54, 56, and Melman and Raviv, *Friends in Deed*, p. 100.

30. Quoted in Bustami, "The Kennedy-Johnson Administrations," p. 114, and Spiegel, *The Other Arab-Israeli Conflict*, p. 99. Kennedy frequently said in speeches that because he felt an emotional attachment to his own ancestral homeland, Ireland, he fully understood the attachment of U.S. Jews to Israel. Spiegel, *The Other Arab-Israeli Conflict*, p. 95.

31. Spiegel, *The Other Arab-Israeli Conflict*, pp. 99–100, and Melman and Raviv, *Friends in Deed*, p. 101.

32. See Spiegel, *The Other Arab-Israeli Conflict*, pp. 107–109, for background on the Hawk sale.

33. See Melman and Raviv, *Friends in Deed*, pp. 95–104, for a description of the discovery of the nuclear complex and U.S.-Israeli discussions about it. When confronted, Israel acknowledged building a reactor and claimed it was for research purposes only, although certain aspects of the construction refuted this contention. Israel has never officially acknowledged possessing nuclear-weapons capability and now employs a standard evasion—that it will not be the first to introduce nuclear weapons to the region. The United States did secure a promise from Israel that it would permit Americans to inspect the Dimona facility, but some Israelis have openly acknowledged that they deceived the U.S. inspection team. Eban has said that the Israelis built false walls, concealed doorways and elevators, and constructed dummy installations when the inspectors arrived so that they would find no evidence of weapons production. Ibid., p. 103.

34. A former CIA official who asked to remain anonymous recalls that "to the intelligence community the evidence was incontrovertible that Israel had

embarked on a nuclear-weapons program. We produced two National Intelligence Estimates by the mid-1960s informing top-level officials of the intelligence community's conclusions."

35. Cited in Andrew Cockburn and Leslie Cockburn, *Dangerous Liaison: The Inside Story of the U.S.-Israeli Covert Relationship* (New York: Harper-Collins, 1991), p. 90.

36. Ibid.

37. Quoted in Kenen, *Israel's Defense Line*, p. 173.

38. Tivnan, *The Lobby*, p. 59, and Spiegel, *The Other Arab-Israeli Conflict*, p. 128.

39. Merle Miller, *Lyndon: An Oral Biography* (New York: Putnam, 1980), p. 477.

40. Tivnan, *The Lobby*, pp. 59–60.

41. See William B. Quandt, *Peace Process: American Diplomacy and the Arab-Israeli Conflict since 1967* (Washington, D.C.: Brookings Institution; and Berkeley: University of California Press, 1993), p. 576, note 42; and Eugene V. Rostow "Resolution 242—a Historical Perspective," in *Can Israel Survive a Palestinian State?* ed. Michael Widlanski (Jerusalem: Institute for Advanced Strategic and Political Studies, 1990), pp. 98–109.

42. Quandt, *Peace Process*, pp. 43, 56, 61, and 515, note 56; Neff, *Fallen Pillars*, p. 139; Donald Neff, *Warriors for Jerusalem: The Six Days That Changed the Middle East in 1967* (Brattleboro, Vt.: Amana Books, 1988), pp. 235–236, 307; Tivnan, *The Lobby*, p. 67; and Spiegel, *The Other Arab-Israeli Conflict*, p. 156.

43. Published as Eugene V. Rostow, "Israel in the Evolution of American Foreign Policy," in *The Palestine Question in American History*, ed. Clark M. Clifford, Eugene V. Rostow, and Barbara W. Tuchman (New York: Arno Press, 1978), pp. 46–104. A version of Rostow's presentation at this symposium was also published as "The American Stake in Israel," *Commentary*, April 1977, 32–46.

44. Quandt, *Peace Process*, p. 377, and untitled article by Eugene V. Rostow in *Approaching Peace: American Interests in Israeli-Palestinian Final Status Talks*, ed. Robert Satloff (Washington, D.C.: Washington Institute for Near East Policy, 1994), pp. 37–40.

45. Spiegel, *The Other Arab-Israeli Conflict*, pp. 126–127, 140; and Quandt, *Peace Process*, pp. 38–40.

46. Lyndon Baines Johnson, *The Vantage Point: Perspectives of the Presidency, 1963–1969* (New York: Holt, Rinehart and Winston, 1971), p. 293; Spiegel, *The Other Arab-Israeli Conflict*, pp. 139, 141; Miller, *Lyndon*, p. 481; and Quandt, *Peace Process*, p. 37. See Quandt, *Peace Process*, pp. 25–48, for a comprehensive description of U.S. actions in the crisis period leading up to the outbreak of war on June 5, 1967. Quandt concludes that as the crisis went on, Johnson's admonition to Israel turned from a "red light" on launching a pre-emptive attack to a "yellow light" that clearly signaled acquiescence to Israel's

initiating action, with the caveat that it could not count on U.S. military intervention. Ibid., pp. 48, 59.

47. Spiegel, *The Other Arab-Israeli Conflict*, p. 129.

48. Ibid., pp. 123–124.

49. Quoted in Bernard Reich, *The United States and Israel: Influence in the Special Relationship* (New York: Praeger, 1984), p. 206.

50. Miller, *Lyndon*, pp. 477–478.

51. Parker, *The Politics of Miscalculation*, pp. 100–104. The remark about the difficulty of dealing with Nasser is by Malcolm Kerr.

52. Neff, *Warriors for Jerusalem*, pp. 102–103.

53. Johnson, *The Vantage Point*, pp. 303–304.

54. Parker, *The Politics of Miscalculation*, p. 38.

55. Ibid., p. 40, and Bustami, "The Kennedy-Johnson Administrations," pp. 113, 126.

56. Helena Cobban, *The Palestinian Liberation Organisation: People, Power and Politics* (Cambridge: Cambridge University Press, 1984), pp. 21–35.

57. The term *myth of Arabism* is used in Khalidi, *Palestinian Identity*, pp. 184–185.

58. See Quandt, *Peace Process*, pp. 54–56, and Neff, *Warriors for Jerusalem*, pp. 235–237.

59. The withdrawal clause of the resolution deliberately omitted the definite article from in front of "territories" in order to leave the extent of the required withdrawal ambiguous.

60. Tessler, *A History of the Israeli-Palestinian Conflict*, p. 433.

61. For a description of the impact of the Holocaust on Israelis, before and since the Eichmann trial, see Tom Segev, *The Seventh Million: The Israelis and the Holocaust*, trans. Haim Watzman (New York: Hill & Wang, 1993).

62. Marc H. Ellis, *Beyond Innocence and Redemption: Confronting the Holocaust and Israeli Power: Creating a Moral Future for the Jewish People* (San Francisco: Harper & Row, 1990), p. 2.

63. Suleiman, "American Public Support," p. 20.

64. Eban, *Personal Witness*, p. 314.

65. Segev, *The Seventh Million*, pp. 353, 425.

66. Ibid., pp. 389–390, 392.

67. Tivnan, *The Lobby*, p. 63; Melman and Raviv, *Friends in Deed*, pp. 136, 139; and Reich, *The United States and Israel*, p. 196.

68. Suleiman, "American Public Support," p. 18.

69. Barrie Dunsmore, "Television Hard News and the Middle East," in *The American Media and the Arabs*, ed. Michael C. Hudson and Ronald G. Wolfe (Washington, D.C.: Center for Contemporary Arab Studies, Georgetown University, 1980), p. 74, and Melman and Raviv, *Friends in Deed*, pp. 365–366.

70. Ellis, *Beyond Innocence and Redemption*, pp. 2–15.

71. Cited in ibid., p. 195, note 21.

72. Interview with a Palestinian American who asked to remain anony-

mous. Palestinian American intellectual Edward Said had a similar experience and marks the beginning of his political activism from it. He recalls walking down Broadway near Columbia University, where he taught, during the war and listening as Americans with transistor radios to their ears commented on how "we" were doing. "It was like a baseball game," he says. "And there was I, a Palestinian without a voice. I was on the wrong side." Pacifica Radio broadcast (25 September 1997) of a speech by Said at a conference in Windsor, Ontario, 20 September 1997.

73. UN official George F. Kossaifi, in *The Palestinian Refugees and the Right of Return,* Information Paper 7 (Washington, D.C.: Center for Policy Analysis on Palestine, 1996), pp. 4–7, estimates the numbers of refugees from the West Bank at 148,000 and from Gaza at 87,000, and gives differing estimates from a number of other sources. Neff, *Warriors for Jerusalem,* pp. 320–321, gives the figures as 178,000 from the West Bank and 38,000 from Gaza.

74. Tessler, *A History of the Israeli-Palestinian Conflict,* p. 426.

75. Ibid., p. 464.

CHAPTER 6. RICHARD NIXON AND GERALD FORD:
AN UNRECOGNIZABLE EPISODE

1. Quandt, *Peace Process,* pp. 65–66, and Henry Kissinger, *White House Years* (Boston: Little, Brown, 1979), pp. 50–51, 563–564.

2. Kissinger, *White House Years,* pp. 347, 351, 564.

3. For a description of the differences between the global and the regional approaches to foreign policy, see Charles F. Doran, "The Globalist-Regionalist Debate," in *Intervention into the 1990s: U.S. Foreign Policy in the Third World,* ed. Peter J. Schraeder (Boulder, Colo.: Lynne Rienner, 1992), pp. 55–71.

4. Parker, *The Politics of Miscalculation,* p. 156, and Kissinger, *White House Years,* pp. 354, 368–369.

5. Quandt, *Peace Process,* pp. 73–74; and Donald Neff, "Nixon's Middle East Policy: From Balance to Bias," in *U.S. Policy on Palestine from Wilson to Clinton,* ed. Michael W. Suleiman (Normal, Ill.: Association of Arab-American University Graduates, 1995), pp. 142–143.

6. Richard Nixon, *RN: The Memoirs of Richard Nixon* (New York: Grosset & Dunlap, 1978), p. 477, and Kissinger, *White House Years,* p. 348.

7. Nixon, *RN,* p. 479; Kissinger, *White House Years,* p. 372; and Quandt, *Peace Process,* pp. 80, 83.

8. For a discussion of the situation in Jordan in 1970, see Cobban, *The Palestinian Liberation Organisation,* pp. 48–52; Alan Hart, *Arafat: A Political Biography* (Bloomington: Indiana University Press, 1989), pp. 284–323; and Quandt, *Peace Process,* pp. 98–108.

9. Quandt, *Peace Process,* pp. 98–108.

10. Kissinger, *White House Years,* p. 594, and Nixon, *RN,* p. 483.

11. Hart, *Arafat,* pp. 277–281, 355; Quandt, *Peace Process,* p. 112; and Neff, *Fallen Pillars,* p. 175.

12. Nixon, *RN*, p. 483.

13. Ibid., pp. 283, 481, 786; Neff, "Nixon's Middle East Policy," p. 133; Quandt, *Peace Process*, p. 524, note 2; and Melman and Raviv, *Friends in Deed*, p. 148.

14. Spiegel, *The Other Arab-Israeli Conflict*, p. 179; Neff, "Nixon's Middle East Policy," pp. 157–158, note 3; and Henry Kissinger, *Years of Upheaval* (Boston: Little, Brown, 1982), pp. 202–203.

15. Nixon, *RN*, p. 481. Emphasis in original.

16. Ibid., p. 249.

17. Kissinger, *White House Years*, p. 341.

18. Edward R. F. Sheehan, *The Arabs, Israelis and Kissinger: A Secret History of American Diplomacy in the Middle East* (New York: Reader's Digest Press, 1976), p. 173, and Tivnan, *The Lobby*, p. 87.

19. Kerr, *America's Middle East Policy*, p. 14.

20. Kissinger, *White House Years*, p. 342.

21. Quandt, *Peace Process*, p. 115.

22. Ibid., pp. 118–119, 146–147, and Spiegel, *The Other Arab-Israeli Conflict*, p. 211.

23. Seymour M. Hersh, *The Samson Option: Israel's Nuclear Arsenal and American Foreign Policy* (New York: Random House, 1991), pp. 209–210, and Cockburn and Cockburn, *Dangerous Liaison*, pp. 76–77.

24. Quandt, *Peace Process*, pp. 119–120, and Mansour, *Beyond Alliance*, pp. 104–105.

25. Neff, "Nixon's Middle East Policy," p. 158, note 14, and Ian Williams, "The US Veto in a Changing World," *Middle East International*, 2 May 1997, 11.

26. Tillman, *The United States in the Middle East*, p. 52.

27. Kissinger, *White House Years*, pp. 1276–1280, 1295–1300.

28. Quandt, *Peace Process*, pp. 114, 116.

29. Quoted in Melman and Raviv, *Friends in Deed*, p. 157. Emphasis in original.

30. Suleiman, "American Public Support," p. 15.

31. Tivnan, *The Lobby*, p. 72.

32. Kenen, *Israel's Defense Line*, p. 109.

33. Mark H. Milstein, "Strategic Ties or Tentacles? Institute for National Security Affairs," *Washington Report for Middle East Affairs*, October 1991, 27–28. Emphasis added.

34. Ibid.

35. State Department statements in October 1970 on the Palestinian issue are cited in Quandt, *Peace Process*, p. 535, note 2, and Shadid, *The United States and the Palestinians*, p. 96.

36. The administration deliberately skirted the Palestinian issue during the two U.S.-Soviet summits in 1972 and 1973. See Kissinger, *White House Years*, pp. 1247–1248, 1494, and Quandt, *Peace Process*, p. 143.

37. *Sunday Times* of London, 15 June 1969.

38. Kissinger, *Years of Upheaval*, pp. 759, 786, 1248–1249, and Sheehan, *The Arabs, Israelis and Kissinger*, p. 108.

39. Sheehan, *The Arabs, Israelis and Kissinger*, p. 135.

40. Kissinger, *Years of Upheaval*, pp. 624–629.

41. The arrangement worked satisfactorily until 1979, when Fatah's intelligence chief, Ali Hassan Salamah, who enforced the agreement by tracking down suspected Palestinian terrorists and warning the CIA and Western governments about planned terrorist operations, was assassinated in Beirut, probably by Israeli agents. For the story of this PLO contact with the United States, see David Ignatius, "PLO Operative, Slain Reputedly by Israelis, Had Been Helping U.S.," *Wall Street Journal*, 10 February 1983, and David Ignatius and Tewfik Mishlawi, "PLO Strife Poses Problem for U.S., Moderate Arabs," *Wall Street Journal*, 6 June 1983.

42. Kissinger, *Years of Upheaval*, pp. 1036–1037.

43. Ibid., pp. 624–625, 1036.

44. Ibid., p. 624.

45. Ibid., p. 1037.

46. Quandt, *Peace Process*, pp. 201–202.

47. Ibid., pp. 217–218, 226–227.

48. Tessler, *A History of the Israeli-Palestinian Conflict*, pp. 485–486.

49. Quoted in Lawrence I. Conrad, ed., *The Formation and Perception of the Modern Arab World: Studies by Marwan R. Buheiry* (Princeton, N.J.: Darwin Press, 1989), pp. 359, 361.

50. Tillman, *The United States in the Middle East*, p. 212.

51. Ibid., pp. 211–212.

52. Harold H. Saunders and Cecilia Albin, *Sinai II: The Politics of International Mediation, 1974–1975*, FPI Case Study 17 (Washington, D.C.: School of Advanced International Studies, Johns Hopkins University, 1993), p. 84, and George Lenczowski, *American Presidents and the Middle East*, p. 152.

53. Saunders and Albin, *Sinai II*, p. 35.

54. Quandt, *Peace Process*, p. 251.

55. See Gerald R. Ford, *A Time to Heal: The Autobiography of Gerald R. Ford* (New York: Harper & Row and Reader's Digest Association, 1979).

56. Saunders and Albin, *Sinai II*, p. 34.

57. Ford, *A Time to Heal*, pp. 245, 286–288.

58. Quandt, *Peace Process*, p. 237; Sheehan, *The Arabs, Israelis and Kissinger*, p. 167; Ford, *A Time to Heal*, p. 286; and Spiegel, *The Other Arab-Israeli Conflict*, p. 221.

59. Sheehan, *The Arabs, Israelis and Kissinger*, p. 176; Ford, *A Time to Heal*, p. 245; and Quandt, *Peace Process*, pp. 237–238.

60. Interview with Harold Saunders, 13 October 1997.

61. Cited in Shadid, *The United States and the Palestinians*, p, 89.

62. Sheehan, *The Arabs, Israelis and Kissinger*, pp. 167–168.

63. Parker, *The Politics of Miscalculation*, p. 114.

64. Saunders credits Congressman Lee Hamilton, then chairman of the

Middle East Subcommittee, for originally suggesting that the State Department testify on the Palestinians. Hamilton convened a hearing on the Palestinian issue in order to produce a library of hearings-based materials for the use of members interested in the issue. Interview with Saunders.

65. U.S. Department of State, "Department Gives Position on Palestinian Issue," *Department of State Bulletin* 73 (1 December 1975): 797–800, contains the full text of the Saunders statement.

66. Saunders and Albin, *Sinai II,* p. 87, and Saunders, *The Other Walls,* p. 9.

67. Saunders, *The Other Walls,* p. 9, and Quandt, *Peace Process,* p. 244.

68. Quandt, *Decade of Decisions,* p. vii.

69. Interview with Saunders.

70. Cited in Shadid, *The United States and the Palestinians,* pp. 90–91. Also see these pages for an earlier speech in the Senate by Oregon's Mark Hatfield showing an unusual degree of understanding of the origins of the Palestinian-Israeli conflict.

71. Georgie Anne Geyer, "The American Correspondent in the Arab World," in *The American Media and the Arabs,* ed. Michael C. Hudson and Ronald G. Wolfe (Washington, D.C.: Center for Contemporary Arab Studies, Georgetown University, 1980), pp. 65–66.

72. Ibid., p. 67.

73. Dunsmore, "Television Hard News and the Middle East," p. 74.

74. Ibid., p. 75.

75. Ibid., pp. 74–75.

76. Geyer, "The American Correspondent," pp. 68, 70.

77. Arthur Fromkin, cited in William J. Drummond and Augustine Zycher, "Arafat's Press Agents," *Harper's,* March 1976, 24–27.

78. Cited in William R. Brown, "The Dying Arab Nation," *Foreign Policy,* spring 1984, 42.

79. Bernard Lewis, "The Palestinians and the PLO," *Commentary,* January 1975, 32–48.

80. Ibid., p. 40.

81. Hisham Sharabi, "A Look Ahead: The Future State of Palestine," in *The Palestinians: New Directions,* ed. Michael C. Hudson (Washington, D.C.: Center for Contemporary Arab Studies, Georgetown University, 1990), pp. 155–156.

82. Saunders, *The Other Walls,* p. 12.

CHAPTER 7. JIMMY CARTER: MAKING A DIFFERENCE

1. Jimmy Carter, *Keeping Faith: Memoirs of a President* (New York: Bantam Books, 1982), pp. 273–275.

2. Harold Saunders, talk on presidents at Hofstra University (15–17 November 1990), rebroadcast by C-SPAN, 24 December 1992.

3. The quote is from Jim Wooten, "The Conciliator," *New York Times Magazine,* 29 January 1995, p. 28. Emphasis in original. Other insights in this and

the preceding paragraph are primarily from William B. Quandt, *Camp David: Peacemaking and Politics* (Washington, D.C.: Brookings Institution, 1986), pp. 30–32. The profile of Carter that follows is taken from these two sources and from the following: Saunders, Hofstra University talk; Zbigniew Brzezinski, *Power and Principle: Memoirs of the National Security Adviser, 1977–1981* (New York: Farrar, Straus & Giroux, 1983), pp. 18, 21–22, 49, 74; Cyrus Vance, *Hard Choices: Critical Years in America's Foreign Policy* (New York: Simon & Schuster, 1983), p. 35; and Robert M. Gates, *From the Shadows: The Ultimate Insider's Story of Five Presidents and How They Won the Cold War* (New York: Simon & Schuster, 1996), pp. 72–73, 572.

4. Quandt, *Peace Process*, p. 259.

5. Reich, *The United States and Israel*, p. 45; Brzezinski, *Power and Principle*, p. 91; and interview with William Quandt, 12 May 1991.

6. Wooten, "The Conciliator."

7. Interview with Harold Saunders, 13 October 1997.

8. Interview with William Quandt, 13 June 1997.

9. Asked during an interview with the *Jerusalem Post* in September 1977 to define what he meant by "homeland," Carter called it a "place for people to live." See Shadid, *The United States and the Palestinians*, p. 134.

10. Carter, *Keeping Faith*, p. 277.

11. Brzezinski, *Power and Principle*, pp. 21–22.

12. Samuel W. Lewis, "The United States and Israel: Constancy and Change," in *The Middle East: Ten Years after Camp David*, ed. William B. Quandt (Washington, D.C.: Brookings Institution, 1988), pp. 226–227.

13. Spiegel, *The Other Arab-Israel Conflict*, p. 316, made a similar observation, noting that Carter and his aides had difficulty understanding the "yearnings and fears" of the U.S. Jewish community. Spiegel apparently did not consider it necessary for Carter to understand Palestinian "yearnings and fears."

14. Saunders, Hofstra University talk.

15. Jimmy Carter, *The Blood of Abraham: Insights into the Middle East* (Boston: Houghton Mifflin, 1985), pp. 115–129.

16. See, for instance, Shadid, *The United States and the Palestinians*, pp. 138–139, 141.

17. Brzezinski, *Power and Principle*, pp. 65–68, 74; Vance, *Hard Choices*, p. 35; and Lewis, "The United States and Israel," p. 228.

18. Carter, *Keeping Faith*, pp. 51–52, and Brzezinski, *Power and Principle*, pp. 18, 22, 64–65.

19. Brzezinski, *Power and Principle*, p. 84.

20. Interview with Quandt, 13 June 1997.

21. Zbigniew Brzezinski, François Duchêne, and Kiichi Saeki, "Peace in an International Framework," *Foreign Policy*, summer 1975, 3–17.

22. *Toward Peace in the Middle East*, Report of a Study Group (Washington, D.C.: Brookings Institution, 1975). Highlights of the Brookings report conclusion are cited in Brzezinski, *Power and Principle*, pp. 85–86, and in Quandt, *Decade of Decisions*, pp. 290–292.

23. Quandt, *Peace Process*, pp. 560–561, note 1, and Saunders, Hofstra University talk.

24. Brzezinski, *Power and Principle*, p. 77, and interview with Quandt, 12 May 1991.

25. The information on Vance in this and the following paragraph is taken from Quandt, *Camp David*, pp. 34–35; Vance, *Hard Choices*, pp. 27–29, 163–167; and interviews with Quandt, 13 June 1997, and Saunders.

26. Brzezinski, *Power and Principle*, pp. 34–35.

27. Janice J. Terry, "The Carter Administration and the Palestinians," in *U.S. Policy on Palestine from Wilson to Clinton*, ed. Michael W. Suleiman (Normal, Ill.: Association of Arab-American University Graduates, 1995), pp. 172–173, note 8.

28. Ibid., pp. 164–165, 169–170; Spiegel, *The Other Arab-Israeli Conflict*, p. 327; and Brzezinski, *Power and Principle*, p. 438. Some pro-Israeli historians and commentators have characterized Carter's administration as lacking any senior official who advocated Israel's position or regarded Israel as a valuable ally. See particularly Spiegel, *The Other Arab-Israeli Conflict*, pp. 326–327. The view that no pro-Israeli official had any impact on policy seriously underestimates the effectiveness of the several pro-Israeli officials described.

29. Quandt, *Camp David*, p. 5. See pp. 6–29 for Quandt's analysis of the political constraints under which Carter operated in making Middle East policy.

30. Brzezinski, *Power and Principle*, pp. 51, 88, and Vance, *Hard Choices*, pp. 169–170.

31. Vance, *Hard Choices*, pp. 169–170, and Carter, *Keeping Faith*, pp. 280–281.

32. Terry, "The Carter Administration," p. 164.

33. Carter, *Keeping Faith*, p. 282; Brzezinski, *Power and Principle*, p. 24; and Vance, *Hard Choices*, pp. 174–176.

34. Vance, *Hard Choices*, p. 184.

35. Ibid., pp. 180–182, and Carter, *Keeping Faith*, p. 291.

36. Carter, Saunders, and Quandt all acknowledge being misled by Begin. Carter, *Keeping Faith*, p. 300; Eric Silver, *Begin: The Haunted Prophet* (New York: Random House, 1984), p. 181; and Quandt, *Camp David*, pp. 82–84.

37. Silver, *Begin*, p. 168.

38. Tivnan, *The Lobby*, pp. 107–110.

39. Carter, *Keeping Faith*, pp. 289, 292, and Brzezinski, *Power and Principle*, pp. 96–97.

40. Tivnan, *The Lobby*, pp. 110–112.

41. Ibid., p. 113.

42. Brzezinski, *Power and Principle*, p. 98.

43. Tivnan, *The Lobby*, pp. 118–119, 124.

44. Ibid., p. 109. Ironically, when the National Security Council staff asked the Israeli embassy for information on Begin in preparation for his first visit, the embassy sent to the White House a newly published, favorable portrait of the new prime minister entitled *Terror out of Zion*. See ibid., p. 115. In the late

1940s, the U.S. Justice Department had briefly imposed a ban on Begin's entry to the United States because he had been a terrorist. McDonald, *My Mission in Israel*, pp. 145–146.

45. Tillman, *The United States in the Middle East*, pp. 192–193.

46. Ibid., p. 194.

47. See *The Jerusalem Post International Edition*, 7 and 14 November 1987. A decade and a half after it had begun to acknowledge that Israel used "extreme physical and psychological pressures," the State Department was still, into the 1990s, shying away from using the word *torture*. Even Amnesty International did not use the word with regard to Israel until its 1990 report. Stanley Cohen, "Talking about Torture in Israel," *Tikkun*, November/December 1991, 24.

48. Suleiman, "American Public Support," p. 18.

49. Melman and Raviv, *Friends in Deed*, p. 215.

50. Quandt, *Camp David*, p. 81, and interview with Quandt, 12 May 1991.

51. Secretary of Defense Brown began a secret strategic dialogue in 1978 with his Israeli counterpart Ezer Weizman and as part of this exercise asked for assessments of the changing balance of power around the world. One official who worked on Middle East aspects was Dennis Ross, then a junior State Department official who would later become a key Middle East policymaker in the Bush and Clinton administrations. A proponent of Israel's strategic importance, Ross urged strengthened contacts between Tel Aviv and Washington but got nowhere during Carter's administration. See Melman and Raviv, *Friends in Deed*, p. 229.

52. Quandt, *Camp David*, pp. 85–87.

53. Tillman, *The United States in the Middle East*, pp. 212–213.

54. Tessler, *A History of the Israeli-Palestinian Conflict*, p. 498.

55. Kissinger himself testified before Congress immediately after concluding the Sinai II agreement, to which this and other promises to Israel were addenda, that the addenda were not binding commitments of the United States but could be altered if circumstances changed. In addition, in a report on the Panama Canal Treaty issued in 1978, the Senate Foreign Relations Committee concluded that because the president has exclusive constitutional authority to negotiate with foreign entities, he may voluntarily commit himself not to negotiate but may not circumscribe the right of a successor to enter negotiations. See Tillman, *The United States in the Middle East*, p. 224.

56. Interview with Quandt, 13 June 1997.

57. Interview with Nicholas Veliotes, 17 March 1998. Harold Saunders, who was involved in negotiating the Sinai II agreement and its codicils, has said that U.S. negotiators deliberately diluted this pledge in order to leave a door open to "an exchange of views in case it became necessary—for example, in moving back to a Geneva Conference—to work out understandings with the PLO about its participation and about its negotiating position." Saunders and Albin, *Sinai II*, p. 84.

58. Tillman, *The United States in the Middle East*, p. 211.

59. Quandt, *Camp David*, pp. 87–91, and Vance, *Hard Choices*, pp. 187–

189, summarize this portion of Vance's trip. See both sources (Quandt, pp. 87–143, and Vance, pp. 187–195), as well as Brzezinski, *Power and Principle*, pp. 101–110, for detailed descriptions of U.S. efforts to start a peace process in the late summer and fall of 1977, before Sadat's trip to Jerusalem in November forced a change of course.

60. Quandt, *Camp David*, p. 101, and Vance, *Hard Choices*, p. 187.

61. Quandt, *Camp David*, p. 94, note 34.

62. Ibid., pp. 101–102.

63. Ibid.

64. Quandt has said that when Arafat responded to the compromise proposal carried by Bolling with demands the United States could not possibly meet, including a demand for a guarantee that a PLO-led independent state would result from negotiations, Brzezinski finally lost patience with the PLO. He concluded that Arafat was not being serious, and the incident caused many in the administration to view the PLO as untrustworthy. Interview with Quandt, 13 June 1997.

65. See Quandt, *Camp David*, pp. 104–134, for a complete review of the negotiations and preparations for Geneva in September and October 1977, including the ill-fated U.S.-Soviet joint communiqué of October 1. The joint communiqué expressed the U.S. and Soviet interest in achieving a comprehensive peace settlement, via a Geneva conference, that would resolve all issues, including assuring the "legitimate rights" of the Palestinian people, and that would incorporate all parties to the conflict, including representatives of the Palestinians. Opposition to the communiqué from Israel and Israeli supporters in the United States was so strong that the United States backed away from it within days of its issuance.

66. Shadid, *The United States and the Palestinians*, p. 144, and Tillman, *The United States in the Middle East*, p. 225.

67. Carter, *Keeping Faith*, p. 302.

68. Quandt, *Camp David*, pp. 160–161.

69. Tillman, *The United States in the Middle East*, pp. 59–60, 221.

70. Quandt, *Camp David*, pp. 95, 322.

71. Former Israeli Prime Minister Rabin told political scientist Steven Spiegel in an interview that he believed Carter would have involved the PLO in the negotiating process had it not been for the Sinai II commitment. Spiegel, *The Other Arab-Israeli Conflict*, p. 474, note 342.

72. Quandt, *Camp David*, pp. 155–156, 168.

73. Ibid., pp. 168–169, and Vance, *Hard Choices*, p. 199.

74. Quandt, *Camp David*, pp. 193–194.

75. Ibid., pp. 162, 204.

76. Ibid., p. 183, and Vance, *Hard Choices*, p. 209.

77. Quandt, *Camp David*, p. 204.

78. See ibid., chs. 10–12 and Appendixes D–I, for a summation of Camp David and its aftermath, as well as texts of the various preliminary and final agreements and of the treaty.

79. Ibid., pp. 261, 322–323.

80. Ibid., p. 265.

81. Tillman, *The United States in the Middle East*, pp. 216–218.

82. Ibid., p. 197, and Harold H. Saunders, "An Israeli-Palestinian Peace," *Foreign Affairs*, fall 1982, 117.

83. Ann Mosely Lesch, *Political Perceptions of the Palestinians on the West Bank and the Gaza Strip* (Washington, D.C.: Middle East Institute, 1980), pp. 6–16

84. Interview with Veliotes.

85. Quandt, *Camp David*, p. 323.

86. This is the conclusion of Quandt in ibid., p. 323.

87. Ibid., p. 321.

88. Saunders, *The Other Walls*, pp. 60–62.

89. Ibid.

90. Brzezinski, *Power and Principle*, pp. 279–280.

91. Ibid., pp. 438–440.

92. Vance believed, as he stated in a speech to the UN shortly after the Camp David accords, that no peace agreement would be "just or secure" if it did not resolve the Palestinian issue in such a way as to assure the Palestinians "that they and their descendants can live with dignity and freedom and have the opportunity for economic fulfillment and for political expression." Cited in Quandt, *Camp David*, p. 289. In January 1979 Vance proposed to Carter that the United States initiate contacts with the PLO in the hope of generating momentum, but the suggestion was treated with near derision by Carter's political aides. Later in the year, Vance, who had always been one of the administration's strongest opponents of Israeli settlement construction, repeatedly urged Carter to show firmness by publicly condemning the settlements and approving reductions in economic aid each time the Israelis built a new settlement. Carter, already disengaged, would not go along and ultimately became irritated with what he characterized as Vance's "dogged" pursuit of the settlements issue. Vance had noticeably lost influence with Carter in Middle East matters when Strauss and later Linowitz assumed the negotiating portfolio. Brzezinski, *Power and Principle*, pp. 278, 440–441.

93. Brzezinski, *Power and Principle*, pp. 442–443.

94. Quandt, *Peace Process*, pp. 328–329, and Reich, *The United States and Israel*, pp. 78–79.

95. Melman and Raviv, *Friends in Deed*, pp. 179–180.

96. Cited in Steve Bell, "American Journalism: Practices, Constraints, and Middle East Reportage," in *The American Media and the Arabs*, ed. Michael C. Hudson and Ronald G. Wolfe (Washington, D.C.: Center for Contemporary Arab Studies, Georgetown University, 1980), p. 99.

97. John Weisman, "Blind Spot in the Middle East," *TV Guide*, 24 October 1981, 8.

98. *Time*, 14 April 1980.

99. Ibid.

100. Ibid., and Tessler, *A History of the Israeli-Palestinian Conflict*, pp. 521, 523, 531.

CHAPTER 8. RONALD REAGAN: MISSED OPPORTUNITIES

1. Lewis, "The United States and Israel," p. 227.

2. Quoted in Quandt, *Peace Process*, p. 338.

3. Quoted in William Safire, "Reagan on Israel," *New York Times*, 24 March 1980.

4. Wolf Blitzer, *Between Washington and Jerusalem: A Reporter's Notebook* (New York: Oxford University Press, 1985), pp. 238–239, 244.

5. Lewis, "The United States and Israel," p. 227.

6. Ronald Reagan, *An American Life* (New York: Simon & Schuster, 1990), pp. 407, 463.

7. Strobe Talbott, "What to Do about Israel," *Time*, 7 September 1981, 18–20.

8. See Leon T. Hadar, "The 'Neocons': From the Cold War to the 'Global Intifada,'" *Washington Report on Middle East Affairs*, April 1991, 27–28, and Michael Lind, *Up from Conservatism: Why the Right Is Wrong for America* (New York: Free Press, 1996), pp. 55–56, 61, for a description of the rise of and the beliefs espoused by neoconservatism. See Leon T. Hadar, "Reforming Israel—before It's Too Late," *Foreign Policy*, winter 1990–1991, 109, for a further description of neoconservative views on Israel.

9. Hadar, "The 'Neocons.'"

10. Alexander M. Haig, Jr., *Caveat: Realism, Reagan, and Foreign Policy* (New York: Macmillan, 1984), pp. 26, 170–171, and Juliana S. Peck, *The Reagan Administration and the Palestinian Question: The First Thousand Days* (Washington, D.C.: Institute for Palestine Studies, 1984), p. 15.

11. Quoted in Peck, *The Reagan Administration*, p. 15, and Reich, *The United States and Israel*, p. 93.

12. Melman and Raviv, *Friends in Deed*, pp. 197, 200–205.

13. Gates, *From the Shadows*, pp. 201, 250, 286.

14. Bob Woodward, *Veil: The Secret Wars of the CIA, 1981–1987* (New York: Simon & Schuster, 1987), pp. 160–161, 216–217.

15. Tivnan, *The Lobby*, p. 142.

16. Churba, who died in 1996, was a long-time friend of Rabbi Meir Kahane, founder of the militantly pro-Israeli and anti-Palestinian Jewish Defense League in the United States and of its Israeli counterpart, Kach. While working as an intelligence analyst for the Air Force, Churba propounded a strongly pro-Israeli position. In 1976, while still an Air Force employee, he released to the *New York Times* an unpublished research paper he had written arguing that Israel was a strategic asset. As a result of his unauthorized release of a classified paper, his highest security clearances were revoked, and he left the Air Force.

Robert I. Friedman, *The False Prophet: Rabbi Meir Kahane — from FBI Informant to Knesset Member* (Brooklyn, N.Y.: Hill, 1990), pp. 58–82.

17. Peck, *The Reagan Administration*, p. 14. Reagan himself apparently took some of his cues from Churba. In 1977, after leaving the Air Force, Churba had written another book, *The Politics of Defeat: America's Decline in the Middle East,* in which he spoke of "the conflict and tension endemic to the region. This condition is traceable largely to the sectarian and fragmented nature of Middle East society." In August 1979, Reagan published an op-ed article in the *Washington Post* so similarly worded as to suggest is was ghost-written by Churba. Reagan wrote, "The Carter administration has yet to grasp that in this region conflict and tension are endemic, a condition traceable largely to the fragmented sectarian nature of Middle Eastern society." Quandt discovered this near identity of wording; *Peace Process,* p. 565, note 1.

18. Milstein, "Strategic Ties or Tentacles?" Stephen Bryen was investigated by the FBI in 1978, when an official of an Arab American organization alleged that he had overheard Bryen, then a Senate staffer, offering classified military information to a visiting Israeli official at a coffee shop in Washington. Bryen denied the charge, and when he was appointed to the Defense Department in 1981, Secretary of Defense Weinberger personally directed an investigation that cleared him. See ibid., and Melman and Raviv, *Friends in Deed,* pp. 286–287.

19. Safire, "Reagan on Israel," and Haig, *Caveat,* p. 334.

20. See Peck, *The Reagan Administration,* pp. 32–35, and Safire, "Reagan on Israel," for Rostow's legal justification of Israel's occupation and settlement construction and for Reagan's early statements on Israeli settlements. For the State Department's position, see David A. Korn, Letter to the Editor, *New York Times,* 1 October 1991.

21. *New York Times,* 3 February 1981.

22. Peck, *The Reagan Administration,* pp. 16–17.

23. Jeane Kirkpatrick, "Dishonoring Sadat," *New Republic,* 11 November 1981,14–16. Kirkpatrick has remained extremely hostile to the PLO and supportive of Israel's Likud governments since leaving office. Rejecting the PLO's conciliatory moves since 1988, she has charged that the organization still seeks Israel's destruction; she has encouraged Israeli settlement construction in the West Bank and Gaza and has not seen the settlements as posing an impediment to peace. See, for instance, Jeane Kirkpatrick, "How the PLO Was Legitimized," *Commentary,* July 1989, 21–28. See also the dissents she made as one of the drafters of a 1997 report on the U.S. role in the peace process, in Presidential Study Group, *Building for Security and Peace in the Middle East: An American Agenda* (Washington, D.C.: Washington Institute for Near East Policy, 1997), pp. 4 and 35.

24. Cited in Ronald J. Young, *Missed Opportunities for Peace: U.S. Middle East Policies, 1981–1986* (Philadelphia: American Friends Service Committee, 1987), pp. 20–21.

25. Hermann Frederick Eilts, "The United States and Egypt," in *The Middle*

East: Ten Years after Camp David, ed. William B. Quandt (Washington, D.C.: Brookings Institution, 1988), pp. 119–120. Ambassador to Israel Lewis has said that Reagan was "often hazy on details" and even in private meetings with Begin had to use index cards to deliver his prepared talking points. Lewis, "The United States and Israel," p. 227.

26. Tessler, *A History of the Israeli-Palestinian Conflict,* pp. 548–552, 564–568.

27. Peck, *The Reagan Administration,* p. 29.

28. Bernard Gwertzman, "Reagan Administration Held 9-Month Talks with P.L.O.," *New York Times,* 19 February 1984, and interview with Nicholas Veliotes, 17 March 1998.

29. Gwertzman, "Reagan Administration."

30. Haig, *Caveat,* p. 335. Haig says he told General Sharon that "unless there was an internationally recognized provocation, and unless Israeli retaliation was proportionate to any such provocation, an attack by Israel into Lebanon would have a devastating effect in the United States." Sharon responded, according to Haig, that no one had the right to tell Israel how to defend its people. The notion that Haig had given Sharon a "green light" was first raised by Israeli journalist Ze'ev Schiff in "The Green Light," *Foreign Policy,* spring 1983, and in considerably greater detail by Schiff and Ehud Ya'ari in *Israel's Lebanon War,* trans. Ina Friedman (New York: Simon & Schuster, 1984), pp. 62–77.

31. Interview with Nicholas Veliotes, 2 May 1991. For an analysis of Israel's objectives in Lebanon, including the restoration of Christian Phalangist power there and the destruction of the PLO, see Tessler, *A History of the Israeli-Palestinian Conflict,* pp. 580–582.

32. Schiff and Ya'ari, *Israel's Lebanon War,* pp. 65–69.

33. Inside administration councils at the beginning of the war, Haig, Kirkpatrick, and Casey all maintained that the invasion was a justifiable act of self-defense by Israel, arguing down suggestions from Vice President George Bush and Defense Secretary Weinberger that the United States should impose sanctions against Israel for using U.S.-supplied weapons in an act of aggression. See Howard Teicher and Gayle Radley Teicher, *Twin Pillars to Desert Storm: America's Flawed Vision in the Middle East from Nixon to Bush* (New York: Morrow, 1993), p. 204.

34. Melman and Raviv, *Friends in Deed,* pp. 216, 487.

35. Rashid Khalidi, *Under Siege: P.L.O. Decisionmaking during the 1982 War* (New York: Columbia University Press, 1986), p. 172

36. Kathleen Christison, "The Arab-Israeli Policy of George Shultz," *Journal of Palestine Studies* 70 (winter 1989): 38.

37. Interview with Veliotes, 17 March 1998.

38. Quandt, *Peace Process,* pp. 344–345. The texts of Reagan's speech and of talking points sent to Prime Minister Begin appear in Appendix H, pp. 476–485.

39. Letter from Walid Khalidi, 12 December 1989.

40. Schiff and Ya'ari, *Israel's Lebanon War*, p. 294.

41. George P. Shultz, *Turmoil and Triumph: My Years as Secretary of State* (New York: Scribner, 1993), p. 65.

42. Thomas A. Dine, "Achievements and Advances in the United States-Israel Relationship," address to the AIPAC Conference, May 17, 1987, reprinted in *Journal of Palestine Studies* 64 (summer 1987): 99–100.

43. Peck, *The Reagan Administration*, pp. 89–90.

44. William B. Quandt, "Reagan's Lebanon Policy: Trial and Error," *Middle East Journal*, spring 1984, 241–242. The full article, pp. 237–266, provides an analysis of the background to and the consequences of the U.S. involvement in Lebanon from 1982 to 1984.

45. Peck, *The Reagan Administration*, pp. 90, 93–94.

46. Ibid., pp. 94–99; William B. Quandt, "U.S. Policy toward the Arab-Israeli Conflict," in *The Middle East: Ten Years after Camp David*, ed. William B. Quandt (Washington, D.C.: Brookings Institution, 1988), p. 366; and Tessler, *A History of the Israeli-Palestinian Conflict*, pp. 621–622.

47. Spiegel, *The Other Arab-Israeli Conflict*, p. 423.

48. Peck, *The Reagan Administration*, pp. 91–92. The Fez Plan grew out of an initiative proposed more than a year earlier by Saudi Crown Prince Fahd. In August 1981, Fahd enunciated eight principles as guidelines for a comprehensive peace settlement, including the major provisions later incorporated into the Fez Plan. The United States failed to encourage the Fahd initiative, claiming it was largely a restatement of previous Saudi positions and emphasizing the points with which it could not agree. Saudi Arabia submitted the plan to an Arab summit meeting in Morocco in November 1981, but the Arab world was badly divided at the time and the meeting broke up almost immediately. Ibid., pp. 39–41, and Reich, *The United States and Israel*, p. 104.

49. Walid Khalidi, *The Middle East Postwar Environment* (Washington, D.C.: Institute for Palestine Studies, 1991), p. 25 (emphasis in original), and Peck, *The Reagan Administration*, p. 92.

50. Teicher and Teicher, *Twin Pillars*, p. 213; Shultz, *Turmoil and Triumph*, p. 100; and *New York Times*, 23 October 1982.

51. Quoted in Tessler, *A History of the Israeli-Palestinian Conflict*, p. 826, note 5.

52. "When Push Comes to Shove," *Time*, 16 August 1982, p. 11, and Neff, *Fallen Pillars*, p. 122.

53. Interview with a former official who asked to remain anonymous.

54. For details on this policy, see testimony before a House subcommittee by Assistant Secretary of State Richard Murphy, 14 December 1987, reprinted in the *Journal of Palestine Studies* 67 (spring 1988): 198–201.

55. Richard Murphy, "United States Policy in the Middle East," in *Proceedings of the Washington Institute Policy Forum, 1988* (Washington, D.C.: Washington Institute for Near East Policy, 1988), p. 12.

56. Interview with the Palestinian American, 11 April 1989.

57. Shultz, *Turmoil and Triumph*, pp. 105–106, 110.

58. Khalidi, *Under Siege*, p. 171. PLO concern to assure the safety of Palestinian noncombatants was acute in light of the massacre of hundreds of civilians by Lebanese Christian forces at the Palestinian refugee camp of Tal al-Za'atar in Beirut at the height of the Lebanon civil war in 1976. PLO leaders negotiating the PLO withdrawal in 1982 were specifically concerned to avoid a repeat of the earlier massacre. Ibid., p. 169.

59. Fisk, *Pity the Nation*, pp. 368–370. Emphasis in original.

60. *Newsweek*, 27 September and 4 October 1982, and *Time*, 27 September and 4 October 1982. *Newsweek's* treatment was highlighted in Fisk, *Pity the Nation*, p. 401. Also "The Horror, and the Shame," *New York Times*, 21 September 1982; "The Latest Horror," *Wall Street Journal*, 21 September 1982; and "Dilemma of Imperfect Freedom," *Wall Street Journal*, 24 September 1982.

61. Fisk, *Pity the Nation*, pp. 370–371.

62. Ibid., p. 366.

63. For descriptions of U.S. policy miscalculations in Lebanon between September 1982 and February 1984, when the U.S. Marine contingent withdrew, see Quandt, "Reagan's Lebanon Policy," pp. 241–250, and Parker, *The Politics of Miscalculation*, pp. 182–211. The United States was first drawn into Lebanon by Israel's invasion. After the assassination of Bashir Gemayel and the Sabra and Shatila massacre, Israel persuaded the administration to put aside its peace initiative in order to focus attention again on Lebanon. When Shultz himself intervened in 1983 to arrange the final details of an accord intended to bring about the withdrawal of both Israeli and Syrian forces in Lebanon, he dealt with the Israelis but failed to negotiate terms with Syria and ignored the warnings of the U.S. ambassador in Damascus that Syrian President Asad would attempt to undermine any agreement concluded between Israel and Lebanon. The result was as predicted; influenced by Syria, Lebanon abrogated the Israeli-Lebanese treaty only months after it was signed in May 1983. The U.S. Marines became deeply embroiled in Lebanon's sectarian violence in September 1983 after Israel, finding itself in the middle of civil strife among Lebanese factions, pulled its forces out of the mountains above Beirut. This retreat left the Marines with no buffer against attack by local militias increasingly opposed to the U.S. presence and to the Israeli-Lebanese accord. In October, a month after the Marines, still technically a peacekeeping force, began exchanging gunfire with Lebanese factions, the Marine barracks was bombed by pro-Iranian elements allied with Syria, with the loss of 241 U.S. military personnel.

64. Christison, "The Arab-Israeli Policy of George Shultz," p. 39.

65. Melman and Raviv, *Friends in Deed*, p. 232.

66. Shultz, *Turmoil and Triumph*, p. 441.

67. Teicher and Teicher, *Twin Pillars*, pp. 221–224.

68. Ibid., pp. 273–274

69. David K. Shipler, "On Middle East Policy, a Major Influence," *New York Times*, 6 July 1987.

70. See Tivnan, *The Lobby*, pp. 135–161, for a description of AIPAC strategy and maneuvering during the AWACS fight.

71. Shipler, "On Middle East Policy."

72. Ibid., and Tivnan, *The Lobby*, pp. 176–177, 180.

73. Melman and Raviv, *Friends in Deed*, p. 248.

74. Ibid.; Robert Pear and Richard L. Berke, "Pro-Israel Group Exerts Quiet Might as It Rallies Supporters in Congress," *New York Times*, 7 July 1987; Shipler, "On Middle East Policy"; Mansour, *Beyond Alliance*, p. 242; and Dine, "Achievements and Advances," pp. 95–106.

75. Blitzer, *Between Washington and Jerusalem*, p. 117.

76. Shipler, "On Middle East Policy."

77. This lament was recalled by a one-time AIPAC staffer writing in the *Washington Post* in 1986, who boasted that State Department "Arabists" hardly received a hearing in Washington anymore. Cited in Neff, *Fallen Pillars*, p. 123.

78. Shipler, "On Middle East Policy"; quote in Tivnan, *The Lobby*, p. 256.

79. Saunders, *The Other Walls*, p. 140.

80. Shimon Shamir, "Israeli Views of Egypt and the Peace Process: The Duality of Vision," in *The Middle East: Ten Years after Camp David*, ed. William B. Quandt (Washington, D.C.: Brookings Institution, 1988), pp. 209–210, and Hadar, "Reforming Israel," p. 123.

81. Blitzer, *Between Washington and Jerusalem*, p. 106, and Young, *Missed Opportunities*, pp. 105–107.

82. See Friedman, "Selling Israel to America," 23–25, for details on the Hasbara Project.

83. Ibid., p. 24.

84. Ibid.

85. Quoted in Said, *The Politics of Dispossession*, p. 255.

86. Friedman, "Selling Israel to America," p. 22, and Weisman, "Blind Spot in the Middle East," p. 12.

87. Quoted in Weisman, "Blind Spot," p. 12.

88. One of the principal expositions of this line in the United States can be found in Daniel Pipes, "Is Jordan Palestine?" *Commentary*, October 1988, 35–42.

89. Peck, *The Reagan Administration*, pp. 16–17.

90. Joan Peters, *From Time Immemorial: The Origins of the Arab-Jewish Conflict over Palestine* (New York: Harper & Row, 1984).

91. Said, *The Politics of Dispossession*, p. 97. Emphasis in original.

92. The book was reviewed by Ronald Sanders in the *New Republic* (23 April 1984), Bernard Gwertzman in the *New York Times* (12 May 1984), John C. Campbell in the *New York Times Book Review* (13 May 1984), Daniel Pipes in *Commentary* (July 1984), Walter Reich in *The Atlantic Monthly* (July 1984), and journalist Sidney Zion in the *National Review* (5 October 1984).

93. Edward Said published an article in the *Nation* summarizing the few critical reviews published in the United States and some published in Europe. See the *Journal of Palestine Studies* 58 (winter 1986): 144–150, for a reprint of the review. The first and most thorough critical review, by Norman Finkelstein,

appeared in the 11 September 1984 issue of the nonmainstream magazine *In These Times.*

94. Yehoshua Porath, "Mrs. Peters's Palestine," *New York Review of Books,* 16 January 1986, 36–39. Interestingly, Porath's critical review is not listed— one must assume through inadvertence—anywhere in the 1986 edition of *The Reader's Guide to Periodical Literature,* under either "Peters," "Porath," or "Palestine" or in the list of book reviews.

95. Erich Isaac and Rael Jean Isaac, "Whose Palestine?" *Commentary,* July 1986, 24–37.

96. Ronald Sanders, "Letting the Record Speak," *New York Times Book Review,* 4 September 1988, contains a dual review of Morris's 1987 book, *The Birth of the Palestinian Refugee Problem, 1947–1949,* and Shlaim's 1988 book *Collusion across the Jordan.*

97. Kathleen Christison, "The Arab in Recent Popular Fiction," *Middle East Journal,* summer 1987, 410.

98. Edmund Ghareeb, *Split Vision: The Portrayal of Arabs in the American Media* (Washington, D.C.: American-Arab Affairs Council, 1983), p. 254.

99. Abuelkeshk, "A Portrayal," pp. 227–232.

100. Evensen, *Truman, Palestine, and the Press,* pp. 1–2.

101. Leon Wieseltier, "Summoned by Stones," *New Republic,* 14 March 1988, 24, 26.

102. Quoted in Friedman, "Selling Israel to America," p. 25. Emphasis added.

103. At a conference of Jewish journalists in Jerusalem in January 1985, he said, "The role of Jews who write in both the Jewish and the general press is to defend Israel, and not join in the attacks on Israel." Criticism, he said, "helps Israel's enemies—and they are legion in the U.S.—to say more and more openly that Israel is not a democratic country." Quoted in ibid., p. 21. Podhoretz did, however, become an outspoken critic of Israel when, under a Labor government, it signed a peace agreement with the PLO in September 1993. Dierdre Carmody, "Veteran Critic of the Left Is Ready to Step Aside," *New York Times,* 19 January 1995.

104. Norman Podhoretz, "J'Accuse," *Commentary,* September 1982, 21–31.

105. Friedman, "Selling Israel to America," p. 25; Robert Sherrill, "The New Regime at the *New Republic,*" *Columbia Journalism Review,* March/ April 1976, cited in Richard H. Curtiss, *A Changing Image: American Perceptions of the Arab-Israeli Dispute* (Washington, D.C.: American Educational Trust, 1986), p. 325. Peretz owned the left-wing magazine *Ramparts* until 1974 but reportedly sold it and bought the *New Republic* when *Ramparts* published an editorial critical of Israel.

106. George P. Shultz, "The Challenge to the Democracies," in *Terrorism: How the West Can Win,* ed. Benjamin Netanyahu (New York: Farrar, Straus & Giroux, 1986), pp. 18–20. Emphasis in original.

107. Cited in Lord Caradon, "Images and Realities of the Middle East Con-

flict," in *The American Media and the Arabs,* ed. Michael C. Hudson and Ronald G. Wolfe (Washington, D.C.: Center for Contemporary Arab Studies, Georgetown University, 1980), p. 80.

108. Saunders, *The Other Walls,* pp. 139–140.

109. Fouad Moughrabi, "American Public Opinion and the Palestine Question," in *Public Opinion and the Palestine Question,* ed. Elia Zureik and Fouad Moughrabi (New York: St. Martin's Press, 1987), pp. 13–48.

110. Ibid., pp. 40–41.

111. Ibid., p. 46.

112. The revisionist, or so-called post-Zionist, historians include Benny Morris, Avi Shlaim, Ilan Pappé, Simcha Flapan, and Tom Segev, whose books were published in the United States between 1986 and 1988. For aspects of the historiographic debate and a discussion of the debate and its effects, see Benny Morris, "The New Historiography: Israel Confronts Its Past," *Tikkun,* November/December 1988, 19ff.; Shabtai Teveth, "Charging Israel with Original Sin," *Commentary,* September 1989, 24–33; Benny Morris, "The Eel and History: A Reply to Shabtai Teveth," *Tikkun,* January/February 1990, 19ff.; Norman Finkelstein, Nur Masalha, and Benny Morris, "Debate on the 1948 Exodus," *Journal of Palestine Studies* 81 (autumn 1991): 66–114; Shlaim, "The Debate about 1948"; and Ilan Pappé, "Critique and Agenda: The Post-Zionist Scholars in Israel," *History & Memory: Studies in Representation of the Past* (ed. Gulie Ne'eman Arad), spring/summer 1995, 66–90.

113. Pappé, "Critique and Agenda," p. 79, and Ilan Pappé, "Post-Zionist Critique on Israel and the Palestinians. Part I: The Academic Debate," *Journal of Palestine Studies* 102 (winter 1997): 33. All discourse on history in Israel, writes Israeli history professor Dan Diner, "is *ipso facto* discourse on legitimacy." The debate about 1948, he says, is a debate on the legitimacy and self-identity of the state and is therefore deeply emotional. Dan Diner, "Cumulative Contingency: Historicizing Legitimacy in Israeli Discourse," *History & Memory: Studies in Representation of the Past* (ed. Gulie Ne'eman Arad), spring/summer 1995, 149.

114. Shlaim, "The Debate about 1948"; Pappé, "Critique and Agenda," p. 71; and Pappé, "Post-Zionist Critique," p. 32.

115. Smith, *Palestine and the Arab-Israeli Conflict,* p. xiii.

116. These books, which broke new ground in bringing aspects of Palestinian history to the fore, include Lesch, *Arab Politics in Palestine;* Ian Lustick, *Arabs in the Jewish State: Israel's Control of a National Minority* (Austin: University of Texas Press, 1980); Khalidi, *Under Siege;* Laurie A. Brand, *Palestinians in the Arab World: Institution Building in the Arab World* (New York: Columbia University Press, 1988); Mattar, *The Mufti of Jerusalem;* and Muslih, *The Origins of Palestinian Nationalism.* A history of Palestinian nationalism published in the early 1970s—William B. Quandt, Fuad Jabber, and Ann Mosely Lesch, *The Politics of Palestinian Nationalism* (Berkeley: University of California Press, 1973)—is virtually the only book of its kind published before 1979.

117. Cited in Young, *Missed Opportunities*, p. 134.

118. In August 1985, Congress added to the two requirements of the Sinai II commitment the further stipulation that the PLO must renounce the use of terrorism. See Quandt, *Peace Process*, p. 572, note 24.

119. For a fuller description of the Jordanian-PLO initiative and maneuvering over it, told from differing perspectives, see Young, *Missed Opportunities*, pp. 141–155; Quandt, *Peace Process*, pp. 351–356; Ann M. Lesch, "The Reagan Administration's Policy toward the Palestinians," in *U.S. Policy on Palestine from Wilson to Clinton*, ed. Michael W. Suleiman (Normal, Ill.: Association of Arab-American University Graduates, 1995), pp. 182–184; Dan Tschirgi, *The American Search for Mideast Peace* (New York: Praeger, 1989), pp. 203–211; Shultz, *Turmoil and Triumph*, pp. 444–462; Samuel W. Lewis, "Israel: The Peres Era and Its Legacy," *Foreign Affairs* 65, no. 3 (1987): 582–610; and Tessler, *A History of the Israeli-Palestinian Conflict*, pp. 654–666.

120. Shultz, *Turmoil and Triumph*, pp. 453–454, 461–462, and Young, *Missed Opportunities*, pp. 143–144.

121. See Quandt, *Peace Process*, pp. 360–363, for details.

122. Lewis, "Israel," p. 598, and Hadar, "Reforming Israel," pp. 121–122.

123. Lesch, "The Reagan Administration's Policy," p. 184.

124. Tessler, *A History of the Israeli-Palestinian Conflict*, pp. 706, 712; for a summary of the factors leading to the *intifada*, see pp. 677–685.

125. See Quandt, *Peace Process*, pp. 364–367, and Lesch, "The Reagan Administration's Policy," pp.184–189, for details on Shultz's efforts in 1988.

126. Lesch, "The Reagan Administration's Policy," p. 185; and Peretz Kidron, "Re-run of an Old Movie," and Donald Neff, "Shultz Leaves a Ticking Time Bomb," *Middle East International* 323 (16 April 1988): 5–6.

127. Quandt, *Peace Process*, pp. 368–369, 372–375.

128. For descriptions of this mediation effort by both of the principals involved, see Mohamed Rabie, *U.S.-P.L.O. Dialogue: Secret Diplomacy and Conflict Resolution* (Gainesville: University Press of Florida, 1995), and Quandt, *Peace Process*, pp. 369–372.

129. Tessler, *A History of the Israeli-Palestinian Conflict*, p. 720.

130. Full texts of the PNC "Declaration of Independence" and the PNC "Political Communique," both dated November 15, 1988, can be found in the *Journal of Palestine Studies* 70 (winter 1989): 213–223.

131. During an Arab summit meeting in Algiers in June 1988, Abu Sharif passed out to the press corps a statement in English declaring the PLO's readiness to coexist with Israel. The statement also expressed the PLO's understanding of "the Jewish people's centuries of suffering" and of the desire for statehood that grew out of that suffering. "We believe," the statement said, "that all peoples—the Jews and the Palestinians included—have the right to run their own affairs, expecting from their neighbors not only non-belligerence but the kind of political and economic cooperation without which no state can be truly secure. . . . The Palestinians want that kind of lasting peace and security for themselves and the Israelis because no one can build his own future on the ru-

ins of another's." Agreeing with Israel's desire for direct negotiations, the statement affirmed that the "key to a Palestinian-Israeli settlement lies in talks between the Palestinians and the Israelis." For the full text, see the *Journal of Palestine Studies* 69 (autumn 1988): 272–275. As previously noted, the U.S. government and press generally ignored the statement.

132. Rabie, *U.S.-P.L.O Dialogue*, pp. 58–61, and Shultz, *Turmoil and Triumph*, pp. 1035, 1037.

133. Quoted in "A Dance of Many Veils," *Time*, 26 December 1988, 23.

134. Shultz, *Turmoil and Triumph*, pp. 1040–1044, and Quandt, *Peace Process*, pp. 374–375. Quandt reproduces the wording of Arafat's statements before the UN session on December 13 and at the press conference the following day. At the UN session, after explicitly naming Israel as one of the parties to the Arab-Israeli conflict, Arafat said the PLO respected "everyone's right to exist, to peace and to security, according to Resolutions 242 and 338." He also "rejected" and "condemned" terrorism but did not "renounce" it. Shultz regarded the statement as not adequate because it did not directly enough recognize Israel's right to exist and did not reject terrorism in a way that admitted to having committed it in the past, a connotation the word *renounce* carries.

135. Shultz, *Turmoil and Triumph*, p. 49. Shultz also complained, somewhat disingenuously, that PLO messages were too indirect and were "delivered through a variety of channels." In fact, of course, the principal channel—that is, talking directly to U.S. officials—was blocked by the U.S. insistence that the PLO first pronounce a prescribed formula.

136. Meron Benvenisti, *The West Bank Data Base Project 1987 Report: Demographic, Economic, Legal, Social and Political Developments in the West Bank* (Jerusalem: West Bank Data Base Project, 1987), pp. 52–55, and Tessler, *A History of the Israeli-Palestinian Conflict*, p. 671.

CHAPTER 9. GEORGE BUSH: NO ILLUSIONS

1. Gates, *From the Shadows*, pp. 454–455.

2. Michael Duffy and Dan Goodgame, *Marching in Place: The Status Quo Presidency of George Bush* (New York: Simon & Schuster, 1992), excerpted in *Time*, 24 August 1992, 32, 38.

3. Quandt, *Peace Process*, p. 383.

4. Bush referred to himself in interviews as "cautious," "prudent," and "diplomatic." Baker was dubbed by former Reagan aide Michael Deaver "the most cautious human being I've ever met." John Newhouse, "The Tactician," *New Yorker*, 7 May 1990, 52.

5. Christopher Ogden, "Vision Problems at State," *Time*, 25 September 1989, 22, and Maureen Dowd and Thomas L. Friedman, "The Fabulous Bush and Baker Boys," *New York Times Magazine*, 6 May 1990, 36.

6. On Baker's political skill, see Dowd and Friedman, "The Fabulous Bush and Baker Boys," pp. 34ff., and Newhouse, "The Tactician," pp. 50–82. For the judgment of another administration official on his political abilities, see Gates,

From the Shadows, p. 456. For a profile of Baker as a policymaker on Middle East issues, see Kathleen Christison, "Splitting the Difference: The Palestinian-Israeli Policy of James Baker," *Journal of Palestine Studies* 93 (autumn 1994): 39–50.

7. Quandt, *Peace Process*, p. 404, and *New York Times*, 8 November 1992.

8. James A. Baker, III, with Thomas M. DeFrank, *The Politics of Diplomacy: Revolution, War and Peace, 1989–1992* (New York: Putnam, 1995), p. xiii.

9. Ibid., pp. 115–117.

10. Dowd and Friedman, "The Fabulous Bush and Baker Boys," p. 67.

11. In one rare example, Baker, touring Kurdish refugee camps in the aftermath of the Gulf war in 1991, was so deeply affected that he organized a relief effort for purely humanitarian reasons. It is an indication of how unusual his reactions to this disaster were that the press wrote about it at the time and that he devoted several pages to it in his memoirs, writing with an unusual degree of feeling. *Washington Post*, 29 April 1991, and Baker, *The Politics of Diplomacy*, pp. 430–435.

12. Washington Institute's Presidential Study Group, *Building for Peace: An American Strategy for the Middle East* (Washington, D.C.: Washington Institute for Near East Policy, 1988).

13. Indyk did not become a U.S. citizen until he was appointed to the Clinton administration National Security Council staff in early 1993.

14. "The Next Step in the Peace Process: A Roundtable Discussion of *Building for Peace*," a symposium with Martin Indyk, Samuel Lewis, William Quandt, and Dennis Ross, November 30, 1988, in *Proceedings of the Washington Institute Policy Forum, 1988* (Washington, D.C.: Washington Institute for Near East Policy, 1988), pp. 31–44.

15. Downplaying the significance of these PLO concessions, Indyk chastised the PLO for having addressed them to the United States and not solely to Israel, despite the fact that the focus of U.S. demands on the PLO had for years been precisely those concessions that would lead to a U.S.-PLO dialogue. Ibid., p. 40.

16. Benvenisti, *Intimate Enemies*, pp. 86–87.

17. Deeming the Middle East a pitfall to be avoided, Baker said in his memoirs, "From day one, the last thing I wanted to do was touch the Middle East peace process." Baker, *The Politics of Diplomacy*, p. 115.

18. In a paper published in 1985, Ross criticized those in the bureaucracy who he claimed "feel guilty about our relationship with Israel and our reluctance to force Israeli concessions." Dennis Ross, *Acting with Caution: Middle East Policy Planning for the Second Reagan Administration*, Policy Paper 1 (Washington, D.C.: Washington Institute for Near East Policy, 1985), p. 32.

19. A brief profile of the two men appears in Jonathan Broder, "The Bush League," *Jerusalem Report*, 22 October 1992, 16–18.

20. The description of these men's Labor Party approach is from ibid. The reference to "impeccable pro-Israeli credentials" and the designation "Israelists" are from Leon Hadar, "High Noon in Washington: The Shootout over the Loan Guarantees," *Journal of Palestine Studies* 82 (winter 1992): 77.

21. Hanan Ashrawi, *This Side of Peace: A Personal Account* (New York: Simon & Schuster, 1995), p. 230

22. Ross, *Acting with Caution,* pp. iv, 2–5.

23. Broder, "The Bush League," and Laura Blumenfeld, "Three Peace Suits," *Washington Post,* 24 February 1997.

24. Aaron David Miller's book on the Palestinians, *The PLO and the Politics of Survival* (New York: Praeger, 1983), is a balanced and nonpolemical exposition of Palestinian and PLO positions; it describes the rise of Palestinian nationalism and the outlook for the Palestinians in the wake of the PLO's dispersal after Israel's 1982 invasion of Lebanon. His second book, *The Arab States and the Palestine Question: Between Ideology and Self-Interest* (New York: Praeger, 1986), is also an unbiased description of the Arab states' relation to and interests in the Palestinian issue. In 1987, Miller wrote an article examining the Arab-Israeli conflict twenty years after the 1967 war; the article viewed the conflict from a middle-of-the-road perspective and showed a realism shared by few in the Reagan administration of the time and by few others on Baker's team two years later; "The Arab-Israeli Conflict, 1967–1987: A Retrospective," *Middle East Journal,* summer 1987, 349–360.

25. Daniel Charles Kurtzer, "Palestine Guerrilla and Israeli Counterinsurgency Warfare: The Radicalization of the Palestine Arab Community to Violence, 1949–1970" (Ph.D. diss., Columbia University, 1976). Kurtzer recognized that the Arab-Jewish conflict in Palestine involved two "national liberation movements" struggling for "political sovereignty."

26. Teicher and Teicher, *Twin Pillars,* p. 146.

27. Richard N. Haass, "Paying Less Attention to the Middle East," *Commentary,* August 1986, 22–26. Richard N. Haass, *Conflicts Unending: The United States and Regional Disputes* (New Haven, Conn.: Yale University Press, 1990).

28. Haass, *Conflicts Unending,* p. 51.

29. Ross, *Acting with Caution,* pp. 25, 40.

30. Dennis Ross, "The Peace Process—a Status Report" (a presentation at the Aspen Institute of the Wye Plantation Fourth Annual Policy Conference, "U.S. Policy and the Middle East Peace Process," Washington Institute for Near East Policy, 1989), pp. 11–12.

31. Quandt, *Peace Process,* p. 388.

32. Broder, "The Bush League," p. 18, and Blumenfeld, "Three Peace Suits."

33. Christison, "Splitting the Difference," pp. 42 and 50, note 19.

34. Thomas L. Friedman, "A Window on Deep Israel-U.S. Tensions," *New York Times,* 19 September 1991.

35. Wolf Blitzer, "How American Pressure Shifted from Israel to the Palestinians," *Jerusalem Post International Edition,* 29 April 1989; David Makovsky, "Shamir's Defiance Aimed at Setting Limits for U.S.," *Jerusalem Post International Edition,* 3 November 1990; and Thomas L. Friedman, "Special Relationship Reaches Its Limits," *New York Times,* 21 October 1990.

36. Rabie, *U.S.-P.L.O Dialogue,* pp. 99–107, describes the dialogue on the

basis of information from Rabie's Palestinian contacts. See also Tessler, *A History of the Israeli-Palestinian Conflict*, p. 723. Hanan Ashrawi has described the dialogue in this way. Pelletreau and PLO negotiator Yasir Abd Rabbo "each brought his insulating bubble to the meetings to make sure that their voices were garbled and that they never made any human contact. Reciting from prepared scripts, neither listened to the other as both were captives of the stilted discourse of rigid officialdom." Ashrawi, *This Side of Peace*, p. 59.

37. Some Palestinians, in fact, believe that the official Tunis channel was undermined by Arafat's acquiescence in the U.S. desire to communicate indirectly and unofficially via the Egyptians. Rabie, *U.S.-P.L.O Dialogue*, pp. 107–156.

38. Quandt, *Peace Process*, p. 389.

39. Ross, *Acting with Caution*, p. 43.

40. Interview with a former government official who asked to remain anonymous.

41. Rabie, *U.S.-P.L.O Dialogue*, p. 145.

42. Baker credits *New York Times* correspondent Thomas Friedman with the idea of threatening to withdraw from the peace process. Noting that he occasionally asked Friedman "to share his thoughts with me on an off-the-record basis," Baker said in his memoirs that Friedman had offered the view that it made no sense to continue with the peace process if the parties were not genuinely interested and that, to get their attention, the United States should let them know it would not be there to help unless they called. Baker himself was the one who decided to do this publicly. Baker, *The Politics of Diplomacy*, p. 131.

43. Abba Eban, "Vision and Hard Facts," *Jerusalem Post International Edition*, 13 January 1990, 8.

44. Hadar, "Reforming Israel," pp. 124–126.

45. Frank Collins, "Borrowing Money for Israel: Annual Interest Alone Exceeds $3 Billion," *Washington Report on Middle East Affairs*, December 1991/January 1992, 33.

46. Tessler, *A History of the Israeli-Palestinian Conflict*, p. 745. A combination of relaxed restrictions on emigration from the Soviet Union, leading to a more than twelve-fold increase in the number of Soviet Jewish emigrants by late 1989, and changes in U.S. immigration laws that increased limits on the entry of those claiming refugee status, together resulted in a huge increase in the numbers of Soviet Jews moving to Israel. In early 1990 the Israeli government was predicting that as many as five hundred thousand Soviet Jews would move to Israel in that year alone. Geoffrey Aronson, "Soviet Jewish Emigration, the United States, and the Occupied Territories," *Journal of Palestine Studies* 76 (summer 1990): 30–45.

47. Dowd and Friedman, "The Fabulous Bush and Baker Boys," p. 67.

48. Ibid., and Glenn Frankel, "The Widening Gulf of Distrust between the U.S. and Israel," *Washington Post National Weekly Edition*, 7–13 May 1990, 17.

49. Baker, *The Politics of Diplomacy*, pp. 127–128. Baker says that White

House Chief of Staff John Sununu, "whose Lebanese heritage caused many to see him as an unabashed Arabist," brought the maps to Bush's attention.

50. Tessler, *A History of the Israeli-Palestinian Conflict*, p. 736.

51. Aronson, "Soviet Jewish Emigration," pp. 30, 37. Immigrants to Israel from all countries for the first ten months of 1990 totaled 122,592; approximately 90 percent were from the Soviet Union. *New York Times*, 2 November 1990.

52. Tessler, *A History of the Israeli-Palestinian Conflict*, p. 745; Geoffrey Aronson, "Settlement Report" (November 1994), reprinted in *Journal of Palestine Studies* 94 (winter 1995): 99; and Rachelle Marshall, "End of the Beginning or Beginning of the End?" *Washington Report on Middle East Affairs*, March 1995, 7.

53. The Security Council initially met outside New York to avoid the issue of whether the United States would again deny Arafat a visa to address the session, as had occurred in 1988, when Secretary of State Shultz refused to allow Arafat to enter the United States for a General Assembly session.

54. Jules Kagian, "Another American Veto," and Daoud Kuttab, "Hunger Strike Gains," *Middle East International*, 8 June 1990, 8–10.

55. Salah Khalaf expressed his concern to Quandt in June 1990. He thought Saddam was planning something big and wanted the PLO in his corner. Khalaf was concerned that this development boded ill for the Palestinians, and he hoped to avoid a break with the United States, but he had been unable to get Arafat to listen to any proposals for a compromise on the Abu al-Abbas issue that would satisfy the United States. Quandt, *Peace Process*, pp. 393–394, and interview with William Quandt, 12 May 1991. (Khalaf was assassinated, most likely by a renegade Palestinian group under orders from Saddam, in January 1991.) Even Baker attributes the Palestinian tilt toward Iraq to the breakdown of the peace process. In his memoirs, Baker observes that "perhaps" because Israel had repudiated its own peace plan, public opinion in the Arab world suddenly began to shift "away from conciliation in the direction of Saddam's truculence," and the Egyptians began to lose influence with the PLO. Baker, *The Politics of Diplomacy*, p. 129.

56. William B. Quandt, "The Middle East in 1990," *Foreign Affairs* 70, no. 1 (1991): 56.

57. Quandt, *Peace Process*, pp. 398–399.

58. Friedman, "Special Relationship Reaches Its Limits," and Michael Kramer, "The Political Interest: Baker's Real Agenda: 1992," *Time*, 27 May 1991, 35.

59. Bush diary entry, early 1991, cited in Herbert S. Parmet, *George Bush: The Life of a Lone Star Yankee* (New York: Scribner, 1997), p. 500.

60. See NBC/*Wall Street Journal* poll, September 25, 1991, reprinted in the *Journal of Palestine Studies* 82 (winter 1992): 163; Gallup poll, December 1992, executive summary reprinted in the *Journal of Palestine Studies* 86 (winter 1993): 167–168; and Fouad Moughrabi, "Polls Show Dramatic Shifts in US

Support for Israel and Palestinians," *Washington Report on Middle East Affairs,* October 1991, 9–10, for the findings of several polls in 1991 and 1992.

61. A political cartoon by Oliphant, for instance, depicted Shamir slapping Baker in the face and then extending his hand; it was labeled "Donations accepted." Reprinted in the *Washington Report on Middle East Affairs,* October 1991, 9.

62. Baker believes that AIPAC's failure to block the request for delay was "a powerful psychological weapon" on the administration's side and meant that AIPAC was no longer perceived in Congress as politically invincible. Baker, *The Politics of Diplomacy,* pp. 549, 555.

63. Quoted in Melman and Raviv, *Friends in Deed,* p. 456.

64. Ashrawi, *This Side of Peace,* pp. 59, 93–94.

65. Baker, *The Politics of Diplomacy,* pp. 414–415, 423.

66. Thomas L. Friedman, "Amid Histrionics, Arabs and Israelis Team Up to Lose an Opportunity," *New York Times,* 3 November 1991.

67. Ashrawi, *This Side of Peace,* p. 93. Ashrawi paints a picture of Baker's team, particularly Ross and Kurtzer, as imperious and patronizing toward the Palestinians, excessively vigilant about preventing any hint of PLO involvement, and extremely careful to accommodate Israel's sensibilities. She alleges that Ross frequently failed to pass on to Baker Palestinian proposals and information on Israeli occupation practices. See, for example, ibid., pp. 99, 108–117, 160, 199–200.

68. Ibid., pp. 83–84, 87, 128, and Baker, *The Politics of Diplomacy,* pp. 466, 493. Baker used the "dead cat" admonition with the Israelis also, urging them to go far enough so that "we can leave this dead cat on the Arab doorstep." Baker, *The Politics of Diplomacy,* p. 450.

69. Baker, *The Politics of Diplomacy,* p. 446.

70. *Washington Report on Middle East Affairs,* July 1991, 15.

71. Richard H. Curtiss, "It's Lift-Off or Abort as Bush-Baker Initiative Nears Point of No Return," *Washington Report on Middle East Affairs,* July 1991, 8.

72. George J. Church, "Finally Face to Face," *Time,* 11 November 1991, 55.

73. CNN broadcast, 5 November 1991.

74. One theme was the "moral-equivalency" argument—the notion that there could be no moral equivalency between Israel and the Arabs and that an evenhanded approach to the peace process was thus unfair to Israel because Israel was the victim of Arab aggression. This theme was enunciated in a full-page ad in the *New York Times* on 26 February 1992 by the Committee on U.S. Interests in the Middle East. Signers included, from the Johnson administration, Eugene Rostow; from the Nixon administration, Leonard Garment; from the Carter administration, Stuart Eizenstat; and from the Reagan administration, Elliot Abrams, William Bennett, Stephen Bryen, Linda Chavez, Alan Keyes, John Lehman, and Richard Perle.

75. David R. Bowen, "Analysis of Loan Guarantee Terms," *CNI Newslet-*

ter, November 1992, reprinted in *Journal of Palestine Studies* 86 (winter 1993): 161.

76. "Settlement Population Growth under Labor," in "Settlement Report," ed. Geoffrey Aronson, reprinted in *Journal of Palestine Studies* 101 (autumn 1996): 130.

77. Quoted in Ashrawi, *This Side of Peace,* p. 90.

78. Anton Shammas, "A Lost Voice," *New York Times Magazine,* 28 April 1991, 48.

79. Ibid.

CHAPTER 10. THE PICTURES IN OUR HEADS

1. Clinton Rossiter and James Lare, eds., *The Essential Lippmann: A Political Philosophy for Liberal Democracy* (New York: Random House, 1963), pp. 140–141.

2. Jervis, *Perception and Misperception,* pp. 146, 156.

3. Stephen S. Rosenfeld, "Political Space for 'Political Islam,'" *Washington Post,* 12 September 1997.

4. Reprinted in *Journal of Palestine Studies* 103 (spring 1997): 162–163.

5. Gore is a former student and a close friend of *New Republic* publisher Martin Peretz, who is strongly pro-Israeli and is also widely characterized as anti-Arab. Gore is believed to be heavily influenced by Peretz.

6. In addition to Ross and Indyk, Aaron David Miller remained in the Clinton administration, on the State Department's Policy Planning Staff, and works on the peace process. Richard Haass left government service after Bush's electoral defeat, moving across town to the Brookings Institution, where he is still actively involved in foreign-policy matters. Daniel Kurtzer became ambassador to Egypt in 1997.

7. Steven Erlanger, "U.S.-Israeli Relations: Real Crisis or Smoke and Mirrors?" (symposium, Center for Policy Analysis on Palestine, Washington, D.C., June 5, 1998).

8. The statement was in the form of a U.S. proposal for an "Israeli-Palestinian Joint Declaration of Principles" and was presented on June 30, 1993, to the Israeli and Palestinian delegations to the ongoing bilateral peace talks. Reprinted, along with the official Palestinian response, dated August 5, 1993, in *Journal of Palestine Studies* 89 (autumn 1993): 111–114.

9. The pertinent sections of the statement of principles asserted that "the inclusion or exclusion of specific . . . geographic areas . . . within the jurisdiction of the [Palestinian] interim self-government will not prejudice the positions or claims of either party and will not constitute a basis for asserting, supporting or denying any party's claim to territorial sovereignty in the permanent status negotiations. . . . Issues related to sovereignty will be negotiated during talks on permanent status." Ibid., p. 112.

10. Ross, *Acting with Caution,* p. 38.

11. Neff, *Fallen Pillars,* pp. 127, 165, 186.

12. Cited in ibid., p. 186.

13. Benvenisti, *Intimate Enemies,* p. 176.

14. William Safire, "Move the Embassy," *New York Times,* 1 July 1996.

15. In the last four years of the five-year loan-guarantee period, the Clinton administration imposed a penalty for that part of Israel's settlement construction that went beyond the limits of the 1992 loan-guarantee agreement, but in three of those years it offset the penalty in order to compensate Israel for redeployment costs under the Oslo agreement or because the offset was deemed "important to the security interests of the United States." Settlement penalties were set at $437 million (from an annual loan-guarantee total of $2 billion) in 1993, $311.8 million in 1994, $303 million in 1995, and $307 million in 1996. There was no offset in 1993, but offsets totaled $95 million (or 30 percent) in 1994, $243 million (80 percent) in 1995, and $247 (80 percent) in 1996. No penalty was levied in 1992, the first year of the loan guarantees. "Loan Guarantees Update," in "Settlement Report," ed. Geoffrey Aronson, reprinted in *Journal of Palestine Studies* 102 (winter 1997): 142.

16. In March and April 1997, UN Ambassador Bill Richardson vetoed two moderately worded resolutions in the Security Council, one drafted by European allies, criticizing Israel's construction of the Har Homa settlement in the Jabal Abu Ghunaym section of East Jerusalem. On two other occasions in the same months, the United States voted with Israel against similar resolutions in the General Assembly. The U.S. position is that the UN should not become involved in an issue that the two parties to the conflict have to settle themselves.

17. Two Israeli human-rights organizations—Hamoked, the Center for the Defence of the Individual, and B'Tselem, the Israeli Information Center for Human Rights in the Occupied Territories—have published a study on the Israeli practices, *The Quiet Deportation: Revocation of Residency of East Jerusalem Palestinians* (Jerusalem: Hamoked and B'Tselem, April 1997).

18. Leon T. Hadar, "The Friends of Bibi (FOBs) vs. 'The New Middle East,'" *Journal of Palestine Studies* 101 (autumn 1996): 91–92.

19. Ian S. Lustick, "The Oslo Agreement as an Obstacle to Peace," *Journal of Palestine Studies* 105 (autumn 1997): 62, 66.

20. Broadcast of the Rush Limbaugh radio show, 9 April 1997.

21. Lustick, "The Oslo Agreement," p. 63.

22. Quoted from a FLAME ad in the *New Yorker,* 8 September 1997.

23. Peretz Kidron, "Triumph in Washington," *Middle East International,* 30 January 1998, 6.

24. Israeli left-wing journalist Haim Baram, for instance, has reported that a prominent Labor Party leader complained to him following the September 1997 visit to Israel of Secretary of State Madeleine Albright—her first involvement in the peace process despite being in office for eight months—that the fate of Israel and of the peace process was now left to "nonentities" like Clinton and Albright, who offered a stark contrast to the "relatively effective" Bush and Baker. Baram also reported that Yossi Sarid of the left-wing Meretz party appeared on Israeli television following the Albright visit and declared

that U.S. pressure on the Likud government would be welcome as the only constructive way to move toward peace. Haim Baram, "The Woman Who Never Was," *Middle East International*, 26 September 1997, 9.

25. Palestinian intellectuals in the United States launched a public campaign in the Arabic and the international press in late 1989 taking the PLO to task for leaving the propaganda field, as always, to Israel and its supporters. See reprint of a critical article by Edward Said in *Journal of Palestine Studies* 74 (winter 1990): 146–151; interview of Ibrahim Abu-Lughod in Foreign Broadcast Information Service FBIS-NES-89-209 (31 October 1989); and Hisham Sharabi, "Two Years of the Intifada: The Impact on the Palestinian Diaspora," *Middle East International* (15 December 1989): 20–21.

26. Edward W. Said, *Peace and Its Discontents: Essays on Palestine in the Middle East Peace Process* (New York: Vintage Books, 1996), p. 27. Emphasis in original.

27. Reich, *The United States and Israel*, p. 179.

28. Mansour, *Beyond Alliance*, pp. 277–278.

29. Gershon Shafir, "Israeli Decolonization and Critical Sociology," *Journal of Palestine Studies* 99 (spring 1996): 29.

30. David Makovsky, *Making Peace with the PLO: The Rabin Government's Road to the Oslo Accord* (Boulder, Colo.: Westview Press, 1996), pp. 19, 26–29; and Jane Corbin, *Gaza First: The Secret Norway Channel to Peace between Israel and the PLO* (London: Bloomsbury, 1994), pp. 66–67, 175–176.

31. Makovsky, *Making Peace with the PLO*, pp. 13, 25, 38–39.

32. Saunders, "An Israeli-Palestinian Peace," p. 121.

33. Corbin, *Gaza First*, pp. 89, 138.

Selected Bibliography

Abuelkeshk, Abdelkarim A. "A Portrayal of the Arab-Israeli Conflict in Three U.S. Journals of Opinion: 1948–1982." Ph.D. diss., University of Wisconsin, 1985.

Acheson, Dean. *Present at the Creation: My Years in the State Department.* New York: Norton, 1969.

Ahmed, Hisham H. "Roots of Denial: American Stand on Palestinian Self-Determination from the Balfour Declaration to World War Two." In *U.S. Policy on Palestine from Wilson to Clinton,* edited by Michael W. Suleiman. Normal, Ill.: Association of Arab-American University Graduates, 1995.

Alcalay, Ammiel. *After Jews and Arabs: Remaking Levantine Culture.* Minneapolis: University of Minnesota Press, 1993.

"The American King-Crane Commission of Inquiry, 1919." In *From Haven to Conquest: Readings in Zionism and the Palestine Problem until 1948,* edited by Walid Khalidi. Washington, D.C.: Institute for Palestine Studies, 1987.

Ashrawi, Hanan. *This Side of Peace: A Personal Account.* New York: Simon & Schuster, 1995.

Baker, James A., III, with Thomas M. DeFrank. *The Politics of Diplomacy: Revolution, War and Peace, 1989–1992.* New York: Putnam, 1995.

Bell, Steve. "American Journalism: Practices, Constraints, and Middle East Reportage." In *The American Media and the Arabs,* edited by Michael C. Hudson and Ronald G. Wolfe. Washington, D.C.: Center for Contemporary Arab Studies, Georgetown University, 1980.

Benvenisti, Meron. *Conflicts and Contradictions.* New York: Villard Books, 1986.

———. *Intimate Enemies: Jews and Arabs in a Shared Land.* Berkeley: University of California Press, 1995.

———. *The West Bank Data Base Project 1987 Report: Demographic, Economic, Legal, Social and Political Developments in the West Bank.* Jerusalem: West Bank Data Base Project, 1987.

339

Blitzer, Wolf. *Between Washington and Jerusalem: A Reporter's Notebook.* New York: Oxford University Press, 1985.

Bowen, David R. "Analysis of Loan Guarantee Terms." *CNI Newsletter,* November 1992.Reprinted in *Journal of Palestine Studies* 86 (winter 1993): 161.

Brzezinski, Zbigniew. *Power and Principle: Memoirs of the National Security Adviser, 1977–1981.* New York: Farrar, Straus & Giroux, 1983.

Brzezinski, Zbigniew, François Duchêne, and Kiichi Saeki. "Peace in an International Framework." *Foreign Policy,* summer 1975, 3–17.

Bustami, Zaha. "The Kennedy-Johnson Administrations and the Palestinian People." In *U.S. Policy on Palestine from Wilson to Clinton,* edited by Michael W. Suleiman. Normal, Ill.: Association of Arab-American University Graduates, 1995.

Caradon, Lord. "Images and Realities of the Middle East Conflict." In *The American Media and the Arabs,* edited by Michael C. Hudson and Ronald G. Wolfe. Washington, D.C.: Center for Contemporary Arab Studies, Georgetown University, 1980.

Carter, Jimmy. *The Blood of Abraham: Insights into the Middle East.* Boston: Houghton Mifflin, 1985.

———. *Keeping Faith: Memoirs of a President.* New York: Bantam Books, 1982.

Christison, Kathleen. "The Arab-Israeli Policy of George Shultz." *Journal of Palestine Studies* 70 (winter 1989): 29–47.

———. "Splitting the Difference: The Palestinian-Israeli Policy of James Baker." *Journal of Palestine Studies* 93 (autumn 1994): 39–50.

Clifford, Clark, with Richard Holbrooke. *Counsel to the President: A Memoir.* New York: Random House, 1991.

Cobban, Helena. *The Palestinian Liberation Organisation: People, Power and Politics.* Cambridge: Cambridge University Press, 1984.

Cockburn, Andrew, and Leslie Cockburn. *Dangerous Liaison: The Inside Story of the U.S.-Israeli Covert Relationship.* New York: HarperCollins, 1991.

Cohen, Michael J. *Truman and Israel.* Berkeley: University of California Press, 1990.

Conrad, Lawrence I., ed. *The Formation and Perception of the Modern Arab World: Studies by Marwan R. Buheiry.* Princeton, N.J.: Darwin Press, 1989.

Corbin, Jane. *Gaza First: The Secret Norway Channel to Peace between Israel and the PLO.* London: Bloomsbury, 1994.

Curtiss, Richard H. *A Changing Image: American Perceptions of the Arab-Israeli Dispute.* Washington, D.C.: American Educational Trust, 1986.

Davidson, Lawrence. "Competing Responses to the 1929 Arab Uprising in Palestine: The Zionist Press versus the State Department." *Middle East Policy* 5, no. 2 (May 1997): 93–112.

———. "Historical Ignorance and Popular Perception: The Case of U.S. Perceptions of Palestine, 1917." *Middle East Policy* 3, no. 2 (1994): 125–147.

———. "Press, State Department and Popular Perceptions of Palestine in the 1920s." Paper presented at the annual meeting of the Middle East Studies Association, November 1994.

Donovan, Robert J. *Conflict and Crisis: The Presidency of Harry S Truman, 1945–1948.* New York: Norton, 1977.

Doran, Charles F. "The Globalist-Regionalist Debate." In *Intervention into the 1990s: U.S. Foreign Policy in the Third World,* edited by Peter J. Schraeder. Boulder, Colo.: Lynne Rienner, 1992.

Doumani, Beshara. "Rediscovering Ottoman Palestine: Writing Palestinians into History." *Journal of Palestine Studies* 82 (winter 1992): 5–28.

Dowd, Maureen, and Thomas L. Friedman. "The Fabulous Bush and Baker Boys." *New York Times Magazine,* 6 May 1990.

Dunsmore, Barrie. "Television Hard News and the Middle East." In *The American Media and the Arabs,* edited by Michael C. Hudson and Ronald G. Wolfe. Washington, D.C.: Center for Contemporary Arab Studies, Georgetown University, 1980.

Eban, Abba. *Personal Witness: Israel through My Eyes.* New York: Putnam, 1992.

Ellis, Marc H. *Beyond Innocence and Redemption: Confronting the Holocaust and Israeli Power: Creating a Moral Future for the Jewish People.* San Francisco: Harper & Row, 1990.

Evensen, Bruce J. *Truman, Palestine, and the Press: Shaping Conventional Wisdom at the Beginning of the Cold War.* Westport, Conn.: Greenwood Press, 1992.

Ferrell, Robert H., ed. *The Eisenhower Diaries.* New York: Norton, 1981.

Findley, Paul. *They Dare to Speak Out: People and Institutions Confront Israel's Lobby.* Westport, Conn.: Hill, 1985.

Finkelstein, Norman, Nur Masalha, and Benny Morris. "Debate on the 1948 Exodus." *Journal of Palestine Studies* 81 (autumn 1991): 66–114.

Finnie, David H. *Pioneers East: The Early American Experience in the Middle East.* Cambridge, Mass.: Harvard University Press, 1967.

Fisk, Robert. *Pity the Nation: The Abduction of Lebanon.* New York: Simon & Schuster Touchstone, 1990.

Ford, Gerald R. *A Time to Heal: The Autobiography of Gerald R. Ford.* New York: Harper & Row and Reader's Digest Association, 1979.

Friedman, Robert I. *The False Prophet: Rabbi Meir Kahane — from FBI Informant to Knesset Member.* Brooklyn, N.Y.: Hill, 1990.

———. "Selling Israel to America: The Hasbara Project Targets the U.S. Media." *Mother Jones,* February/March 1987, 21–52.

Fromkin, David. *A Peace to End All Peace: The Fall of the Ottoman Empire and the Creation of the Modern Middle East.* New York: Avon, 1989.

Gates, Robert M. *From the Shadows: The Ultimate Insider's Story of Five Presidents and How They Won the Cold War.* New York: Simon & Schuster, 1996.

Gerner, Deborah J. "Missed Opportunities and Roads Not Taken: The Eisenhower Administration and the Palestinians." In *U.S. Policy on Palestine from Wilson to Clinton,* edited by Michael W. Suleiman. Normal, Ill.: Association of Arab-American University Graduates, 1995.

Geyer, Georgie Anne. "The American Correspondent in the Arab World." In

The American Media and the Arabs, edited by Michael C. Hudson and Ronald G. Wolfe. Washington, D.C.: Center for Contemporary Arab Studies, Georgetown University, 1980.

Ghareeb, Edmund. *Split Vision: The Portrayal of Arabs in the American Media.* Washington, D.C.: American-Arab Affairs Council, 1983.

Goodwin, Doris Kearns. *No Ordinary Time: Franklin and Eleanor Roosevelt: The Home Front in World War II.* New York: Simon & Schuster, 1994.

Grabill, Joseph L. *Protestant Diplomacy and the Near East: Missionary Influence on American Policy, 1810–1927.* Minneapolis: University of Minnesota Press, 1971.

Graham-Brown, Sarah. *Palestinians and Their Society, 1880–1946.* London: Quartet Books, 1980.

Grose, Peter. *Israel in the Mind of America.* New York: Knopf, 1983.

Haass, Richard N. *Conflicts Unending: The United States and Regional Disputes.* New Haven, Conn.: Yale University Press, 1990.

———. "Paying Less Attention to the Middle East." *Commentary,* August 1986, 22–26.

Hadar, Leon T. "The Friends of Bibi (FOBs) vs. 'The New Middle East.'" *Journal of Palestine Studies* 101 (autumn 1996): 89–97.

———. "The 'Neocons': From the Cold War to the 'Global Intifada.'" *Washington Report on Middle East Affairs,* April 1991, 27–28.

———. "Reforming Israel—before It's Too Late." *Foreign Policy,* winter 1990–1991, 106–127.

Haig, Alexander M., Jr. *Caveat: Realism, Reagan, and Foreign Policy.* New York: Macmillan, 1984.

Hamoked, the Center for the Defence of the Individual, and B'Tselem, the Israeli Information Center for Human Rights in the Occupied Territories. *The Quiet Deportation: Revocation of Residency of East Jerusalem Palestinians.* Jerusalem: Hamoked and B'Tselem, April 1997.

Hart, Alan. *Arafat: A Political Biography.* Bloomington: Indiana University Press, 1989.

Heckscher, August. *Woodrow Wilson.* New York: Scribner, 1991.

Hentsch, Thierry. *Imagining the Middle East.* Translated by Fred A. Reed. Montreal: Black Rose Books, 1992.

Hersh, Seymour M. *The Samson Option: Israel's Nuclear Arsenal and American Foreign Policy.* New York: Random House, 1991.

Hudson, Michael C. "The Media and the Arabs: Room for Improvement." In *The American Media and the Arabs,* edited by Michael C. Hudson and Ronald G. Wolfe. Washington, D.C.: Center for Contemporary Arab Studies, Georgetown University, 1980.

Hughes, Emmet John. *The Ordeal of Power: A Political Memoir of the Eisenhower Years.* New York: Atheneum, 1963.

Hurewitz, J. C. *The Struggle for Palestine.* New York: Norton, 1950.

Indyk, Martin. "Peace without the PLO." *Foreign Policy,* summer 1990, 30–38.

Jacobs, David. *An American Conscience: Woodrow Wilson's Search for World Peace.* New York: Harper & Row, 1973.

Jervis, Robert. *Perception and Misperception in International Politics.* Princeton, N.J.: Princeton University Press, 1976.

Johnson, Lyndon Baines. *The Vantage Point: Perspectives of the Presidency, 1963–1969.* New York: Holt, Rinehart and Winston, 1971.

Kenen, I. L. *Israel's Defense Line: Her Friends and Foes in Washington.* Buffalo, N.Y.: Prometheus, 1981.

Kerr, Malcolm H. *America's Middle East Policy: Kissinger, Carter and the Future.* IPS Papers 14(E). Washington, D.C.: Institute for Palestine Studies, 1980.

Khalidi, Rashid. *Palestinian Identity: The Construction of Modern National Consciousness.* New York: Columbia University Press, 1997.

———. *Under Siege: P.L.O. Decisionmaking during the 1982 War.* New York: Columbia University Press, 1986.

Khalidi, Walid, ed. *From Haven to Conquest: Readings in Zionism and the Palestine Problem until 1948.* Washington, D.C.: Institute for Palestine Studies, 1987.

———. *The Middle East Postwar Environment.* Washington, D.C.: Institute for Palestine Studies, 1991.

Kimmerling, Baruch. "Academic History Caught in the Cross-Fire: The Case of Israeli-Jewish Historiography." *History & Memory: Studies in Representation of the Past,* spring/summer 1995, 41–65.

Kirkpatrick, Jeane. "Dishonoring Sadat." *New Republic,* 11 November 1981, 14–16.

———. "How the PLO Was Legitimized." *Commentary,* July 1989, 21–28.

Kissinger, Henry. *White House Years.* Boston: Little, Brown, 1979.

———. *Years of Upheaval.* Boston: Little, Brown, 1982.

Kurtzer, Daniel Charles. "Palestine Guerrilla and Israeli Counterinsurgency Warfare: The Radicalization of the Palestine Arab Community to Violence, 1949–1970." Ph.D. diss., Columbia University, 1976.

Kurzman, Dan. *Genesis 1948: The First Arab-Israeli War.* New York: New American Library, 1970.

Lee, Martin A., and Norman Solomon. *Unreliable Sources: A Guide to Bias in News Media.* New York: Carol, 1990.

Lenczowski, George. *American Presidents and the Middle East.* Durham, N.C.: Duke University Press, 1990.

Lesch, Ann Mosely. *Arab Politics in Palestine, 1917–1939: The Frustration of a Nationalist Movement.* Ithaca, N.Y.: Cornell University Press, 1979.

———. *Political Perceptions of the Palestinians on the West Bank and the Gaza Strip.* Washington, D.C.: Middle East Institute, 1980.

———. "The Reagan Administration's Policy toward the Palestinians." In *U.S. Policy on Palestine from Wilson to Clinton,* edited by Michael W. Suleiman. Normal, Ill.: Association of Arab-American University Graduates, 1995.

Lewis, Bernard. "The Palestinians and the PLO." *Commentary*, January 1975, 32–48.

Lewis, Samuel W. "Israel: The Peres Era and Its Legacy." *Foreign Affairs* 65, no. 3 (1987): 582–610.

———. "The United States and Israel: Constancy and Change." In *The Middle East: Ten Years after Camp David*, edited by William B. Quandt. Washington, D.C.: Brookings Institution, 1988.

"Loan Guarantees Update." In "Settlement Report," edited by Geoffrey Arronson. Reprinted in *Journal of Palestine Studies* 102 (winter 1997): 142.

Lustick, Ian S. "The Oslo Agreement as an Obstacle to Peace." *Journal of Palestine Studies* 105 (autumn 1997): 61–66.

Makovsky, David. *Making Peace with the PLO: The Rabin Government's Road to the Oslo Accord*. Boulder, Colo.: Westview Press, 1996.

Mansour, Camille. *Beyond Alliance: Israel in U.S. Foreign Policy*. Translated by James A. Cohen. New York: Columbia University Press, 1994.

Manuel, Frank E. *The Realities of American-Palestine Relations*. Washington, D.C.: Public Affairs Press, 1949.

Mattar, Philip. *The Mufti of Jerusalem: Al-Hajj Amin al-Husayni and the Palestinian National Movement*. New York: Columbia University Press, 1988.

McCullough, David. *Truman*. New York: Simon & Schuster, 1992.

McDonald, James G. *My Mission in Israel 1948–1951*. New York: Simon & Schuster, 1951.

McGhee, George. *Envoy to the Middle World: Adventures in Diplomacy*. New York: Harper & Row, 1983.

Melman, Yossi, and Dan Raviv. *Friends in Deed: Inside the U.S.-Israel Alliance*. New York: Hyperion, 1994.

———. *The Imperfect Spies: The History of Israeli Intelligence*. London: Sidgwick & Jackson, 1989.

Michalek, Laurence. "The Arab in American Cinema: A Century of Otherness." *Arab Image in American Film and Television*, supplement to *Cineaste* 17, no. 1 (n.d.), copublished with the American-Arab Anti-Discimination Committee.

Miller, Aaron David. "The Arab-Israeli Conflict, 1967–1987: A Retrospective." *Middle East Journal*, summer 1987, 349–360.

———. *The Arab States and the Palestine Question: Between Ideology and Self-Interest*. New York: Praeger, 1986.

———. *The PLO and the Politics of Survival*. New York: Praeger, 1983.

Miller, Merle. *Lyndon: An Oral Biography*. New York: Putnam, 1980.

———. *Plain Speaking: An Oral Biography of Harry S. Truman*. New York: Berkley, 1974.

Milstein, Mark H. "Strategic Ties or Tentacles? Institute for National Security Affairs." *Washington Report for Middle East Affairs*, October 1991, 27–28.

Morgan, Ted. *FDR: A Biography*. New York: Simon & Schuster, 1985.

Morris, Benny. *The Birth of the Palestinian Refugee Problem, 1947–1949.* New York: Cambridge University Press, 1987.

———. *1948 and After: Israel and the Palestinians.* Oxford: Clarendon Press, 1994.

———. "A Second Look at the 'Missed Peace,' or Smoothing Out History: A Review Essay." *Journal of Palestine Studies* 93 (autumn 1994): 78–79.

Moughrabi, Fouad. "American Public Opinion and the Palestine Question." In *Public Opinion and the Palestine Question,* edited by Elia Zureik and Fouad Moughrabi. New York: St. Martin's Press, 1987.

Muslih, Muhammad Y. *The Origins of Palestinian Nationalism.* New York: Columbia University Press, 1988.

Naff, Alixa. *Becoming American: The Early Arab Immigrant Experience.* Carbondale: Southern Illinois University Press, 1985.

Neff, Donald. *Fallen Pillars: U.S. Policy towards Palestine and Israel since 1945.* Washington, D.C.: Institute for Palestine Studies, 1995.

———. "Nixon's Middle East Policy: From Balance to Bias." In *U.S. Policy on Palestine from Wilson to Clinton,* edited by Michael W. Suleiman. Normal, Ill.: Association of Arab-American University Graduates, 1995.

———. *Warriors for Jerusalem: The Six Days That Changed the Middle East in 1967.* Brattleboro, Vt.: Amana Books, 1988.

Newhouse, John. "The Tactician." *New Yorker,* 7 May 1990.

"The Next Step in the Peace Process: A Roundtable Discussion of *Building for Peace.*" A symposium with Martin Indyk, Samuel Lewis, William Quandt, and Dennis Ross, November 30, 1988. In *Proceedings of the Washington Institute Policy Forum, 1988.* Washington, D.C.: Washington Institute for Near East Policy, 1988.

Nixon, Richard. *RN: The Memoirs of Richard Nixon.* New York: Grosset & Dunlap, 1978.

Pappé, Ilan. *The Making of the Arab-Israeli Conflict, 1947–1951.* London: I. B. Tauris, 1994.

———. "Post-Zionist Critique on Israel and the Palestinians. Part I: The Academic Debate." *Journal of Palestine Studies* 102 (spring 1997): 29–41.

Parker, Richard B. *The Politics of Miscalculation in the Middle East.* Bloomington: Indiana University Press, 1993.

Parmenter, Barbara McKean. *Giving Voice to Stones: Place and Identity in Palestinian Literature.* Austin: University of Texas Press, 1994.

Peck, Juliana S. *The Reagan Administration and the Palestinian Question: The First Thousand Days.* Washington, D.C.: Institute for Palestine Studies, 1984.

Peters, Joan. *From Time Immemorial: The Origins of the Arab-Jewish Conflict over Palestine.* New York: Harper & Row, 1984.

Podhoretz, Norman. "J'Accuse." *Commentary,* September 1982, 21–31.

Porath, Yehoshua. "Mrs. Peters's Palestine." *New York Review of Books,* 16 January 1986, 36–39.

Quandt, William B. *Camp David: Peacemaking and Politics.* Washington, D.C.: Brookings Institution, 1986.

———. *Decade of Decisions: American Policy toward the Arab-Israeli Conflict, 1967–1976.* Berkeley: University of California Press, 1977.

———. *Peace Process: American Diplomacy and the Arab-Israeli Conflict since 1967.* Washington, D.C.: Brookings Institution; and Berkeley: University of California Press, 1993.

———. "Reagan's Lebanon Policy: Trial and Error." *Middle East Journal,* spring 1984, 237–266.

———. "U.S. Policy toward the Arab-Israeli Conflict." In *The Middle East: Ten Years after Camp David,* edited by William B. Quandt. Washington, D.C.: Brookings Institution, 1988.

Quandt, William B., Fuad Jabber, and Ann Mosely Lesch. *The Politics of Palestinian Nationalism.* Berkeley: University of California Press, 1973.

Rabie, Mohamed. *U.S.-P.L.O. Dialogue: Secret Diplomacy and Conflict Resolution.* Gainesville: University Press of Florida, 1995.

Reagan, Ronald. *An American Life.* New York: Simon & Schuster, 1990.

Reich, Bernard, ed. *An Historical Encyclopedia of the Arab-Israeli Conflict.* Westport, Conn.: Greenwood Press, 1996.

———. *The United States and Israel: Influence in the Special Relationship.* New York: Praeger, 1984.

Roosevelt, Eleanor. *The Autobiography of Eleanor Roosevelt.* Reprint, New York: Da Capo Press, 1992.

Ross, Dennis. *Acting with Caution: Middle East Policy Planning for the Second Reagan Administration.* Policy Paper 1. Washington, D.C.: Washington Institute for Near East Policy, 1985.

Rossiter, Clinton, and James Lare, eds. *The Essential Lippmann: A Political Philosophy for Liberal Democracy.* New York: Random House, 1963.

Rostow, Eugene V. "The American Stake in Israel." *Commentary,* April 1977, 32–46.

———. "Israel in the Evolution of American Foreign Policy." In *The Palestine Question in American History,* edited by Clark M. Clifford, Eugene V. Rostow, and Barbara W. Tuchman. New York: Arno Press, 1978.

———. "Resolution 242—a Historical Perspective." In *Can Israel Survive a Palestinian State?* edited by Michael Widlanski. Jerusalem: Institute for Advanced Strategic and Political Studies, 1990.

———. [No title.] In *Approaching Peace: American Interests in Israeli-Palestinian Final Status Talks,* edited by Robert Satloff. Washington, D.C.: Washington Institute for Near East Policy, 1994.

Said, Edward W. *Orientalism.* New York: Vintage Books, 1979.

———. *Peace and Its Discontents: Essays on Palestine in the Middle East Peace Process.* New York: Vintage Books, 1996.

———. *The Politics of Dispossession: The Struggle for Palestinian Self-Determination, 1969–1994.* New York: Pantheon Books, 1994.

Sanders, Ronald. *The High Walls of Jerusalem: A History of the Balfour Dec-

laration and the Birth of the British Mandate for Palestine. New York: Holt, Rinehart and Winston, 1983.

Saunders, Harold H. "An Israeli-Palestinian Peace." *Foreign Affairs*, fall 1982, 100–121.

——. *The Other Walls: The Politics of the Arab-Israeli Peace Process*. Washington, D.C.: American Enterprise Institute for Public Policy Research, 1985.

Saunders, Harold H., and Cecilia Albin. *Sinai II: The Politics of International Mediation, 1974–1975*. FPI Case Study 17. Washington, D.C.: School of Advanced International Studies, Johns Hopkins University, 1993.

Schiff, Ze'ev, and Ehud Ya'ari. *Israel's Lebanon War*. Translated by Ina Friedman. New York: Simon & Schuster, 1984.

Segev, Tom. *The Seventh Million: The Israelis and the Holocaust*. Translated by Haim Watzman. New York: Hill & Wang, 1993.

Sha'ban, Fuad. *Islam and Arabs in Early American Thought: The Roots of Orientalism in America*. Durham, N.C.: Acorn Press, 1991.

Shadid, Mohammed K. *The United States and the Palestinians*. New York: St. Martin's Press, 1981.

Shafir, Gershon. "Israeli Decolonization and Critical Sociology." *Journal of Palestine Studies* 99 (spring 1996): 23–35.

Shamir, Shimon. "Israeli Views of Egypt and the Peace Process: The Duality of Vision." In *The Middle East: Ten Years after Camp David*, edited by William B. Quandt. Washington, D.C.: Brookings Institution, 1988.

Sharabi, Hisham. "A Look Ahead: The Future State of Palestine." In *The Palestinians: New Directions*, edited by Michael C. Hudson. Washington, D.C.: Center for Contemporary Arab Studies, Georgetown University, 1990.

Sheehan, Edward R. F. *The Arabs, Israelis and Kissinger: A Secret History of American Diplomacy in the Middle East*. New York: Reader's Digest Press, 1976.

Shiblak, Abbas. "Residency Status and Civil Rights of Palestinian Refugees in Arab Countries." *Journal of Palestine Studies* 99 (spring 1996): 36–45.

Shlaim, Avi. *Collusion across the Jordan: King Abdullah, the Zionist Movement, and the Partition of Palestine*. New York: Columbia University Press, 1988.

——. "The Debate about 1948." *International Journal of Middle East Studies* 27, no. 3 (August 1995): 287–304.

Shultz, George P. "The Challenge to the Democracies." In *Terrorism: How the West Can Win*, edited by Benjamin Netanyahu. New York: Farrar, Straus & Giroux, 1986.

——. *Turmoil and Triumph: My Years as Secretary of State*. New York: Scribner, 1993.

Silver, Eric. *Begin: The Haunted Prophet*. New York: Random House, 1984.

Smith, Charles D. *Palestine and the Arab-Israeli Conflict*. 3d ed. New York: St. Martin's Press, 1996.

Spiegel, Steven L. *The Other Arab-Israeli Conflict: Making America's Middle*

East Policy, from Truman to Reagan. Chicago: University of Chicago Press, 1985.

Stephens, John Lloyd. *Incidents of Travel in Egypt, Arabia Petraea, and the Holy Land.* Reprint, Norman: University of Oklahoma Press, 1970.

Stevens, Art. *The Persuasion Explosion: Your Guide to the Power and Influence of Contemporary Public Relations.* Washington, D.C.: Acropolis Books, 1985.

Stivers, William. *America's Confrontation with Revolutionary Change in the Middle East, 1948–83.* New York: St. Martin's Press, 1986.

Suleiman, Michael W. "American Public Support of Middle Eastern Countries: 1939–1979." In *The American Media and the Arabs,* edited by Michael C. Hudson and Ronald G. Wolfe. Washington, D.C.: Center for Contemporary Arab Studies, Georgetown University, 1980.

———. "Palestine and the Palestinians in the Mind of America." In *U.S. Policy on Palestine from Wilson to Clinton,* edited by Michael W. Suleiman. Normal, Ill.: Association of Arab-American University Graduates, 1995.

A Survey of Palestine, Prepared in December 1945 and January 1946 for the Information of the Anglo-American Committee of Inquiry. Reprint, Washington, D.C.: Institute for Palestine Studies, 1991.

Teicher, Howard, and Gayle Radley Teicher. *Twin Pillars to Desert Storm: America's Flawed Vision in the Middle East from Nixon to Bush.* New York: Morrow, 1993.

Temko, Ned. *To Win or to Die: A Personal Portrait of Menachem Begin.* New York: Morrow, 1987.

Terry, Janice J. "The Carter Administration and the Palestinians." In *U.S. Policy on Palestine from Wilson to Clinton,* edited by Michael W. Suleiman. Normal, Ill.: Association of Arab-American University Graduates, 1995.

Tessler, Mark. *A History of the Israeli-Palestinian Conflict.* Bloomington: Indiana University Press, 1994.

Thomson, William. *The Land and the Book: Biblical Illustrations Drawn from the Manners and Customs, the Scenes and Scenery of the Holy Land.* Reprint, Grand Rapids, Mich.: Baker, 1954.

Tillman, Seth P. *The United States in the Middle East: Interests and Obstacles.* Bloomington: Indiana University Press, 1982.

Tivnan, Edward. *The Lobby: Jewish Political Power and American Foreign Policy.* New York: Simon & Schuster Touchstone, 1988.

Toward Peace in the Middle East. Report of a Study Group. Washington, D.C.: Brookings Institution, 1975.

Truman, Harry S. *Memoirs.* Vol. 1, *Year of Decisions.* Garden City, N.Y.: Doubleday, 1955.

———. *Memoirs.* Vol. 2, *Years of Trial and Hope.* Garden City, N.Y.: Doubleday, 1956.

Tschirgi, Dan. *The American Search for Mideast Peace.* New York: Praeger, 1989.

————. *The Politics of Indecision: Origins and Implications of American Involvement with the Palestine Problem*. New York: Praeger, 1983.

Twain, Mark. *The Innocents Abroad, or The New Pilgrim's Progress, Being Some Account of the Steamship* Quaker City's *Pleasure Excursion to Europe and the Holy Land*. Reprint, Pleasantville, N.Y.: Reader's Digest Association, 1990.

U.S. Department of State. "Department Gives Position on Palestinian Issue." *Department of State Bulletin* 73 (1 December 1975): 797–800.

————. *Foreign Relations of the United States 1948*. Vol. 5, *The Near East, South Asia, and Africa*. Washington, D.C.: U.S. Government Printing Office, 1976.

Vance, Cyrus. *Hard Choices: Critical Years in America's Foreign Policy*. New York: Simon & Schuster, 1983.

Vogel, Lester I. *To See a Promised Land: Americans and the Holy Land in the Nineteenth Century*. University Park: Pennsylvania State University Press, 1993.

Ward, Geoffrey C. *A First-Class Temperament: The Emergence of Franklin Roosevelt*. New York: Harper & Row, 1989.

Washington Institute's Presidential Study Group. *Building for Peace: An American Strategy for the Middle East*. Washington, D.C.: Washington Institute for Near East Policy, 1988.

Weisman, John. "Blind Spot in the Middle East." *TV Guide*, 24 October 1981.

————. "Why the Palestinians Are Losing the Propaganda War." *TV Guide*, 31 October 1981.

Wilson, Evan M. *Decision on Palestine: How the U.S. Came to Recognize Israel*. Stanford, Calif.: Hoover Institution Press, 1979.

Wooten, Jim. "The Conciliator." *New York Times Magazine*, 29 January 1995.

Young, Ronald J. *Missed Opportunities for Peace: U.S. Middle East Policies, 1981–1986*. Philadelphia: American Friends Service Committee, 1987.

Index

Aaron, David, 166
Abbas, Muhammad (Abu al-Abbas), 263, 334n. 55
ABC television, 8, 151, 224
Abd Rabbo, Yasir, 332–33n. 36
Abdul Aziz, King, 54–56
Abdullah, King, 6, 58, 88, 225
Abdul-Shafi, Haidar, 269
Abrams, Elliot, 198, 335n. 74
Abu al-Abbas. *See* Abbas, Muhammad
Abu Sharif, Bassam, 238, 296n. 23, 329–30n. 132
Acheson, Dean, 64, 66, 102
Achille Lauro, 235, 263
Acting with Caution (Ross), 252
AIPAC. *See* American Israel Public Affairs Committee
Ajami, Fouad, 11
Albright, Madeleine, 279, 285, 337–38n. 24
Algeria, 164
Allen, Richard, 200–201
Allenby, General Edmund, 28
American Board of Commissioners for Foreign Missions, 29
American Enterprise Institute, 282
American Federation of Labor, 301n. 56
American Israel Public Affairs Committee, 42, 101, 102, 137, 166, 168, 249; during Bush administration, 256, 335n. 62; growth and impact on policymaking during Reagan years, 210, 219–21, 222–23
American Jewish Committee, 52
American Jewish Congress, 223
American Palestine Committee, 51
American University of Beirut, 23, 29
American Zionist Emergency Council, 52, 68, 73
Amnesty International, 173, 318n. 47
Anatolia, 23
Andersson, Sten, 237, 238, 239
Anglo-American Committee, 75, 76
Anglo-American Convention, 34
anti-Semitism, 24, 34–35, 43, 46, 47–48, 51, 130
Arab Americans, 34, 42, 59, 74, 146, 286
Arab Higher Committee, 76–77
The Arabian Nights, 17, 19
Arab Information Office, 56
Arab-Israeli conflict. *See separate listings*
Arabists. *See* U.S. State Department, Arabists
Arab League, 213
Arab Legion, 88
Arab revolt, against Turkey during World War I, 31

Arabs (*see also specific countries and peoples*): compared to Nazis, 102, 104, 117–21; referred to as Turks, 19–20, 37, 38–39; U.S. public perceptions of, 3, 8, 9, 19, 24, 37–41, 42–44, 53, 62, 86, 102–4, 124, 136, 152

The Arab States and the Palestine Question (Miller), 332n. 24

Arab summit meetings: Algiers (1988), 8, 329–30n. 131; Fez (1982), 212 (*see also* Fez Plan); Rabat (1974), 141–42, 145

Arafat, Yasir, 128, 145, 152 (*see also* Palestine Liberation Organization); and Bush administration, 258–59, 333n. 37, 334n. 53; and Declaration of Independence (1988), 196; early organizing efforts, 115, 122; and Oslo process, 283, 290, 291–93; overtures to U.S., during Carter administration, 175–78, 319n. 64; —, during Nixon administration, 140–43; —, during Reagan administration, 8, 205, 208; and Persian Gulf crisis, 263–64, 286, 334n. 55; reaction to Camp David accords, 185–86; and Reagan Plan, 212; statement leading to U.S.-PLO dialogue, 238–239, 330n. 134; U.S. public image of, 153, 231, 269, 275–76, 283, 285–86

archaeology, in Palestine, 17, 20

Arens, Moshe, 173–74

Armenia, 23, 29, 38–39

al-Asad, Hafiz, 125, 147, 168, 179, 325n. 63

Ashrawi, Hanan, 251, 267–69, 335n. 67

Associated Press, 217

Aswan formula, 180

Atomic Energy Commission, 107

AWACS aircraft, sale of to Saudi Arabia, 197, 219–20

AZEC. *See* American Zionist Emergency Council

Baghdad Pact, 99

Baker, Howard, 142–43

Baker, James: allows 1989–1990 peace process to languish, 243, 245, 255, 262–64, 271, 334n. 55; attitude toward Israel, 255, 262, 276; change in negotiating tactics, 255, 267–69; compared unfavorably to Reagan administration by Israel, 256–57; friendship with George Bush and similarities of style, 244–45; influence of cautious, pro-Israeli advisers, 242–43, 247–55, 285, 335n. 67; interest in process over substance, 242–43, 244–45, 270, 272; Israeli elections proposal, 258–60, 333n. 42; lack of sentimentality toward Israel and Palestinians, 245–47, 256, 268; Palestinian-Israeli negotiations following Persian Gulf crisis, 264–67; personal meetings with Palestinian representatives, 247, 251, 267–69; personal style, 242–43, 244–47, 251, 330n. 4, 331nn. 11, 17; perspective on Palestinian situation, 246–47, 258, 267–69, 270, 272; preparations for Madrid conference, 268–69, 335n. 68; relations with Shamir, 246, 259–60

Balfour, Sir Arthur, 30–31, 32, 33, 34, 41

Balfour Declaration, 8, 13, 27–28, 34, 35, 36, 42–43, 48, 52, 59, 66

Ball, George, 111, 146

Begin, Menachem, 6, 163, 188, 194, 220, 221, 222; background as terrorist, 170, 172, 317–18n. 44; initial U.S. reaction to, 170–172; relations with Carter, 166, 167, 168–70, 174–75, 180, 181–85, 186, 189, 261, 317n. 36; relations with Reagan, 198; U.S. popular acceptance of, 170–72, 173, 185, 194

Beilin, Yossi, 290–91

Bellow, Saul, 226

Ben-Gurion, David, 47, 52, 62, 106, 107
Bennett, William, 335n. 74
Benvenisti, Meron, 5, 153, 250, 280
Biltmore Program, 52
The Birth of the Palestinian Refugee Problem (Morris), 5
Blackstone, William, 23, 30
Bliss family, 23
Blitzer, Wolf, 220–21
B'nai B'rith, 113, 197
Bolling, Landrum, 177–78, 319n. 64
Boston Herald, 75
Bourguiba, Habib, 213
Brand, Laurie, 328n. 116
Brandeis, Louis, 27, 28, 29, 30, 33, 41, 46–47, 49
Britain. *See* Great Britain
British Broadcasting Corporation, 5
British Mandate. *See* Mandate for Palestine
Brookings Institution, 164–65, 247
Brown, Harold, 162, 318n. 51
Bruce, David, 146
Bryen, Shoshanna, 201
Bryen, Stephen, 201, 322n. 18, 335n. 74
Brzezinski, Zbigniew, 146, 182, 276; background and beliefs, 163–64; criticized by supporters of Israel, 165, 166, 171; relations with Carter, 162, 163, 189; views of PLO, 164, 178, 179, 319n. 64
B'Tselem, 337n. 17
Bundy, McGeorge, 146
Bush, George, 88, 220, 247, 248, 249, 250, 252, 258, 284–85, 287–88 (*see also* Baker, James); alters conventional view of Palestinians and Israelis, 243, 266–67, 269, 270; anti-Palestinian actions before Persian Gulf crisis, 263–64; attitude toward Israel, 243, 255–56, 323n. 33; attitude toward Palestinians/PLO, 255, 268, 270–71; background and beliefs, 242–44, 251; election calculations as factor in peace process, 265–66; failure to follow through after Madrid, 271, 290; lack of sentimentality toward Israel, 243, 244, 246, 256–57; preoccupation with Israeli settlements, 261–62, 271; readiness to move in peace process after Persian Gulf war, 264–66; readiness to pressure Israel, 243, 255, 260–62, 265–67; relationship with Yitzhak Shamir, 244, 259–61, 264, 271; similarities to Baker in personal style, 242–43, 244–45, 270, 330n. 4
Buxton, Frank, 75–76

Camp David (Quandt), 167
Camp David accords, 166, 167, 177, 178, 180; linkage, 182, 184, 185, 187; negotiations leading to, 181–84; Palestinian autonomy plan and negotiations for, 181–82, 184–85, 186–88, 190–91, 208; Palestinian opposition to, 185–88; proposals for Israeli withdrawal, 182–83, 184, 187; proposed freeze on Israeli settlement construction, 184, 186–87; U.S. failure to understand Palestinian position on, 185, 188
Carlucci, Frank, 276
Carter, Jimmy, 10–11, 149, 156, 195, 199, 202, 205, 220, 239, 243, 247, 259–60, 261, 287 (*see also* Camp David accords; Egyptian-Israeli peace treaty; peace process, early attitude toward involvement of Palestinians in); alters conventional wisdom, 157–62, 167, 191–92, 240; anti-Israeli votes in UN, 183, 189–90; approach of foreign-policy team of, 162–66; background and beliefs, 158–63; domestic political pressures on, 157, 167, 171–72, 177–78, 180–81, 183–84, 185, 188, 190; influence of pro-Israeli advisers, 166–67, 189, 317n. 28; interest

Carter, Jimmy (*continued*)
in human rights, 160–61, 162,
165–66, 172; and lead-up to Camp
David, 181–84; misjudges Likud determination, 170, 185; perspective
on Palestinian situation, dealings
with Palestinians/PLO, 157–62,
172, 175–81, 319n. 71; position on
Palestinian self-determination/
statehood, 161, 162, 177, 179–80,
182, 316n. 9; post–Camp David dis-
couragement, 189; relations with
Arabs, 159, 168; relations with Is-
rael, 158, 159, 161, 167–72, 174–
75, 189, 194, 316n. 13, 317n. 36;
U.S.-Soviet communiqué (1977),
319n. 65
Casey, William, 200, 323n. 33
CBS television, 172, 224
Central Intelligence Agency, 35, 87,
98, 107–8, 140, 200, 309–10n. 34
Chacour, Elias, 269
Chancellor, John, 224
Chavez, Linda, 335n. 74
Chicago Tribune, 38
Childers, Erskine, 295n. 12
Christian Science Monitor, 227
Christopher, Warren, 278, 280, 285,
291
Churba, Joseph, 200–201, 321–
22n. 16, 322n. 17
Clifford, Clark, 63, 69–72, 79
Clinton, Bill, 275, 288; general tilt
toward Israel/pro-Israeli policy
changes, 276–80, 281–82, 337–
38n. 24; impact of pro-Likud political pressures, 282, 284–85; influence of pro-Israeli advisers, 249,
255, 285; lack of interest in details,
285; limited involvement in peace
process, 277, 279–80, 281, 284–85,
290–91; personal affinity for Israel,
276; position on UN resolutions,
279–80; relations with Netanyahu,
277, 284–85
CNN, 269
Commager, Henry Steele, 102

Commentary, 154, 199, 226, 228–29,
253
Conference of Presidents of Major
American Jewish Organizations,
171, 172
Conflicts Unending (Haass), 253
conservatives, U.S., anti-peace lobbying of, 282–85
conventional wisdom. *See* "frame of
reference" on Palestinian-Israeli
issues
Crane, Charles, 32
Crossman, Richard, 76
Crusades, 19, 20, 25

Deir Yassin massacre, 6, 172
Democratic Party, 45, 51, 53, 71, 166
Dillon, Douglas, 146
Dimona, 107, 309n. 33
Dine, Thomas, 219–20
Dodge, Cleveland, 23, 29, 38
Dole, Robert, 248
Duffy, Michael, 244
Duke, Angier Biddle, 226
Dulles, Allen, 35, 36
Dulles, John Foster, 91, 97, 99, 100,
102
Dunsmore, Barrie, 150, 151

Eagleburger, Lawrence, 218, 247, 276
Eban, Abba, 74, 87, 93, 96, 101–2,
110, 112, 118, 120, 130, 260, 267,
309n. 33
Egypt, 87, 97, 107, 116, 117, 129, 130,
131, 176, 181, 265 (*see also specific
Arab-Israeli wars; specific U.S. administration policies; individual
Egyptian leaders; specific peace
agreements*); and Camp David accords, 184, 185; impact of Camp
David on role of in Arab-Israeli
conflict, 187; intermediary in Bush
administration negotiating efforts,
257, 259, 333n. 37, 334n. 55; negotiations leading to Camp David,
178, 181–83; 1973 war and aftermath, 135, 140, 143, 151; and Pales-

tinians, 84, 90, 114–15, 179, 180, 190–91; relations with Reagan administration, 199

Egyptian-Israeli peace treaty, 136, 157, 166, 178, 184, 185, 189, 191

Eichmann, Adolf, 117–20

Eilts, Hermann, 203–04

Eisenhower, Dwight, 74, 102, 104, 105, 107, 113, 116, 265, 287; actions/attitude toward Israel, 96–97, 98, 157; background and beliefs, 96–97; efforts to thwart Soviet advances, 98–99; Eisenhower Doctrine, 99; ignorance of Palestinians, 97–98, 99–100, 122; relations with Arab states, 97–99

Eizenstat, Stuart, 166, 335n. 74

Ellis, Marc, 120

Elon, Amos, 213

Epstein, Eliahu, 72

Eretz Israel, 7. *See also* Israel, "Greater Israel" policy

Erlanger, Steven, 277

Evensen, Bruce, 79, 80

Evron, Ephraim, 109

Exodus (Uris), 103–4, 118, 119, 121, 227, 266–67

Exodus 1947, 75

Fackenheim, Emil, 118, 120–21

Fahd, Prince, 142–43, 324n. 48

Fahd Plan, 213, 324n. 48

Fairbanks, Richard, 205, 276

Fatah, 100, 115, 122, 128, 140, 175, 314n. 41

Faysal bin Abdul Aziz, Prince, 66

fedayeen, 127–29, 132, 155

Feinberg, Abraham, 109, 110

Fez Plan, 212–14, 324n. 48

Findley, Paul, 186

Finkelstein, Norman, 326–27n. 93

Fish, Hamilton, 37

Fisher, Max, 130

Fisk, Robert, 7, 216–18, 297n. 2

FLAME (Facts and Logic about the Middle East), 284

Flapan, Simcha, 328n. 112

Ford, Gerald, 124, 136, 148, 149; ignorance of Palestinian issue, 144–45; influence of Henry Kissinger on, 125, 144–45; reassessment of policy toward Israel, 145–47

Foreign Policy, 164

Foreign Service. *See* U.S. State Department

Fortas, Abe, 109, 110, 112

Fourth Geneva Convention, 202

"frame of reference" on Palestinian-Israeli issues (*see also* orientalism; scholarship on Palestinian-Israeli conflict; *and specific U.S. administrations*): anti-Palestinian cast of public mindset after 1960s, 153–56, 157–58, 168, 195–96, 203; assumption, that all Palestinians are refugees or terrorists, 7, 90, 130–31, 140–41, 150, 153, 193, 202, 216–18; —, that Arabs are warlike, primitive, 19, 32, 36, 37–40, 42, 50, 70, 76, 81, 102–4, 150, 287; —, that burden of compromise is on Palestinians, 248–49, 252, 253; —, that criticism of Israel endangers it, 171–72, 183, 229, 256–57, 327n. 103; —, that Palestine should be Jewish, 19, 21–22, 25, 26, 33, 36, 38, 42, 45, 46, 52, 53, 54, 59, 63, 77, 274, 287; —, that Palestinian/Arab hostility to Israel is irrational, 1, 2, 5–6, 61, 65, 89, 90–91, 111, 120–21, 130, 159–60, 185, 197; —, that Palestinians lack sense of nationalism, as held during British Mandate period, 36, 44, 57–58, 88; —, that Palestinians lack sense of nationalism, as held during 1960s and 1970s, 111, 116, 148, 154, 162, 168; —, that Palestinians lack sense of nationalism, as held during Reagan-Bush years, 195–96, 198, 202–3, 204, 225–27, 240, 249, 250–51, 254; —, that Palestinians not attached to Palestine, 5, 16, 85, 90–91, 104, 297n. 2; —, that Palestin-

"frame of reference" (*continued*)
ians/PLO unalterably radical, 181,
187, 215–16, 246, 249–50; assumption of unique U.S. bond with Israel, 2, 5, 82, 95, 101–4, 119–20,
136, 192, 218, 257, 287–89; changes
in, beginning after 1960s, 125, 149,
151, 152–53, 155, 191–92, 270;
changes caused by new scholarship,
232–33; changes caused by peace
process, 269–70, 275–76; definition, 2, 3–4, 5; effect of on open
discourse, 155, 172, 230–31; effect
of Palestinian/Arab militancy and
terrorism on, 50, 56–57, 78, 92–
93, 96, 124, 152–54, 183, 285; effect
of Palestinian statelessness on, 12,
92, 95, 98, 272–73; effect of on
prolongation of conflict, 275, 289–
93; enduring nature of, despite
factors for change, 228, 269–70,
276–77, 280–85; as framework
for/constraint on policymaking, 1,
3, 14–15, 26, 33, 161, 287–88, 290;
—, during Carter administration,
157–58, 167, 180–81, 183–84, 188,
191–92, 194; —, during Kissinger
era, 125, 129, 134–35, 136, 137–
38, 145, 155–56; —, in 1980s and
1990s, 195–96, 218, 221, 222–23,
227, 228, 240–41, 251, 275, 284;
—, in 1950s and 1960s, 97–98,
101–2, 104, 110–11, 112, 114,
115–17; —, during Truman administration, 69–72, 80, 86, 90–91; inherent inequity in U.S. mediation
efforts resulting from, 180–81,
191, 275, 293; Palestinian absence
from discourse/ignorance of Palestinian grievances, 2, 3, 275, 287–
89; —, before 1948, 19–20, 21–22,
25, 26, 30, 42–44, 49, 53, 54, 57,
59–60, 274–75; —, from 1948 to
1967, 62, 65–66, 77, 82, 84, 90–91,
92–94, 97–98, 110–11, 112, 114,
115–17, 121–23; —, since 1967,

8–9, 130–31, 132, 134–35, 138,
141, 144–45, 152, 154, 156, 161–
62, 202–3, 218, 232, 239–41, 250,
253; shaped by personal knowledge/
experience, 150, 247, 267–69, 292–
93; shaped by terminology, 6–8,
43, 159, 296n. 20; shaped from
Zionist/Israeli perspective, 287–
89; —, before 1948, 2–3, 5–6, 8,
11, 43, 54, 60, 61–62, 72–73, 76,
80–86; —, since 1948, 104, 108–9,
116, 123, 172, 174–75, 191–92,
202, 218, 275; virtually automatic
nature of support for Israel, 171,
173, 174, 222–23, 224, 229–30, 232;
zero-sum effect of Israeli vs. Arab
images, 92–94, 96, 118–19, 121,
168, 171, 174–75, 272–73, 335n. 74
France, 33, 97, 98, 103, 164, 210, 216
Frankel, Max, 222
Frankfurter, Felix, 33, 47
Friedman, Thomas, 245, 257, 268,
333n. 42
From Time Immemorial (Peters),
225–27, 254, 327n. 94
Fulbright, William, 146, 147, 149

Garment, Leonard, 130, 335n. 74
Gates, Robert, 200
Gaza, 87, 98, 100, 116, 122 (*see also*
West Bank/Gaza; Israel, "Greater
Israel" policy; Israeli settlements
in occupied territories)
Gemayel, Bashir, 210, 325n. 63
Genesis 1948 (Kurzman), 4
Geneva conference, 139, 146–47, 168,
176, 178
Germany, 27, 28, 29, 47, 55, 56
Geyer, Georgie Anne, 150–52
Gilbert, Martin, 226
Golan Heights, 116, 135, 197
Goldberg, Arthur, 109, 110, 146,
170–71, 226
Gompers, Samuel, 301n. 56
Goodgame, Dan, 244
Gore, Al, 276, 336n. 5

Great Britain, 7–8, 38, 97, 98, 103, 225; in Palestine, 31, 33, 34, 39, 48, 49–50, 56–57, 60, 65, 74, 75, 77, 274–75 (*see also* Balfour Declaration; Mandate for Palestine); and Transjordan, 58, 88; white papers, 33, 48, 49

Greenberg, Irving, 120

Grose, Peter, 2–3, 24, 32

Haass, Richard, 248, 249, 251, 252–54, 255, 258, 270, 336n. 6

Habash, George, 128

Habib, Philip, 206, 207, 209, 210

Haddad, Wadi, 128

Haig, Alexander, 199–200, 201, 276; disinterest in Palestinian issue, 199, 203, 205, 206; "strategic consensus" policy, 199–200; support for Israeli invasion of Lebanon, 205–6, 323nn. 30, 33

The Haj (Uris), 227

Halperin, Morton, 133

Hamilton, Lee, 149, 314–15n. 64

Hamoked, 337n. 17

Harding, Warren, 34, 35

Har Homa. *See* Jerusalem, Israeli actions in East Jerusalem

Harriman, Averell, 146

Harrison, Benjamin, 23

Harrison, Earl, 63–64

Hasbara Project, 223–24

Hatfield, Mark, 315n. 70

Hauser, Rita, 130

Hebron, 6, 39, 42, 277

Henderson, Loy, 70, 88–89

Hentsch, Thierry, 18

Heritage Foundation, 282

Hertzberg, Arthur, 119

An Historical Encyclopedia of the Arab-Israeli Conflict (Reich), 6

Hitler, Adolph, 45, 47, 49, 119

Holocaust, 45, 53, 65, 77, 86, 103, 132, 155, 246, 272, 316n. 13; "Holocaust theology," 120–21; increased awareness of, in 1960s, 117–21;

Jewish refugees in Europe, 46, 47, 62, 63–64, 68, 75, 77; U.S. reaction to, 2, 61–62, 74, 118, 150, 158, 161, 196

Holy Land. *See* Palestine

Horne, Alistair, 164

Hughes, Charles, 34

Hull, Cordell, 48, 51

Humphrey, Hubert, 170–71

Hussein, King, 113, 115, 168, 213; and Jordan civil war, 128–29, 135; and Palestinians, 179, 234; reaction to Camp David accords, 186; reaction to Reagan Plan, 212

Hussein, Saddam, 255, 263–64, 286, 334n. 54

Hussein, Sherif, of Mecca, 31

Husseini, Faisal, 238, 263

al-Husseini, Haj Amin, 56–57, 77, 88, 118–19, 287

Ibn Saud. *See* Abdul Aziz, King

Incidents of Travel in Egypt, Arabia Petraea, and the Holy Land (Stephens), 17, 20

Indyk, Martin, 220, 249–51, 252, 276, 331nn. 13; 15

The Innocents Abroad (Twain), 16–17

In These Times, 326–27n. 93

intifada, 8, 57, 214, 215, 228, 230, 241, 242, 255, 262; factors leading to, 235, 240; message/implication of, 196, 236, 238, 240, 250, 272–73; U.S./Israeli reaction to, 57, 233, 236–37, 242, 248–49, 250, 256, 266, 286

Iran, 98–99, 189

Iraq, 31, 33, 49, 105, 128, 197, 200, 263–64 (*see also* Hussein, Saddam)

Irgun, 6, 109, 163, 170, 172

Islam. *See* Muslims; Palestinians, Islamic fundamentalism among

Israel (*see also various Arab-Israeli wars; specific U.S. administration policies; individual Israeli leaders; specific peace agreements*): com-

Israel (*continued*)
mitted core of pro-Israeli sympathizers, 231–32, 266; diminished
U.S. sympathy for in 1980s, 223–
24, 231, 266–67; fear of Palestinian legitimacy, 139, 141, 148, 153–
54, 168, 169, 213–14, 250, 272,
289–90, 292–93; "Greater Israel"
policy pursued by Begin, 167, 169–
70, 171, 174, 185, 186, 193–94;
"Greater Israel" policy pursued by
Shamir, 242, 256, 259–60, 261, 262
(*see also* Israeli settlements in occupied territories); hospitable to
journalists, 80, 120, 151; housing
loan guarantees for, 262, 266, 271,
281, 337n. 15; increased U.S. sympathy for following Eichmann trial
and 1967 war, 117–21, 311–12n.
72; internal impact of U.S. support
for Likud, 221–22, 235–36, 260,
267, 284, 337–38n. 24; issue of
repatriation of Palestinian refugees,
89–90, 100, 105, 307–8n. 97;
military superiority, 107–8, 117,
133, 145 (*see also specific Arab-
Israeli wars*); nuclear program,
107–8, 133, 309n. 33, 309–10n.
34; opposition to Palestinian/PLO
involvement in peace process, 157,
167–70, 185, 213–14, 234–35; romantic appeal of to U.S. public,
61–62, 63, 82–83, 103–4, 119–20;
Soviet Jewish immigrants, 261, 262,
333n. 46, 334n. 51; U.S. affinity
for, 2–3, 5, 86, 95–96, 136; U.S.
diplomatic recognition of, 67, 72,
91–92; U.S. perception of Israeli
security vulnerability, 183, 223,
249, 254; U.S. public perceptions of,
2–3, 8, 101–4, 136; as U.S. strategic asset, 3, 92, 132–33, 134, 174,
198–201, 220, 221, 252, 318n. 51
Israel in the Mind of America (Grose),
3, 24
Israeli settlements in occupied territories, 111, 168–70, 184, 186, 190,
210, 266, 276, 277, 280; numbers
of settlers and settlements, 193–94,
204, 240–41, 261, 262, 271–72;
significance of to Palestinians, 262,
269; U.S. position on settlements,
during Bush administration, 244,
246, 261–62, 271–72; —, during
Carter administration, 168–70, 182,
186–87, 190, 194, 320n. 92; —,
during Clinton administration, 279,
281–82, 337n. 15, 337nn. 15, 16;
—, during Reagan administration,
199, 201–2, 208, 211, 218, 240
Italy, 210, 216
Ivanhoe (Scott), 25, 37

Jabber, Fuad, 328n. 116
Jackson, Henry, 136, 199
Jacobson, Eddie, 68–69
Jennings, Peter, 150, 151
Jerusalem, 6, 17, 38, 39, 83, 190; Hebrew and Arabic names for, 296n.
20; Israeli actions in East Jerusalem,
241, 261–62, 271, 277, 281–82,
283, 337nn. 16, 17; status of, 182,
185, 279, 280–82
Jerusalem Post, 229, 256
Jewish Agency in Palestine, 47, 70, 71,
72, 74
Jewish Defense League (Kach), 321–
22n. 16
Jewish Institute for National Security Affairs, 137, 138, 198, 199,
200
Jewish intellectuals in United States,
118, 120–21
Jewish organizations in United States,
9 (*see also* lobby, pro-Zionist/
Israel; U.S. Congress, pressures
from pro-Israel lobbyists; Zionist
movement; *and specific organizations*); anti-peace lobby among,
282–85, 327n. 103; early efforts
to generate public support, 101–2;
lobbying/educational efforts with
government officials, 137–38
Jewish Telegraph Agency, 40

JINSA. *See* Jewish Institute for National Security Affairs
Johnson, Lyndon, 95, 287; actions/policies during and after 1967 war, 111–12, 116–17, 310–11n. 46; animosity toward Arabs/ignorance of Palestinian perspective, 109, 110, 113–14, 122–23; friendship with Israel, 109–10, 112, 113; influence of pro-Israeli friends/advisers on, 109–11, 112, 116
Jordan, 31, 105, 117, 176, 199, 225, 236 (*see also* Abdullah, King; Hussein, King); control over Arab areas of Palestine, 6, 58, 87–88, 90, 98; 1970 civil war, 124, 127–30, 132–33, 135, 138; 1985 Jordanian-PLO initiative, 234–35; Palestinian cross-border raids into Israel from, 98, 100, 115, 122; and Palestinians, 84, 86, 89, 90, 140, 154; proposals to link Palestinian control of West Bank with, 149, 161, 164, 175, 177, 208, 254–55; renounces responsibility for West Bank, 237; response to Reagan Plan, 211–12, 214; role in peace process, 141–42, 149, 179, 184, 190
Jordan, Hamilton, 189
Judea and Samaria. *See* West Bank/Gaza

Kahane, Meir, 321–22n. 16
Kampelman, Max, 198–99
Karameh, 122, 127
Kedourie, Elie, 226
Kenen, I. L., 42, 74–75, 102
Kennedy, John, 95, 109, 113; attitude toward Israel, 104, 106–7, 309n. 30; ignorance of Palestinians, 105–6, 122; and Israel's nuclear program, 107–8, 309n. 33, 309–10n. 34; military aid to Israel, 107–8; relations with Arab states, 104–6
Kennedy, Ted, 190

Kerr, Malcolm, 1, 2, 62, 110–11, 132, 146
Keyes, Alan, 335n. 74
Khalaf, Salah, 263–64, 334n. 55
Khalid, King, 176
Khalidi, Rashid, 7, 328n. 116
Khalidi, Walid, 208–9, 213
Khomeini, Ayatollah, 189
Kimmerling, Baruch, 7–8, 289
King, Henry, 32
King-Crane Commission, 32–33, 34, 36
King David Hotel, 6, 172
Kirkpatrick, Jeane, 198–99, 203, 322n. 23, 323n. 33
Kissinger, Henry, 4, 10, 14, 130, 137, 151, 153, 165, 199, 247, 276, 318n. 55; calculated refusal to become involved in mediation efforts, 126, 132, 135, 138; diplomatic assurances to Israel, 133–34, 139–40, 143–44; diplomatic complacency, 135–36, 291; global/Cold War approach to policy, 125–29; ignorance of Arab-Israeli issues, 131–32; ignorance of and efforts to circumvent Palestinian issue, 124, 125, 127–29, 131–32, 138–44, 147–49; importance of Israel in thwarting Soviets, 125, 126, 129, 132–33, 134, 135; importance of Israel personally, 131; negotiations with Israel and reassessment, 145–47; view of Arabs as radical, pro-Soviet, 125, 126, 129
Kollek, Teddy, 103
Koppel, Ted, 269
Krauthammer, Charles, 282, 283
Krim, Arthur, 109, 110, 112
Krim, Mathilde, 109, 110, 112, 116
Krock, Arthur, 79
Kurtzer, Daniel, 251, 252–53, 256, 332n. 25, 335n. 67, 336n. 6
Kurzman, Dan, 4–5

The Land and the Book (Thomson), 17, 20

Landau Commission, 173
Lansing, Robert, 30, 35
League of Nations, 27, 34, 39, 43
Lebanon, 7, 31, 84, 89, 90, 99, 102, 105, 203, 214, 325n. 58; Israeli attacks in, 134, 183, 192 (*see also* 1982 Israeli invasion of Lebanon); Palestinian cross-border attacks from, 115, 183
Ledeen, Michael, 201
Lehman, John, 335n. 74
Lehrer, Jim, 227
Lenczowski, George, 66
Lesch, Ann, 186, 236, 328n. 116
Lewis, Anthony, 9
Lewis, Bernard, 11, 154, 226
Lewis, Samuel, 161, 191, 193, 197, 234
Life magazine, 120, 121
Limbaugh, Rush, 283–84
Linowitz, Sol, 166, 189, 190–91, 205
Lippmann, Walter, 274
Lipshutz, Robert, 166
lobby, pro-Zionist/Israel, 37, 41–42, 71, 72–74, 130, 286 (*see also* Jewish organizations in United States; *and specific organizations*); pressures during Carter administration, 165, 167–68, 171, 190; pressures during Nixon/Ford administrations, 136–38, 145, 146–47, 148; strength of during Reagan administration, 195–96, 209, 219–21, 222–24
Lodge, Henry Cabot, 25, 37
London Times, 172
Long, Breckinridge, 47, 51
Los Angeles Times, 38, 39
Lowenthal, Max, 69–72
Lustick, Ian, 283, 328n. 116

MacNeil-Lehrer News Hour, 227
Madrid peace conference, 242, 245, 251, 267, 269, 271, 275 (*see also* Baker, James); as a landmark in Palestinian-Israeli history, 242, 270; procedural steps toward convening, 247, 268–69, 272
Mahfouz, Naguib, 9

Mandate for Iraq (British), 31
Mandate for Lebanon and Syria (French), 31
Mandate for Palestine (British), 31, 34, 39, 43, 56, 78, 80, 93, 111, 131, 154, 225 (*see also* Great Britain, in Palestine)
Mansour, Camille, 289
Manuel, Frank, 36, 84
Marching in Place (Duffy and Goodgame), 244
Marcus, Yoel, 214
Marines, U.S., 7, 99, 102, 211, 218, 325n. 63
Marshall, George, 68, 72
Marshall Plan, 67
Mattar, Philip, 57, 328n. 116
McCloy, John, 146
McCormick, Anne O'Hare, 82–83, 84
McDonald, James, 83, 85
McGovern, George, 142
McMahon, Henry, 31
McNamara, Robert, 146
McPherson, Harry, 109, 113
media (*see also specific newspapers, journals, and television networks*): ability to influence policymakers, 78–80, 151, 228–30; ability to influence public opinion on policy issues, 79–80, 151, 153, 204; criticism of Carter, 189, 192; criticism of Israel, 223, 227, 229, 266, 282, 335n. 61; disproportionate coverage of Israel, 227; efforts of Israeli supporters to influence, 223–24; hostile/stereotypical treatment of Arabs/Palestinians, 8–9, 38–40, 53–54, 81, 82, 84–85, 102–3, 142, 192, 204, 224–25, 227; improved treatment of Palestinians beginning in 1970s, 125, 149–52, 192–93, 223, 227; improved treatment of Palestinians following *intifada* and peace process, 236, 275–76; increase in conservative anti-peace commentary, 282, 283–84; increased Middle East coverage after 1967 and 1973

wars, 120, 150–52; influence of elite media on policymakers, 228–30; pro-Israeli sympathies of, 223–24; pro-Zionist treatment of Palestine, 37–40, 53–54, 75, 78–82; radio talk shows, 283–84; self-perpetuating aspect of pro-Israeli coverage, 227–28, 230–31; treatment of Israel/Israelis, 82–83, 101, 102, 118, 120, 121, 170, 172–73, 192; treatment of Sabra/Shatila massacre, 217–18, 223
Meir, Golda, 133, 139
Middle East Watch, 173
Miller, Aaron David, 251, 252–53, 256, 332n. 24, 336n. 6
mind-set, in United States about Arabs and Israel. *See* "frame of reference" on Palestinian-Israeli issues
missionaries in Middle East, 38–39; involvement in Arab independence movement, 29; missionaries to Palestine, 17, 19–20, 21, 22–23, 29; missionary-led educational and wartime relief efforts in Middle East, 23, 29
Mondale, Walter, 162, 166, 170–71, 183, 189, 190, 247
Morris, Benny, 5, 6, 61, 85, 226–27, 328n. 112
Moses, Alfred, 166
motion pictures, depiction of Arabs and Israelis in, 40–41, 53, 74, 103 (see also *Exodus*)
Moughrabi, Fouad, 232
Mroz, John, 205
Mufti of Jerusalem. *See* al-Husseini, Haj Amin
Murphy, Richard, 215
Muslih, Muhammad, 328n. 116
Muslims, 23, 89; in Palestine, 19–20, 25, 37, 38, 42, 70, 84
Mussadegh, Muhammad, 98–99
myths. *See* "frame of reference" on Palestinian-Israeli issues
Myths and Facts (AIPAC), 137

Nablus, 20
nakba. See Palestinians, dispossession and flight in 1948
Nasser, Gamal Abdel, 98, 99, 104–5, 111, 113, 115, 119; U.S. perceptions of, 102–3, 130
Nation, 81, 84–85, 102, 227
National Review, 102–3
National Security Council and staff, 87, 99–100, 137, 162–63, 164
Nazi Atrocities (motion picture), 74
Nazis, 52, 53, 56–57, 117, 120, 121
Near East Report (AIPAC), 137
neoconservatives, 198–99, 201, 203 (*see also* conservatives)
de Nerval, Gérard, 21
Netanyahu, Benjamin, 229–30, 276–77; and peace process, 277, 283; relations with United States, 276, 281, 284–85; and U.S. conservatives, 282, 283–84
New Republic, 79, 81, 84, 203, 228–29
Newsweek, 217
New Yorker, 284
New York Post, 84
New York Review of Books, 226, 327n. 94
New York Times, 6, 37, 38–40, 78–79, 82–83, 170, 173, 217, 227
Nightline, 8, 269
Niles, David, 69–72, 79
1982 Israeli invasion of Lebanon, 187, 197, 198, 205, 208–9, 210, 224, 227, 229, 325n. 63; internal Israeli criticism of, 22, 223; Israeli bombing and siege of Beirut, 187, 207, 210, 223, 224; Lebanon-Israel peace agreement, 214, 325n. 63; multinational peacekeeping force, 210–11, 216; Reagan sympathy with plight of Palestinians during, 206–7; Sabra and Shatila massacre, 210–11, 216–18, 223; U.S. guarantees to Palestinians, 216, 325n. 58; U.S. support for invasion, possible collusion, 205–6, 323nn. 30, 33

1956 Arab-Israeli war, 96, 97, 98, 99, 102, 116, 120

1948 Arab-Israeli war, 6, 61–62, 88, 95, 97–98, 111, 120, 132 (see also Palestinians, dispossession and flight in 1948); intercommunal fighting following partition, 80; Jewish-Arab military balance, 81; Jewish certainty of victory in, 81

1973 Arab-Israeli war, 6, 11, 125, 131, 137, 139, 140, 143, 155; aid to Israel during, 133, 137; increased U.S. public interest in Middle East after, 150–51; Israeli military weakness revealed by, 233; postwar policy changes induced by, 126, 135–36, 150–51

1967 Arab-Israeli war, 6, 11, 110, 111–12, 115–17, 121, 124, 125, 135, 151; Arab reaction to, 124; fears of another Holocaust, 119; increased popularity of Israel after, 119–21, 311–12n. 72; Israeli military superiority, 111–12, 116; Palestinian refugees created by, 122, 312n. 73; postwar implications of, 122–23, 129

1969–1970 War of Attrition, 135

Nixon (motion picture), 4, 14

Nixon, Richard, 136, 137; assurances to Israel about peace process, 133–34; attitude toward Israel, 129–30; global/Cold War approach to policymaking, 125–29; ignorance of Palestinians, 124, 127–31, 132, 138; influence of Henry Kissinger on, 126, 132, 134; intention to pursue "even-handedness," 126, 127; military aid to Israel, 132–33; unnuanced view of Arabs, 125, 129, 130

Norway, 290–92

Ochs, Adolph, 40

oil, 67, 79, 98, 150–51

Oliphant, 335n. 61

orientalism, 17, 18–19, 25, 59; colonialism's disregard for Arab political interests, 21–22, 30, 31–32, 50, 100

Orientalism (Said), 3

Oslo peace process, 2, 275, 278, 279, 281; crises in, following Netanyahu election, 277, 283; initial U.S. skepticism about, 290–92; Israeli withdrawals required by, 277; secret PLO-Israeli negotiations, 278, 290–91, 292–93; U.S. pro-Likud pressures opposing, 282–85

The Other Arab-Israeli Conflict (Spiegel), 212

Ottoman Empire. See Turkey

Palestine: Arab history in, 20, 22, 26, 93; Arab Revolt (1936–1939), 49, 53–54, 56–57; extent of proposed Jewish National Home in, 33, 45, 48, 53; fate of independent Arab state proposed by partition, 6, 86, 87–89; Jewish immigration to, 45, 48–49, 53, 55, 56, 64–65, 67, 73, 75, 302n. 12; Jewish statehood in, 45, 52, 58, 59–60, 65, 67, 68; nineteenth-century descriptions of, 16–17, 20, 297n. 2; nineteenth-century travel to, 16–18, 19–20; Ottoman rule in, 22, 28; partition of, 60, 65–66, 74, 76, 77–78, 80 (see also United Nations, partition plan); population, 20, 31, 32, 35, 43, 48–49, 60, 65, 66; status of Arab self-determination in, 30–33, 66, 67, 88–89, 93, 131; U.S. government position on Jewish settlement in/partition of, 33–34, 59–60, 63, 64, 67; U.S. public support for Jewish settlement/statehood in, 19, 23–24, 43, 52–53, 54, 73

Palestine and the Arab-Israeli Conflict (Smith), 233

Palestine Liberation Front, 263

Palestine Liberation Organization, 148, 152, 159, 160, 164, 165, 182,

237–39, 246, 268 (*see also* Palestinians; *and specific member organizations, U.S. administrations, and peace agreements*); acceptance of two-state solution, 142, 175, 179, 186, 208, 213, 238, 242, 250; allegiance of Palestinians to, 162, 215, 258, 272; Arab states press U.S. contacts with, 147, 203; Declaration of Independence (1988), 196, 238, 246, 259, 286; declared "sole legitimate representative" of Palestinians by Arab states, 141–42, 145, 153; and Lebanon, 205–6, 207, 209, 210, 211, 216–17, 325n. 58; negotiations with Bush administration, 257–59; organization and early days of, 114–15, 122; overtures to Israel/United States (*see also* Palestine Liberation Organization, Declaration of Independence), during Carter administration, 175–81, 185–86, 319n. 64; —, during Nixon administration, 140–43, 314n. 41; —, during Reagan administration, 8–9, 205, 208, 212–13, 231, 238, 240, 329n. 131; Palestine National Charter and demands for amendment, 256, 283; pursuit of diplomacy over military action, 175; renunciation of terrorism, 153, 330n. 134; response to Reagan Plan, 211–12, 214; terrorist acts by renegade PLO group, 235, 263; U.S. demands imposed for U.S.-PLO dialogue, 143–44, 148, 165, 175–76, 177–78, 235, 238–39, 329n. 118, 330n. 134; U.S. failure to probe PLO overtures, 140–41, 142, 155–56, 208–9, 211–12, 213–14, 236, 239, 240–41, 324n. 48; U.S.-PLO dialogue during Bush administration, 255, 257, 263, 264, 332–33n. 36, 333n. 37; U.S. refusal to deal with, 125, 143–44, 153–56, 190, 213, 234–35 (*see also* Sinai II

agreement); use of terrorism, 128, 138, 140, 152, 183, 235; viewed as Soviet agent, 125, 128–29, 132, 195–98, 200

Palestine National Council, 142, 175, 238, 250, 283

Palestinian guerrillas. See *fedayeen*

Palestinian-Israeli conflict. *See separate listings*

Palestinian issue as heart of Arab-Israeli conflict, 117, 123, 125, 142, 147–49, 153, 155, 167

Palestinians (*see also* Palestine Liberation Organization; *and specific administration policies*): alleged broadcast orders to leave Palestine, 4–5, 85, 295n. 12; Christians, 21, 23, 32, 70; cross-border raids into Israel, 98, 100, 115, 122, 127–28, 152; dispossession and flight in 1948, 1, 2, 3, 5–6, 83, 84–85, 90, 155, 231; early nationalism, 22, 43–44, 58, 303n. 42; growing frustration over stalled 1990 peace process, 262–64; growing international awareness of as political issue, 122–23, 125, 139, 141–42, 144–45, 147–49, 152–53, 192; growing U.S. public support for Palestinian statehood, 231–32, 266; increased activism/sense of nationalism following 1967 war, 117, 122; Islamic fundamentalism among, 262, 277; opposition to partition of Palestine, 66, 76–78, 92–93; opposition to Zionism, 32, 35, 36, 39, 42, 49, 53, 65, 301n. 58; perceived immorality of for opposing Israel, 93; political invisibility of, 2, 3, 7–9, 24–25, 30, 31, 33, 53; —, during British Mandate, 42–44, 60, 82; —, following defeat in 1948, 62, 82–84, 90–91, 92–94; —, in 1950s and 1960s, 95, 97–98, 100, 102, 113–17; poor political organization/public relations, 22, 42–44, 56–59, 76, 151–

Palestinians (*continued*)
52, 285–86, 305–6n. 52; refugees
from 1948 war, 84–85, 89–91, 94,
99–100, 103, 105, 117; relations
with Arab states, 95, 100, 105–6,
114–16, 141, 178, 179; status of
self-determination for, since 1948,
142, 147, 149, 164, 166, 175, 177,
179–80, 184, 186, 188, 213, 234,
279; U.S. attempts to find West
Bank alternative to PLO, 214, 249,
257–58, 290; U.S. public perceptions of, 2, 5, 37, 76, 183 (*see also*
Arabs, U.S. public perceptions of);
—, during partition debate and immediately after, 76–78, 86; —, following upsurge in terrorism, 152–
53; —, in 1950s and 1960s, 102–4,
117–21; —, in 1980s and during
intifada, 223, 231–32; —, in nineteenth century, 16–25; —, as result of peace process, 243, 269–70,
275–76
Palestinian state, 164, 208, 231–32;
U.S. opposition to, 40, 87–88, 90,
140, 161, 162, 177, 179–80, 182,
207, 256
Palestinian Students' Union, 115
pan-Arabism, 58, 105, 115–16,
303n. 42
Pappé, Ilan, 6, 232–33, 328n. 112
Paris Match, 179
Parker, Richard, 12–13, 126
Pasha, Nuqrashi, 65
peace process, 135–36, 140, 145–46
(*see also specific agreements and
processes*); Bush administration efforts to bypass PLO in, 257–58,
290; consequences of stalled 1990
peace process, 262–64, 334n. 55;
early attitude toward involvement
of Palestinians in, 139, 147, 148,
149, 155–56, 157–62, 165, 168,
172, 175–81; growing public support for in 1980s, 231–32; initial
Bush administration mediation efforts, 257–60; 1989 Israeli West

Bank/Gaza elections proposal, 257–
59; Rabie-Quandt initiative (1988),
237–39; Reagan administration at-
titude toward, 199, 203, 234–36;
Swedish initiative (1988), 237–39
Peel Commission, 88
Pelletreau, Robert, 257, 332–33n. 36
Peres, Shimon, 234–36, 276–77, 291
Peretz, Martin, 229, 327n. 106,
336n. 5
Perle, Richard, 199, 201, 335n. 74
Persian Gulf crisis, 243, 255, 264,
268; atmosphere in aftermath of,
264–65
Peters, Joan, 225–27, 254, 327n. 95
Peterson, Peter, 146
Philippines, 72
Pipes, Daniel, 199, 226, 326n. 88
Pipes, Richard, 199
PLO. *See* Palestine Liberation
Organization
The PLO and the Politics of Survival
(Miller), 332n. 24
Podhoretz, Norman, 199, 228–30,
327n. 103
policymakers, U.S. (*see also specific
administrations, departments, and
programs*): failure to challenge preconceived assumptions, 1, 3, 9–13,
59–60, 61, 274–75; globalist vs. regionalist perspective, 10–11, 126–
27, 134; ignorance of Palestinian
situation/perspective, 1, 3, 8, 12,
26, 50, 58, 59–60, 92, 93, 95–96,
98, 100, 114, 115–16; impatience
with history, 234; susceptibility to
pro-Israeli pressures, 101–2; tendency to ignore history/expert advice, 11–13, 146–47; tendency to
misjudge Israeli flexibility, 61, 170,
171, 185, 259–60; tension between
non-political careerists and politicians, 86, 134
The Politics of Defeat (Churba),
322n. 17
Popular Front for the Liberation of
Palestine, 128

Porath, Yehoshua, 226, 327n. 94
post-Zionists. *See* scholarship on
Palestinian-Israeli conflict, revisionist Israeli scholars
Presbyterian General Assembly, 30
press. *See* media
Protestant activity in Middle East.
See missionaries in Middle East
public opinion polls, 82, 118, 120, 136,
171, 173, 193, 231–32, 234, 266 (*see
also specific polling organizations*)

Quakers, 23
Quandt, William, 149, 160, 162,
164–65, 166, 245, 255, 317n. 36,
328n. 116; and Camp David process,
182–83, 187; on domestic constraints on Carter, 167, 180, 183;
involvement in 1988 peace initiative, 237–39; on Persian Gulf crisis,
264

Rabie, Mohamed, 237–39
Rabin, Yitzhak, 10, 167–68, 271, 277,
280, 319n. 71
*Reader's Guide to Periodical Litera-
ture*, 327n. 94
Reagan, Ronald, and administration
of, 11, 111, 193, 194, 244, 249, 259–
60, 279, 287, 288 (*see also* Shultz,
George; *and other officials*); adherence to conventional wisdom, 197,
228, 239–41; anti-Palestinian viewpoint of, 195–96, 198, 200, 202–4,
214, 225; anti-Soviet viewpoint of,
196, 198–201, 203; belief Palestinian issue a distraction, 198, 199,
203; change of heart about Palestinians during 1982 Lebanon fighting, 206–7; disinterest in Palestinian autonomy negotiations, 199,
203, 204–5, 234; effort to exclude
PLO from peace process, 234–36,
237; embroiled in Lebanon, 210–
11, 218, 219, 325n. 63; establishment of dialogue with PLO, 196,
238–39, 241; failure to confront Is-

rael over disagreements, 211, 214,
231, 237; globalist perspective of,
198, 200, 203, 234; influence of elite
media on, 228–30; influence of pro-
Israeli neoconservatism on, 195,
198–201, 228–29, 322n. 17; missed
opportunities for peace, 196, 211–
15, 234–36, 237, 239, 240–41;
oblivious to new trends in public
discourse, 231–34; occasional efforts to resolve Palestinian problem,
207, 208, 214; opposition to international peace conference, 235; orientation toward Israeli viewpoint,
195–202, 203–4, 212, 213–14,
218–19, 221, 222–23, 240–41, 242,
256; reaction to *intifada*, 236–37;
Reagan beliefs and personal style,
196–97, 322–23n. 25; strong opposition to PLO, 195–96, 202–3,
205, 208–9, 213–16; support for/
failure to criticize Israeli anti-PLO
moves, 195, 202, 204, 205–6,
209
Reagan Plan, 207–8, 222, 256; Arab
response to, 210, 211–15; autonomy provisions of, 207–8; Israeli
rejection of, 210, 211, 212; U.S. failure to pursue, 211–12, 214, 234
*The Realities of American-Palestine
Relations* (Manuel), 84
refugee resettlement/repatriation efforts. *See* Palestinians, refugees
from 1948 war; United States, refugee resettlement efforts
Reich, Bernard, 5, 288
Republican Party, 53, 71, 282
Resolution 242. *See* United Nations,
Security Council Resolution 242
Retreat from Freedom (Churba), 200–
201
revisionism. *See* scholarship on Pal-
estinian-Israeli conflict, revisionist
Israeli scholars
Ribicoff, Abraham, 220–21
Richardson, Bill, 337n. 16
Roche, John, 109

Rockefeller, John D., 24
Rogers, William, 124, 126, 127, 132
Rogers Plan, 127, 137
Roosevelt, Eleanor, 46, 47, 59, 86
Roosevelt, Franklin, 51–53, 59, 62, 67, 69, 109; background and beliefs, 45–46; failure to assist Jews during World War II, 46, 47; poor understanding of Palestine situation, 48–50, 55–56; support for Zionism, 46–50, 55; views on Arabs, 49–50
Rosenfeld, Stephen, 275
Rosenthal, A. M., 282
Ross, Dennis, 13, 249, 318n. 51, 331n. 18; attitude toward Palestinians, 254–55, 258, 335n. 67; during Bush administration, 248, 251–53, 254, 270; during Clinton administration, 276, 277, 285; criticized by Likud in Israel, 256; misjudges Shamir's flexibility, 259–60; proposes changes in territory-for-peace concept, 278–79
Rostow, Eugene, 109, 110–11, 112, 146, 201–2, 335n. 74
Rostow, Walt, 109, 110, 112
Rubinstein, Danny, 9
Rusk, Dean, 110, 125, 146

Sabra and Shatila massacre. See 1982 Israeli invasion of Lebanon
Sadat, Anwar, 179; and Carter, 168, 180; and Kissinger, 135, 147; negotiations with Israel, 178, 181; and Reagan, 203–4; role in changing U.S. public perceptions of Arabs, 125, 152, 173, 181, 192, 287
Saddam Hussein. See Hussein, Saddam
Safire, William, 130, 281, 282
Safran, Nadav, 146
Said, Edward, 3–4, 18, 286, 311–12n. 72
Salamah, Ali Hassan, 314n. 41
Samuels, Gertrude, 83
Sanders, Edward, 166
Sarid, Yossi, 337–38n. 24

Saudi Arabia, 31, 54–56, 105, 176, 179, 183, 197, 199, 203, 205, 213
Saunders, Harold, 10–11, 13, 86, 205, 221, 231; Carter administration, 158, 160, 161–62, 164–65, 188, 317n. 36; Nixon administration, 143, 147–49, 291, 318n. 57
Saunders Document, 147–49, 153, 155
A Savage War of Peace (Horne), 164
Savir, Uri, 292
Schifter, Richard, 199
Schindler, Alexander, 171, 172
scholarship on Palestinian-Israeli conflict, trends in (see also individual scholars): national Israeli debate sparked by, 232–33, 328nn. 112, 113; revisionist Israeli scholars, 5, 6, 61, 85, 226–27, 232–33, 289, 328n. 112; U.S. scholarship on Palestinians, 233, 328n. 116
Scott, Sir Walter, 25
Scowcroft, Brent, 276
Scranton, William, 146
Seelye, Talcott, 129
Segev, Tom, 328n. 112
self-determination. See Wilson, Woodrow; Palestine, status of Arab self-determination in; Palestinians, status of self-determination for, since 1948; Palestinian state
Shafir, Gershon, 289–90
Shaftesbury, Lord, 298n. 29
Shah of Iran, 99
Shalev, Menachem, 223–24
Shamir, Yitzhak, 172, 235, 237, 268–69; and Bush administration, 242, 244, 261–62, 264, 266, 271, 272, 335n. 61; electoral defeat, 260, 267; maneuvering during 1989–1990 negotiating effort, 257–60
Shammas, Anton, 272–73
Sharabi, Hisham, 155
Sharon, Ariel, 205–6, 209, 216, 283, 323n. 30
Shechem. See Nablus
Sheehan, Edward, 147

Shin Bet, 173
Shlaim, Avi, 6, 61, 226–27, 328n. 112
Shultz, George, 146, 213, 229–30;
    attitude/policies toward Israel,
    209–10, 211, 214, 218–19, 256–57,
    276; authorship of Reagan Plan,
    207–8; early views/style of, 206–7,
    209–10; effect of domestic pro-
    Israeli pressures on, 209, 214; frus-
    tration with Arabs, 210, 212, 214,
    218; hostility to PLO, 208–9, 213–
    16, 234–36, 239, 240–41; obstacles
    imposed to dialogue with PLO,
    238–39, 330nn. 134, 135; policy/
    actions toward Lebanon, 210–11,
    214, 216; Shultz initiative (1988),
    237
Silver, Abba Hillel, 52, 68
Sinai Peninsula, 96, 111, 116, 135
Sinai II agreement, 143–44, 146,
    148, 149, 186; as defined by Ford
    administration, 318nn. 55, 57; as
    interpreted and augmented by
    Reagan administration, 196, 238–
    39, 329n. 118, 330n. 134; as inter-
    preted by Carter administration,
    165, 175–76, 178, 190, 319n. 71
Six-Day War. *See* 1967 Arab-Israeli
    war
Smith, Charles, 233
South Africa, 170
Soviet Union, 111, 139, 141, 147,
    264–65, 279; and 1982 Israeli in-
    vasion of Lebanon, 210; perceived
    impact of partition of Palestine on
    world role of, 67, 70, 79, 87; Reagan
    administration belief U.S. losing
    influence to, 198–201; relations
    with Arabs, 107, 108, 124, 126,
    128–29, 135; U.S. efforts to thwart
    role of in Middle East, 125–29, 130,
    134, 135; U.S.-Soviet communiqué
    (1977), 319n. 65; U.S.-Soviet com-
    petition for influence, 79, 96, 98–
    99, 104, 174, 240; U.S.-Soviet sum-
    mits (1972, 1973), 313n. 36
Sparkman, John, 114

Spiegel, Steven, 212, 316n. 13
Stephens, John Lloyd, 17, 20, 21
Stern Gang, 172
Stettinius, Edward, 55
Stone, I. F., 230–31
Stone, Oliver, 4
Stone, Richard, 165
Stowe, Harriet Beecher, 17–18
Strauss, Robert, 166–67, 189, 204–5,
    276
Suez Canal, 98, 102–3, 135
Suez crisis. *See* 1956 Arab-Israeli war
Sunday Times of London, 139
Sununu, John, 333–34n. 49
Sweden, 1988 peace initiative of. *See*
    peace process, Swedish initiative
Syria, 23, 29–30, 31, 33, 36, 131, 134,
    135, 149, 151, 175, 207, 217 (*see*
    also al-Asad, Hafiz; Golan Heights);
    1982 Israeli invasion of Lebanon,
    210–11, 325n. 63; and Palestinians,
    58, 84, 90, 115, 128–29, 178, 179
Syrian Protestant College. *See* Ameri-
    can University of Beirut

The Talisman (Scott), 25
Tal al-Za'atar refugee camp, 325n. 58
Teicher, Howard, 201, 213, 219
television. *See* media
terrorism, 7, 124, 138, 152–53, 170,
    172, 200, 230, 263, 277, 285 (*see*
    also Palestine Liberation Organiza-
    tion, use of terrorism)
Tessler, Mark, 43, 117, 194, 236
Thomson, William, 17, 20
Tillman, Seth, 186
Time, 193, 217, 269
Time-Yankelovich poll, 193
Transjordan. *See* Jordan
Truman, Harry, 55, 73, 96, 97; back-
    ground and beliefs, 62–63, 67–68;
    "brain trusts," 70–71; influence of
    domestic politics on, 62–63, 67;
    influence of pro-Zionist advisers on,
    67, 68–72, 79; lack of interest in
    Arab concerns, 63, 64, 65–66, 67;
    position on partition and recogni-

Truman, Harry (*continued*)
tion of Israel, 66–67, 69–70, 72, 78, 79, 80, 91–92; proposal to allow Jewish immigration to Palestine, 64–65; pro-Zionist view of self-determination in Palestine, 66; relations with media, 78, 80; relations with State Department, 67–68; relations with Zionists, 68; support for Zionism/Israel, 62–68 trusteeship plan for Palestine. *See* United Nations, trusteeship debate
Tuchman, Barbara, 226
Turkey, 23, 27, 28, 29, 31, 32, 35, 38–39, 92
TV Guide, 192
Twain, Mark, 16–17, 20, 21, 297n. 2

United Jewish Appeal, 73
United Nations, 60, 75, 86, 89, 111, 189–90, 279–80; anti-Israeli resolutions and U.S. vetoes of, 134, 262–63, 281–82, 337n. 16; General Assembly Resolution 194, 89, 100, 279; international desire to ensure credibility of during partition debate, 62, 67, 77–78, 79, 81; Israeli Likud interpretations of Resolution 242, 169–70, 183, 184; later Palestinian acceptance of partition as basis for peace, 213, 238; Palestinian reasons for opposing Resolution 242, 117, 143, 176, 178; partition plan, 65–66, 67, 72, 73, 76, 77, 78–79, 231; pro-Palestinian actions/resolutions, 142, 145, 153; Security Council Resolution 242, 116–117, 143, 165, 175–78, 184, 238, 311n. 59; Security Council Resolution 338, 143; trusteeship debate, 69, 78–79, 80; UN Special Committee on Palestine, 75, 76–77, 79; U.S. alteration of territory-for-peace concept, 278–79, 336nn. 8, 9; U.S. position on various provisions of Resolution 242, 127, 131, 140, 169, 176, 182, 208

United States (government) (*see also specific administrations, departments, and programs*): acceptance of Israel's existence as *fait accompli,* 87, 90, 91, 92, 98; Arab perception United States has no control over Israel, 186, 212; change in immigration laws, 334n. 51; commitment to Balfour Declaration/Zionism, 33–34, 45, 54, 59–60, 66, 287; desire to preserve stability/status quo in Middle East, 62, 88, 96, 97–99, 135; effect of U.S. aid on Israeli willingness to compromise, 126, 133, 134, 145, 221–22, 235, 237, 254, 260, 281, 284; refugee resettlement efforts, 89–90, 99–101, 104–5, 113, 140; U.S. military and economic aid to Israel, 107–8, 110, 126, 132–33, 134, 145–46, 182, 218–19, 220, 237; —, during Bush administration, 261, 266, 335n. 61; —, during Clinton administration, 281, 284, 337n. 15
UNSCOP. *See* United Nations, UN Special Committee on Palestine
U.S. Congress, 42, 47, 55, 149, 245, 264, 265, 314–15n. 64; antipathy toward/ignorance of Arabs, 53, 113, 168; arms sales to Arab states, 183, 197, 219; mandates move of U.S. embassy to Jerusalem, 281; pressures from pro-Israel lobbyists, 102, 137, 155, 168, 219, 220, 282, 284, 335n. 62; support for Israel, 97, 136, 145–46, 168, 173–74, 220–21, 222, 236–37, 242, 263, 282; support for Zionism, 36–37, 41, 45, 51–53, 59, 73
U.S. Defense Department, 87, 137
U.S. intelligence, 11, 112 (*see also* Central Intelligence Agency)
U.S. Joint Chiefs of Staff, 87, 92
USS *Quincy,* 54
U.S. State Department, 9, 24, 33, 42, 55, 71, 84, 101, 102, 149, 180, 214, 238 (*see also* policymakers, U.S.;

and specific administrations); annual report on human rights, 172–73, 318n. 47; Arabists, 11, 23, 34–35, 50, 162, 201, 251, 252, 326n. 77, 331n. 18, 333–34n. 49; bypassed during Reagan administration, 201–2, 221, 326n. 77; during Kissinger era, 126–27, 129, 132, 133, 134, 137, 138, 146; line offices shut out under Baker, 251; obstruction of Jewish immigration during World War II, 46, 47–48, 51; Office of Near Eastern and African Affairs (also Division of Near Eastern Affairs, or Bureau of Near Eastern and South Asian Affairs, or Near East Bureau), 24, 35, 51, 70, 251, 298–99n. 37; policy on partition of Palestine, 67–68, 69, 70, 78–79, 80, 86–89; policy toward Zionism/Palestine, 34–36, 50–51; views of Arabs/Palestinians, 36, 76, 88–89, 90
Uris, Leon, 103–4, 227

Vance, Cyrus, 10–11, 146, 162, 163, 190, 243, 276; attitude toward Israel, 166, 168–69, 181–82, 183; efforts to resolve Palestinian problem, 165–66, 167, 175–77, 189–90, 320n. 92; regionalist perspective on Middle East, 165; willingness to deal with PLO, 165
Vatikiotis, P. J., 226
Veliotes, Nicholas, 186–87, 205, 206, 207
Versailles Peace Conference, 23, 28, 29, 30, 36
Vietnam, 110, 111, 119, 140, 151, 199
Voyage en Orient (de Nerval), 21

Wagner, Robert, 51–52
Wall Street Journal, 9, 217, 283
Walters, Vernon, 140
War of Independence. *See* 1948 Arab-Israeli war

Washington Institute for Near East Policy, 220, 276, 279; access of to policymakers, 249; 1988 report, Israeli perspective of, 247–51, 252, 253, 255, 257
Washington Post, 9, 38, 173, 227, 322n. 17
Watergate scandal, 124
Wattenberg, Ben, 109
We Belong to the Land (Chacour), 269
Weinberger, Caspar, 200, 322n. 18, 323n. 33
Weizman, Ezer, 318n. 51
Weizmann, Chaim, 28, 46, 49, 69, 79, 85–86
Welles, Sumner, 50–51
West Bank/Gaza, 8, 87, 88, 98, 149, 164, 167, 175, 211, 214 (*see also* Israel, "Greater Israel" policy; Israeli settlements in occupied territories; *and specific peace agreements*); autonomy for (*see* Camp David accords, Palestinian autonomy plan; Reagan Plan); concept of transitional arrangement for, 176, 181–82, 184, 237; growing popular Israeli opposition to occupation, 204, 221, 260; Israeli occupation of, 9, 116–17, 122, 141, 152, 170, 171, 232, 262; Israeli treatment of Palestinians in, 160–61, 162, 172–73, 174, 193–94, 204, 215, 218, 229, 240, 253–54, 262–63, 280, 318n. 47; justifications for Israel's occupation of/settlements in, 110, 111, 201–2, 322n. 23; U.S. proposal to improve "quality of life" for Palestinians, 214, 236; West Bank/Gaza uprising (see *intifada*)
Wiesel, Elie, 118, 120, 226
Wieseltier, Leon, 228
Will, George, 282, 283
Wilson, Woodrow, 8, 34, 35, 40, 45, 66, 106, 287; background and beliefs, 26–27, 299n. 3; endorsement of Balfour Declaraton, 27–28, 33; influence of Protestant missionary

Wilson, Woodrow (*continued*)
  friends, 29; and principle of self-
  determination, 27, 30–33, 66; support for Zionist program, 27–28,
  29, 33, 36, 41
Wirthlin, Richard, 231–32
Wise, Stephen, 28, 46–47, 55
Wye agreement, 277, 283, 284–85

Yad Vashem, 119, 272
Yale, William, 36
Yom Kippur war. *See* 1973 Arab-
  Israeli war
Yost, Charles, 146
Young, Andrew, 190, 192

Zionist movement, 22, 25, 32 (*see
  also specific organizations*); connections to U.S. policymakers, 28, 30,
  41, 45, 46–47, 59, 70–71; divisions
  in, 46, 52; inconsistency with self-
  determination in Palestine, 30–32,
  50; leadership and organization in
  Palestine, 57–58, 71; relations with
  Congress, 36–37, 41, 45, 51–52, 59;
  relations with U.S. media, 78, 80,
  81; romantic appeal of, 38, 39, 75–
  76, 78; U.S. membership, 41–42,
  73; U.S. organizations and activities, 33, 34, 41–42, 51–52, 54, 59,
  70–71, 72–74; U.S. public perceptions of, 36, 41, 42–43, 48, 53,
  54, 82, 301n. 56
Zionist Organization of America, 28,
  37, 41–42, 46, 284

Text:	10/13 Aldus
Display:	Aldus
Composition:	G & S Typesetters, Inc.
Printing and binding:	Thomson-Shore, Inc.